2009 BPM and Workflow Handbook

2009 BPM and Workflow Handbook

Methods, Concepts, Case Studies and Standards in Business Process Management and Workflow

Spotlight on BPM in Government

Published in association with the
Workflow Management Coalition

Workflow Management Coalition

W f M C

15 Years of Thought-Process Leadership

Edited by

Layna Fischer

Future Strategies Inc., Book Division

Lighthouse Point, Florida

2009 BPM and Workflow Handbook

ISBN-13: 978-0-9777527-9-9

ISBN-10: 0-9777527-9-8

11 10 09 9 10 11

Published by Future Strategies Inc., Book Division

2436 North Federal Highway #374
Lighthouse Point FL 33064 USA
954.782.3376 fax 954.782.6365
www.FutStrat.com; books@FutStrat.com

Cover by Petal Design Studio, London

Publisher's Cataloging-in-Publication Data
Library of Congress Catalog Card LCCN No. 2009927319

2009 BPM and Workflow Handbook:
/Layna Fischer (editor)
p. cm.
Includes bibliographical references, appendices and index.

ISBN 978-0-9777527-9-9

1. Business Process Management. 2. Workflow Management.
3. Technological Innovation. 4. Information Technology. 5. Total Quality Management. 6. Organizational Change 7. Management Information Systems. 8. Office Practice Automation. 9. Business Process Technology. 10. Electronic Commerce. 11. Process Analysis

Fischer, Layna

TABLE OF CONTENTS

SECTION 2—THE BUSINESS VALUE OF WORKFLOW AND BPM

SECTION 3—BPM IN STANDARDS AND TECHNOLOGY

SECTION 3—DIRECTORIES AND APPENDICES

Foreword 2009

Most of the world's economies are in recession and the credit crunch has steepened the slide. Policy makers around the word are racing to contain the damage and there are calls for the expansion of government spending, taxes and regulation. In some quarters, there are calls for a radical revision of current economic systems and the end of capitalism. The current situation was created by a perfect storm of mutually reinforcing trends and policy mistakes: in the United States the loose monetary policy by the Fed post 9/11, the housing policy that encouraged home ownership by those less able to pay, the growth of leverage and the use of complicated derivatives, poor and lacking governance and an oil price shock. All of these factors resulted in a housing bubble that became a recession.

The change that world is now going through is what recessions are all about. Fast, inevitable and unavoidable. The restructuring of the world economies is going to be immense. It's not at all clear which direction organizations will be pushed in but they do not have to be passive onlookers while these forces do their worst. They can be harnessed as an opportunity and for inspiration one can look no further than the words of the Sage of Omaha—Warren Buffett—for inspiration; "A simple rule dictates my buying: Be fearful when others are greedy, and be greedy when others are fearful. And most certainly, fear is now widespread, gripping even seasoned investors."

To lead in this business environment is to embrace change. That means business processes must be both thorough and yet still quickly adaptable. It's no longer just what you do that counts, it's how you do what you do—and how quickly you can modify your methods to take on new opportunities and challenges that's really important. So it is inevitable that business leaders are looking for new ways to use computing power to meet their needs.

The perfect storm and the changes in the New World Order means that organizations cannot afford to waste time, human and financial resources on processes that can rapidly and easily be automated and managed. Businesses must transform themselves into agile operations capable of turning a constantly changing business environment into opportunities. Process innovation and speed of change are the key opportunities for competitive differentiation moving forward.

Unfortunately the IT organization, responsible for facilitating changes demanded by the business, often falls short of being able to do just that. Many studies and surveys show that changes to IT infrastructure and applications are fraught with complexity, costing much more and taking much longer than initially anticipated. It is not uncommon for an IT organization to take five or more years to make significant enterprise-wide changes; this pace just doesn't support the business initiatives required in today's business climate. This constant friction between the business desire to achieve a rapid pace of change and the ability of IT to deliver it resulted in what is infamously known as the "IT Gap." Instead of being in a position to help the business to become more competitive, IT has to invest most of its budget in maintenance of existing legacy systems and applications.

Being able to invest more in "new development" and innovation to increase business agility and efficiency are top priorities for most progressive CIOs, who understand that in today's business environment it's no longer only what you do that counts, it's also how quickly you can do it in the midst of changing business conditions that's equally important.

A key solution area that helps organizations become more efficient and agile is Business Process Management (BPM). Simply put, BPM is designed to help businesses to discover how their processes work and how to measure, manage and optimize them. Properly implemented, BPM helps organizations to pin-point and resolve process bottlenecks, monitor and anticipate business activity and quickly react to the constantly changing business environment. Many now recognize BPM as one of the most important enterprise software market segments, and it is not surprising to find many vendors attempting to address the growing demand.

One emerging trend is the notion of cloud computing—we haven't seen the impact this is going to have—but we will very soon. This cloud of computing resources will have profound implications for the organization. On one level the cloud will be a huge collection of electronic services based on standards. Many web-based services are built to be integrated into existing business processes. IT systems will permit organizations to become more modular and flexible and this will lead to further specialization. In the cloud it will become even easier to outsource business processes, or at least those parts of them where firms do not enjoy a competitive advantage. This also means that companies will rely more on services provided by others. Furthermore, there will be not just one cloud but a number of different sorts: private ones and public ones, which themselves will divide into general-purpose and specialized ones. People are already using the term "intercloud" to mean a federation of all kinds of clouds, in the same way that the internet is a network of networks. And all of those clouds will be full of applications and services.

There will be many ways in which the cloud will change businesses and the economy, most of them hard to predict, but one theme is already emerging. In the current economic environment businesses will have to become more like the technology itself: more adaptable, more interwoven and more specialized.

"When it comes to the future, there are three kinds of people: those who let it happen, those who make it happen, and those who wonder what happened." John M. Richardson, Jr.

Organizations should use this *Perfect Storm* as an opportunity to get fit and healthy. There is an idiom that states "a better built ship can weather a storm". Organizations should take a good look at what it does but most importantly it should take a long hard look at how it does things. As a final point we should turn the clock back ten years when the world was obsessed with the Millennium. It is unclear exactly how much was spent on IT to ensure a successful transition into the Millennium—although an estimate of around $200 Billion sounds plausible. Whilst organizations were checking millions of lines of code two students took another look at an everyday problem.

The students focused on how searching across the internet worked. The major search engines of the day were turning themselves into web portals and destinations. The students came up with an elegant solution and Google was born—the rest is history.

Once again, on behalf of everyone involved in the Coalition and those that work tirelessly behind the scenes, mostly in their own time, I sincerely thank you for continuing to support us. As I have said on many previous occasions, it never ceases to amaze me just how much can change and the progress that can be made in a 12-month period. Enjoy the book.

Jon Pyke, Chair WfMC
and Chief Strategy Officer, Cordys.

Section 1

Spotlight on BPM in Government

An Open Letter to President Obama: It's Time to Fix Broken Government

Clay Richardson, Forrester Research, USA

Dear President Obama:

The world paused on a remarkable day in January 2009 as you took the oath of office and promised to usher in a new era in American government. In many ways, the country and the world continue to bask in the afterglow of that historic day. However, critical observers closely interpreted your speech as a challenge to roll up our collective sleeves and recommit ourselves to good deeds, hard work and innovation. A call to employ the best minds, the boldest ideas, and the most innovative technologies to wage a war against the economic malaise brought on by the market crash of 2008. During the speech, you pointed out:

> "Our economy is badly weakened, a consequence of greed and irresponsibility on the part of some but also our collective failure to make hard choices and prepare the nation for a new age... Starting today, we must pick ourselves up, dust ourselves off, and begin again the work of remaking America."

To "remake America" we must first pinpoint the process and policy failures that brought us to the brink of collapse. Yet, given the current state of affairs, we can ill afford to become frozen in paralysis analysis—studying every government process like Sherlock Holmes searching for minute clues on where the train went off the tracks.

Turn to C-SPAN for a "Cliff Notes" version of agency processes run amuck. Take, for example, the congressional oversight hearing on the failure of the SEC to detect the Bernie Madoff[1] Ponzi scheme scandal. The hearing, broadcast on C-SPAN, provided a valuable lesson on failed processes that cost Americans billions—directly impacting investors bilked by Madoff and indirectly impaling the already-deflated balloon of confidence of American taxpayers.

Of course you probably don't have time to study all of the congressional oversight hearings, so here's a neat tag cloud that sums them all up:

---

[1] http://en.wikipedia.org/wiki/Bernard_Madoff

Figure 1: Congressional oversight hearings tag cloud (created with Many Eyes)

A CRASH COURSE IN BUSINESS PROCESS MANAGEMENT (BPM)

Take a close look at the tag cloud floated in the previous section. Now, circle the most prominent words. Notice you circled: "act," "management," "implementation," "review," "programs," "improve," "consider," "efforts," "information," and "reform." According to the Policy Agendas Project, these are the most popular terms used to describe agency oversight hearings called by the U.S. House of Representatives and the U.S. Senate[2]. Coincidentally (or maybe not so coincidentally), many of these terms also describe a practice that has gained momentum among public and private sector leaders: "Business Process Management," or BPM, for short.

Figure 2: The White House Technology Agenda

Let's agree that most of government's (and business' for that matter) problems are rooted in broken and misunderstood business processes. As a practice, BPM provides the methodologies and innovative tools needed to understand and improve these broken business processes, business rules, and cross-agency collaboration.

---

[2] Policy Agenda's Project, http://www.policyagendas.org/codebooks/hearings.html

In short, there are three specific elements of BPM that align with your administration's Technology Agenda[3]:

- **Improve transparency, accountability, and participation.** BPM's visual modeling capabilities allow agencies to quickly document process knowledge and publish this knowledge on-line to be viewed and accessed by citizens.
- **Improve the Exchange of Information**. Once agencies capture process knowledge, agencies can move on to automate these processes to improve interaction and exchange of information with citizens—most importantly automation capabilities provide visibility into running processes and potential bottlenecks.
- **Improve Interagency Collaboration.** When combined with Service-Oriented Architecture (SOA), BPM represents the government's best shot at promoting interagency collaboration. This combined approach allows government to orchestrate business processes that span multiple agencies without forcing agencies to adopt new onerous policies or tools.

Of course BPM is not the silver bullet, and if done haphazardly, it's just like anything else—garbage in, garbage out. However, if implemented properly, BPM provides a cost-effective framework for continual process improvement that connects organizational objectives to auditable results.

USE BPM TO ELIMINATE TRANSPARENCY ROADBLOCKS

Okay, now you're equipped with some basic knowledge on BPM. Your CTO is probably shaking his head, saying, "Just what I need, the President quizzing me about yet another technology idea somebody planted in his head." Before that picture settles in, rest assured that your CTO has BPM on his radar—considering its growing popularity and exposure to IT and business leaders, both inside and outside of government. BPM methodologies and tools have been around for decades, with many pointing to Motorola and GE as original pioneers in the space.

Enough with the history lesson; we're all about the future here, right? Looking to the future, I think it's critical to highlight current trends in BPM that can help you plow through the transparency roadblocks you will encounter. In particular, government agencies and businesses should harness the latest trends in BPM to:

- **Consolidate institutional process knowledge.** According to OPM[4], something like 1.2M government workers will retire in the next 10 years. Unfortunately, for you, the bulk of them will retire with a wealth of institutional process knowledge. Of course they will leave behind rafts of policy manuals and guides that will collect dust. Let's face it, policy manuals are so, um how shall we say it, 20th Century. We're in the 21st Century, it's time to deploy "process wikis" that empower employees at all levels to contribute and maintain process knowledge—think "Wikipedia," but for *processes*. Best of all, agencies can publish their processes on the web and share processes and process knowledge with other agencies. These tools are lightweight, collaborative, and easy to use. Take a look at Lombardi Blueprint, Software AG AlignSpace, or Itensil for examples of pretty cool process wikis.

---

[3] Barack Obama's Blueprint for America

[4] US Office of Personnel Management: http://www.opm.gov/

- **Aggregate just-in-time process information.** "Mashup" was the tech buzzword of 2008. In 2009, the term will mutate and take on many different forms. In the BPM world, "process mashups" will become the buzzword *du jour*. Mashups aggregate data from multiple data sources to create new insights that improve the quality of decision making—think Frankenstein with Albert Einstein's brain. While basic mashups only aggregate data, **process mashups** aggregate data, workflows, and content from numerous business processes. The primary objective of process mashups is to minimize the "application switching" phenomena that forces employees to constantly navigate between numerous desktop applications to complete a task or answer a simple question. With process mashups, all of the processes, applications, and content are consolidated into a single view that empowers users to answer questions before they're asked. Take a look as Serena Business Mashups for a good example of how process mashups work.
- **Connect processes to trusted data sources.** Public and private sector CIOs are all abuzz about improving data quality and identifying trusted data sources. For some reason, these same CIOs never connect their BPM initiatives to their master data management (MDM) initiatives. In fact, this is a dirty little secret in the BPM world—since business processes usually cut across numerous data sources, there's typically a heavy development lift on BPM projects to synchronize process data with source systems. Sometimes this can mean several man-months of unbudgeted work to map and integrate processes to the appropriate trusted data sources. In 2009, leading BPM vendors will tackle this issue to provide built-in capabilities that improve data design and integration with existing MDM initiatives.

SET AN EXAMPLE: GOVERNMENT MUST BECOME LEAN AND MEAN

After reading the excellent chapters within this handbook, many agencies will declare BPM as a panacea. As pointed out earlier, BPM is not the silver bullet, and agencies should not go on a spending spree buying BPM software and services thinking that it will cure all ills. In fact, many public and private sector BPM initiatives reported failure due to poorly managed expectations, poor coordination, and lack of governance[5].

Unlike the economy, just throwing money at BPM won't solve the problem—in many cases it simply makes it worse. In tackling the country's most challenging process problems, agency heads should adopt "Lean BPM" strategies that:

- **Harness BPM software-as-a-service.** Instead of purchasing on-premise BPM solutions that can be costly, public and private sector organizations should explore pay-as-you go alternatives delivered via software-as-a-service (SaaS) models—also commonly referred to as "cloud computing"[6]. BPM SaaS alternatives allow you to better align your BPM technology investment with the actual return. In other words it takes the Vegas-style risk-taking vibe out of investing in new technologies, such as BPM.
- **Embrace process frameworks and accelerators.** You don't always need to start from scratch to fix broken processes. Process frameworks and ac-

---

[5] BPM Center of Excellence

[6] Talking To Your CFO About Cloud Computing

celerators provide a foundation for kick-starting process initiatives when most of the requirements are well-known for a particular problem. For example, leading BPM vendors provide "case management" accelerators that provide foundational best practices and technology components needed to quickly develop and deploy case management solutions. Process accelerators and frameworks also promote configuration over coding, thereby minimizing contractor labor costs.

- **Accept the reality of ad-hoc processes.** Many agencies will wiggle out of fixing their broken processes with the old refrain of "my processes are too unstructured for BPM." These ad-hoc, unstructured processes are the very ones that keep agency heads up late at night praying that nothing slips through the cracks. Fortunately, in recent years BPM vendors stepped up to the plate to support ad-hoc and unstructured process management. This means you can kick-off a process, assign it to an initial staff member who can then decide where it needs to go from there. Agencies heads implementing ad-hoc BPM solutions sleep well at night, knowing that they have visibility into the status and progress of key unstructured processes.

During this year of crisis, government needs to show business that it is possible to tackle tough process problems from a smart and lean mindset—with a sharp eye on the lookout for bloated process projects that don't create value. Business and public sector leaders around the world are watching and prepared to follow your lead. They are asking whether America can finally fix its broken processes.

Of course, the answer is: *Yes We Can!*

Measuring Readiness for BPM: Insights from Corporate Entrepreneurship and Organizational Change Research

Daniel T. Holt, Air Force Institute of Technology, United States

ABSTRACT

In this chapter, a framework that has been used by Department of Defense leaders to understand two fundamental issues that are keys to readiness for and sustainment of continuous improvement is presented. First, leaders must understand the extent to which the environment will support long-term, sustained improvement efforts, focusing on the top management's support, work discretion, rewards and reinforcements, and time availability. Second, leaders must understand how members view any specific BPM effort, understanding whether improvements are needed, are appropriate, can be done, and will be beneficial.

INTRODUCTION

In July 2008, the senior leaders at a Southwestern Air Force Base faced a perplexing problem. One of their shops that maintained and refurbished jet engines lost nearly $16 million over 18 months. With this news, the leadership immediately pulled together a cross-functional team of technical experts from across the organization to examine the issue and answer two key questions. "How did this happen?" and, more importantly, "What could be done to keep it from happening again?" Using a structured process improvement method, the team discovered that, as parts were being tested and calibrated by one group of technicians, replacement pieces were being ordered by others. As a result, the replacement parts on hand exceeded the shop's needs dramatically. To understand how this happened, the team began mapping the process of requesting, ordering, and receiving engine parts. They found a confusing, redundant, paper-based process that had evolved over the years where orders were often made on hunches. Then, those who actually tested and calibrated parts placed additional orders without regard to inventory or previous orders. In essence, the process was outdated, responsibilities were misunderstood, and over-ordering was inevitable. As one team member noted, "Supply management and parts integrity are a critical area of our business. Simple mistakes in procedure can cost the government and ultimately the taxpayers millions of dollars." Accordingly, the team devised a new process that involved everyone working on the engine, incorporated necessary data, significantly reduced costs, and eliminated steps that were the source of 60 percent of ordering errors.

This particular vignette represents a significant success story within the Air Force's broad *Air Force Smart Operations for the 21st Century* program. Coined AFSO 21 within Air Force circles, the program codifies Air Force leaders' focused and dedicated effort to maximize value and minimize waste in all of its processes. Be it jet engine maintenance, aircraft ground-time, deployment processing, pharmacy operations, or looking at excess aircraft weight to conserve fuel—all individuals and teams within the Air Force have been encouraged to leverage their collective expertise, process improvement tools, and observed best practices to improve. As small successes are realized through this program, Air Force leaders, perhaps more importantly, hope to cultivate a culture of continuous process improvement whereby improvement efforts are not only initiated and directed from the top-down but simultaneously and continuously emerge from the bottom up. Conveying this sentiment, a member of the team that refined the jet engine supply ordering process said, "I hope the culture of continuous improvement becomes ingrained, because there's always room for improvement."

Diffusing this type of culture within any organization, public or private, is difficult and often requires organizational members at all levels to adopt new perspectives, philosophies, and work practices. To help these perspectives and practices take hold, leaders find themselves asking, "Where do I start?" and "Is my organization ready?" Research in corporate entrepreneurship and organizational change indicates that, as a first step, managers should comprehensively examine their organization's underlying readiness to embrace any change to include those that might come with process improvements. [1] Through this examination, differences that may exist between leaders' beliefs about the environment and a particular initiative and the organizational members' beliefs are highlighted. If the differences are large, especially with regards to the supporting environment, and nothing is done to close those gaps, sustaining the desired perspectives, philosophies, and practices would likely be unsuccessful. In essence, an assessment of an organization's readiness can serve as a guide to leaders as they plan and implement improvement initiatives.

Unfortunately, the assessment of an organization's readiness for continuous improvement initiatives poses a challenge because there does not appear to be a structured framework available. To fill this gap, the considerable bodies of research that have examined readiness for change and that which has suggested "enablers" of organizational innovation were examined. [1, 2, 3] From this, a diagnostic framework is presented that has been used to help Department of Defense leaders understand their organization's readiness and guide them as they try to transform and manage processes. The proposed readiness framework was guided by both practical and theoretical considerations. Practically, Air Force leaders were interested in efficiently understanding the readiness of their organizations. So they needed a conceptual framework that focused on the most salient issues. Theoretically, this conceptual framework needed to be evidence-based, drawing on previous empirical findings and used diagnostic measures that were valid and reliable.

Table 1 presents this framework as a sequence of steps. While most organizations have strategies and goals, the first step entails the translation of these strategies and goals into specific actions. While not the focus of this chapter, this step is critical. Slogans like "stomp out red tape" are compelling goals within a bureaucracy but must have tangible activities associated with them if leaders hope to successfully rid themselves of unnecessary administrative burdens. Translating this particular slogan into action, managers in one organization were asked to look at any document they were asked to sign and count the number of individuals who had signed it previously. In one case, six signatures, one of which belonged to a General, appeared on a request to order office supplies. Rather than increasing oversight, it was watering it down with each person assuming others would scrutinize the request. Thus, to "stomp out red tape", leaders engaged in a specific action, asking themselves, "What value did my signature (and presumed review) add when three others had already reviewed a request?" By articulating this unambiguous action, several inefficient processes were identified, evaluated, and, subsequently, stream-lined without diminishing oversight.

With the first step fulfilled, leaders may still encounter several impediments as they try to create a culture of continuous improvement. First, the environment may not support the desired activities. Thus, it is important for leaders to understand the extent to which the environment is conducive to long-term, continuous improvement efforts. While a supportive environment may be a necessary precondition for success, it may not be sufficient for groups to embrace any particular process change efforts. So, leaders must also understand the extent to which the members embrace specific improvement efforts.

ASSESSING KEY FACETS OF THE INTERNAL ENVIRONMENT

I argue that continual process improvement requires more than technical prowess or some clever diagnosis. It requires a climate with aligned systems and individuals behaving in a coordinated way to advance goals, refine methods as needed, and improve. Researchers in the area of corporate entrepreneurship have provided key insights toward understanding the factors that might enhance or inhibit continual process improvements like the Air Force's AFSO 21 efforts [3, 4].

Step 1. Specify performance in actionable terms.

Step 2. Diagnose the internal environment, examining the following:

Dimension	Definition	Example Item
Management support	An environment where managers have encouraged innovative behaviors	People are often encouraged to take calculated risks with ideas around here.
Rewards & reinforcement	An environment where managers have reinforced innovative behavior by explicitly linking innovative performance and achievement to rewards	The rewards I receive are dependent upon my work on the job.
Work discretion	An environment where managers have provided broad decision making latitude and delegated authority	This business unit provides the freedom to use my own judgment.
Time availability	An environment that has allowed or facilitated personnel to pursue innovative efforts in support of short and long-term goals	My co-workers and I always find time for long term problem solving.

Step 3. Diagnose the attitudes members have toward any particular improvement effort, examining the following:

Dimension	Definition	Example Item
Need for improvement	A belief that there are legitimate reasons and needs to revise the focal process.	There are legitimate reasons for us to analyze and change this process.
Appropriateness	A belief that the proposed strategies and solutions address the identified needs.	The time we are spending on this improvement should be spent on something else.
Capability to execute	A belief that the system is capable of executing activities associated with revisions.	I do not anticipate any problems adjusting to the work I will have when this improvement is adopted.
Personal benefits	A belief that implementing changes will lead to benefits.	My future in this job will be limited because of these improvements.

Table 1. Framework to Assess Readiness for Continuous Improvement

Briefly, corporate entrepreneurship refers to the entrepreneurial behaviors in larger, existing organizations that lead to innovative activities, including new product development, process improvement, and service improvement [5]—in essence, activities related to BPM. At the individual level, it is demonstrated through each members' (a) anticipatory, forward-leaning planning (i.e., pro-activeness); (b) creative, novel problem solving (i.e., innovation); and (c) calculated experimenting (i.e., prudent risk-taking). [5] Moreover, creating an internal work environment that cultivates employees' interest and commitment to these activities could arguably be the centerpiece of any process improvement culture where managers and leaders at all levels feel responsible for its development.

Indeed, empirical findings have indicated that engaging in corporate entrepreneurial behaviors has positively affected organizations' performance. [6] To capitalize on these successes, several researchers have attempted to identify the environmental factors that encourage these attitudes. This focus on the internal work environment assumes that given the appropriate setting members within an organization have some basic capability to be proactive, innovate, and take prudent risks. While there is no question that success would also be a function of other factors like individual capabilities, changes to the internal work environment are within the discretion of most leaders. Findings focused on identifying the key factors have converged around four key dimensions [3], namely, *management support, rewards and reinforcement, work discretion*, and *time availability.*

Leaders must be willing to, first, look at themselves and examine the cues they are giving organizational members through their actions. *Management support* represents the belief that top-level managers are willing to facilitate and promote innovative endeavors. Several empirical efforts have supported the link between a supportive leadership climate and results. Damanpour, for instance, found that innovation in organizations was related to the perceptions that employees had regarding their managers' attitudes toward innovation. [7] Kuratko and his colleagues state that management support is manifested by top level managers who explicitly promote pro-activeness, innovation, and risk taking and champion creative ideas. [8] More recently, Ireland, Kuratko, and Morris extend this, stating that leaders should establish goals, a system of feedback, and results-based rewards. [5]

While the establishment of goals is consistent with the first step of the readiness framework posited (see Table 1), the reward climate should be examined as the internal environment is diagnosed. Specifically, rewards and reinforcement concerns the extent to which organizational members feel rewards are contingent on performance, encouraging the pursuit of improvement efforts. There is a rich academic literature that has linked individual performance with rewards. Twomey and Harris, in their study of the links between Human Resource Management systems and corporate entrepreneurship, found a positive relationship between reward and recognition systems and entrepreneurial activities. [9] The use of extrinsic rewards like pay may be difficult for some managers like those in a military organization that has a fixed pay scale. Even in these organizations, however, there is the possibility for additional financial support through other programs. The DoD has the Innovative Development through Employee Awareness (IDEA) program that will reward members for their significant suggestions. Moreover, DoD civilian employee compensation includes an annual bonus that should be linked to performance.

The other elements of the internal context involve the design of jobs. *Work discretion* refers to the extent to which individuals feel that they are given decision making latitude and freedom, giving them the authority and responsibility to adjust processes. In turn, *time availability* refers to the extent to which individuals and groups feel they have the time needed to pursue innovations and that their jobs are structured in ways that allow them to pursue short- and long-term goals. The logic underlying these factors is straight forward. Leaders should not expect proactive and innovative process improvements if individuals do not feel they have the authority to suggest and test improvements nor the time to do so. Empirical tests, indeed, have indicated that improvement activities in organizations are affected by these factors. [10]

An instrument is available that validly and reliably measures these climate dimensions. [3, 11] Using this measure in an organization, the understanding of these particular facets of the climate was very useful as leaders of a large Department of Defense agency were trying to jumpstart their process improvement efforts. In this case, the organization's leaders had initiated a broad program that created a series of cross-functional teams chartered to examine several acquisition and administrative processes. As is often the case, after a year, the leaders had seen few results. The leaders assumed that the performance problems resided at the individual- and team-level, suggesting that individuals needed technical training with regards to the tools needed for process analysis and the groups needed training on effective team management. Rather than simply accept that assumption, the leaders were willing to gauge the overall climate of the organization to determine whether it was conducive to the activities they had hoped for. When the climate was measured and compared to benchmark organizations within DoD that had been recognized for their continuous process improvement climates [10], the data indicated that the global climate was inhibiting their efforts (i.e., *management support, rewards and reinforcement, work discretion,* and *time availability* were lower than the model organizations) not the individuals. From these data, an action plan was developed that first targeted work discretion, ensuring that the individuals within the organization felt that they could truly make changes. Overtime, rewards (financial and non-financial) were provided to support this and several significant improvements followed.

ASSESSING ATTITUDES TOWARD SPECIFIC IMPROVEMENTS

The internal work environment characterizes the circumstances, or existing conditions, that influence improvement efforts. Regardless of these circumstances, the organizational change literature has indicated that readiness is also shaped by the attitudes individuals have with regard to a specific change. [1] Foremost is a general belief among individuals that a changes or improvements are necessary. Armenakis, Harris and Mossholder dubbed this an acknowledged discrepancy or recognized differences between current performance levels and some more desired performance, suggesting that organizational members tend to reject changes that they believe are unwarranted because of current performance. [1] Within the process management context, this presents a vexing problem. Most would agree that there is "always room for process improvements" and a continuous improvement climate is predicated on members recognizing this and behaving accordingly. Unfortunately, leaders must recognize they will always be working against a mindset that believes, "If it ain't broke, don't fix it!" This inherent tension reinforces the importance of the framework's second step, ensuring the internal environment is aligned such that this mindset is challenged.

Armenakis, Harris, and Feild later suggested that individuals will evaluate the appropriateness of any change, the capability to execute a new process, and the value that comes with change. [12] As with the environmental factors, these elements have been strongly related to change success. The capability to execute the new process, for instance, refers to individuals' judgments regarding their ability to perform certain tasks and has been related to the amount of effort and persistence they are willing to put forth toward goals. [13] When they do not believe they can succeed, little effort is put forth and efforts are abandoned when obstacles are encountered. Research findings have indicated that these perceptions are more salient during taxing situations like those that come as new management practices are introduced. [14]

Like the internal environment, these beliefs can be measured validly with a questionnaire and the information garnered can be useful to leaders. [2] In one particular situation, the questionnaire was used to gauge the readiness of DoD members who were embroiled in a contentious process improvement effort that had been directed by the Office of Management and Budget. [15] This effort dictated that all government agencies study the activities they perform to decide whether the activity was so important that it must be accomplished using government resources and manpower or could be accomplished by private sector service providers—put simply, all activities were being studied for outsourcing. If the analysis showed that the private sector could accomplish the activities, government organizations, ideally, would improve their processes by reducing overhead and refocusing resources on functions directly related to the public's interests.

One of the larger more complex divisions within one DoD agency that appeared ripe for this type of assessment was the engineering division responsible for facility design, construction, and maintenance at installations throughout the world. This engineering division's functions had already been outsourced to varying degrees. For instance, the private sector maintained utility systems at some installations. Given this, it was not surprising when the readiness assessment found a widely held perception that no further changes were necessary (i.e., low discrepancy). More detailed comments indicated that members viewed this as nothing more than an edict from a remote agency with little understanding of their organization's functions. With this information, leaders crafted an appeal to managers, asking them to candidly reflect on the extent to which they had thoroughly analyzed all of their functions and processes to determine if the edict made sense. With a frank assessment, managers found that there were indeed additional opportunities worth exploring and several agency-wide processes changes were introduced.

Conclusion

The Department of Defense is engaged in a dizzying array of missions from applying force in austere places like Afghanistan and Iraq, to assisting in the response to natural disasters, to maintaining defenses around the United States, to operating satellites in deep space. To fulfill these missions in a resource-constrained environment, leaders have called for an examination and transformation of the myriad processes that support and sustain these diverse missions. All processes involved must be scrutinized to see if new, innovative methods can be applied to fulfill the organization's obligations more efficiently. More importantly, leaders seek a culture of continuous improvement that flourishes beyond the current budget constraints.

Change lies at the heart of these efforts! The diffusion of change within any bureaucratic firm, whether public or private, is challenging. Elements of the organizations' climate as well as the characteristics of the efforts themselves may be impediments to success. By measuring the key internal climate factors that influence proactive, innovative, and risk taking activities, leaders can create action plans to reshape the environment to cultivate the desired culture. Then, as specific alternatives are developed, attitudes toward those should be gauged. Armed with this information, leaders will understand whether their employees are ready for a particular effort and have clear path to better develop their employees' understanding when necessary.

What makes this framework unique? First, it focuses on the individual. Most leaders recognize that organizations by themselves do nothing—even the most collective activities require the fusion of actions taken by individuals. Organizations, therefore, will proactively and innovatively improve processes through the coordinated actions of individuals, making their perceptions and evaluations of the environment and specific efforts critical. Second, it blends two areas of research, namely, the research examining corporate entrepreneurship and organizational change, to provide novel insights into process management. Third, it provides actionable guidance to leaders. The recommendations regarding change implementation, for instance, are often too vague to be helpful. Almost any change prescription will tell leaders to communicate but often does not identify the important messages that should be conveyed. Those that do often stop after stating leaders should explain the needs and benefits that come with change. While helpful, research indicates that appropriateness and capability are also key messages important to success and often overlooked. Thus, even when attitudes cannot be measured using the instruments available, leaders at all levels still have a framework that can facilitate a self-assessment. Finally, this framework can be used by leaders in the private, for-profit sector as well as researchers who can use this to systematically test the efficacy of implementation alternatives. Armed with this information leaders may reap more significant returns on the considerable investments made in process improvements.

REFERENCES

1. Armenakis, A. A., Harris, S. G., & Mossholder, K. W., "Creating readiness for organizational change". *Human Relations,* Volume 46, pp. 681-703, 1993.
2. Holt, D. T., Armenakis, A. A., Harris, S. G., & Feild, H. S., "Readiness for organizational change: The systematic development of a scale". *Journal of Applied Behavioral Science.* Volume 43, Issue 2, pp. 232-255, 2007.
3. Hornsby, J.S., Kuratko, D. F., & Zahra, S. A., "Middle managers' perception of the internal environment for corporate entrepreneurship: Assessing a measurement scale". *Journal of Business Venturing,* Volume 17, pp. 49-63, 2002.
4. Hornsby, J.S., Kuratko, D. F., & Montagno, R. V., "Perception of internal factors for corporate entrepreneurship: A comparison of Canadian and U.S. managers". *Entrepreneurship Theory and Practice,* Volume 24, pp. 9-24, 1999.
5. Ireland, R. D., Kuratko, D. F., & Morris, M. H., "A health audit for corporate entrepreneurship: Innovation at all levels, Part I". *Journal of Business Strategy,* Volume 27, pp. 21-30, 2006.
6. Zahra, S. A. & Garvis, D., "International corporate entrepreneurship and firm performance: the moderating effect of international environmental hostility". *Journal of Business Venturing,* Volume 15, pp. 469-92, 2000.
7. Damanpour, F., "Organizational Innovation: A Meta-Analysis of Effects of Determinant and Moderators". *Academy of Management Journal,* Volume 34, pp. 555-590, 1991.
8. Kuratko, D. F., Ireland, R. D., Covin, J. G., & Hornsby, J. S., "A Model of Middle-level Managers' Entrepreneurial Behavior". *Entrepreneurship Theory & Practice,* Volume 29, pp. 699-716, 2005.
9. Twomey, D. F. & D. L. Harris., "From Strategy to Corporate Outcomes: Aligning Human Resource Management Systems with Entrepreneurial Intent". *International Journal of Commerce and Management,* Volume 10, pp. 43-55, 2000.
10. Wood, C. C., Holt, D. T., Reed, T. S., & Hudgens, B. J., "Entrepreneurial mindset in United States Air Force organizations: Antecedents and outcomes". *Journal of Small Business and Entrepreneurship.* Volume 21, pp. 117-132, 2008.

11. Hornsby, J. S., Holt, D. T., & Kuratko, D. F., "The dynamic nature of corporate entrepreneurship constructs: An assessment of the Corporate Entrepreneurship Assessment Instrument (CEAI)". *Best Paper Proceedings of the Annual Meeting of the Academy of Management*, Anaheim, CA, August 8 – 13, 2008.

12. Armenakis, A. A., Harris, S. G., & Feild, H. S., "Making change permanent: A model for institutionalizing change interventions". *Research in Organizational Change and Development*, Volume 12, pp. 97-128, 1999.

13. Bandura, A., "Self-efficacy mechanism in human agency". *American Psychologist*, Volume 37, pp. 122-147, 1982.

14. Bernerth, J., "Expanding our understanding of the change message". *Human Resource Development Review*, Volume 3, pp. 36-53, 2004.

15. Holt, D. T., Self, D. R., Thal, A. E., & Lo, S. W., "Facilitating organizational change: A test of leadership strategies". *Leadership and Organization Development Journal*, Volume 24, pp. 262-272, 2003.

Streamlining Research and Development Case Files at the Air Force Research Laboratory (AFRL)

Charles Joesten, PMP, ICOR Partners LLC, USA

ABSTRACT

The United States Air Force Research Laboratory (AFRL) provides leadership in scientific and technological research and development for Department of Defense, commercial, and academic organizations. Key artifacts that ultimately improve warfighting technologies are assembled into official records known as laboratory case files. From 2002-2005 AFRL set out to streamline the management of its case files using improved processes and modern workflow tools. This case explores the challenges AFRL faced and its approach to better process, workflow, and records management of science and technology projects.

Practitioners in the field of workflow management and process improvement face a variety of challenges with each agency they support. Administrative, bureaucratic, and logistical challenges were all considered in determining the best business process management solutions for AFRL. Additionally, many challenges related to the unique nature of the content generated and managed at the lab, including rocket science.

INTRODUCTION

This case highlights the approach and results of a team of AFRL scientists and engineers to define, analyze, and streamline the workflow of the lab's case files. The team targeted areas for improvement including data collection, forms population, automation of case file folders, protocol constraints, and improved access to case files for auditors or fellow researchers. A tool was selected and piloted to support the improved processes, and the approach to automating the case file workflow gleaned valuable lessons learned.

UNITED STATES AIR FORCE RESEARCH LABORATORY

AFRL was a young command, a 1997 consolidation of four Air Force laboratory facilities and the Office of Scientific Research, with an annual budget of more than two billion dollars. At the time, AFRL employed nearly six thousand civilian and military personnel spread across eight locations nationwide. Each location was the site of one or more technical directorates that each specialized in a particular research discipline including: air vehicles, space vehicles, propulsion, directed energy, human effectiveness, information, materials, munitions, sensors, and scientific research. Initial logistical challenges in conducting basic, applied, and advanced technology research were evident due to the numerous locations, directorates, and fractionalized ways that research was planned, managed, and documented.

In the spring of 2002, AFRL embarked on an ambitious initiative to transform their organization and deploy enterprise tools. One key goal was to capture, automate, streamline, and track their mission-critical artifacts—research and development case files. The challenges associated with this effort resulted from non-

standard formats and protocol, inconsistent data, varying content security designations, numerous review and approval triggers, redundant regulatory compliances, external downstream handoffs, voluminous storage requirements, and shrinking numbers of administrative support staff. Additionally, the key stakeholders were the scientists and engineers of the lab, an incredibly talented and intellectual team of several hundred, but one functioning in antiquated and manual processes and procedures by modern workflow standards. These issues presented great risks to the research function of the lab, ultimately jeopardizing its warfighting capability, security, and innovation.

THE ENTERPRISE BUSINESS SYSTEM INITIATIVE

In January 2000, AFRL kicked off the Enterprise Business System (EBS) initiative as a strategic investment to improve and integrate the lab's business processes. This was a large and complex effort due to the varying practices for managing research projects in the geographically remote Technical Directorates (TDs). The program was intended to overhaul the technical infrastructure, build an integrated architecture, and deploy collaborative applications to improve business operations and mission-critical systems. It focused on delivering functional solutions and cross-functional solutions. Included in the functional process scope was research and information management, operational integration, budget planning and programming, financial management, human resource management, and customer relationship management. Cross-functional solutions included document and records management, task management, business intelligence, data warehousing, and web-based portal services. Though extensive collaboration and input came from the remote Technical Directorates (TDs), most of the program deliverables and direct inputs came from the AFRL headquarters complex at Wright-Patterson Air Force Base in Dayton, Ohio.

The entire AFRL community invested in the EBS program in some way, financially or by assigning staff resources to support. After awhile however, folks in the field began to wonder why no tangible impacts or improvements were making their way to the TDs. Extensive analysis, requirements gathering, process mapping, and technical drawings led to system acquisitions. A business intelligence tool and financial management system were deployed and tested. A robust content management system with implementation support had also been acquired. Many antiquated or duplicate legacy systems were analyzed for integration or absorption options. These accomplishments showed progress, but not a return on the substantial TD investment. Senior stakeholders decided to complement the top-down solution implementation approach with a bottom-up data gathering effort and more input from the users in the remote TDs. Ultimately the strategic architecture and operational inputs would meet to provide a more robust system and one achievable and visible to a greater audience in a shorter timeframe.

> Lesson Learned #1: Identify and support core business drivers.

An EBS program team was formed to canvas the lab and find a user base that could help provide the visibility and value of the program out to the field. Some process work and requirements from early in the program were revisited and it was determined that AFRL's bench-level scientists and engineers (S&Es) could serve as the user sample to test EBS functionality with actual TD users. The S&Es made up the largest population of the AFRL staff and were the core of the Air Force's superior research and development brain trust. However, with the staff shrinking each year, the S&Es were becoming ever burdened by administrative tasks and bureaucratic procedures which kept them from their scientific specialties. An initiative called Information Technology for the Scientist and Engineer began, and the team recruited representatives from each of the TDs and at least one representative from each geographical site location. The invitation for participation was a success in the field, and the TDs especially appreciated getting first-hand insight into the EBS program progress but more importantly being able to contribute to tangible results. The program team realized that including the S&Es was an important lesson in fostering more customer buy-in, validating requirements from the source, reducing the implementation lifecycle with parallel but complimentary efforts, and improving program communications throughout a geographically dispersed organization.

> **Lesson Learned #2: Know and include your audience.**

INFORMATION TECHNOLOGY FOR THE SCIENTIST AND ENGINEER

The Information Technology for the Scientist and Engineer (ITSE) project had its own budget and plan, with a dynamic group of representatives from all over the lab. Many of the team had been in the lab for decades and the chairman for over thirty years. These representatives drew remarkable respect from their colleagues in the field, other fellow researchers. The first challenge was to spearhead a solution that could positively benefit any TD or type of research. One pain point that was felt by all was in the area of managing research with respect to the contractual and administrative documentation required for each research project. Of particular concern was that the Air Force was quite generous in publishing mandatory guidance and directives for particular elements of research projects, but little guidance to standardize the overall way research projects were managed and documented. The directors at each remote site, made up of one to many TDs, essentially determined their own way of performing and reporting research. The team ascertained that the most value with the least effort would come from automating administrative research processes for the S&Es.

An initial query found three manuals from three different TDs that helped S&Es outline the administrative processes managing science and technology projects. One common attribute on which all three manuals were based was the work unit. Synonymous to a defined project, the work unit was the smallest segment of a research and development effort with a defined beginning, end, and tangible deliverables. By rebuilding lab processes and procedures based on the work unit, solutions could be built that would translate to any TD, any scientific discipline, and at any location. The next step involved consolidating and integrating the existing manuals to create one that was useful to the entire S&E community.

With advice and guidance from the Air Force Records Manager, the resulting document became an official Air Force Manual. The manual became a required document for guidance on project management under the title "AFRLMAN 61-204, AFRL Scientist and Engineer (S&E) Manual." The manual provided a checklist for every phase of managing work units as a bench-level scientist or engineer. Hyperlinks were used within the document to provide a streamlined, user-friendly artifact that could be easily navigated given the dependencies of the particular project and user decision path. In print form, the twenty-seven page document was relatively "light-weight" compared to many voluminous Air Force handbooks. Useful references included links to forms, a detailed glossary, lifecycle timelines, roles and responsibilities, earned value measures, standardized and validated acronyms, and a two-page version of a checklist for printing as a desk reference. From the very onset, the manual was written with the work unit process in mind, and a process standardized for everyone in the lab. So streamlined was the document with its procedural approach and integrated links to more detailed or related content, it nearly served as a design document for its companion website. It was easily web-enabled and available to AFRL users via their intranet. The web version helped create one standard set of processes and procedures for managing research and development projects throughout all of the remote TDs.

The AFRL S&E Manual was a major milestone for the lab in that it was created and put in practice through the collaborative voice of all of the TDs. It was written by the S&Es, for the S&Es, which helped build critical mass for support of the enterprise program. However, though more and more projects became standardized, this did not help relieve the administrative burden placed on the S&Es. A more robust tool would be required to actually automate the work unit management process.

> **Lesson Learned #3: Find a process champion, then get consensus.**

RESEARCH AND DEVELOPMENT CASE FILE MANAGEMENT

In addition to the work unit being the mechanism that all S&Es could relate to, research and development (R&D) case files were something that all S&Es were responsible for when conducting science and technology research. The collection of artifacts from a project was stored in a physical case file folder, and could include requirements documentation, contracts, work orders, receipts, data outputs, test results, or even physical pieces of equipment or test apparatus. However, little standardization and predominantly manual collection processes led to a multitude of inconsistencies, missing contents, and rework. Actual folders were stored in file cabinets and an administrative assistant helped catalogue where cabinets and particular folders could be found in the event of an audit.

In some cases attention paid to record-keeping and reporting deadlines helped ensure the case files were built and maintained in compliant, though not always, consistent order. However, many of the case files for busier labs or larger projects were updated just before reporting deadlines or when an audit was imminent. This practice and resulting scramble to comply was much like compiling a tax return the night before the due date. With a shrinking workforce, AFRL had fewer and fewer administrative resources each year. The most important requirement for maintaining an orderly case file was to capture the research or experimentation that was being performed because it could ultimately be archived as an official record. After interviews and workshops to collect feedback on the S&E Manual and possible next steps, consensus showed that the case file was ripe for improvement to:

- Reduce the effort for building, maintaining, and retiring case files
- Make compliance audits easier and quicker by allowing electronic files to serve as official records
- Streamline and automate case file process steps

The stage was set and the next tasks were to map the case file business process and data models.

The R&D Case File Business Process

Modeling the case file process was based on the work that had previously been completed for the AFRL S&E Manual. The key process steps were closely related to the Project Management Institute's Guide to the Project Management Body of Knowledge (PMBOK), Third Edition process groups:

- Initiate Work Unit (similar to PMBOK's Initiating Process Group)
- Plan Work Unit (similar to PMBOK's Planning Process Group)

- Implement Work Unit (similar to PMBOK's Executing Process Group)
- Maintain Active Work Units (similar to PMBOK's Monitoring and Controlling Process Group)
- Complete Work Unit (similar to PMBOK's Closing Process Group)

The process lexicon for managing work units included processes and subprocesses with varying levels of detail mapped. The ITSE team focused on processes that related to the case file, hence the variations in detail. The processes modeled by the team represented the initiation, planning, implementation, maintenance, and completion of case file phases as specified in the S&E Manual. The map in Figure 1 shows the processes for managing a work unit. The planning in processes "1.0 Initiate Work Unit" and "2.0 Plan Work Unit" led to artifacts that required the generation of the R&D case file. The "3.0 Implement Work Unit" process was where the case file was created and when the work unit was implemented as a project.

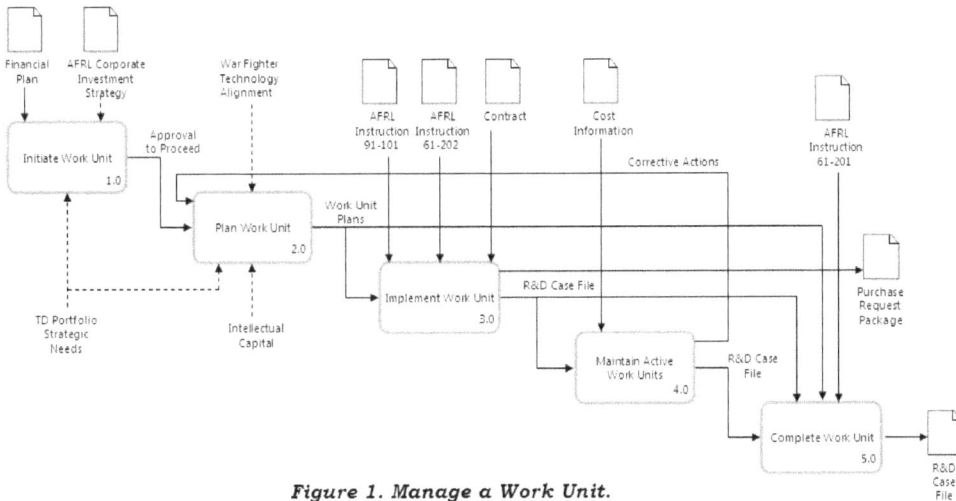

Figure 1. Manage a Work Unit.

The highest level process steps under the "Manage a Work Unit" lexicon were drilled-down to the lowest levels necessary to capture the key inputs and artifacts relevant to the work unit. Not all processes required this detail, but the "2.0 Plan Work Unit" process was where the majority of required forms, planning artifacts, contractual agreements, S&E office data, purchase requests, reviews, and approvals were performed in order for the proposed research to mature into an actual project.

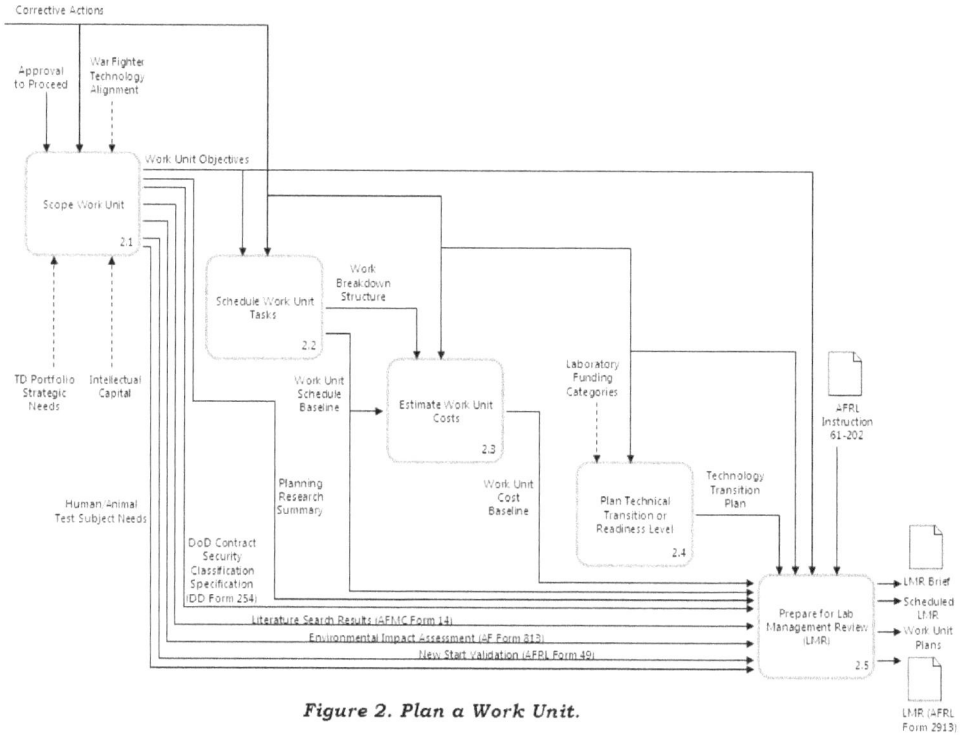

Figure 2. Plan a Work Unit.

Following the process lexicon to a greater level of detail, Figure 2 shows the drill-down of the "2.0 Plan Work Unit" process. At this level of detail the ITSE team captured the workflows and data for the many forms and project artifacts required to build a project proposal. Work units were scoped, scheduled, budgeted, and valued in order to present them for approval or disapproval in a Lab Management Review (LMR). The LMR committee determined the fate of a work unit getting funded by AFRL for continued research and development, being transitioned to an outside entity, or being archived as a record for future potential use.

The case file process detail generated by the ITSE team served many important purposes. Because the case file was a permanent mission record that was ultimately retired to the Washington National Records Center, it was important to understand where the case file contents exactly originated. This helped in the automation of the process and in setting up the legal encoding of the file folder. The models also provided an excellent baseline for discussion among all process owners and participants to fine-tune and standardize. Consensus was reached to make the processes relevant to S&Es in all TDs, as well as provide a blueprint for the automation solution so desired in the lab.

> **Lesson Learned #4: Document and understand the process.**

Building the Data Model

Another benefit of the thorough process modeling exercise was that it gleaned valuable information on the myriad forms, instructions, constraints, protocols, reviews, and approvals required to build and manage a case file. The ITSE team determined that for the scope of the case file automation prototype, data would be captured from within a data "zone of control," meaning within AFRL control. In other words, as long as data was generated by the S&Es, regardless of who owned what form or instruction, the data would be part of the ITSE Logical Data Model (LDM). The LDM followed a construct of entities, relationships, attributes, and cardinalities. These mapped to the construct of a Relational Database (RDB), one partition of the EBS data warehouse. Figure 3 shows the mapping of the LDM to the RDB with examples of the S&E data. This mapping was necessary in order to determine the relationships between the various forms and also their respective form numbers. The mapping was crucial for taking the unstructured form data and structuring it into the LDM, providing a framework for the case file management system data store.

Logical Data Model	Relational Database		Official Form Requirements	Example
Entity	Table		Form	AFRL Form 2913
Relationship	Property	...relates to...	Detail	DD, AF, AFMC, AFRL or 254, 813, 14, 2913
Attribute	Record		Element	Work Unit Manager Name
Cardinality	Alias		Same Element	Work Unit Manager Name = Project Manager Name

Figure 3. Logical Data Model Mapping.

The majority of data captured by S&Es was discovered to come from 22 different forms: Department of Defense (DD), Air Force (AF), Air Force Material Command (AFMC), Air Force Research Lab (AFRL), and Standard (SF). Each form was analyzed element by element to determine how many were unique. Across all forms it was determined that 1100 data elements were captured by the S&Es to initiate, plan, manage, and submit a work unit. An initial comparison showed at least ten percent being redundant and many more outside of the predetermined data scope. More detailed analysis and follow-up with records managers had to be performed to normalize attributes across forms. For example, a DD form might refer to a user as a "Program Manager," while an AF form might refer to the same user as a "Project Manager." All elements had to be normalized before they could become attributes in the LDM. Because this normalization would potentially take enormous effort or might never get resolved across commands, the data scope was narrowed to AF and AFRL-owned forms, and forms critical for the case files. Some attribute duplication was inevitable when normalization answers could not be obtained. This realistic approach helped keep the case file management initiative on track.

> **Lesson Learned #5: Establish a "zone of control" for data modeling.**

To recap the extent of data captured for the LDM, the following is the sequence of forms required to initiate, plan, and implement a work unit and resulting R&D case file:

- *DD Form 254*—Contract Security Classification Specification
- *AFMC Form 14*—Request for Computer-Aided Literature Search
- *AF Form 813*—Request for Environmental Impact Assessment
- *AFRL Form 49*—New Start Validation
- *AFRL Form 2913*—Lab Management Review
- *AF Form 2519*—All Purpose Checklist, R&D Case File Checklist Page 1-2
- *AFRL Form 1a*—R&D File Folder Contents/Index, Extramural Efforts

- *AFRL Form 1b*—R&D File Folder Contents/Index, Technology Transfer Efforts
- *AFRL Form 1c*—R&D File Folder Contents/Index, In-house Efforts
- *AFRL Form 5*—Laboratory Safety Permit
- *DD Form 250/250Z*—Material Inspection and Receiving Report
- *AF Form 1279*—Disclosure and Record of Invention
- *SF 298*—Report Documentation Page
- *AFMC Form 476*—Contractor Invention Monitoring
- *AFMC Form 36*—Purchase Request
- *AF Form 9*—Request for Purchase
- *AFRL Form 12*—Test Hazard Analysis
- *AFRL Form 19A*—Safety Review Board
- *AFMC Form 19*—Technical Library Materials Request
- *DD Form 1423*—Contract Data Requirements List
- *AFMC Form 607*—Budget Estimate Agreement
- *DD Form 448*—Military Interdepartmental Purchase Request

The extensive analysis on the relevant forms also uncovered obvious duplications that could eventually be addressed with the AF Records Manager. An example was that the AF Form 9 and AFMC Form 36 were essentially duplications of effort for requesting a purchase. Though probably fulfilling unique or differentiating requirements, these two forms could potentially be combined, though not without extensive coordination and approvals between the AF Headquarter and AFMC records managers. In addition to duplications, a few forms could seemingly be captured in one instance. This was evident in the AFMC Form 14 and AFMC Form 19, both requesting library-related services. Consolidating form elements might be easier to propose to AFMC records managers, but out of the ITSE scope. With case file data identified and a subset of required forms normalized, the team was ready to build a prototype business process management system for the S&Es.

AUTOMATING THE CASE FILE PROCESS

A commercial-off-the-shelf (COTS) enterprise content management system was selected to provide the lab-wide operational repository and archive for documents and records. AFRL research and development case files, documentation, and published articles required careful management, maintenance, and adherence to records protocol. The Open Text Corporation's Livelink content management and workflow engine was extremely robust yet relatively easy to configure, so it provided a relevant framework for the automation of the case file and management of work units. Automating the work unit process and building the case file and its embedded artifacts involved numerous steps, but ones that were well defined in the S&E Manual. Mapping these processes and related data inputs provided operational views and a comprehensive set of requirements. The intent with the ITSE prototype was to best capture and automate the data required to populate the forms required for new work units, streamline and automate the case file process, and best prepare the S&Es for the Lab Management Review (LMR) with easy access to auditable files. The prototype was developed in three modules: data capture mechanisms, workflow processes, and case file automation.

Data Capture Mechanisms

The scope of the first module for capturing S&E planning data was to develop what was termed the "Turbo S&T," the automated tool for science and technology projects. The application simulated popular consumer tax preparation software where prompts guided S&Es through a sequence of screens to capture preliminary information that was stored in a single repository. For each subsequent request, the system saved and reused data already entered, without users retyping it all as they had to previously on the numerous paper forms. Some data was populated automatically, drawing from other applications after manual entries triggered transparent queries. Before the EBS integrated the corporate systems, each application maintained its own data store, interfacing with companion systems to share data, but only when prompted. The Turbo S&T prototype stored its own data as well, pulling in what it needed from other applications, based on entries from the user. For example, when the user entered their name, a transparent query to the AFRL global address list in Microsoft Exchange returned office and contact information related to the user and automatically populated that section of the database for later use. The architecture at this stage of development was still very transactional, but at least electronic and not in file cabinets.

Workflow Processes

Many features of the workflow engine satisfied S&E requirements with little configuration. Workflows were built for each of the process areas in the "Manage a Work Unit" lexicon and the more detailed "2.0 Plan a Work Unit" sub-processes. This way planning work was presented to the S&Es, with resulting data capture, in smaller bursts. If a user wanted to save work in progress and return to it later, the entry screens remained the same as when last used. Additionally, some workflows could be initiated in parallel so that the user was not tied to sequential processing limitations.

Another key feature was the process logic built into the entry screens. Selections on drop box lists and checked boxes determined the next screens, sections, or questions. This logic was derived from the S&E Manual and its checklist approach. Additionally, certain text windows required a minimum length entry or else they would signal an error and prompt the user to comply. An S&E might have to describe or justify a human use experiment for example. These checks, balances, and logic-enhanced prompts saved S&Es much effort by embedding corporate protocol and limiting the risk of duplication or rework. Once the user completed all of the necessary screens in each workflow, the next workflow started. Ultimately the system helped the S&E prepare for the Lab Management Review (LMR) with all of the data necessary to populate the required planning forms and artifacts to implement a work unit, build a case file, and start a project.

Case File Automation

Upon project approval, an accession number from the Defense Technical Information Center (DTIC) was generated for the case file, making it an official record. The forms required for the case file were stored virtually in the system, but if required in paper form, could be printed and assembled as in the legacy process. Physical items relating to the case file, such as data disks or shrapnel from a rocket engine failure, were historically stored with the physical case file. If the item was too large for a file cabinet, its storage location was noted in the case file folder. With the electronic version, storage locations for physical items were noted in the case file, and maps of the base with drawings of the buildings were linked so that the exact location of the item could be easily and accurately located. The ability to quickly and easily access case file information and contents dramatically improved the audit scores for case file compliance. Finally, official retirement dates of case files could trigger automated reminders to file owners, in order to prompt their preparation and submission to the Washington National Records Center. In all, the automation of the case file made the S&Es' lives easier and helped them focus more of their attention on scientific and technological research. Additionally, moving manual and paper-based processes to electronic format helped preserve the information, make it available to S&Es across all TDs, and reduce content errors and administrative overhead during audits.

> **Lesson Learned #6: Automate the process to eliminate errors.**

LESSONS LEARNED AND RESULTS

The Enterprise Business System at AFRL had many projects in parallel stages of development. The Scientists and Engineers of the lab drove additional value into the enterprise tools by injecting rigorous process standards into automated workflows to improve a specific, though impacting need. The enterprise content management tool was pressed and tested to its capability limit, with features that may now seem standard in enterprise resource planning or customer relationship management applications. Throughout the effort, many lessons were learned about which processes were core to the mission, which deserved the most attention, how to get buy-in to support change, and how to implement automated tools in a manual and bureaucratic culture.

The following Lessons Learned were highlighted in this case:

- Lesson Learned #1—Identify and support core business drivers. Many enterprise integration projects go on for years before any return on investment is realized. In the AFRL improvement effort, the ITSE team realized the importance of the voice of the bench-level scientists and engineers in the remote technical directorates. Streamlining their processes provided direct, tangible benefits to the core product of AFRL, the advancement of research and technology.
- Lesson Learned #2—Know and include your audience. Do not operate under a "build and they will come" approach because most likely requirements will be missed or misinterpreted. Users must help drive development to some extent, with the strategic framework based on corporate goals and objectives governing the integration of processes and solutions.
- Lesson Learned #3—Find a process champion, then get consensus. For a price, technology can be developed to perform nearly any possible function or service. Where technology cannot, business rules provide the cohesion to processes to maintain efficiency. Gaining consensus in a complex organization is sometimes near impossible, but fine-tuning standard processes and procedures to gain majority buy-in from the user base is a key factor to success. Partnering with an internal process champion helps tell the story to the masses "in their language."
- Lesson Learned #4—Document and understand the process. As COTS packages and product suites become more robust, with added features to lure one-stop shoppers, it is easier to let technology drive the way organizations do business. Traditional business process reengineering, as viable as ever, dictates that the process comes first, with technology in support as an enabler.
- Lesson Learned #5—Establish a "zone of control" for data modeling. This lesson was particularly relevant at AFRL, where numerous forms required for research and development projects were mandated by a variety of commands. Trying to normalize forms across parent commands presented insurmountable challenges so AFRL defined scope around data

that it could control. This approach helped prove the concept of standardization and consolidation of administrative procedures.

- Lesson Learned #6—Automate the process to eliminate errors. Automating any process does not guarantee that process is error-free. Processes must define the best way of performing a task and then embed logic to reduce the user input required to proceed. As processes can perform more tasks behind the scenes, there is less demand for input and potential error on the part of users or other applications.

CONCLUSION

The Air Force Research Laboratory attempted to completely overhaul its business system infrastructure with commercial, integrated, and secure systems. The scope of the Enterprise Business System program was vast and years of planning and preparation helped establish a business model and architecture to support the solution. In order to increase visibility of the program to its Technical Directorates, AFRL established a team to represent the largest user group and build a prototype to support them using the enterprise tools. The Scientists and Engineers of the lab seized the opportunity and set about to create a prototype to streamline the generation of their work products, specifically research and development work units and case files. The prototype was a success for AFRL in terms of process improvement, integration discovery, content management system testing, and cultural breakthroughs in communication and collaboration. The savings attributed to the work of the ITSE team was evident in preparation and planning time savings, reduced paper-based processes, improved access to case files and records, standardization across remote Technical Directorates, more timely return on investment, and official guidance published as a result of process improvement.

How Converging Methodologies and Technologies Effect Adoption and Success of BPM

Linus K. Chow, Oracle Corporation, USA

Government Enterprises faced with incredible changes with multiple crises and political upheaval are trying to adapt their operations to handle increased workload, cut costs, and be more agile. BPM has indeed been very effective at addressing this need, but as BPM and other capabilities have evolved, governments are expanding their evaluation and use of BPM to include this convergence of technology and methodology.

BPM does not operate in a vacuum. In fact BPM has come to be the bridge among stakeholders, methodology, systems, and legacy applications. Especially in government, BPM plays a key role in not only cutting costs and increasing efficiency, but also in adding agility to their Enterprise Architecture (EA). For many in the government this is a new and radical change to the way they are used to doing business. Here are stories of some early adopters of BPM to provide insight into their success and the way they leveraged BPM to provide capability to their constituents.

We will analyze several different BPM use cases that cross both technology (SOA, Document / Records Management, Application Integration), as well as methodology (Center of Excellence, Program / Portfolio Management, BPM vs. Development) from successful implementations. You will easily see why BPM enables an Agile EA that can encompass existing system while providing adaptability.

In our first case, BPM is seen in its traditional setting of automating paper-based processes. What BPM provides here is a lightweight agile platform enabling a flexible solution for the end user while leveraging other technologies like document / records management and applications (ERP & CRM) for government entities.

THE CASE FOR BPM IN CASE MANAGEMENT

Art Randles and Randy Blevins[5]

For government entities, the concept of a case is a known form of collaboration around a topic or incident. The legal industry's "court case," the healthcare industry's "customer case," and the investigator's "evidence tracking" are but a few examples. Case handling can follow many defined processes cleanly, but often requires careful, undefined ad-hoc situations as well. Case management requires a great deal of knowledge work, undefined interactions among all stakeholders, lengthy resolution situations, hefty human interactions, and multiple process fragments. BPM is flexible enough to accommodate both sequential and non sequential business processes that occur within the same value chain. In addition, requirements for data capture and case management technologies and their integration with BPM software form a suite of tools that supports the entire investigative value chain regardless of the sequential or non-sequential nature of the individual business processes will be identified.

Collaborative BPM Systems was made for case management, and numerous examples exist, which demonstrate how BPM is well suited for solving the case management dilemma for government entities. One such example is automating electronic Freedom of Information Act (eFOIA) inquiries. eFOIA is a process with which all government entities must comply when responding to requests to release information in a timely manner, yet ensuring that sensitive information is not released without proper approvals. This eFOIA process contains a multitude of human checks and balances and is satisfied by few application vendors. Additionally, the eFOIA solution has to be simple to execute, yet scalable and adaptable to each government entity's specific requirements.

The traditional implementation of a CRM or ERP solution to meet this requirement is overkill, and yet building a point application loses the ability to properly account for the sensitivity of the information and auditing of the process. With a BPM solution integrated with underlying document and records management for tracking original and redacted content, the system provides instantaneous visibility into the processes and audit control with DOD 5015.2 / 4 certifications if required.

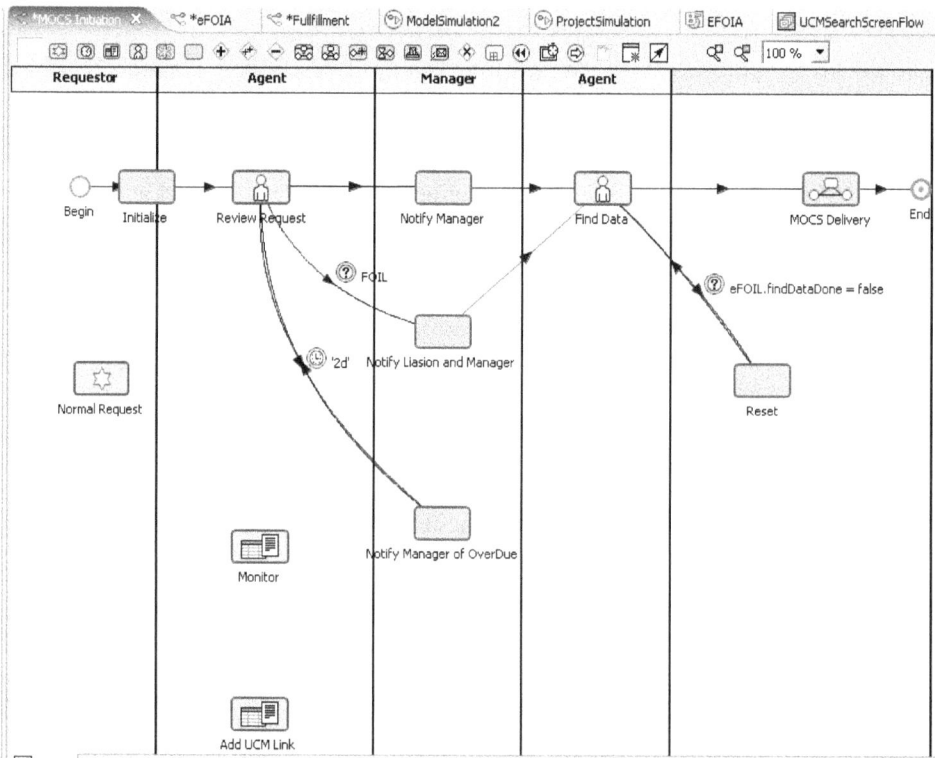

Fig 1: Example: eFOIA main process used by a large US city Mayor's Office

An example of the eFOIA process steps would be the review and removal of Personal Identity information, such as Social Security Numbers or classified information. Figure 2 below provides a screenshot of a pre-redacted working copy from EDAC Systems, Inc's automated redaction product, VeriDact. At this stage in the business process, the reviewer may approve or reject the highlighted areas and may add others for redaction.

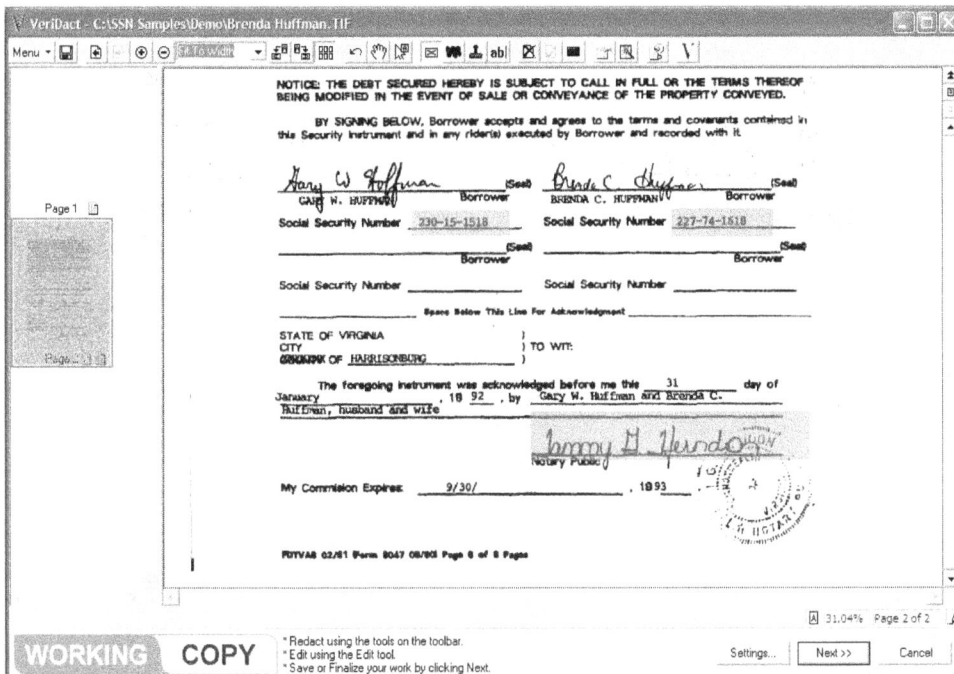

Figure 2: Pre-Redacted Working Copy

The next step in the process may be to route the approved copy to the final reviewer or to the individual responsible for relaying the information onto the inquirer. Figure 3 demonstrates the redacted version with an exemption code signifying the type of redaction it is.

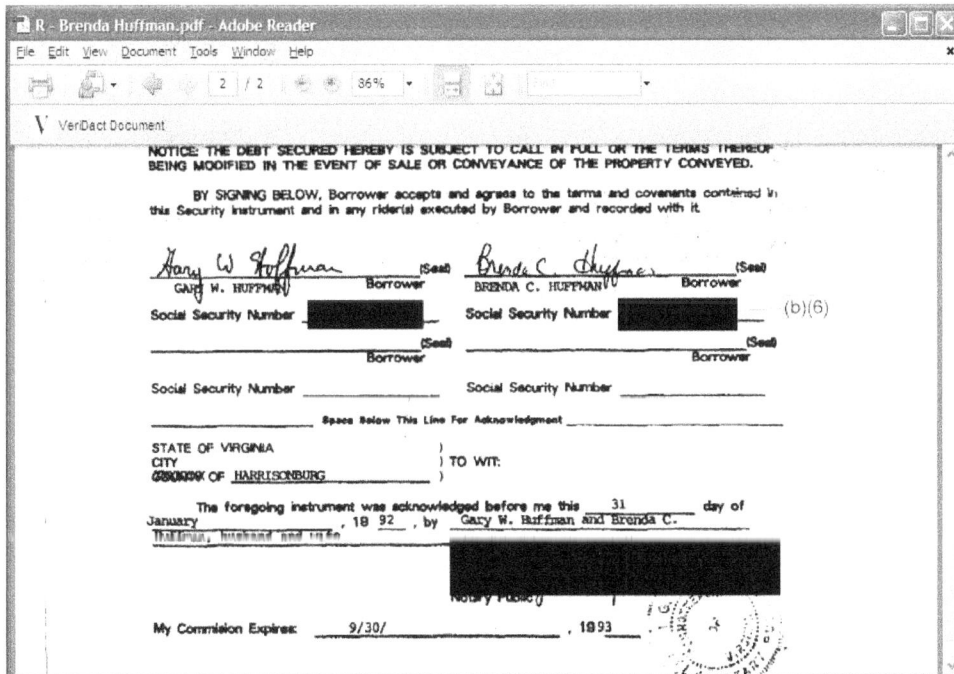

Figure 3: Redacted Version with Exemption Codes.

Court and law enforcement processes, such as e-Filing and Evidence Tracking, are a little more complicated and potentially require more integration to legacy systems and may expand additional SOA components. However, these processes involve a lot of human tasks, collaboration, and monitoring. These processes usually have more process fragments (e.g. each piece of evidence has its own life and can be associated with one or more crime cases). Only BPM can create and manage the potential process complexity and yet allow the solution to fit the specific needs of that organization (e.g. each state may do things slightly differently but may have to pass information to each other and the federal government).

As depicted in Figure 4 below, BPM provides the visibility into the system and each step therein.

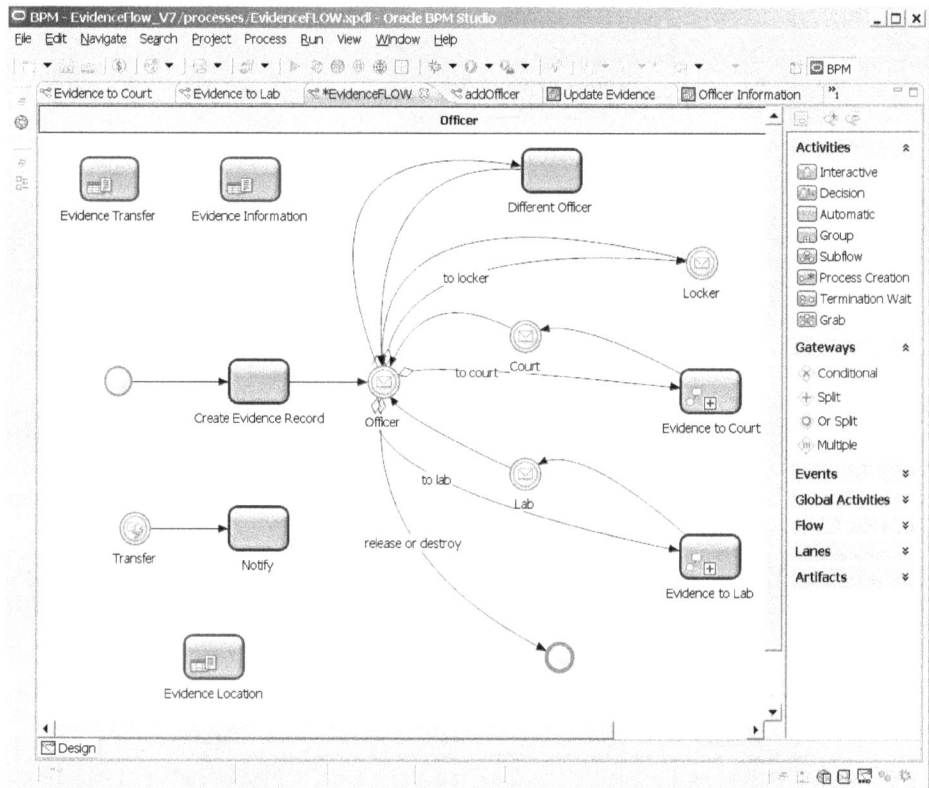

Figure 4: Evidence Tracking Process in use by West Virginia Police

According to Lt. Chris Kutcher of the Charles Town, WV Police Department, "Our previous process was manual in nature and it could take anywhere from five minutes to an hour to find a specific piece of evidence. With the new CaseFLOW Evidence Tracking system, we can tell where the evidence is by a quick check of the graphical display. Our department never wants to be in a position where perpetrators are released because evidence was misplaced."

Finally, BPM provides agility and orchestration to Enterprise deployments with applications (CRM, SCM, and ERP). BPM fills the gaps when it does not make sense to customize the applications workflow to meet and also connects multiple applications and legacy systems together without being forced into point-to-point integration. Frequently, process inefficiencies are the direct result of "gaps" that exist between these silos; the manual handoff of a purchase order from sales to finance, for example, can create the need to enter the same data twice into two different systems. Gaps among systems, people, business units, and geographies undermine the efficacy of the business overall.

BPM and SOA together provide even greater flexibility than ERP systems because they allow easier integration with other enterprise applications and business partner applications and are overall easier to change with requirements that continually evolve. Additionally, many BPM suites provide better visibility into process progress and performance than currently available within the ERP suites directly.

In our second case we see that BPM is a key tool bringing IT concepts to a broader business audience through our educational process. This is only possible due to the evolving standards surrounding BPM and the convergence between the modeling and run-time implementations of processes.

RELATING TECHNOLOGY TO BUSINESS LEADERS WITH BPM

Professor H. Mark McGibbon[1]

Many IT leaders struggle to understand how to improve their businesses. Many business schools profess to educate the future business leaders in the tools required to successfully lead a business. Yet, once the Master's in Business Administration (MBA) student graduates, the new business leader may become frustrated with knowing so little about the realities of running a small business, large corporation, or government entity. It is not that U.S. academic institutions do not teach relevant business information; rather, it is the business professor's inability to *connect-the-salient-points* presented throughout the MBA program curriculum. This can even be more challenging in programs targeted toward senior Government Executives (including CIOs) where they are balancing real-time swift changes in both policy and technology.

MBA schools are also in the education business to make profit. The school's reputation means everything for repeat business and word-of-mouth. Satisfied MBA students will help recruit new students only if the end-result produces the expected educational outcome. The expected educational outcome is more than simply understanding the functional areas of business such as marketing, sales, production, etc.

MBA students need to understand how the functional areas are related to the organization's internal and external operations. Understanding each stakeholder's perceptions will assist in measuring business performance. Most MBA schools present their students with the various perceptions that stakeholders may possess; however, it is usually presented in a homework assignment reading or a lecture, which is often not retained long after the student reads or hears the material.

Overcoming the mental retention problem has been challenge within the education field for years. One solution is for students to reinforce their readings and lectures via hands-on exercises. The hands-on exercises also assist MBA schools in connecting-the-salient-business-points and functional business competency areas.

BPM assists MBA students in understanding how organizational structures and functional areas interact. The old cliché "a picture is worth a thousand words" is a gift from the BPM Gods especially when students are assigned a massive amount of vapid reading material. Processing pictures in our visual cortex for frontal lobe reasoning is a much quicker mental process than reading thousands of words that convey the same meaning as the BPM picture. MBA students can easily comprehend pictorial representations of voluminous textbooks for deeper meaning and to answer *who, what, why, where, when and how* questions faster and with increased retention. BPM can also be easily programmed to visually execute business issues and problems via modeling and simulation.

Academic institutions have the opportunity to incorporate BPM tools within their labs to help prepare our future business leaders in cognitively understanding the holistic business picture, which comprises myriad other business areas. By allowing students to use BPM software within an academic lab (or personal computer) learning is done in a safe setting where mistakes can be made without financially hurting anyone but the student's pride. Educators also understand the business world relies on performance. Hiring the MBA student with top grades does not guarantee that the MBA student will be able to perform well in a work setting. In contrast, many successful leaders failed to do well in school, but went on to be successful in their fields—Albert Einstein, Winston Churchill and Ronald Reagan to name a few.

Applying what one learns, whether in an academic setting, or self-study, is crucial to deep understanding. Business and technology professors assist business leaders in educating business students how to apply BPM for effective and efficient decision making, budget planning, budget execution, monitoring processes, vision planning, social network mapping, organizational structuring (hierarchies, decentralized networks, centralized networks, etc.), collaboration, program / project management, process improvement, technology assessment, as well as a myriad other business-related disciplines. These business-related disciplines are conveyed more easily to the Generation-X (Gen-X) and Generation-Y (Gen-Y) populations using BPM technology since for the most part, these generations grew up using technology to understand their world.

Gen-X and Gen-Y within the United States have achieved higher education credentials compared to the Baby-Boomer generations. Gen-X and Gen-Y willingly accept technology and are socially connected using technology. Many baby boomers are now retooling their skills through education and seek technology to reduce complexity. Technically-savvy MBA students, categorized as Gen-X or Gen-Y and baby boomers willing (or forced) to retool, will reap the educational benefits from the academic institutions that incorporate BPM into their curricula. The educational benefits should in turn equate to a financial advantage within the business world making winners of both MBA students and businesses in which they are employed. For government executives BPM can provide better focus on the "Business" and "Management" side of BPM while enabling them to control technology innovation versus having their technology control them.

BPM definitely enables business to have better control of technology. Likewise, without properly thought-out and supported implementation methodologies BPM implementations would be destined for failure.

The Office of the Secretary of Defense (OSD) AT&L used a CoE to successfully manage "Agile software development" with BPM and Enterprise 2.0.

SMALL & SIMPLE WITH BIG IMPACT: A CENTER OF EXCELLENCE DOESN'T MEAN ADDING COMPLEXITY

Shaundra Eberhardt, Brian H. Kim[6]

Implementing a Center of Excellence (CoE) to manage BPM and Enterprise 2.0 solutions does not have to mean making projects large and slow moving. Presenting change in small bite-sized components go along way in smoothing stakeholder acceptance. The Keep-it-Simple Stupid (KISS) is an axiom we live by. Also, we made sure to have continued engagement and a true change management processes, knowing that we wouldn't get it right 100 percent the first time. We ran customer surveys to measure the usability of the new processes. The feedback allowed focus on the customer and to change features as required. Key to a CoE's success is a proper chain-of-command with clear lines of authority and responsibility. Forming the CoE with core staff and representation from the all stakeholders was the next step. Regularly briefing the chain of command on progress was another key factor for success. Finally, a proper change management and governance structure enabled them to control change, risk, and scope. A CoE with the right strategy actually ensures projects through KISS.

The Office of the Secretary of Defense (OSD) AT&L, like many government entities, learned from former mistakes of creating multi-year, complex, never-ending projects. Its current vision is focused on deploying a very agile and collaborative-driven solution leveraging the latest technologies and methodologies in BPM and Enterprise 2.0 to create a self-service environment supporting over 7,000 US Department of Defense's end-users across over 60 communities with over 600 Collaboration Projects. This could only be successful by several development spirals (capability releases) in three-month or less increments.

With a focus on the end-user since its first production release the OSD ATL net has achieved significant benefits for the end users. Currently, over six successful implementations are in production with enhancements and additional projects in the works. OSD ATL has now been recognized and awarded the 2008 gold award by the Global Awards for BPM and Workflow for North America[1].

Deployed on both SIPR and NIPR networks fully vetted and compliant with OSD EA, incorporating DoD CAC and PKI encryption technologies, this framework now supports six production processes: Training Request, IT Ticketing and Support, External Visit Request, External Account Creation System, Common Access Card Location Finder, and Acquisition Information Management System. With only 10 staff on average and maintaining over a 98 percent positive feedback rating was only possible with a properly structured CoE with a focus on the end-user experience.

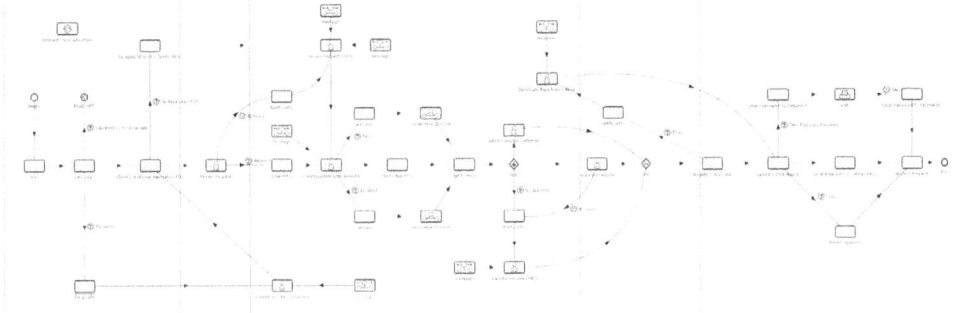

---

[1] More information on the annual *Global Awards for Excellence in BPM and Workflow* can be found at bpmf.org

Acquisition Information Management System
BSM Energy_TDS_2009MAR6_DRAFT_v5 • Download

Welcome, sponsor

You are logged in as: SPONSOR

LOGOUT

Home
Document History
End Coordination

Approve for Signature
Request Revision

Manage Comments
Current: 5 (3 new)
Outstanding: 4

Create Email

BSM Energy_TDS_2009MAR6_DRAFT_v5

Coordination Summary

Program: BSM Energy
Document Type: Technology Development Strategy
DoD Service: Army

Date Submitted: March 2, 2009

Comments Summary

Total Number of Comments Submitted	15	
Accepted Comments	8	53%
Partially Accepted Comments	1	6%
Rejected Comments	1	6%
Resolved Comments	4	44%

Coordination Status
Document Review

Suspense Date
3/9/2009
There are **3** days remaining before the selected suspense date.

Participants

Originator
Oscar Originator

Sponsor
Sally Sponsor (5)

Reviewers
Brian Kim (4)
William Rees (0)
Richard Reviewer (6)

For questions, please contact the Web & Portal Services Team at 703-602-2626 (Option #0) or ousdatl.portal@osd.mil

AT&L External Account Creation
OFFICE OF THE UNDER SECRETARY OF DEFENSE FOR ACQUISITION TECHNOLOGY & LOGISTICS

Please use the form below to submit an External Account Request

First Name:
Middle Initial:
Last Name:
Title:
Phone:
Extension:
Email:
Agency:
Grade:

Submit   Cancel

For questions, please contact the Web & Portal Services Team at 703-602-2626 or ousdatl.portal@osd.mil

AT&L External Account Creation
OFFICE OF THE UNDER SECRETARY OF DEFENSE FOR ACQUISITION TECHNOLOGY & LOGISTICS

Thank You!

Your request has been successfully submitted for review.
You will receive an email with login information when your account has been approved.

Web & Portal Services
ousdatl.portal@osd.mil

CAC Locations
Home

Write   Design

Hoffman Buildings 1 & 2 - Rm 7N63
Updated Dec 12, 2007 3:13 PM by Janet Towles
View Record | Delete Record | Edit Record

Crystal City Polo Building - Rm 9W20
Updated Dec 12, 2007 3:13 PM by Janet Towles
View Record | Delete Record | Edit Record

Pentagon Pass Office - 1I 1084
Updated Dec 12, 2007 3:12 PM by Janet Towles
View Record | Delete Record | Edit Record

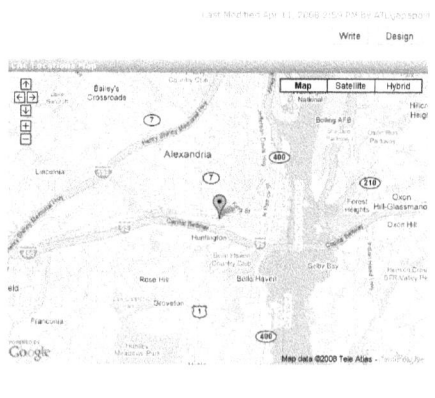

Pentagon Air Force Badge Office - 5A202
Updated Dec 12, 2007 11:56 AM by Janet Towles
View Record | Delete Record | Edit Record

Add Record

Example Process and End-User Experience

The result is not only a better experience for the end-users, but also a secure self-service environment with Return on Investment (ROI) that justified further process projects.

Across the six production projects there are substantial reductions in wait and execution times. Two estimated examples are:

150 support requests / month * 12 months * 9 days (from 2 weeks to 1 day)	= 16,200 person/days
50 External Visit Requests / month * 12 months * 9 days (from 2 weeks to 1 day)	= 5,400 person/days

All the other projects also produce significant user time reductions in content access.

BPM and Enterprise 2.0 technologies are great tools to make EA more agile, but without a proper approach it would not matter how great the technologies are. Management and control by a well-structured CoE ensures that vision of implementation agility is maintained and protected and ensures a successful iterative implementation model.

Large government entities are always trying to avoid the high risk rip-and-replace approach when modernizing. US MEPCOM successfully used SOA and BPM in its efforts to not only avoid unpalatable risk, but also to extend its enterprise to external partners.

EXTENDING THE ENTERPRISE: EA MODERNIZATION WITH SOA AND BPM

Kevin Moore[4]

US MEPCOM is undertaking a holistic Architecture Driven Modernization (ADM) across both Business and IT domains. US MEPCOM is attempting a non-invasive transformational Service Oriented and Business Process modernization of its legacy information systems. This approach is used to incrementally evolve from its existing Enterprise Architecture (EA) to a more agile SOA/BPM enable EA to meet the rapidly-changing mission. The United States Military Entrance Processing Command (USMEPCOM) processes and qualifies individuals applying for military service in any one of five Armed Services (Army, Navy, Marine Corps, Air Force and Coast Guard) and their subcomponents (i.e. Reserve, National Guard). They are required to process over one million records a year with potential spikes of 18,000 per day (5.6 million a year) and to maintain over 60 million current records across all the armed services. Each Service has its own unique Recruiting System and the only interface to US MEPCOM was either a flat file or manual re-keying of data. The system is actively used by over 15,000 recruiters and 2,700 MEPS employees across the US. Additionally, US MEPCOM exchanges data with a variety of Federal, state and private agencies such as the Social Security Agency, FBI, the Office of Personnel Management, Departments of Motor Vehicles and medical laboratories. Building and maintaining these capabilities in a secure and trustworthy architecture across such a broad set of internal and external stakeholders is a hefty challenge.

The genesis of the BPM and SOA project was a business requirement to make the exchange of data more efficient and real-time. The original project, named by the functional proponent, Data Exchange/Top of System Interface Process (DE/TOSIP) was intended to address the interface with the Armed Services. The Office of the CIO saw an opportunity to expand beyond the Armed Services and to address all of the data interface requirements of the command. BPM and SOA were seen as a way to provide an agile and flexible architecture to meet this growing requirement, increase data quality, and reduce the cost and risk of adding new capabilities. Additionally, this would permit USMEPCOM to move to the future of virtual processing, with the goal of reducing processing time from about 2.6 days to one day or less.

Using BPM and SOA, USMEPCOM planned on prequalifying 90 percent of applicants for military Service without a visit to an actual USMEPCOM facility. Additionally, BPM and SOA provided standardization without having to reengineer all the legacy systems; more accurate estimates of project time / costs (key for budget planning, mission planning, accurate projections and auditing); better governance and control; added agility due to BPM (rapid development of processes, change control and management, error reduction or "six sigma" capabilities); reusability of BPM and SOA components once added to the SOA Architecture; and cost savings in development and support once a library of components were built.

Collaboration across DoD, other government agencies and even with some commercial entities (e.g. employment and credit verifications) was also streamlined with an accepted standards-based SOA interface. The BPM and SOA governance structure was enhanced to a more robust model that includes the USMEP leadership, staff, customers (Recruiting Services), etc. Finally, the USMEPCOM CIO (J6) staff had to be compliant with the Defense Information System Agency (DISA) newly-defined system requirements for the future DoD net-centric architecture.

The challenge was that its existing IT Enterprise Architecture (EA) could not modernize to meet the growing demands of the US Military in its current form US MEPCOM was faced with two choices; build a completely new modern IT EA while still running the existing system and then change over, or "wrap" the existing EA with SOA and BPM and then manage the legacy resources either to migration or support scenarios. The obvious lowest risk and fastest path was to use SOA and BPM. It was not feasible to rebuild the existing systems as this could mean waiting over five years for a new system to be in place.

The new "Enterprise Service Oriented Architecture" provided the abstraction layer required for US MEPCOM to allow standardized access to its existing resources, while allow for new business interactions to take place without changes to the these legacy resources.

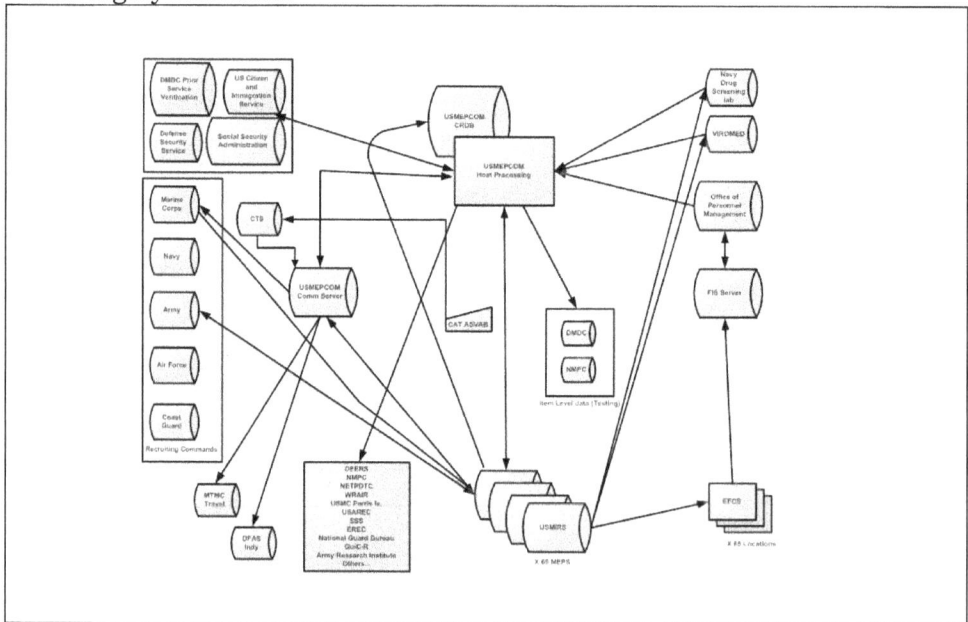

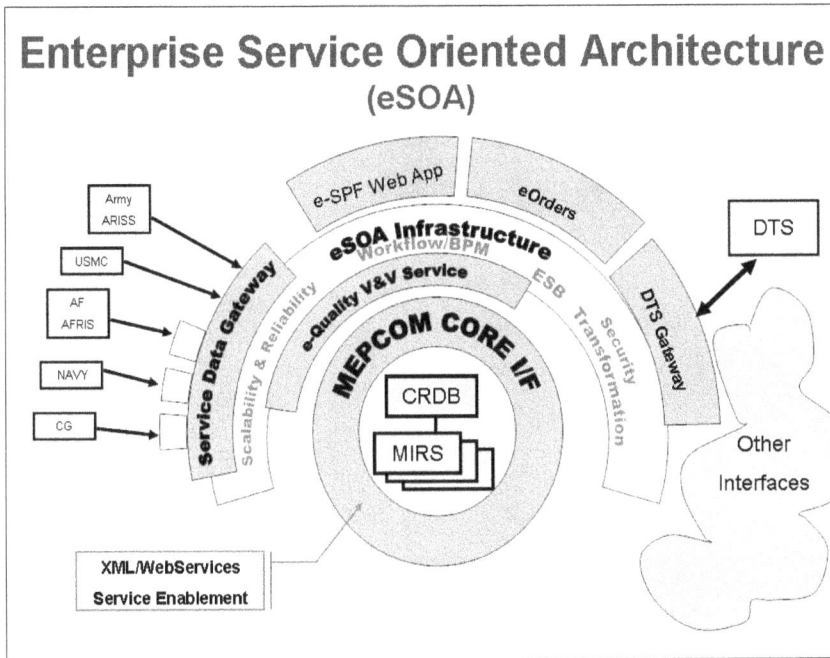

The US government and the US Military in particular have had to adapt to a much more interconnected, real-time environment with many new business challenges. US MEPCOM faced numerous challenges in meeting its mission to serve its DoD branch (Army, Air Force, Navy, Marines, Coast Guard) customers with its aging and inflexible systems. Additionally, many legacy systems were built in stove-pipes, lacked sufficient documentation, and/or were created by programmers that had left or were soon to retire. Added to this, US MEPCOM's business is dependent on highly interconnected, high-volume processes spanning defense, civilian, and commercial entities with sensitive information. Transforming its EA to a SOA-based standard with automated processes and full SOA governance was the only path to successfully supporting its customers' current and future requirements.

One of new areas of interest now being tied to BPM is Event Driven Architecture (EDA). This is where processes move beyond transaction-centric to real-time situationally-aware processes. BPM is combined with Business Activity Monitoring (BAM), EDA, sensors, and other technologies.

BPM ENABLING REAL-TIME DECISION MAKING

Dilip Rane and Stacey Camp[2]

Advances over traditional offerings of situational awareness lie in how traditional situation awareness is interlaced with collaboration, hence creating a unique approach to execute mission scenarios. We developed a Collaborative Situational Awareness and Decision Making (CSADM) framework that brings the collaboration, situational awareness (Gather It, Analyze It and Visualize It) and Analytical tools together in a manner where "Context" of the situation isn't lost while working with any of the tools. For example, a workflow task and a chat conference room can be tied to a particular sourcing requirement that several users may be working on.

BearingPoint, through its innovative approach of integrating context aware, real-time collaboration with situational awareness using information gathering, fusion, rich visualization and analytical techniques, achieves unparalleled mission effectiveness by providing actionable information to the authorized users. CSADM is based on strong architectural foundation using BearingPoint's SOA Framework. It is developed using proven, production tested, standards-based COTS components as opposed to custom developed components. Many components are already in use in many of the DoD agencies. BPM, Data Fusion and Visualization, GIS, Web 2.0 technologies such as Wikis, Social Networking, Bookmarking and Chats provide new ways of Net Centric, Web-enabled collaboration. CSADM also provides context sensitive analysis of the situation for better and informed decision making. All of these capabilities are integrated in CSADM within a context of a situation or an event.

CSADM focuses on five key areas:

- Situational Awareness (Data Fusion and Visualization)
- Decision Making
- Collaboration (using process flows, portals, Wikis and other Web 2.0 technologies, Instant Messaging, Notifications etc.)
- Information Analysis: Analysis of information through situational awareness and collaboration that feeds back into the decision making process (Entity Link Analysis)
- Identity and Access Management including Federated Identity and Access Management and Cross Domain Information Sharing (Security)

This paper focuses on the key area of BPM that pulls together all of the areas within the context of a mission. The following section will describe the CSADM solution and how SOA principles and BPM technology has helped BearingPoint put together such a solution in an open architecture, open standard environment.

Collaborative Situational Awareness and Decision Making

Our approach to providing an integrated, collaborative situational awareness and decision making solution is to use commercial off-the-shelf (COTS) products that can be adapted with relative ease and integrated and configured using standards based integration techniques using BPM, XML, SOAP/XML, Web Services standards and Service Oriented Integration techniques.

Following are the key components of the CSADM Solution:

Situational Awareness

CSADM's rich visualization, analysis, alerting, anomaly detection capabilities and its integration with various visualization tools, including Geospatial display such as Google Earth, makes it the perfect accelerator for situational awareness. Furthermore, its in-memory efficient data models, compression algorithms and equally efficient communication between different nodes provide tremendous performance for real-time situational awareness.

Collaborative Workflow or Business Process Management

BPM is the key piece of CSADM solution as it holds together various systems, data sources and users in the context of a give situation. It implements the techniques, tactics and procedures (TTPs) and the military doctrine and provides a seamless user experience without having to go through the manuals when instant action from the war fighters is warranted for the success of the mission.

BearingPoint believes that although automating business processes brings some structure and discipline, it is necessary to configure such processes so that they are flexible enough for handling ad-hoc activities or ad-hoc processes. Assignments, re-assignments, approval cycles and collaborative research are some examples where flexibility is required. Overruling certain decisions made by the BPM engine with justification may also be required in some cases. A dynamic change to the paths taken by a business process based on the results of analysis is required to successful implementation of BPM/Workflow technology.

In CSADM, an integrated architecture for collaborative business process management is achieved through the following components:

- Portal and User Experience: Provides the foundation services for delivering a volume and variety of applications and user experiences: authentication and provisioning, data and content integration, assembly, personalization and presentation.
- Workflow and Business Process Management: A complete business process management platform, delivering rich process modeling, simulation, development, integration, automation and measurement capabilities for optimizing processes that span systems and people.
  - Balance between structure and flexibility in business processes
  - Maintenance and enrichment of the context throughout the processes
  - Dynamic allocation of activities to people based on constantly updated profile and roles of people. For example, one may require assistance from a subject matter expert who has been instrumental in handling a similar situation in the past may be chosen over another person while allocating a certain task based on their profile and history of the work. This is going beyond the traditional allocation of activities based on roles and responsibilities.

Wikis

CSADM uses Wiki as a shared knowledgebase where information can be shared freely by users yet controlled by access controls on who can edit, view certain information. Wikis provide the flexibility to users on how they would like to organize the information as opposed to the traditional content management tools. Although Wikis aren't replacement for the traditional content management tools, they are excellent platform for collaboration without any delay. Wiki facilitates communication and augments the business process flows for ad-hoc collaboration.

Instant Messaging

Instant Messaging integrated with portals and BPM along with a context services described below provides meaningful "context aware" chats that can help prevent human errors due to information sharing without a meaningful context. Standards based (XMPP) instant messaging integrated into the CSADM solution conforms to the DoD/Chat presence architecture.

Information Analysis and Search

Information Analysis for decision-making falls into two types:

- Historical information analysis to identify trends and patterns so that decision makers can more readily identify the patterns and make decisions accordingly.
- Real-time information analysis, where both of the following can occur: comparison of planned information with the actual event information for any anomalies; and comparison of current information with any historical information to fit the current incident into any of the patterns identified.

CSADM screen shots

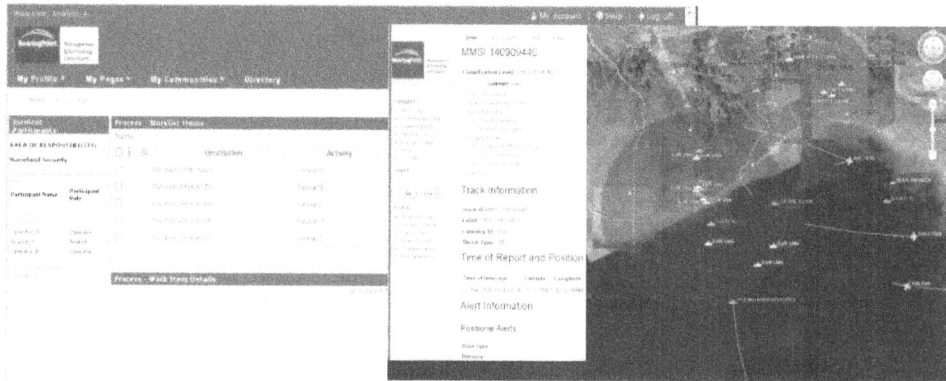

CSADM and Applicable Domains

The CSADM solution is applicable in various domains as shown below. Examples show Emergency Management and Healthcare Networks monitoring a situation of a disease or monitoring a situation of emergency where healthcare providers need to collaborate in order to handle such a situation.

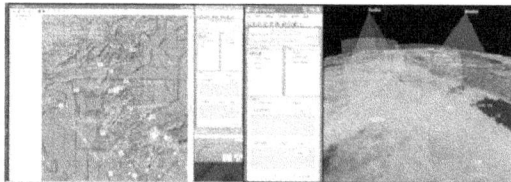
Defense – Battle Space Management

Critical Infrastructure Protection

Examples
1. Health Care Network
2. Emergency Management
3. Disease Control
4. Blue Force Protection
5. Improvised Explosive Devices
6. Collection Management
7. Time Sensitive/Critical Targeting
8. Search and Rescue
9. Disease Control
10. Threat Reduction
11. Natural Disasters
12. Border Patrol
13. High Profile Events

Public Safety Incident Management

Transportation (Air, Sea, Land)

Finally, looking forward we can clearly see the trend of BPM's value being its focus on the *business* users and allowing more insight into how things work through the entire lifecycle of processes and process implementations. It can also provide "shared" insight across organizational and even partner and customer boundaries.

A BUSINESS PROCESS MANAGEMENT CONTEXT TO SHARED SERVICES

Mateo Almenta Reca, Linus Chow[3]

Bringing technology and business closer together has been the driving value of BPM. BPM now encompasses collaboration between both humans and systems providing proven enterprise value with measureable ROI. Recent developments in BPM standards, such as Business Process Modeling Notation (BPMN) have also opened a path to converge Enterprise Architecture (EA) modeling closer to regular Business Analysts. And as BPM matures as the driving force of Service Oriented Architecture (SOA) it will be a key technology in enabling service components to be related in a business context. The future of BPM is to focus on its leadership in abstracting technology so that it allows more and more non-technical users to add value to the enterprise.

EA modeling was around even before the Business Process Reengineering (BPR) days of the 80s. Key reference models such as The Open Group Architecture Framework (TOGAF) and Department of Defense Architecture Framework (DoDAF) are prevalent. The challenge with EA is to enable a broader stakeholder audience to collaborate and understand processes. BPMN[2] is the emerging standard that could fit into this niche as part of these reference models that are much more easily understood by average subject matter experts and end-users and not just IT Architects. There is still much to be negotiated and matured in the BPMN standard, but it is seen as the best hope for a standard supported by customers and product vendors alike. One of the key advantages of BPMN is that it enforces one common language between two disparate worlds, Business and IT, closing the gap between them and making it easier to collaborate and understand each other.

SOA has been successful in bringing about abstraction and reuse for information technologies. As a first step, BPM has provided an abstracted orchestration layer for SOA providing business users insight and influence over how processes are built and run. Recently, Cloud Computing which incorporates SOA as well as Software as a Service (SaaS) and Web 2.0 has sparked a lot of interest. This could also potentially bring applications (such as Financials, Human Resource Management, and Customer Relationship Management) into a virtualized and / or services framework. BPM could further this realization by sharing the "business process context" of Cloud Objects. Imagine, if you will, being a consumer of a Cloud Service without understanding the "process context" that it is part of. Furthermore, slightly changing the underlying process from the base template using BPM would enable you regain some control of the process without having to worry about the infrastructure details. Finally, if that design-time environment was web-based, secure, and version-controlled then governance and control over the process lifecycle could involve more business stakeholders. Finally, exposing web-based runtime capabilities to business users empowers them to change and evolve the business processes, putting them at the driver's seat.

---

[2] More information on this OMG standard can be found at BPMN.org

BPM as both a technology and a concept is undergoing momentous change at this time. Its value is moving up the stack from a pure technology play to reach the business community, allowing them greater control of the enterprise which today has more and more information systems. As the only technology tool to effective bridge the gap between IT and business, it has the potential to truly drive the enterprise and transform the way we run our processes.

REFERENCES:

1. H. Mark McGibbon is a professor who has lectured at four universities in the U.S. and two universities in the U.K. and Germany. He holds a Doctorate in Business Administration (DBA) and a M.S. in Information Technology Management (ITM). He is currently a professor and is writing his last chapter for a PhD in Business Administration. Working 27 years in Europe and five years in the U.S. as an IT leader and a part-time professor has allowed him to apply academic theories and concepts in the real-world.

2. Dilip Rane, Senior Manager, Systems Architect, Public Sector Solutions Architecture Group, 1-214-732-1182; Stacey N. Camp, PMP Senior Manager, PS Solution Architecture Group BearingPoint, Management and Technology Consulting, BearingPoint.

3. Mateo Almenta Reca, Oracle BPM Sr. Principal Product Manager, Oracle United States, Linus Chow Principal Consultant Oracle Public Sector,

4. Kevin D. Moore was the CIO for US Military Entrance Processing Command (USMEPCOM) at North Chicago, IL. He has over 26 years of leadership experience and has held several senior level positions in the US Department of Defense (DoD). Kevin is a published author, active speaker, and has been interviewed for the successful transformation that is occurring in MEPCOM. He is also a Lieutenant Colonel in the U.S. Army Reserve, and a graduate of the United States Military Academy at West Point. USMEPCOM is the Gold Winner of the 2008 Global Awards for BPM and Workflow for North America and the 2009 OMG's BPM Application that Demonstrates the Best Return on Investment

5. Arthur Randles, Director Integration Technology, Randy Blevins, EDAC Systems. Inc.

6. Shaundra Eberhardt is the Program Manager for CACI and Brian H. Kim is the Senior Principal Consultant for Oracle for The Office of the Secretary of Defense (OSD) AT&L, OSD AT&L is an award-winning finalist of the 2008 Global Awards for BPM and Workflow for North America.

Optimizing the National Corporation for Development (CND), Uruguay

Lucía Wainer, Corporación Nacional para el Desarrollo; Juan J. Moreno, INTEGRADOC / Universidad Católica and Martín Dauber INTEGRADOC, Montevideo, Uruguay

ABSTRACT

The National Corporation for Development (CND—www.cnd.org.uy) is an organization governed by civil law whose capital belongs in 100 percent to Uruguayan government. It is the main organization that promotes corporate development, fostering the creation of new companies, strengthening the existing ones and eventually participating in them.

In order to continue the growth of the last years, in 2008 CND focused on improving internal business processes, incorporating a local BPM solution for its documents flows. In an extremely short four-month period, all documents flows that support CND operations were automated in electronic forms. An agile software engineering methodology was used to analyze requirements, to model the business processes, implement the solution and finally train users in the new system. Business Experts from CND were integrated to the team and engaged in the project in order to achieve said objective. This chapter summarizes the project, its threats, unanticipated events, changes management and results achieved.

INTRODUCTION AND BUSINESS CONTEXT

This chapter is divided into four main sections. In this introductory section we illustrate the business context and the definition of the problem. Next, we include a short summary of previous and related work. After that, the proposed solution is described, and finally conclusions and future work are presented.

BUSINESS CONTEXT

The National Corporation for Development is the main organization in Uruguay that promotes corporate development, fostering the creation of new companies, strengthening the existing ones and eventually participating in them.

The CND's current vision contemplates two major areas:

1. The National Development Agency, including areas of financial services, micro, small and medium enterprises (99 percent of Uruguayan companies) and non-financial services (distributed in several public programs)
2. Coordination of Private-Public Associations for Infrastructure Projects (basically with government counterparts). Among them:
   - Bridges and Highways: Ministry of Transport and Public Works of Uruguay (Ministerio de Transporte y Obras Públicas del Uruguay - MTOP).
   - Electric interconnection with Brazil: National Administration of Electric Plants and Transmissions (Administración Nacional de Usinas y Trasmisiones Eléctricas--UTE)

- Trains: National Trains Administration (Administración de Ferrocarriles del Estado--AFE)
- Ports: National Ports Administration (Administración Nacional de Puertos--ANP)

CND's activities are varied and diverse, driving various business sectors of the country. In reference to credit for micro, small and medium enterprises, is worth mentioning that CND in 2007 granted approximately US$6,000,000 in credit lines. CND also created and is still managing the "Corporación Fomenta" program, for partnership projects, aimed at generating added value, preferably for export or for import substitution, involving analysis, preparation of business plans, structuring the business, seeking financing and accompanying control management professionals in charge of the project. CND also created and operates the UruguayFomenta.com.uy Web Site in an effort to gather all the programs that support the productive sector in the country.

In order to perform all these activities, CND has a staff of over 150 employees, all of them with different professions and activities. They participate in the business processes that support the Corporation's operations, and therefore, they are potential users of the BPM solution to be implemented.

CND has fulfilled its strategic goals to date. One of the goals for 2008 was installing technologies that will further optimize its performance, achieving new challenges. In this context, one of the key points was to incorporate BPM technology for documents flows' management. After a thorough selection process, and considering its documents flows' needs, CND decided to incorporate INTEGRADOC [1].

There was also an important temporary condition to meet: the project must begin in September 2008 and the modeling, implementation, and users' training had to be completed by the end of the year.

Involved Business Process

The main document types that support the operation of the Corporation and the documents flows that should be modeled and automated are:

1. Board of Director's minutes
2. Personnel contracts
3. Works Certificates
4. Judicial Records
5. Payrolls
6. Collection
7. Notes
8. Procurements and Tenders
9. Legal department's documents

These types of documents, and their associated processes, concentrate much of the CND's organizational knowledge [2][3].

The following section describes some of the types of documents and the business problems to be solved, in the context of the National Corporation for Development.

Board of director's minutes

The corporation's board of directors holds periodical meetings in order to deal with the topics set by the different managers of all the departments that form the organization. The Board of Directors note these proposed topics, as well as the decisions taken.

This is one of the most important documents of the organization, since it is related to almost every other document through the above-mentioned resolutions. A clear example may be found when hiring employees. In general, the need for this arises within a department and the relevant manager puts forth this issue to be dealt with in the following meeting of the board. In case the decision for a call is made, the personnel selection process shall be carried out by the Human Resources Department, ending up in a contract of employment (which is another type of document within the organization).

Personnel contract

When bringing new personnel into the corporation becomes necessary, the Human Resources Department is in charge of studying the new post in order to define the profile of the person needed and the characteristics of the call to be carried out. After these items have been defined, the department's personnel carry out a thorough study of the CVs received and after that, there is a series of personal interviews in order to find the person that better fits the profile. This process involves a great amount of information which, until the present, the corporation was used to managing manually on paper. Besides, in many cases, it is necessary to consult other departments regarding some technical characteristics, so it is not a process in which only the Human Resources department is involved. Finally, once the person for the job has been selected, all important information is sent to the Legal department, where the contract of employment is drawn.

This type of document, known as personnel contract, refers not only to the contract of employment (which is the contract, per se), but also to the whole process of personnel selection, including the formal employment contract.

ORGANIZATIONAL CLIMATE.

Given the varied activities of the Corporation, the profile of its members is extremely heterogeneous. They participate in a collaborative work involving different professionals (engineers and other areas, accountants, economists, lawyers, etc.), along with administrative roles that perform tasks of vital importance in the management of the organization. Each of these people has different business visions, IT skills, work history, experience, etc. This makes that any system to be implemented will face a significant risk related to target users that will use it. In order to mitigate these risks, three main objectives were identified, aligned with INTEGRADOC's implementation methodology for successful BPM projects. To wit:

- Engaging key users throughout the project implementation, in order to ensure a proper business model and to generate natural leaders within the organization who act as sponsors of the BPM system.
- Providing a simple user's interface for all user profiles but at the same time powerful and agile enough to be used by the most experienced ones.
- Defining mechanisms for interactive training, including all the users involved in the system, thus achieving a proper acceptance of it.

PROBLEM DEFINITION

The problem to be addressed in this work is automating every business process previously described, addressing their complexities and particularities, managing business users and assuring project success within the four-month time constraint in order to achieve strategic goals for year 2008.

Given the growth of CND's operation, in terms of projects, contracts, loans, etc, the managing of documents and their flows inside the organization has been increasingly difficult. In this context, CND identified an important opportunity for improvement in moving important documents from personal e-mail boxes, paper or desktops PCs to a centralized knowledge base. After achieving this, the next step was to automate these processes, improving the collaboration in the documents flows, allowing users to make their part of the job in the system.

There are some important differences between CND's business context and traditional applications of document's approval. The team had to take special care about them in every stage of the implementation. Some of them are:

- The reduced time frame to complete the project required a methodology and tools which minimize errors and allow business users to really define their processes (without Computer Engineers intervention or programming)
- The nature of the business process was very heterogeneous, covering users and needs from the Legal Department to the Board of Directors, as well as the Secretariat and the Financial and Planning Departments, among others. This fact implied the need to use techniques for process modeling and document's type definitions suitable for these profiles. These techniques had to be very agile, flexible and not requiring strong technological skills or training by the users.
- Integration with specialized digitalization tools in order to process high volumes of paper and transferring resulted files to INTEGRADOC, using Web Services in a Service Oriented Architecture.
- The electronic documents must present some special features in order to meet current legislation and CND's needs: digital signatures, grouping and ungrouping of documents (milling paper based documents), alerts for expiration of documents in an office, managing mixed documents (paper based and electronic forms), automatically routing a document after a time limit is met, etc.

PREVIOUS AND RELATED WORK

When business processes have to be implemented in a real organization, it is necessary to follow a methodology, addressing main risks and forecasting problems, in order to mitigate them before they impact the schedule. In this section, we summarize the methodology used in INTEGRADOC BPM projects in order to achieve these results. This methodology is aligned with Rational Unified Process, using the same stages and being complemented with specific elements of documents flow modeling.

INTEGRADOC METHODOLOGY

The methodology used consists of a series of employees' training stages, demonstrations of the system and requirements specification meetings in which the principal aim is to strongly involve the organization's key users. First of all, after the project manager has been appointed by the customer, INTEGRADOC's experts present the working methodology to the main users involved in the different processes of the organization. At this stage, the survey lists must be paid attention to. These lists are the foundations of this methodology since they are designed to allow the customer's autonomy when filling them, and, on the other hand, they have very valuable information for the technicians to work in an efficient manner when searching for a solution.

Illustration 1 shows the Document Type template. There is a template to define each topic, which is useful to better characterize each document type with additional features that only apply to such topic.

TIPO DE DOCUMENTO

ORGANIZACIÓN:
FECHA / LUGAR:
COMENTARIOS:

CONTRAPARTES QUE ESPECIFICAN:

TIPO DE DOCUMEN' TIPO DE RUTA	Elem.Fisicos	Titulares	Asignaciones	Movimientos	Actuaciones	Agregados
o Ad-HOC o Predefinida->	o Si | o No	o Si | o No	o Si | o No	o Si | o No	o Si | o No	o Si | o No
					Vinculados	Alertas
					o Si | o No	o Si | o No

Descripción del Tipo de Documento:

Campo Espec.	Nombre	Requerido	Mascara	Tipo
1		o Si | o No		o Num | o Txt | o Fch | o Otro
2		o Si | o No		o Num | o Txt | o Fch | o Otro
3		o Si | o No		o Num | o Txt | o Fch | o Otro
4		o Si | o No		o Num | o Txt | o Fch | o Otro
5		o Si | o No		o Num | o Txt | o Fch | o Otro
6		o Si | o No		o Num | o Txt | o Fch | o Otro
7		o Si | o No		o Num | o Txt | o Fch | o Otro
8		o Si | o No		o Num | o Txt | o Fch | o Otro
9		o Si | o No		o Num | o Txt | o Fch | o Otro
10		o Si | o No		o Num | o Txt | o Fch | o Otro
11		o Si | o No		o Num | o Txt | o Fch | o Otro
12		o Si | o No		o Num | o Txt | o Fch | o Otro
13		o Si | o No		o Num | o Txt | o Fch | o Otro
14		o Si | o No		o Num | o Txt | o Fch | o Otro
15		o Si | o No		o Num | o Txt | o Fch | o Otro
16		o Si | o No		o Num | o Txt | o Fch | o Otro
17		o Si | o No		o Num | o Txt | o Fch | o Otro
18		o Si | o No		o Num | o Txt | o Fch | o Otro
19		o Si | o No		o Num | o Txt | o Fch | o Otro
20		o Si | o No		o Num | o Txt | o Fch | o Otro

Comentarios a campos específicos marcados con *:

Illustration 1 Document Type Spreadsheet

Once the working methodology has been presented, some groups are appointed to be constantly trained and to start to survey the first types of documents of the organization. These groups shall be integrated by INTEGRADOC's experts and users with experience in the business. The main objective, at this point, is that users get to acquire command over the lists, so as to be able to continue with the survey of their own processes, thus achieving autonomy, and at the same time, allowing the parallel surveying of many processes involving less personnel super-vision.

The survey of the types of documents, as well as of the topics, involves different processes. These processes may be ad-hoc or may be pre-defined. When facing how to model pre-defined processes, there are many options, including—but not limited to—State Diagrams [4], Activity Diagrams [5], Petri Nets [6], States and Activities Diagrams (DEA) [7], Flow Charts [8], Data Flow Diagrams, (DFD) [9]. Due to their simplicity for flow representation and good results achieved in Uruguay, we used DEAs in this project.

Finally, once all the types of documents and their associated processes have been surveyed, it is time to pass to the following stage "outside" the customer--the creation of a solution which the IT technicians are in charge of--and after that, the system starts to operate.

AD-HOC PROCESSES IN GOVERNMENT

As introduced in the previous section, the processes may have associated predefined flows or *ad-hoc* flows. Predefined flows are those in which the electronic document path is defined when designing the process. That is, the BPMS is who defines the next state and next user, assigning the document as a new work item for them.

On the other hand, ad-hoc processes are those in which the electronic document path is defined at runtime. Each participant decides the next step to continue processing the electronic document. The user is the one who "sends" the document to the participant or office that he/she chooses.

Ad-hoc processes are widely used in government, given the unstructured nature of the procedures to be performed and the inability to predict and model the whole casuistry at design time. In spite of the fact that many document types have a pre-defined process, there are many others that need to be evaluated in each phase and each participant defines where and by whom it should be followed. For this reason, it is essential to provide in addition to the predefined processes, the support for ad-hoc processes.

Exceptions management

Ad-hoc also could be seen as a general approach for exception management in predefined flows. This is very common in the government, where the higher authorities are entitled (by law) to modify the flow and to send documents out of the predefined flow, to other participants, in order to obtain their opinion. This kind of behavior is completely supported by ad-hoc processes, and this is why they are so important for Uruguay's Government.

PROPOSED SOLUTION

The proposed solution could be conceptually divided in three main stages:
- Building the project team, integrating CND's business analyst with INTEGRADOC's engineers, for the modeling of processes.
- Implementing the processes and putting them in production.
- Training users and assuring the adoption of the process oriented tool.

In the following sections, we will be discussing the way they were implemented.

BUILDING THE PROJECT TEAM AND MODELING THE BUSINESS PROCESSES

During the process modeling and requirements specification, four teams were formed with staff from the Law, Human Resources, the Public-Private Partnerships (PPP) Departments and the Secretariat. In turn, these groups were composed by the area manager and several employees of the department.

As an example, we will analyze the case of the type of document called "**Board of Director's minutes**" defined with the Secretariat. The rest of the document types were modeled in the same way.

After the team was built, under the oversight of INTEGRADOC's Engineers, business users defined each of the specific parameters required for the "**Board of directors' minutes,**" as shown in Illustration 2. Note that in a single spreadsheet (most suitable for business users), they defined fields such as dates, combo boxes and numeric fields as well as tabs relevant to this document type.

INTEGRADOC		TIPO DE DOCUMENTO					

ORGANIZACIÓN:	CND	CONTRAPARTES:	
FECHA / LUGAR:	02/09/2008 - CND		
COMENTARIOS:			

TIPO DE DOCUMEN'	TIPO DE RUTA		Elem.Físicos	Titulares	Asignaciones	Movimientos	Actuaciones	Agregados
ACTA de DIRECTORIO	PREDEFINIDA		NO	NO	NO	NO	SI	NO

		Vinculados	Alertas
		SI	SI

Comentarios al tipo de documento:		Campo Espec.	Nombre	Requerido	Mascara	Tipo	*
		1	Número	SI	NN / NNNN	Numérico	*
		2	Fecha	SI	DD/MM/AAAA	Fecha	
		3	Horario	NO		Texto	
		4	Participantes	SI		Texto	
		5	Dirección	NO		Texto	
		6	Adm. y Operaciones	SI		Combo manual	**
		7	Finanzas y Riesgo	SI		Combo manual	**
		8	MIPYMES	SI		Combo manual	**
		9	Productos y Servicios	SI		Combo manual	**
		10	Asociaciones Público-Privadas	SI		Combo manual	**
		11	Legal	SI		Combo manual	**
		12	Corporación Fomenta	SI		Combo manual	**
		13	RRHH	SI		Combo manual	**
Comentarios a campos específicos marcados con *:	* Nª 1ª/2008	14	Comunicaciones	SI		Combo manual	**
		15	Varios	SI		Combo manual	**
	** Combo con la opción SI o NO.	16		o Si | o No		o Num | o Txt | o Fch | o Otro	
		17		o Si | o No		o Num | o Txt | o Fch | o Otro	
		18		o Si | o No		o Num | o Txt | o Fch | o Otro	
		19		o Si | o No		o Num | o Txt | o Fch | o Otro	
		20		o Si | o No		o Num | o Txt | o Fch | o Otro	

Illustration 2 "Board of directors' minutes" Spreadsheet

It should be noted that the worksheets are in Microsoft ® Excel ® format, widely accepted by users worldwide, which contributes to breaking down the barrier between the business analyst and technical staff.

Timing of this stage

This stage took 8 weeks, considering every document type.

IMPLEMENTING BUSINESS PROCESSES

Following the "Board of directors' minutes" example, the predefined flow was defined by using DEA, inferring the state diagram shown in Illustration 3.

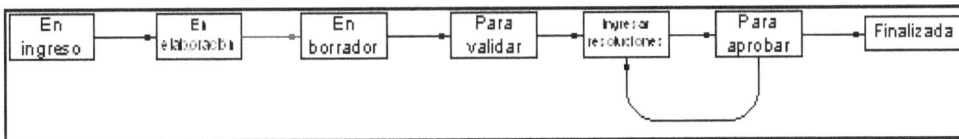

En ingreso	En elaboración	En borrador	Para validar	Ingresar resoluciones	Para aprobar	Finalizada

Illustration 3 Inferred State Diagram

From the State Diagram and its associated document type spreadsheet, the solution is customized to meet all the requirements established in conjunction with the client. It is interesting to observe how the professionals of INTEGRADOC make up the solution in a very short period of time, due to the efficiency of the previous stage and the lack of programming tasks. This short example demonstrates the full potential of the methodology.

INTEGRA						Documento ⊕ ✎ ⊗

<table>
<tr><td>◇ Inicio</td><td colspan="2">Info</td><td>Actuaciones</td><td>Alertas</td><td>Docs Vinc</td></tr>
</table>

Navigation menu:
- ◇ Inicio
- **Mis Pendientes (2)**
- Notificaciones
- ◇ Crear Documento
- Nuevo Documento
- ◇ Docs mi Depend.
- Por Referencia
- Por Tema
- Vencidos
- Vencidos Urgentes
- ◇ Nóminas
- Crear Nominas
- Nominas Emitidas
- Recibir Nominas
- ◇ Mi Perfil
- Cambiar Contraseña
- Cambiar Clave Firma

Imprimir Documento

Los campos con * son obligatorios.

*Organización	*Gerencia	Tipo	Número	Año	Anexo	Bis
CND	20	Acta de Directorio	1	2009	10	0

Fecha: 02/02/2009	Referencia: CND/20/15/1/2009

Prioridad	Normal
Resumen	

Situacion actual

Dependencia Actual	CND/20/20 Secretaría
Fecha de Ingreso	02/02/2009
Plazo de tenencia	30 días

Campos adicionales al documento

Numero	23
Fecha	02/02/2009 14:30
Participantes	Gerentes de todas las áreas; Directorio
Dirección	
Adm y Operaciones	NO
Finanzas y Riesto	NO
MYPIMES	NO
Productos y Servicios	NO
Asociaciones Publico Privadas	NO
Legal	NO
Coporación Fomento	NO
RRHH	NO
Comunicaciones	NO
Varios	NO

Documento sin firmar

Illustration 4 Customized Form for Board of directors' minutes.

In Illustration 4, the customized worksheet for the Board of Director's Minutes is presented. In this electronic form, the reader should recognize all the fields defined in the document type spreadsheet built in the previous stage. The BPM solution allowed definition, not only every field, but also its type (numeric, date, text, combos, etc.) as well as setting whether they are mandatory or not. All of this is made without programming, which speeded up the customization phase and significantly decreased risks of misunderstanding business users' needs when transferring them to programmers.

Timing of this stage

This stage took four weeks.

TRAINING AND ASSURING ADOPTION

After installing the beta version of the customized system, the training phase began. Small groups of at most four users with different profiles were formed. Each group was conducted by two INTEGRADOC's professionals in a two-hour training workshop, in which they went through the solution, showing the main features and particular characteristics of each document type used by the users involved in the workshop. Not all users were presented with all document types, but only the ones that were relevant for them. This helped to keep a high degree of attention and participation.

The final product of this stage is obtaining a set of key users trained in the basic BPM features so they can begin to use it in its beta version. By using the software, users will be validating everything defined (by themselves) while getting familiar with the solution in the context of their real jobs. As it can be seen, this stage has much to do with the quality assurance of the proposed solution.

Finally, with the information obtained from the use of the product in its beta version, the solution is adjusted to get the final version to be put in production. Led by the key users who participated in the workshops (and not by the supplier Engineers), the system is finally delivered to the whole company, obtaining the formal acceptance.

Timing of this stage

This stage took four weeks.

KEY PERFORMANCE INDICATORS (KPI)

As defined in [10]: KPIs are financial and non-financial metrics used to help an organization define and measure progress toward organizational goals. KPIs can be delivered through Business Intelligence techniques to assess the present state of the business and to assist in prescribing a course of action.

Given the importance of the documents flows modeled and implemented in this project, to monitor and analyze the evolution of KPIs is a major issue. It is also important to manage exceptions to the normal flows based on monitoring these KPIs [11].

INTEGRADOC includes a Business Intelligence Tool, which is based in predefined data warehouses to collect main KPIs related to documents flows. Good examples of pre-configured KPIs are:

- the number of documents created in a given time frame
- the number processed by a set of users
- the amount of time it takes to finish a business process
- the amount of time the process spends in each stage of the flow

Reports showing the analysis based in these KPIs are available to CND's users and analysts, who can navigate and configure them in order to continually improve its business processes.

CONCLUSIONS

This article summarizes the implementation of BPM Technology in the public-funded institution for Corporate Development in Uruguay (CND) using INTEGRADOC's methodology and the BPM tool. CND is a legal person governed by civil law whose capital belongs in 100 percent to Uruguayan government.

The methodology and BPM tools used allowed the team to satisfy the time constraints for the project completion, starting in September, 2008 and finishing in December, 2008, including training stages and quality assurance. This allowed CND to meet its strategic objective relating to the incorporation of BPM technology in their business processes in 2008.

The project team addressed the organizational problem which was modeling, optimizing and automating every documents flow that supports the Corporation's operations. In this context, the nine main document types were identified, and their related business processes modeled.

The methodology was able to cover the three identified main objectives: involving CND's users in every step of the project, providing a simple and quick-to-use system and defining an interactive training program in order to maximize the acceptance of the system. Indeed, during all the stages of the modeling, CND's business users were the ones to model and define the business processes. This allowed us to decrease Computer Engineers participation in these stages, significantly reducing errors and the length of this phase. This participation also facilitated a much more agile and effective training, which would not have been possible if users had not known the system previously.

A key element to make it possible was the inclusion of easy-to-use spreadsheets to model document types and topics. These spreadsheets were also very powerful and flexible to support every document type and topic, for each CND's department. This allowed us to use business users' time in defining the documents flows: the users adding extra value, rather than only learning how to use complex modeling techniques and tools.

The solution addressed integration issues using Web Services in a Service Oriented Architecture. The legislation requirements were also met, including digital signatures, grouping and ungrouping of documents, supporting mixed documents (part electronic and part in paper), warning and automatic routing of expired documents, etc.

The system also includes a Business Intelligence tool that continuously monitors automated business processes. This tool generates Key Performance Indicators (KPIs), useful for making decisions related to the optimization of automated processes, based in objective indicators rather than in manager's perceptions.

At the time of writing this chapter, CND is starting to use the system, with remarkable positive results. Future work includes process improvements derived from the analysis of KPIs collected by the BI tool.

ACKNOWLEDGEMENTS

The authors would like to thank all the members of Corporación Nacional para el Desarrollo who took part in this project. We also would like to thank INTEGRADOC's (http://www.integradoc.com) professionals and the Process Automation Working Group of Universidad Católica del Uruguay (http://www.ucu.edu.uy), for the rich discussions of concepts and experiences presented in this chapter.

REFERENCES

[1] INTEGRADOC Business Process Management Suite optimized for documents flows. http://www.integradoc.com (revised January 30th, 2009)

[2] Moreno, Juan J.; Aldaz, Guillermo and Joyanes, Luis. Knowledge extraction in environments automated with Workflow Management Systems. (Extracción de conocimiento en ambientes automatizados con Sistemas de Gestión de Workflow). Proceedings of the III International Symposium of Information Systems and Software Engineering in the Knowledge Society. (SISOFT-2005). Santo Domingo, República Dominicana. ISBN 846893411-9. 2005.

[3] Moreno, Juan; Joyanes, Luis. Applying Knowledge Management to exploit the potential of information stored in a Business Process Management System (BPMS). Workflow Handbook 2006. Future Strategies Inc. Book Division. Lighthouse Point, Florida, USA. 2006

[4] Booth, Taylor. Sequential Machines and Automata Theory. 1967

[5] UML. Unified Modeling Language, Version 2.1.2. Object Management Group. http://www.omg.org/technology/documents/formal/uml.htm (revised January 30th, 2009)

[6] Petri, Carl; Reisig, Wolfgang. Petri net. Scholarpedia, http://www.scholarpedia.org/article/Petri_net. Petri Nets were invented in 1939. (revised January 30th, 2009)

[7] Morales, Pablo. Process architecture for workflow models. (Arquitectura de procesos para modelos de workflow). Professionals community ICTNet – Workflow & BPM Section (http://ictnet.es/). 2002

[8] Gilbreth, Frank. Presentation "Process Charts—First Steps in Finding the One Best Way". American Society of Mechanical Engineers (ASME). 1921

[9] Constantine, Larry; Stevens, W; Myers, G. Structured Design. IBM Systems Journal. 1974.

[10] Wikipedia, the free encyclopedia. Key performance indicator http://en.wikipedia.org/wiki/Key_performance_indicators (revised January 30th, 2009)

[11] Moreno, Juan; Laborde, Alejandro. Business Activity Monitoring y Business Rules para el manejo de excepciones en las políticas en un sistema de gestión de procesos de negocios. (Business Activity Monitoring y Business Rules para el manejo de excepciones en las políticas en un sistema de gestión de procesos de negocios) Proceedings of the IV International Symposium of Information Systems and Software Engineering in the Knowledge Society. (SISOFT, 2006). Cartagena de Indias, Colombia. ISBN 846900258-9. 2006

Delivering Case Management with BPM in the Public Sector: Combining Knowledge with Process

Michael White, Singularity, United Kingdom

ABSTRACT

Case management is the most common pattern of work in collaborative knowledge environments in Government. It is different from other types of process pattern because it is ad-hoc, non-sequential, non-deterministic and driven primarily by human discretion and judgment. This article defines Case Management in more detail and explains why case oriented Business Process Management [BPM] is the best way to address collaborative Case Management.

INTRODUCTION

Case management is critical to the work of most public sector organizations but is often intensely manual, paper-driven and subject to delay and poor visibility. Primarily that is because Case Management requires supporting knowledge work, where many of the important steps take place in people's heads or through collaboration with colleagues, making these knowledge intensive processes difficult to analyze and structure. Also, because cases are primarily driven by human participants reacting to changing context, cases do not follow a predetermined path defined in advance—they lack predictability, making them difficult to automate.

Various technologies have been proposed for supporting Case Management, including Customer Relationship Management systems and Content Management Systems. While these technologies play a role, they are not in themselves sufficient to meet the challenges of Case Management.

Case-oriented Business Process Management is the ideal way to help public sector knowledge workers become more effective in their work. Case-enabled BPM enables government organizations to strike the correct balance between proceduralizing repetitive and mundane aspects of knowledge work while providing scope for the creative and discretionary elements. BPM-based Case Management can combine knowledge and process effectively, supporting the ad-hoc and unpredictable nature of cases, and can coordinate a range of other technologies to appropriately support knowledge intensive work.

WHAT IS CASE MANAGEMENT?

There are no universally accepted definitions available for case management. We define it as follows:

> Case Management is the management of long-lived collaborative processes that coordinate knowledge, content, correspondence and resources to progress a case to achieve a particular goal; where the path of execution cannot be predetermined in advance of execution; where human judgment is required to determine how the end goal can be achieved;

and where the state of a case can be altered by external out-of-band events.

Case management (also known as case handling) describes the way organizations such as government agencies handle complex customer and service interactions. When a customer initiates a request for some service, for example when they apply for social welfare benefits, the set of interactions with that customer and other relevant participants from initiation to completion is known as the 'case'. In the past, cases would have been managed using a manila folder of documents and records, with the folder moving through a department or organization from one in-tray to the next while the case was evaluated and progressed. Evaluation of the case would involve correspondence, phone calls, meetings and notes being appended to provide a record of the progress of the case. The staff working on the case, known as 'case workers', would be knowledgeable about their organization and how previous cases had been progressed, and would be empowered to use their judgment and discretion when deciding how some part of the current case should be handled. Cases might follow a general pattern, but each particular case would take its own unique path from initiation to resolution depending on the circumstances of the individual whose case was being handled.

Area	Case type
Government	Social welfare benefits applications
	Immigration applications
	Complaint management
	Regulatory monitoring
	Licensing and permits management
	Freedom of Information Enquiries
	Planning applications
	Industrial Health and Safety Enforcement
Law enforcement	Firearms licensing
	Forensics management
	Investigations

Table 1 Common Case Types in the Public Sector

Case management is often very manual, with only isolated parts of the process automated by legacy systems or spreadsheets. There are two main reasons why case management is so poorly supported.

- Firstly, cases are inherently more difficult to automate than other processes because of the extent to which cases processes must support human knowledge, judgment and discretion to determine their outcome. It is harder to manage the complexity and unpredictability of a case than, say, automating payroll processing or credit card transaction processing.
- Secondly, until recently the available technology has not been able to support the requirements for dynamic-user driven changes to cases as they progress.

We will look at the characteristics of case management a little more closely before considering how it can be properly supported by technology.

CHARACTERISTICS OF CASE MANAGEMENT

Case management scenarios share many common characteristics:

- **Knowledge-intensive**: Typically case management processes require the intervention of skilled and knowledgeable personnel. Staff acquire their knowledge through their experience of working on similar cases and through collaboration with more experienced colleagues, becoming thoroughly familiar with the tacit and explicit rules governing how cases should be managed. These staffers have to deal with issues that can be ambiguous and uncertain and that require judgment and creativity. Managing knowledge so it stays within the organization and is passed quickly to new members of staff is a challenge.

- **Variability**: While a particular type of case will share a general structure (e.g. handling benefits applications), it is not possible to predetermine the path that a particular instance of a case will take[i]. A case can change in unpredictable, dynamic and ad-hoc ways as it is progressed through an organization.

- **Long running**: Cases can run for months or years, and are generally much longer running than the shorter interaction cycles handled by standard customer relationship management (CRM) systems. Because a case is long running, it changes hands over time, different people work on different aspects and no single individual has an accurate view of the case as a whole.

- **Information Complexity**: Emails, meeting notes, case documents and correspondence related to a case must be easily accessible to the appropriate case worker at the right time. This information is often organized manually and retrieving the correct information required at a particular decision point therefore depends on the knowledge of the case worker and an adequate physical filing system.

- **Collaboration and coordination:** Case workers usually need to co-ordinate interviews and meetings among interested parties e.g. scheduling an interview with an applicant, with other staff in the organization, with legal representatives. Many cases require a team-based approach, with different specialists working on different aspects of a case or acting as consultants to their colleagues.

- **Multiple Participants, Multiple Roles**: There are often a range of involved parties, either directly or indirectly related to a case, who play different roles during the lifetime of the case—e.g. applicant, witness, claimant, injured party, appellant etc. And case workers can fulfill different roles in different types of cases.

- **Cases can be interrelated**: The outcome of separate cases may have an impact on each other. For example, an application for citizenship by an individual may be affected by the success or failure of an application by a spouse or immediate relative. Cases can be explicitly linked or they may be linked by inference and conducted with this inferred link in mind.

- **Critical nature of timescales**: While cases may have great variability in how they are completed, very often there are inflexible requirements for end-to-end timescales, driven by legislation or Service Level Agreements.

- **External events affect cases**: External, out-of-band events and intervention can change the state of a running case e.g. a phone call from a lawyer or the unscheduled arrival of compliance documentation.

- **Difficulty in Gaining Visibility of Case Progress**: This is a common characteristic of case management as it is implemented today, although it is not an inherent characteristic. While case workers may have a good understanding of how they are progressing individual cases, it is often difficult to monitor progress when work has been passed to colleagues within their own unit or to an external department. At a higher level, managers usually have poor visibility of how long it takes to progress a case on average, how much a case costs to process, and what the expected completion time is for a particular case. It may also be difficult to obtain information on which cases are stalled waiting for an external communication and which steps in a case are repeatedly causing bottlenecks. The result is that processing of cases is often serialized, because to run them in parallel, while more efficient, is just too difficult for many organizations to manage.

- **Strong reporting requirements**: There is usually a significant requirement to report on and analyze information derived from case handling, for example workload analysis of cases by stage, by individual and by department and case performance versus target.
- **History:** The case history is the organization's defense mechanism against any allegations of failure to perform, particularly in cases which have high cost or personal impact. Every action performed, every decision taken and every piece of correspondence received has to be tracked, not just for audit purposes, but also to provide guidance for future similar cases.
- **Security**: There is a requirement to provide fine-grained control over who has access to particular information and functionality. In certain environments, these security requirements assume particular significance e.g. policing, health care and child protection.
- **Isolated pockets of automation**: This is a characteristic of case management as it is generally implemented today, rather than an inherent characteristic. Case management is usually only partly automated and there is disjoint between those pockets of automation. Legacy systems automate slices of the processes, but the end-to-end management of a case still relies too heavily on paper documentation, physical folders, spreadsheets and email.

WHY IS CASE MANAGEMENT IMPORTANT?

Why should people care about the characteristics of cases or the issues raised when trying to automate them? Primarily because Case Management is the most common approach to supporting knowledge workers with technology, particularly in the public sector, but it is not done well today. According to Gartner's Marc Kerremans,

> "In collaborative environments, where knowledge workers work together on a process deliverable, the case management representation is the predominant process representation" [ii]

Tom Davenport has defined knowledge workers as "people whose primary job is to do something with knowledge: to create it, distribute it, apply it"[iii]

> "Knowledge workers think for a living. They solve problems, they understand and meet the needs of customers, they make decisions, and they collaborate and communicate with other people in the course of doing their work".[iv]

In the late 1950s and 1960s the economist Fritz Malchup first tried to formalize the size of the knowledge sector of the economy, suggesting it was growing two times faster than other sectors[v], and management author Peter Drucker highlighted the growing importance of knowledge workers and their productivity.[vi] More recently, research in the US, Canada and the UK suggests that between 25 percent and 40 percent of the workforce can be classified as knowledge workers, and that this proportion will increase[vii].

Knowledge workers are important not just because they make up a growing proportion of the workforce, but also because of their disproportionate impact on the organizations and economies they work in.

> Even if they're not a majority of all workers, they have the most influence on their economies. They are paid the most, they add the most economic value and they are the greatest determinant of the worth of their companies. Companies with a high proportion of knowledge workers—let's call them knowledge intensive—are the fastest growing and most successful in the United States and other leading economies, and have generated most of these economies' growth in the past couple of decades.[viii]

> Knowledge workers tend to be closely aligned with the organization's growth prospects. Knowledge workers in management roles come up with new strategies. Knowledge workers in R&D and engineering create new products. Knowledge workers in marketing package up products and services in ways that appeal to customers. Without knowledge workers there would be no new products and services, and no growth.[ix]

Over the past hundred years the automation of work focused first on automating manufacturing, then automating clerical work with the introduction of computers at the second half of the twentieth century, through to automating knowledge-centric work today. For much of the past four decades computer automation was directed at areas that were clearly defined and fairly predictable at 'design-time', mainly operational and administrative processes. Examples include bank automation, airline booking automation and manufacturing production automation. These kinds of processes could be complex, but the complexities could be analyzed, anticipated and accommodated at the design phase. When we went to execute these processes, the 'system' dictated most of the sequence of events to the human participants, based on logic embedded in software. This kind of automation has meant that old-fashioned clerical roles are largely disappearing. However, as these roles have reduced, there has been an increase in roles that demand greater skills and knowledge. But despite the growth in the number of knowledge workers and their importance to organizational success, there has been limited systematic effort made to improve the management of knowledge centric processes:

> Process improvement has mostly been for other workers: transactional workers, manufacturing workers, people in call centers. All the serious approaches to improving work have largely escaped knowledge work.[x]

A recent report by McKinsey reinforces this message

> Companies have been automating or off-shoring an increasing proportion of their production and manufacturing (transformational) activities and their clerical or simple rules-based (transactional) activities. As a result, a growing proportion of the labor force in developed economies engages primarily in work that involves negotiations and conversations, knowledge, judgment and ad hoc collaboration—tacit interactions, as we call them. By 2015 we expect employment in jobs primarily involving such interactions to account for about 44 per cent of total US employment, up from 40 percent today. Europe and Japan will experience similar changes in the composition of their workforces. The application of technology has reduced differences among the productivity of trans-

formational and transactional employees, but huge inconsistencies persist in the productivity of high-value tacit ones."[xi]

Tom Davenport, in his book 'Thinking for a Living', emphasizes the same point:

> For about fifteen years I've been doing research on business processes and how they can be improved. I've come to the conclusion that the most important processes for organizations today involve knowledge work. In the past, these haven't really been the focus of most organizations—improving administrative and operational processes has been easier—but they must be in the future. [xii]

So, knowledge workers are the most important and fastest growing section of the workforce, but the processes they use in their work are not well supported by technology; and generally they haven't been the focus of systematic process improvement initiatives.

THE IMPORTANCE OF COMBINING PROCESS AND KNOWLEDGE

It is self-evident that there should be good linkage between knowledge-centric processes and the underlying knowledge needed to carry out those processes.[xiii] However, process and knowledge are generally *not* well integrated. In a 2005 article, L. Russell Records of CSC Consulting discussed the parallel evolution of business process reengineering and Knowledge Management, highlighting the lack of integration between the two:

> There was (and still is) a general lack of understanding of how valuable the fusion of processes and knowledge can be. The thought of actually taking the distilled knowledge and making it easily available to people executing the process was somehow overlooked. Employees would only stop to access the available knowledge base when the process execution came to a screeching halt due to an inability on the part of the employee to continue. Many times this would involve looking up information in an offline source like a procedures handbook or calling a friend who might know the answer[xiv]

It's worth providing a little historical background to this issue. Paul Harmon, editor of BPTrends, described in a 2006 article how approaches from cognitive psychology and computer science were used in the 1980s to capture and embed knowledge in software systems (known as 'expert systems')[xv]. According to Harmon:

> Ultimately expert systems have not proven very viable. It turns out that human expertise—if it's worthy of the name—needs to be constantly maintained. Human experts attend conferences, read books and research papers, and constantly interact with peers while trying to solve hard problems. All this leads to their reformulating their knowledge. It turns out that it is expensive to capture human knowledge from an expert system, but it is much more expensive to maintain that knowledge.

The next major attempt to focus on the use of knowledge in work was the Knowledge Management movement, which gained momentum in the late 1990s. Knowledge Management aimed to capture knowledge effectively, categorize it and then make that knowledge available across an organization.

> For the most part, it wasn't particularly successful, because we didn't look closely at how knowledge workers did their work.... Most organizations simply created one big repository for all knowledge and all workers. The only way to get people to use knowledge on the job is to understand how they do their jobs and then figure out some way to inject knowledge into the course of their day-to-day work, not make it a separate thing you have to

> consult when you need knowledge. ... The best way is to use technology to bake the knowledge into the job.[xvi]

This inability to access the right information at the point in a process when it is needed is a problem:

> Process execution normally stops when someone has to retrieve knowledge that has not been provisioned for them to use. When this occurs in a customer-facing process, the cost to execute the process skyrockets.[xvii]

While it seems obvious that integrating knowledge at the correct points in a process is a good idea, how does this relate to Case Management? Well, as we previously noted, Case Management is the most common pattern of work in collaborative environments where knowledge workers work together on process deliverables. We hope to demonstrate that an effective Case Management solution based on Business Process Management technology provides the best mechanism for supporting the appropriate creation, dissemination and retrieval of knowledge for knowledge workers within a process. The goal is to provide the information the knowledge worker needs at the point in a process when he needs it, rather than force him to go searching for it when he hits a problem. The supporting technology should capture useful, shareable knowledge from workers so it can be distributed to others doing the same kind of work. L. Russell Records states that the goal

> "...is to diligently and selectively move the knowledge into the IT infrastructure so that it can be used to improve the execution of key business processes. [xviii]

We would emphasize the word 'selectively' here. It should not be a goal, explicit or implicit, to try to move all knowledge out of workers heads and into the IT infrastructure. As Paul Harmon pointed out, knowledge is constantly being created, knowledge workers are constantly learning, so only certain elements of the knowledge relevant to a particular type of work can be transferred to automated systems. But we should provide tools that let knowledge worker capture new insights and information so that it can be reused by themselves and their colleagues at appropriate steps in a process, and that gather knowledge about how processes are performed for analysis and ongoing improvement of knowledge processes.

THE CHALLENGES OF AUTOMATING CASE MANAGEMENT

The characteristics of Case Management we outlined earlier indicate where the challenges lie when trying to more fully automate this style of work. As with the automation of any business processes, the technology has to support "exception handling, collaboration, decision making, unstructured information, negotiations and paper flows"[xix]. But the fundamental challenge in automating case management is using the technology to support the unpredictable ways cases progress and people work in practice. Traditional automation assumes that a sequence or pattern can be determined in advance by careful initial analysis and catered for by good design. More formally, it assumes that the logical flows can be understood *a priori*. As noted by van der Aalst et al[xx], in a traditional approach the designer has to specify what is permitted. Any routing which is not specified at design time will not be supported by the system at runtime. However, when seeking to automate cases, there is no predetermined sequence, and new tasks and processes can be added at any point during the life cycle of the case as the need for them arises. The emphasis must be on supporting the ad hoc nature of cases. As Lucy Suchman puts it:

"the trick …. is to introduce bits of automation that will fit in to the work and do useful things, and then make it possible for people to work with those bits of automation embedded in the systems while leaving them the discretionary space to exercise the kind of judgment they need to exercise to really get the work done"[xxi]

The challenges specific to automating Case Management include:

- **Striking a balance between Practice and Procedure**: Almost any job today has both clearly defined, predictable elements and less well defined, more ambiguous aspects where workers exercise their judgment. Different types of job, and the activities within a particular job, can be thought of as a spectrum running from 'well defined procedure' to loosely defined 'discretionary practice'. Someone working in a call center generally doesn't exercise great discretion in how they carry out their job, while a senior investment analyst probably does.

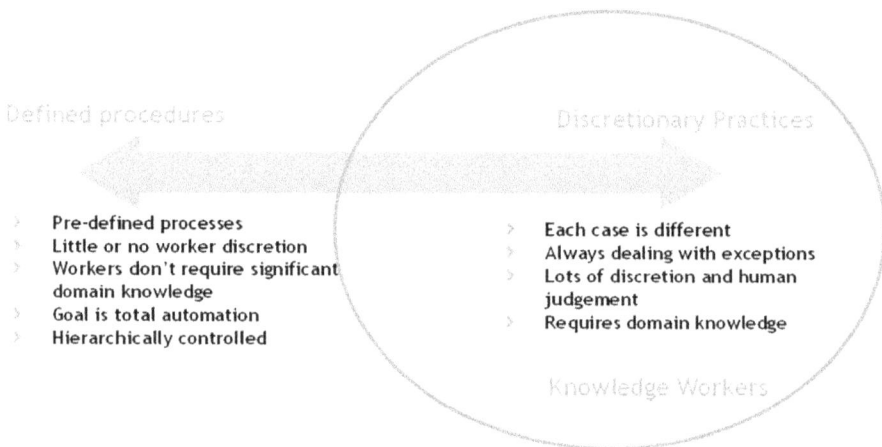

Defined procedures

- Pre-defined processes
- Little or no worker discretion
- Workers don't require significant domain knowledge
- Goal is total automation
- Hierarchically controlled

Discretionary Practices

- Each case is different
- Always dealing with exceptions
- Lots of discretion and human judgement
- Requires domain knowledge

Knowledge Workers

Source: adapted from Derek Miers[xxii] and Paul Harmon[xxiii]

There is a danger of aiming to fully proceduralize processes when reengineering knowledge work, ignoring the 'Practice' side of the spectrum. However, this is counterproductive, because when a case occurs that doesn't match the rules prescribed in the procedure, workers are either brought to a halt or forced to create an unofficial workaround.[xxiv] A careful balance must be maintained between prescribing defined procedures for fully understood and repeatable aspects of work, while respecting the parts of work that should be left to the discretion of knowledge workers.

> Every effort to change how work is done needs a dose of both process—the design for how work is to be done—and practice, an understanding of how individual workers respond to the real world of work and accomplish their assigned tasks.[xxv]

It should be a goal that, as particular workers become more experienced, they will be able to formalize and standardize aspects of what they do, and these standardized procedures can then be made available for use by colleagues.[xxvi]

- **Capturing Implicit Rules and Tacit Knowledge:** This challenge is related to the point made about Practice versus Procedure. Many case management processes will never have been previously automated. They rely on paper forms and tacit and implicit rules governing how cases should be managed in addition to documented and explicit policies and procedures. The challenge here is to discover these implicit rules and tacit knowledge and, where appropriate, try to support their automation, while leaving room for those steps and decisions that should continue to depend on individual discretion.

- **Formalizing experience—supporting learning:** A good Case Management solution should help an organization learn from previous cases. This learning could be exhibited in the definition of new processes, new procedures, better online help etc., where lessons learned by knowledge workers during a previous case were quickly applied to process definitions to improve them. We use the phrase 'formalizing experience' to describe this process of changing a practice into an automated step where appropriate, or supporting some other action that will assist in the processing of future cases.

There is a related area of research, called Case Based Reasoning (CBR), which has some obvious applicability to Case Management. Case Based Reasoning is the process of solving new problems based on the solution of similar past problems: it's based on two tenets, "similar problems have similar solutions. Consequently, solutions for similar prior problems are a useful starting point for new problem-solving" and "the types of problems an agent encounters tend to recur. Consequently, future problems are likely to be similar to current problems"[xxvii]. CBR consists of four steps — look at a given case or problem and try to think of a previous case or cases it might match; consider how the solution to the previous case could be applied to the current case; test the solution on the existing case and revise it if necessary; then record the new case, and the solution that eventually worked, for future reference.

- **Supporting Ad-hoc change**: It is not possible to fully analyze and define at design time how a case will actually unfold at 'runtime'. A range of outcomes may arise at each stage in the case, unpredictable at design time, and these outcomes then determine the next stage or stages.
- **Involving Participants in the Design of Knowledge Processes**: the challenge here is to let knowledge workers influence the design of those processes they participate in, helping them make changes to processes or innovating new ones. Any solution needs to support, fast easy change initiated by a worker.
- **Supporting Collaboration**: collaboration is a key requirement, but it is not simply a matter of enabling instant messaging or document sharing. Case workers need to share everything related to a case, including history, discussions, correspondence and previous decisions. The collaboration support for case management must ensure that the correct information is made available to team members at the correct time, without losing the context or current state of progress of the case. This requires a 'smart' system that knows who needs what when. Conversely, it is important that irrelevant information is not provided at the wrong time, and that confidential information is not made available to inappropriate recipients.
- **Supporting Decisions**: case workers are the key decision makers in determining how a case will progress, supported where appropriate by automated rules. Automation of cases must recognize that control will

continue to reside with human case participants, rather than seeking to encapsulate everything in an increasingly complex rule-base.

- **Effectively coordinating participants**: effective case management requires that work is routed to participants at the appropriate time and in the appropriate sequence, given the history of the case to date. This coordination requires sophisticated workflow routing, synchronization of process flows, and monitoring of milestones at a case, process and activity level. Any delays must be quickly identified and remediating actions initiated where necessary.
- **Managing complexity**: information and data has to be organized and presented to all case workers in a useful way so they do not become overwhelmed or confused by the documentation, records and notes related to a case. The user interface workers use is a key determinant of the success of any case management solution.
- **Managing artifacts**: beyond the presentation of case information to the user, there is a need to effectively store, manage and retrieve information related to a case. Case history and associated records may need to be retained for specific periods, as a result of legislation or organizational policy. Content may be structured or unstructured, and may reside on multiple supporting systems such as databases, content management systems and electronic record management systems. Any case management solution must manage this content efficiently and effectively.
- **Integrating Disparate Systems:** there are almost always some important legacy systems in use at an organization. Effective case management requires the smooth integration of these existing systems into any future solution.

SOME APPROACHES TO CASE MANAGEMENT

We have discussed the characteristics and the challenges to be overcome when automating case management. The question then turns to the most appropriate technology to use to support case management. Until recently the main approaches advocated have been:

- Custom-built applications;
- Customer Relationship Management (CRM) systems
- Electronic Document and Record Management (EDRMS) systems

None of these approaches are appropriate, for the following reasons.

- Firstly, developing a custom-built application will make it difficult to support the ad-hoc and dynamic nature of case management. Developing a custom application assumes that all the possible paths for the execution of a case can be identified up-front and catered for through careful analysis and design, or can be subsequently supported through programmatic changes to the system. But as described, the nature of cases means there will always be significant exceptions to whatever paths are identified at the design stage. Another objection to the development of a custom application is that the business logic will be buried in software code and so will be inaccessible to the case workers who work with the system on a day-to-day basis, making it difficult to maintain and change. Finally, this approach is inadvisable for the same reasons that gave rise to the birth of commercial software products; it is generally preferable to select a commercial off-the-shelf (COTS) product rather than to build a custom solution, because of the benefits in terms of cost, reliability, pre-built integration points to popular systems and ongoing support.

- Customer Relationship Management (CRM) systems are also proposed as a way to automate case management. However, CRM systems are generally optimized for short-lived, high-volume customer interactions, not cases that can last for months or years. They have usually focused on interactions with a single client, not in the management of multiple external parties that potentially belong to several organizations. They also suffer from the problem cited for custom applications, in that the process logic governing the management of the case is buried within the application and so cannot be easily manipulated and changed by case workers and managers. Most importantly, they provide little or no support for ongoing ad-hoc and dynamic process change during the execution of a case.[xxviii] . While CRM systems are likely to be an important element in a case management solution (e.g. for storing customer data), they are not sufficient of themselves to meet the full range of requirements.
- Lastly, while Electronic Document and Record Management Systems (EDRMS) will form a crucial element in most case management solutions, as they are needed to store, manage and retrieve content related to a case, they too have minimal support for complex interactions and long-lived case management. These systems are optimized to manage the storage and retrieval of content, not the management of dynamic processes and complex human interactions over long periods of time. Also, case content will frequently be distributed across multiple data stores and EDRMS systems.

BPM-BASED CASE MANAGEMENT

Case management is about the successful coordination of a number of different technologies in order to provide a supporting environment that enables knowledge workers to achieve an outcome. Successful case management, when all of the tools and technologies are correctly aligned, enables efficient working. The focus on supporting knowledge workers is critical; removing many of the mundane tasks such as tracking progress, managing and generating the required artifacts, guiding them through critical aspects of the process. Equally there is a need to support appropriate decision making by knowledge workers, as well as a need to support the impact of external events on cases.

Case-oriented Business Process Management (BPM) represents the best approach to the automation of case management. A case-centric BPM solution can provide support for well-defined processes that interact with each other in a range of ways determined during the execution of the case, not at design time. It meets the requirement of orchestrating disparate technologies, while also supporting the need for dynamic change and ongoing adaptability. A BPM system that supports case management can present one unified interface to the user, enabling case workers to gain a single view of a particular case and the corresponding content, regardless of where that content is held.

Specifically, case-oriented BPM overcomes the limitations of the other proposed technologies through its support for:

- Explicit graphical modeling of business processes, so that these are visible to and can be managed and changed by case workers
- Execution of complex processes that interact with and coordinate multiple systems

- Support for frequent, rapid and dynamic change to cases, initiated by case workers and case managers as well as by the system
- Support for knowledge capture and knowledge sharing, through process models, process history, integration to content repositories, case user interfaces and knowledge wikis
- Support for team collaboration through workflow, scheduling and calendars
- Integration to multiple supporting content repositories

To provide this support, we believe the BPM system needs to adhere to the following guiding principles:

- The primacy of the case rests with the human case workers, not the supporting systems. By this we mean the system must support the way people work, not force them to change how they work to suit the constraints of the system.
- The end-to-end activity flow of a case does not have to be fully determined in advance at design time. In real life, new tasks and processes may be added to a case at runtime.
- Maximum flexibility in case 'disposition' (i.e. how it is progressed) must be maintained, within specified time and budget constraints.
- All case documentation, including emails, meeting notes, and correspondence, must be organized and readily accessible to participants working on the same case.
- The state of a particular case may be changed by unpredictable external 'out of band' events, such as a phone call, thereby by-passing some or all of the steps laid out in the standard case definition.
- The outcome of a case can be affected by the disposition of other separate but related cases.
- Meetings among parties to the case may need to be scheduled and coordinated.

Case Management Architecture

Singularity has implemented a case oriented BPM architecture based on the concept of a two-tiered hierarchy of process types, with the first being a Case process and then, at a lower level, a Process Fragment.

In conventional business process management systems, execution of a process runs from start to finish along a pre-defined path. Even with complex nesting and chaining logic, what happens is fully predictable, based on a process model produced at design-time. For example, if we have a process model that contains a decision point with 10 different possible paths to choose from, we know that one of those 10 will be executed at run time—standard BPM doesn't enable the selection of an arbitrary new 'path 11' at execution. Also, in conventional business process automation, an executing process has access to its own data and that of any embedded or sub-processes, but not that of other independent processes.

Standard BPM

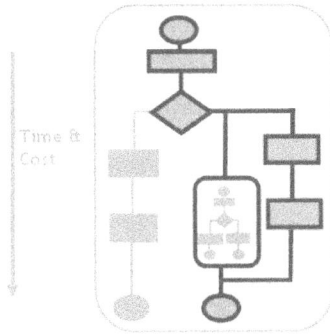

- Process defined at design time
- Decision logic specified as business rules
- Rule evaluation is automated
- Embedded processes invoked according to design
- Execution can only follow the steps specified by the designer, even though these may include complex nesting and chaining logic
- Executing process only has access to its own variables and data

However, for Case Management we have to be able to coordinate a collection of independent processes, all of which are leading to a common goal, but which may be initiated in any order. These processes need access to a common set of case related data, and may need to synchronize with each other at different times or stages, but apart from that they are independent processes that execute autonomously, and they are invoked in an order that is driven by human case workers and external events.

To support these requirements, we have developed the concept of a "Case Definition". A Case Definition can be thought of as a container used to hold a set of 'process fragments' and their associated context. These process fragments are available to the Case at runtime for invocation, although some or all of them may not be invoked. At design time we use the Case Definition to define

- The Start and End Points for the case
- Case Attributes such as **Milestone** dates for the case, overall **Budget** for the case, and allowed **Roles** that can work on that case
- **Case Data**—the case-level data that will be available to all process fragments as they execute
- **Virtual Case Folder**—a folder containing references to documents and other content pertaining to the case and held on external data stores.
- Case **States**—a set of 'states' can be defined, defining different stages in a case lifecycle such as 'Create', 'Prepare Case', 'Review Case', 'Archive Case' etc.

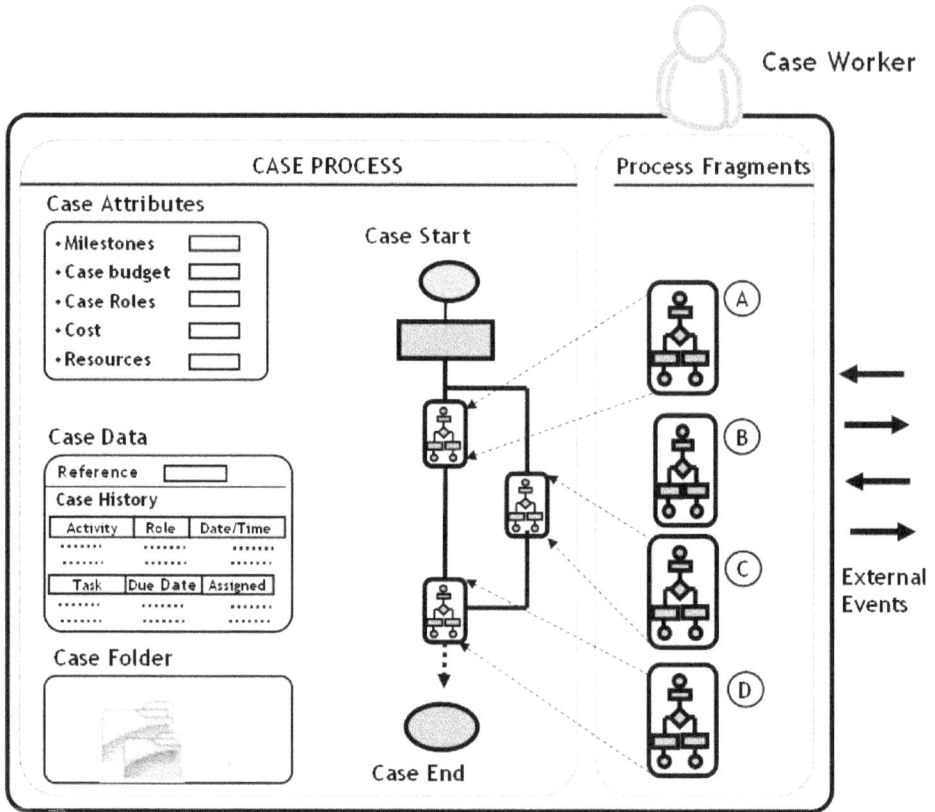

Figure 1 Executing Case Process

When we initiate a case, an instance of the Case Definition is created. This instance consists of the attributes, data and a set of executing process fragments, along with the associated content held for the case and referenced via the Virtual Case Folder. During the execution of a case, process fragments are invoked depending on the choices made by the human participants, the arrival of external events such as 'document inserted on content management system' and the outcome of other executing process fragments. There is no predefined order to this execution; fragments can be invoked in any order. Only the start point of the case and the end goal are defined, how that goal will be achieved will be determined during execution. The executing process fragments can be thought of as a collection of independently executing business processes that share a context (the goal or end-point of the case, overall milestones, and common case data).

Supporting this overall architecture are a range of case-specific features such as pre-emptive case escalation, case-based role definitions, wiki integration for context-sensitive case knowledge storage and retrieval, milestone recalculation etc.

CONCLUSION

Through the course of this article we have defined Case Management and its characteristics, and highlighted its link to knowledge workers. We emphasized the growing importance of knowledge workers and the current poor support for knowledge work automation. We also discussed the challenges in supporting this kind of knowledge work. We considered three competing approaches to supporting Case Management; the 'grow your own' self build option, or else using a Document Management or CRM system to meet the requirements. However, none of these approaches are adequate. Case-oriented Business Process Management [BPM] is the ideal way to support knowledge workers as they strive to become better and more effective in their work. BPM enables organizations to strike the appropriate balance between proceduralizing repetitive and mundane aspects of knowledge work while providing scope for the creative and discretionary elements. BPM-based Case Management combines knowledge and process effectively, supporting the ad-hoc and unpredictable nature of cases, and coordinate a range of other technologies to appropriately support knowledge intensive processes.

Fundamentally, we believe Case management is important because Knowledge Work is important. As we noted, the most important processes in most organizations involve knowledge work—they add the most value and have the greatest impact on long-term success. But processes and the knowledge required to execute them have generally been badly integrated, which means that knowledge work has been poorly supported by technology. With case-oriented Business Process Management, there is now an effective way to address knowledge intensive processes.

REFERENCES

[i] Van der Aalst, Wil M.P., Weske, M., Grünbauer, D., *"Case Handling: a new paradigm for business process support"*, Eindhoven, 2004, p1

"Unlike workflow management, which uses predefined process control structures to determine what should be done during a workflow process, case handling focuses on what *can* be done to achieve a business goal. In case handling, the knowledge worker in charge of a particular case actively decides on how the goal of that case is reached, and the role of a case handling system is assisting rather than guiding her in doing so.

[ii] Kerremans, Marc, "Case Management is a Challenging BPMS Use Case", *Gartner Research*, ID G00162739, 8 December 2008, p1

[iii] Quoted in Alter, Allen, "Knowledge workers need better management", CIOInsight.com, 5 Aug 2008

[iv] Davenport, Tom, "Thinking for a Living", Harvard Business School Press, 2005, p10

[v] Malchup, Fritz, *"The Production and Distribution of Knowledge in the United States"*, Princeton University Press, 1958

[vi] "To make knowledge work productive will be the great management task of this century, just as to make manual work productive was the great management task of the last century", from Peter Drucker, *"The age of Discontinuity"*, New York, Harper & Row, 1969,

"The productivity of knowledge and knowledge workers will not be the only competitive factor in the world economy. It is, however, likely to become the decisive factor, at least for most industries in the developed countries", from Peter Drucker, *"The future that has already happened"*, Harvard Business Review, Sep – Oct 1997

Both quoted by Tom Davenport in "Thinking for a living", p. 8

[vii] Davenport, Tom, "Thinking for a Living", Harvard Business School Press, 2005, p5

[viii] Davenport, Tom, "Thinking for a Living", Harvard Business School Press, 2005, p4

[ix] Davenport, Tom, "Thinking for a Living", Harvard Business School Press, 2005, p7

[x] Quoted in Alter, Allen, "Knowledge workers need better management", CIOInsight.com, 5 Aug 2008

[xi] "The McKinsey Quarterly- Eight business technology trends to watch", December 2007

[xii] Davenport, Tom, "Thinking for a Living", Harvard Business School Press, 2005, pp9-10

[xiii] For example, "integrating knowledge management into business processes" was selected as the most important issue of knowledge management in a 2002 survey of academics

engaged in KM research – see First Global Delphi Study, "The Future of Knowledge Management", Humboldt University, Berlin, March 2002

[xiv] Records, L. Russell, "The Fusion of Process and Knowledge Management", BPTrends, September 2005

[xv] Harmon, Paul, *Review of "Working Minds: A practitioner's guide to cognitive task analysis" by Beth Crandall, Gary Klein and Robert R. Hoffman*, BPTrends, October 2006

[xvi] Quoted in Alter, Allen, "Knowledge workers need better management", CIOInsight.com, 5 Aug 2008

[xvii] Records, L. Russell, "The Fusion of Process and Knowledge Management", BPTrends, September 2005

[xviii] Records, L. Russell, "The Fusion of Process and Knowledge Management", BPTrends, September 2005

[xix] "BPM: A change from business as usual", Gartner, Janelle Hill, February 2007

[xx] "The Case Handling Case", Reijers, Rigter and Van der Aalst, Eindhoven University

[xxi] Quoted in *"Process Innovation and Corporate Agility: balancing efficiency and adaptability in a knowledge centric world"*, Derek Miers, BPMFocus, 2006, p6

[xxii] Miers, Derek, *"Process Innovation and Corporate Agility: balancing efficiency and adaptability in a knowledge centric world"*, BPMFocus, 2006, p3

[xxiii] Harmon, Paul, *Review of "Working Minds: A practitioner's guide to cognitive task analysis" by Beth Crandall, Gary Klein and Robert R. Hoffman*, BPTrends, October 2006, Fig. 1, p3

[xxiv] In a paper by Brown and Duguid, cited by Davenport and others, the authors studied the work of a group of IT support technicians, finding that the formally defined procedures imposed on them were counterproductive, forcing staff to carry out strenuous workarounds in order to solve problems while being seen to comply with company rules – see Brown, John Seely, Duguid, Paul, "Organizational Learning and Communities of Practice", The Institute of Management Sciences, 1991

[xxv] Davenport, Tom, "Thinking for a Living", Harvard Business School Press, 2005, p74

[xxvi] Miers, Derek, *"Process Innovation and Corporate Agility: balancing efficiency and adaptability in a knowledge centric world"*, BPMFocus, 2006, p3

"When someone starts in a new position, they tend to follow the rules. After 3 months, they might have a good feel for those rules that are important and those rules that are safe to ignore or break. After 3 years of experience, they may even help establish the rules that govern their position"

[xxvii] Leake, David, "Case Based Reasoning in Context: the Present and the Future", AAI Press/MIT Press, 1996, p2

[xxviii] Miers, Derek, "Business Processes and Customers—Difficult domains to integrate", BPMFocus, 2007

BPM in eGovernment: a Genuine Virtual Counter

Cédric Tumelaire, City of Waterloo, Belgium, Laurent Bagnoud, University of Applied Sciences Western Switzerland and Rémy Tzaud, Xpert.Ivy, Switzerland

INTRODUCTION

This novel approach, based on BPM combined with RIA Technology, will show how processes are managed across different administration levels without predetermining the choice of technologies, platforms and tools made by each organization. This will allow them to preserve autonomy while providing task execution integrated from bottom to top of the organization.

The city of Waterloo figures among the pioneers of 'Cyberadministration' clearly illustrated by W@tson, an innovative platform of exchange between administration and population. Agoria, the federation of technology industries, has honored Waterloo and its virtual agent W@tson with the E-Gov Awards 2007.

The agent consists of a robot with a data base coupled to an artificial intelligence engine able to recognize natural language. This agent can be accessed via Windows Live Messenger. It suffices adding watson@waterloo.eu to the contacts in order to be able to interrogate on matters concerning the community. Thereby the communal administration has become accessible during 24 hours a day and seven days a week. It has been a European premiere in eGovernment. After this very positive experience a new strategic goal has been set: to integrate BPM (Business Process Management) at the heart of Waterloo's IT. Recognizing the necessity to manage processes via a very simple interface between administration and users an appropriate BPM tool had to be found. The typical government processes imply a number of different participants as well as different technological environments within the administration. It will be shown how BPM offers the perfect approach to meet integration and flexibility needs. An important objective for Waterloo is the possibility to federate processes between different cities or communities having quite similar needs but requiring the possibility of adaptation to their peculiarities.

The Belgian market seems particularly receptive for BPM within eGovernment after having recently introduced ID cards with an integrated chip. Waterloo has been one of the first cities to provide this card to its population. Therefore, already being able to individually identify each citizen in a secure way, process-based online services should help markedly to improve the quality of government services to its citizens.

Key objectives of this new eGovernment are the following:
- Provide for citizens the best quality and responsiveness in services
- Assure high performance of process execution and follow-up of tasks in public administrations
- Realize the needed flexibility to promote decentralization of task execution while securing and keeping a centralized data management.

Public administrations all over the world are built on multiple levels, whether their organization model is centralized or decentralized. The more decentralized the administrations, the more decisive workflow management (BPM) will become to control and optimize their processes.

BPM PLATFORM AS A COLLABORATIVE TOOL

The implementation of a BPM platform in the eGov process brings an answer to the problems of services availability with regard to the needs of the population. This technology enables a citizen to initiate a request 24-7 and to ensure its follow-up so that the applicant gets an answer as soon as possible.

The notion of virtual retail or administrative counter replacing the physical shop or office counter takes all its sense within the framework of administrative processes intended for the population. Like placing an online order or making a payment via Internet, it seems henceforth 'normal' to be able to carry out a change of address, to claim an attestation or make a complaint without having to be concerned with the office's location or the administration's schedule.

The procedure itself makes the approach complex; who has never gone to the administration counter in order to make a claim and realise then that his/her personal file is incomplete? The consequence is that the person has to plan a later appointment and is often strongly displeased. Indeed, some administrative or legal procedures can be complex and difficult to understand and the authorities must scrupulously respect this legal framework. More than proposing the notion of the virtual counter, the BPM technology enables the creation of a real-time interactivity with the user. The user is guided step by step in the different procedures according to the particular nature of his request. Each person receives in real time a personalized and intuitive answer, without any risk of a mistake.

Some BPM solutions such as Xpert.Ivy allow us to publish the process itself by a BPMN (Business Process Modelling Notation) chart. The requester can also study the flow of the process before initiating it or know its progression, either through the BPMN model or by an email notification.

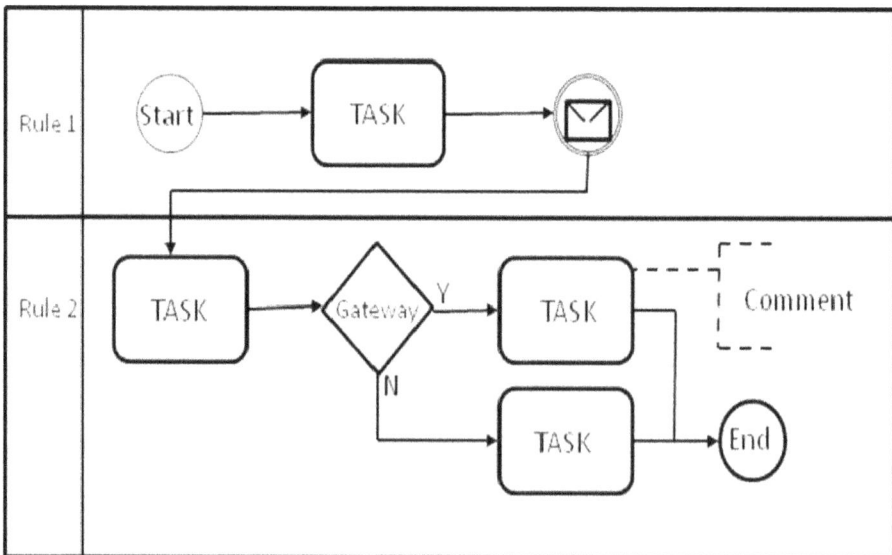

(Fig 1. BPMN diagram)

Beyond these constraints, the tool also enables to bring an answer to the linguistic problems as the same process can be published in different languages and therefore satisfy the multiple communities concerned. Whether it is a foreign tourist, an immigrant or a businessman, the process will guide him in his language, whichever it is, and bring a service which is sometimes difficult to produce in a physical counter.

This process management allows us to offer the user at all times an interactive on demand service in his language, but it also mainly enables us to coordinate later the back office processing. Indeed, according to the complexity of the file, multiple internal or external contributors will be involved in the processing. Thanks to the BPM integrating the tasks management, each contributor will be called at the appropriate time with the right information in order to process the request. The progression of the different tasks in the process ensures the continuity of the flow and its processing from start to finish in the respect of rules and without any disruption.

The definition of deadlines and management rules in case these deadlines are not respected ensures a high level quality of services to the population close to the practice of the world of services (SLA; Service Level Agreement). The BPM also brings an answer to the requests of citizens accustomed to quick and precise answers. Xpert.Ivy manages the surplus all the absences and substitutions problems with the same concern of quality and flexibility.

Parallel activities

The originality of the BPM also lies in its capacity to launch independent or parallel sub processes, by the initiation of a main process. The management of a paper file generally runs sequentially to a file transmitted from department to department, but the BPM enables us to allocate the process in parallel to several sectors.

As long as the rules of management allow it, each department is therefore questioned at the same time. The time spent on the whole development of the process is therefore greatly reduced, without altering the performance or the information in any way within the administration. The collaborative environment allows everyone to know the status of the file, its progression level and any comment or remark brought by the different contributors.

This approach is all the more important since the process can concern external contributors such as for example: engineer offices, social organisations or other governmental authorities. This capacity to launch independent but also controlled processes ensures a treatment of quality without disruption.

The BPM enables therefore to optimise the process without any concession to the information, to the rules or to the quality of the service.

Synchronization of the existing applications

The previous chapters showed the contribution of a Business Process Management solution as a 'vehicle' of information in the execution of the process, stage by stage and task by task. The perfect running of the process would, however, not be complete without a total integration of the existing information system. Indeed it is not conceivable, as much from a qualitative perspective as from an operational point of view, to have a disruption in the development; for example with a task calling a department which has to enter information in a third application. The process would thus have no control whether the information has been entered by the user or if it has been entered correctly.

The BPM must therefore be totally integrated to the existing environment, whichever it is and whatever its technology. This is mostly at this level that we will be able to differentiate a simple project of Workflow from the logic of business process totally integrated to the organisation and to the information system. Thanks to this approach, the user is questioned with a task and he enters his information in a form proposed by the process; then this same process transfers this information in a secure way in the third application. This information can then be checked by the process and disruption in the development is therefore discarded.

These integrations are located at different levels and first at a transactional level. By the integration of SOA (Service Oriented Application) technologies, we guarantee secured and standard exchanges. Moreover they are potentially quite simple to implement and to maintain. The SOA approach thus brings a functional aspect which is adapted and freed from risks for the model of data. Some solutions such as Xpert.Ivy also integrate the WSDL (Web Service Description Languages) which simplifies the configuration of these integration functions with the help of an assistant.

Other transactional methods are also conceivable according to the level of opening offered by the applications to integrate. For example; JavaBeans, API (Application Program Interface), XML files or even possibly a JDBC access (Java Data Base Connectivity). This latest method should be privileged for some accesses in reading only, unless you master totally the data model; the risk of integrity for the database is indeed particularly high with damaging consequences.

Beyond the transactional aspects which are obviously the most important, the BPM must also satisfy to the needs of communication and to be interfaced with SMTP messaging services. This integration allows first to solve the questions of notifications; for example to notify the incoming of a new task to process, a prospective delay or yet an information on the progression of the file processing. The e-mail can furthermore launch a process by entering a form in the virtual counter but it can also be launched by the reception of an e-mail (or a fax, as the technologies are henceforth similar). Finally an answer to a question or an agreement can also be requested or processed by the exchange of e-mails and totally managed by the process.

The last level of integration concerns the security with the advantage of leaning on the LDAP (Lightweight Directory Access Protocol) for the authentication of the users and potentially the management of their role. This approach supplies the user with the single sign-on and simplifies management for the organisation's security administrator.

Finally there are still other interesting possibilities of integration such as the synchronisation of agendas or in another topic, the flow of the BI (Business Intelligence) with data of the process in order to feed the control panels.

POPULATION; ADMINISTRATION INTERACTIVITY

Beyond the availability and the level of service, the keys of approval by the users go through an interface which is efficient, attractive, comfortable and reliable. The City of Waterloo in Belgium brings an innovative answer with its service W@tson.

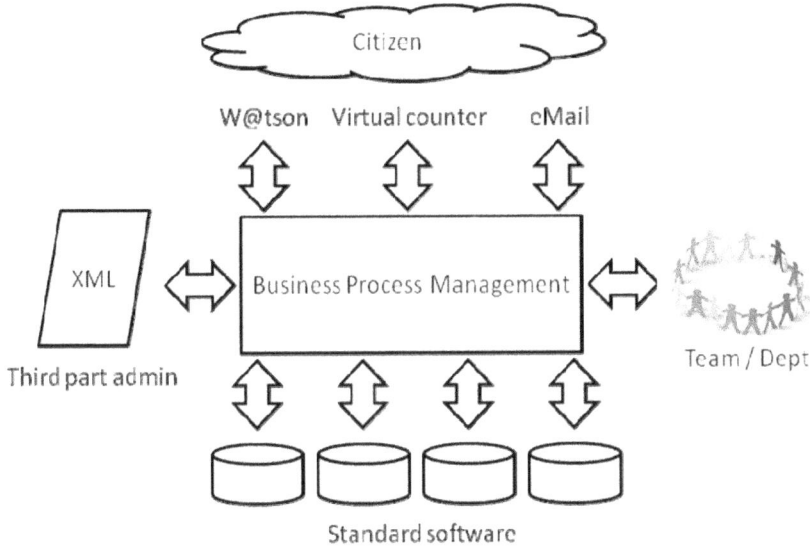

(Fig 2. BPM interactivity)

By coupling an MSN-type interface in the virtual counter with the process management, Waterloo has acquired a playful tool accessible to everyone, inviting the population to use it and to master it. The solution runs on a concept of 'chat' on which the customer can ask a question or surf through the menus. This interactive exchange depends on a database (knowledge base) which brings real time answers to the requester according to context. If the answer is not available, the robot launches the appropriate process so that the department can then process the request. This approach meets the concepts of the Web 2.0 which aims at processing the information in a rich interface, functionally more user-friendly than the traditional HTML displays.

BPM and Rich Internet Application

This level of interactivity and acceptance is important for the end-user, but it is just as important for the departments implicated in the processing of the file during the course of the process. It is in this spirit that Xpert.Ivy associates the technologies of RIA (Rich Internet Application) to the BPM.

For their ease of use, the departments need to gather multiple information emanating from different sources, for example; simultaneous display of several files in different tabs, parallel information coming from various applications, display of documents, etc. The RIA enables us to fulfil this need by compiling the components of screens which are assembled to offer the user a complete and totally integrated working environment. The advanced features allow us then to play with tabs, shutters or drop-down menus to adapt the screen to our needs. The user thus benefits from an application as complete as currently possible in client/server environments with the interactivity and the flexibility of today's web applications. All the functions familiar to the user in the Windows world, for example the personalisation of the working environment, drag and drop, etc. are also available.

Reliability and zero deployment

The technology used is based on Java, ensuring thus a high level of reliability in its features while solving the problem of deployment. By adopting the RIA concepts no application requires installation on the client stations. The richness of the interface can be used via the Web like a traditional HTML application can be used through the Internet browser.

Efficiency

Each component contains the information required to exchange with other components. The advantage of these features in a BPM tool also relates to the integration with third party systems.

For example, Belgium is already equipped with ID cards integrating a chip following the example of other countries which are still only at the project stage. All city of Waterloo inhabitants are holders of these smart cards. The administration can therefore authenticate the interlocutor in the flow of the process similar to electronic signature transactions; the BPM integrates the data coming from the chip in its components, guaranteeing the protection of the data and the traceability of the file.

Finally, each component is re-usable with no need to re-enter the information, as the process propagates the information through the various third party systems. A component which displays an official document in a naturalisation procedure can be used again to display a plan in a structural procedure. The Return on Investment from the implementation of new processes and the efficiency as a result are significant.

Flexibility

The axis of flexibility is henceforth essential for all the organisations. The time of the applications with hundred of parameters to which the structures must adapt is definitely gone. Today the BPM brings a process to which everyone can adapt.

The BPM is not approached by a vertical functional philosophy but indeed in a business and transversal logic, whether the roles impacted by the process, the processing order or yet the management rules, each administration can adapt the processes to its real functioning. The appeal of this personalisation also reflects in the constant improvement or the adaptation of the processes according to the legislative or organisational evolutions. Beyond the flexibility of the BPM processes typically used by business analysts, the modularity of RIA technology allows users to adapt visual display to his needs, create or assemble new components.

BPM as a complement to ERP has been noted by leading analysts such as Gartner Group, Butler Group, CXP etc.

INTERACTIVITY AMONG DIFFERENT ADMINISTRATIONS

Public administrations worldwide are built on multiple levels, whether the organization model is centralized or decentralized. The more decentralized the administrations, the more decisive workflow management (BPM) will become to control and optimize their processes. In Switzerland the federal system is based on three levels: "Community", "Canton" and "Confederation". In these organizations, we have horizontal processes inside each administration as well as vertical processes within these three levels.

Each interaction between a citizen and his administration as well as between administrations themselves implies managing information flow and executing task in an efficient and well coordinated way. In order to work properly, BPM in public administration requires that process owners take defined responsibility for the processes across participating administrations.

As an example, Switzerland replaced its social welfare number (with 11 numbers and not anonymous) by a new number with 13 digits which is anonymous and used more generally than for the social welfare only. Moreover the former number was only allocated to the income-producing citizens; the new number is allocated to the whole population. This project required gathering of information from multiple sources in the country, namely from the cantons, the social insurances, the private insurances but also from the communes, before the new number could be allocated to a person. Switzerland created a national working group in order to determine the standard of electronic exchanges which could then be applied to all the levels of Cyber administration. This group called eCH (www.ech.ch), not only integrates representatives from the administration but also specialists of the market and software editors.

One of the first tangible signs concerns the SEDEX project which aims at the harmonisation of the population data, the homes and accommodations. The first objective is to automate the official census of the Confederation in 2010. Beyond the specification of the data, the methods of exchange via XML have not only been defined to feed SEDEX for the census but also to use SEDEX to feed the processes in the communities. When managing the process of arrival of a new inhabitant or in case of a building construction, it is henceforth possible to integrate the centralized data (from the Confederation) in a decentralized process of the commune.

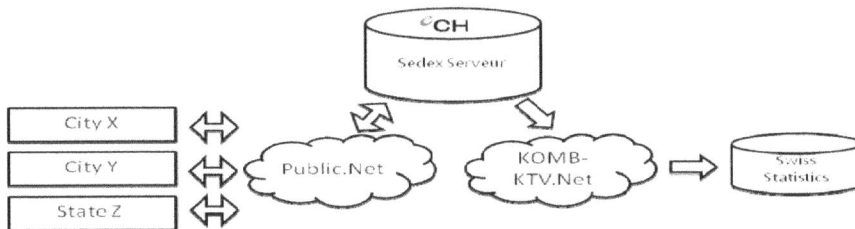

(Fig 3. Sedex concept)

This concept is important as the centralization of the data through non-redundancy of the information. By contrast, the processes of proximity are generally more efficient as they are related to the local specificities and to the linguistic or cultural questions. The parallel implementation of standards which cover all the administrative and business process management layers, ensuring flexibility, brings the advantages of both the centralization and the decentralization.

This is our vision of an extended public administration integrating citizens, politicians, multiple administrations, partners and external suppliers. In such an environment, support is needed for the execution of asynchronous processes exchanging data in a standardized way.

From Business Process Analysis to Business Process Management

Aware of the stakes of the mastery of processes at all levels of the administration, eCH, beyond developing standards of the Cyber administration, has the ambition to encourage the modelling of the processes of all the communes of the country.

The first stage consisted in determining the rules and the standards which would be applied nationally. The working group appointed for this BPM Starter Kit project and driven by ISB (Information Strategy Bund) and entrusted to the HESSO (University of Applied Sciences Western Switzerland) first validated the BPMN [1]concepts as a basic standard for the realisation of the project.

---

[1] More information on this OMG standard can be found at BPMN.org

A working group composed of the BPM Starter kit team and the pilot communes has the objective to model the basic processes as certified BPMN. All the processes (in the end the totality of the communes processes) will be integrated in an exhaustive portal called 'Landkarte' (Process landscape). Each commune has then the possibility to take the 'Landkarte' on its account in order to select the processes which concern it and adapt these to their own functioning.

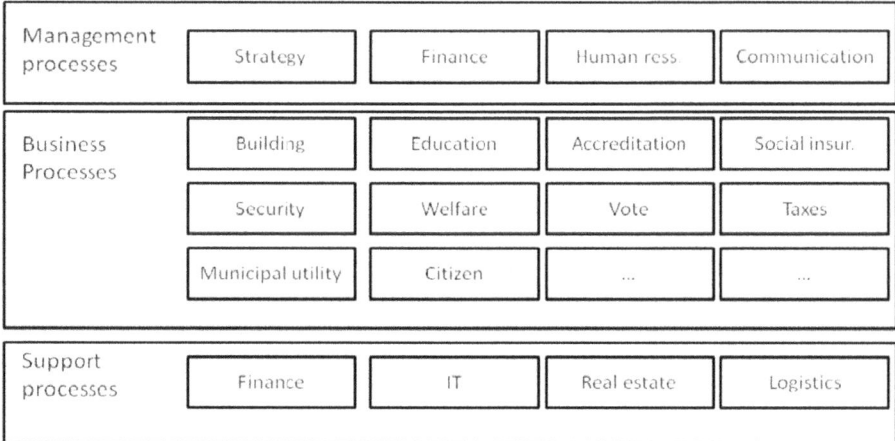

Management processes	Strategy	Finance	Human ress	Communication
Business Processes	Building	Education	Accreditation	Social insur.
	Security	Welfare	Vote	Taxes
	Municipal utility	Citizen	...	...
Support processes	Finance	IT	Real estate	Logistics

(Fig. 4 Landkarte – Process tree inventory)

BPM Starter Kit plans in parallel the creation of a web community on which every structure will be able to share its experiences or good practices with all the other participants. Whether it is for processes, comments, suggestions or communications, this community will doubtless have a determining impact on the development of the BPM concepts at all levels of the Swiss administration. Training is also planned for BPM and BPMN.

This approach of promotion of the BPMN in the administration represents an important step towards the generalization of the Cyber administration in Switzerland. Indeed, from the moment the processes will be mastered, participants will be able to the use of BPM solutions allowing their execution.

The big winners of this initiative will first be the inhabitants of the country who will benefit from this virtual government administrative, or retail, counter adapted to their needs and from on-line services which are up to their expectations. As for the administrations, they will benefit from the flexibility and the optimization of their processes; this will allow them to step back from daunting tasks and to concentrate on the added value they bring to the society.

CONCLUSION

Behind the genius of a virtual counter such as it is understood in the concepts of Cyber administration, clearly hides a technology of Business Process Management not only destined to rule the exchanges between the inhabitant and the administration, but also for the administrations among themselves. The needs of flexibility, reliability, integration of the data or relationships among the processes, are only for us some examples of the necessity to promote the BPM.

The process has already been initiated by some pioneers but the success lies in the political will to pursue the normalization of the exchanges and to demonstrate the benefits by the example. The technologies are henceforth available and the competences exist.

Transforming Health Care through Enterprise Architecture and BPM

Christine Robinson, CSC, United States

ABSTRACT

Health Care is one of President Obama's top priorities for the nation according to his 2009 State of the Union Speech and many other statements he and others have made. This area demands radical change to increase the accessibility and affordability of health care, find new cures for disease (especially a cure for cancer), assure privacy of patient data, lessen health care's draining effects on our economy, cut waste and fraud in Medicaid and Medicare, have greater participation in global health initiatives, accelerate health care's role in Emergency Preparedness and Disaster Recovery, and facilitate information sharing environments between organizations. These are some of the major objectives the United States must fulfill to improve our lives as individuals, as a nation, and as members of the global community. This calls for new ways of providing health care across the nation and beyond. With the frameworks and models already in place today, we can achieve profound improvements through adopting an Enterprise Architecture (EA) approach empowered by Business Process Management (BPM) and enabling technologies toward improving affordability and accessibility of health care while protecting the privacy of patient data.

PROMISE OF ENTERPRISE ARCHITECTURE AND BUSINESS PROCESS MANAGEMENT

President Obama named improving health care as one of his top priorities in his first address before the American people on February 24th, 2009. He has said reforming US Health Care is critical to preventing the United States from becoming bankrupt from skyrocketing medical costs and has repeatedly invited everyone in the nation to brainstorm to find ways in which we can improve health care and all ideas are welcome. The devastating effects of our present health care crisis affect every one of us in some way on an individual basis as well as on a global basis. As a nation, the health care drain on our economy threatens our ability to compete in the global economy. From an individual standpoint, health care costs are the leading cause of personal bankruptcy in the United States, constituting about half of them. Maintaining the privacy and security of patient data further adds to the cost and complexity of health care for organizations that must satisfy HIPAA information security requirements. Of disastrous consequences to an increasingly greater number of Americans due to the economic meltdown, tremendous disparities exist in the ability to have access and to afford adequate health care. These are only a fraction of the issues.

An unknown fact, for many thus tasked, the Federal Government and health care providers don't have to look too far to find professional disciplines cut out specifically for the daunting task of health care reform, from both a micro to a macro level. The existing bodies of knowledge within EA and BPM already possess the frameworks with which to capture all the inputs and come up with improved strategies and business processes along with the enabling technologies to support them. The EA community understands design, of both the business side, as well as the enabling technology side, and works closely with Business Architects and countless other professional disciplines required to design health care systems and systems of health care systems. BPM seeks to improve business processes and use enabling technologies whereas the Enterprise Architecture scope spans the entire length and breadth of the health care provider's architecture and beyond.

EA and BPM are poised to take on a major role in health care reform. EA and BPM offer powerful human and technology tools which can help achieve desperately needed improvements in health care on a Federal, state, local, and even international basis. John Teeter, Deputy Chief Information Officer for Health and Human Services at a February 2009 Architecture Plus meeting in Washington, DC, stated that "Architecture needs to have a seat at the table" with health care leaders and decision-makers.

In the words of Linus Chow, head of the Public Sector group for the Workflow Management Coalition, "EA and BPM are poised to bridge the gap between the health care providers, the business architects, and techies who are so often relegated to behind-the-scenes or the Information Technology shop."

Dr. Gary Kaplan, Clinical Associate Professor at Georgetown University and Medical Director and founder of the Kaplan Center for Integrative Medicine, said that, "I recognize that improved processes for providing health care and technology are indispensable in providing our patients with the highest quality of medical care. I also recognize that technology will continue to transform the way we will practice medicine in the future. Unfortunately, due to complexity and the lack of cohesive guidelines, the implementation of electronic medical records and other medical technologies in their present form provides a tremendous distraction from the practice of medicine at almost overwhelming costs. The benefits of improved processes and fully integrating technology into the practice of medicine have to offer Americans cannot be understated but it also cannot be accomplished without the leadership and guidance that only the government can provide."

"The successful administration of health care requires making optimal use of often scarce resources," says Nathaniel Palmer, Executive Director of the Workflow Management Coalition and Chief BPM Strategist of SRA International. "These also happen to be the more profound benefits offered by EA and BPM. Successful EA and BPM initiatives come from understanding these not as means for automation, but for enabling better decisions through improved communications and greater visibility into the linkage between actions and consequences."

EA and BPM achieve vast improvement in these significant areas of concern, just to highlight a few:

- Health care providers requiring to learn technicalities to improve the way they deliver health care—Enterprise Architecture and BPM exist to bridge that gap,
- The need for models required to achieve innovative transformation of health care,
- How to harness technologies as agents of change to improve health care,
- Waste, fraud, and inefficiency of the Medicaid system on all levels,
- Emergency Preparedness and Disaster Recovery on a Federal, state, local, and even international basis,
- Protection of patient data and satisfying Health Care Insurance Portability and Accountability Act of 1996 (HIPAA) information security requirements,
- Less-than-effective information sharing environments on a Federal, state, local, and even international level, and

- Contribute to the global community to track and prevent the spread of disease.

Enterprise Architecture and BPM can become the bridge between health care providers and the army of professionals and technologies that can facilitate vast improvements in health care. A short list of improvements would include electronic health records, information-sharing between various organizations that need a patient's health information, medical intake processes, and tracking medical histories over time, to mention just a few examples. The Enterprise and Business Architects translate the health care providers' understanding of how they deliver health care into business processes and technologies that enable them, working closely with experts across the continuum necessary to transform health care delivery. This holistic and intricately integrated micro and macro EA view of government agencies, hospitals, medical centers, the public, and other elements comprising the health care community and how all the pieces fit together will help lead the health care community to help achieve vast improvements according to priority and those areas targeted to receive development funds.

Important message for health practitioners and decision-makers

Health care providers and patients are not required to understand the technology of the EA and BPM enabling components in order to mend our broken health care system. It is important to know, however, that Enterprise Architecture and BPM have the appropriate tools and resources to bridge the chasm between the health care providers and the persons designing the processes and technology systems that can help transform health care.

The Enterprise Architects also provide the translation among the business architects studying the business requirements and processes for health care service delivery and the designers of technology systems necessary to transform health care service delivery. EA and BPM translate health care requirements through specific models and frameworks that capture and analyze information to improve health care delivery processes such as patient intake and insurance eligibility.

Health care providers who love their Blackberries and laptops and are LinkedIn- and FaceBook-savvy will not have to learn yet another technology skill. EA and BPM cover every aspect of networking, computing, and storage requirements for providing local health care services to underserved communities as well as facilitate global disease detection and containment. EA and BPM harness the arsenal of professionals and technologies for health care business and technology improvements no matter how broad or focused.

Take Advantage of Existing EA Frameworks and Bodies of Knowledge

"Granting Architecture a seat at the table," holds great promise to achieve transformation in health care accessibility, affordability, privacy of patient data, and raise the standard of health care for all Americans.

Frameworks already exist to help improve health care. The Federal Enterprise Architecture (FEA), Department of Defense Architecture Framework (DODAF), and other formal EA models can help us inject "disruptive" innovations that transform current practices for delivering health care services and their supporting technologies with entirely new ones. Disruptive models neither sustain the status quo nor evolve it incrementally as they offer an entirely different model. Examples of disruptive technologies are the telephone, the internet and the computer, which overturn the status quo and cause evolution of the current thought. Today many providers provide the same or similar services but often each one does it differently and shared potential is lost. Through these frameworks we can identify common models, reuse instead of recreate every time, and build for change. We tie in strategy, budget, performance, and life-cycle management of the health care enterprise all as part of planning within these EA frameworks.

We desperately need disruptive business models and disruptive technologies to help us transform health care that don't just sustain or improve upon how we deliver health, but actually provide whole new ways of providing health care services.

Although FEA and DODAF slice the health care enterprise differently, the two models study the entire enterprise from different perspectives and actually complement each other very well. Whereas, the FEA looks at the enterprise via Business, Technical, Service, Performance, and Data reference models defined within the FEA framework, the DODAF 1.5 slices the enterprise into 26 different system and operational "views" that can study the same information as the FEA. The two may be used in concert with one another. Within these frameworks, Enterprise Architects use powerful analytic tools to study every relevant piece of information from the very inception of the business process to the implementation and life cycle of processes and match the enabling technology tools. Sophisticated software modeling tools design and implement changes in software by changing the business processes themselves within the modeling software.

EA frameworks and others adapt to relevant industry standards. These EA frameworks can incorporate Capability Maturity Model Integration known as CMMI originated for improving software development, Lean Six Sigma for improving quality, Information Technology Infrastructure Library (ITIL) for managing all aspects of Information Technology, Disaster Recovery International for improving Emergency Preparedness and Disaster Recovery, and a whole host of other industry models, depending on strategy, relevance, need, and budget.

Health care innovations will arise on many fronts. Disruptive innovations may create health care success stories compared to, for example, what Amazon.com is to the book industry, Toyota to the auto industry, eBay and Paypal to on-line buying communities, Cisco to the telecommunications networking industry, and TurboTax to the accounting and tax preparation industry, just to name a few.

EA looks at each of these communities, not as separate entities, but as systems of systems with inter-related parts that provide different aspects of our health care either as suppliers or consumers. In their lowest common denominator, they represent business processes, business rules, and technology enablers.

Working with health care providers, the Enterprise Architect prioritizes initiatives, weighs alternatives, enlists the stakeholders and Subject-Matter-Experts, and aligns these with the agency's mission and strategic objectives. They assimilate Health Care 2.0, HIPAA, Federal Information Security Management Act requirements, information sharing environments, and other areas on behalf of the health care practitioners, incorporating BPM to synthesize Lean Six Sigma, CMMI, ITIL, DRII, BPML and that vast world of acronyms frequently mysterious to the health care individual.

Enabling Technologies

The health care delivery system consists of incredibly complex and inter-related systems of systems on an infinite number of levels, both internal and external to the organization itself that can vastly benefit from existing Commercial-Off-The-Shelf (COTS) products and existing EA and BPM capabilities. Custom solutions may still also be necessary to address certain requirements, although for the most part, COTS products are available for every part of designing and management.

Each health care scenario required certain EA and BPM depending upon complexity, budget, clientele, criticality, and many other criteria. Because every state has Medicaid and Medicare and every health care provider has some form of patient intake processing and case management, it is possible to reuse processes and architectures. Enhancements transforming health care delivery range from simply upgrading hardware and software to refining business processes. On a grand scale for a Federal Agency such as Health and Human Services, Service Oriented Architecture (SOA), BPMS, and a host of other technology solutions accelerate health care improvements to deliver better services more efficiently.

The combination of EA and BPM improve upon business processes by matching the most appropriate technology solutions to the particular needs of the organization. Chief among transformative technologies, BPM software (BPMS) and SOA used together transform existing health care architectures regarding patient data, information security capabilities regarding access and usage and data-sharing among various resources. SOA allows the business services to be only minimally aware of one another on a technical level while taking advantage of each other's capabilities, treating them as reuseable building blocks. BPMS and SOA are used in conjunction with a number of integrated technologies within a system and within systems-of-systems from the physical layer up to the application layer.

BPMS range from fairly simplistic packages that improve routine processes and provide document management capabilities to packages that integrate an array of other technology components and execute commands within them using off-the-shelf and custom code integration. Such packages include PeopleSoft, Siebel, HP Openview, ArcSight, TDI, Borland, IBM, and others, to name just a few integration options. The more sophisticated BPMS packages can supervise and execute processes across an entire enterprise or segment architecture through other systems with which they are integrated.

Today's technology enablers hold great promise in Emergency Preparedness and Disaster Recovery. Agencies using BPMS integrated solutions can execute a Continuity of Operations Plan or IT Contingency Plan for an entire agency. BPMS integrated solutions can also execute an external Emergency Preparedness and Disaster Recovery response for agencies with health care responsibilities such as EPA, FEMA, HHS, Coast Guard, USDA, and others. Emergency response in this context can be viewed as exceptions to normal operations with preplanned scenarios for response for health care providers and other participants.

BPMS allows health care providers to place their institutional knowledge in software that can exponentially improve their ability to deliver medical services. BPMS provides many customers case management and call center operations capabilities to improve their operations, quality, and process improvement. BPMS and business rules engines can automatically decide who is authorized to receive certain types of health care services, where they are allowed to access them, and the cap on the amount of the health care services they are authorized to receive.

One of the "Blue" health care insurance companies with 9,000 employees and 3.4 million members radically transformed its clinical health care delivery processes using leading BPMS software to improve:
- Pre-certification of elective services
- Medical review of inpatient hospitalizations and other medical services and equipment
- Discharge Planning, and
- Case Management

This particular insurance company placed 5700 different medical procedures and 130 completely different processes using separate spreadsheets through which insurance company employees previously had to hunt and peck for information are now business rules and business processes in BPMS. Prior to BPMS implementation, the processes were manual and highly inefficient, with many medical review decisions requiring individual professional medical review. Using BPMS, the insurance company transformed itself into having the flexibility to adapt to evolving business needs, focus minimal intervention for routine tasks, become extremely responsive with quick turnaround for routine changes, supply documentation through the BPMS, make possible sharable information between parties and applications, provide transactions that became traceable and auditable, and build in data reuse for building medical case management histories and other key information. *Now, it takes only 10 minutes to train users in the system and two minutes to change or maintain a rule.*

Harnessing BPMS and other enabling technologies allows health care providers not only to pre-plan their responses and execute some processes instantaneously, but some also offer the capability to provide continuous health care delivery process improvement using the BPMS and other software itself. Some of these packages enable agencies to capture results, analyze results, play what-if analysis, and other capabilities to develop process improvements for health care delivery. BPMS ultimately places more power in the hands of the decision-makers and enables professionals to spend more of their limited time and resources on delivering improved health care services rather than continually dealing with difficult-to-use resources and processes, waste, inefficiency, and redundancy.

Waste, Fraud, and Inefficiency of the Medicaid System

EA and BPM can help reduce and protect against waste and fraud through improved processes and enabling technologies. Health care providers can build rules in business rules engines and BPMS that can execute instantaneously for when and how to provide services to patients and make payments while achieving substantial efficiencies across the spectrum of processes used to deliver health care. Compare this to maintaining data in multiple spreadsheets, multiple binders in which procedures are housed, institutional knowledge held only in people's heads, and other typical means of performing work in many organizations today. For instance, BPMS with the appropriate rules and processes built in can instantaneously detect and remediate fraud. Also, effective EA and BPMS can identify when a patient is submitting for services using multiple addresses using business rules and business processes in an information sharing environment comprising a system of systems.

The Centers for Medicaid and Medicare (CMS) Medicaid Information Technology Architecture (MITA) Maturity Model perhaps represents one of the most classic examples of using EA and BPM to supply health care services with enabling technologies in a phased approach. This model holds great promise as more and more Medicaid entities adhere to it and evolve through the five phases as evidenced through their self-assessments. This model serves as the architecture framework for 51 individual Medicaid enterprises that must adhere to it over time in order to receive their funding and is used by CMS, states, and vendors. It shows health care business transformation over time, capturing the way the business looks at five milestones covering a ten-year time-frame that takes into consideration dependencies on technology advances, changes in state and federal policies, and legislation on many levels.

The MITA transformation path divides into two separate tracks, one for business and one for technical. The business track maps to the business process model and the technical track enables the business services while mapping to MITA goals and objectives. MITA does not specify technology enablers but does name Web Service Definition Language (WSDL) at Level 3, leaving it up to the Medicaid enterprises and states to determine whether they should use .Net or J2EE or any custom or Commercial-Off-The-Shelf (COTS) packages they wish. The qualities of each level of maturity are defined by timeliness between initiation and result, accuracy and ease of access to data, the level of effort required to perform a function, cost effectiveness, quality, and the value or utility to stakeholders.

Emergency Preparedness and Disaster Recovery

Health care providers play a critical role in Emergency Preparedness and Disaster Recovery. We can use the same EA and BPM approach to handle Emergency Preparedness and Disaster Recovery with pre-planned scenarios driven by different rule-sets planned as exceptions to normal operations. Typically, Emergency Preparedness and Disaster Recovery planning is at best a parallel effort and is often not addressed or funded adequately. Using this approach, we can create plans that we can use among multiple organizations and prepare more easily executable plans that are pre-thought out and even practiced before an emergency occurs. These plans can alert authorities and emergency workers automatically, provide the means for collaboration for situational awareness, access multiple resources within an information sharing environment such as medical information and health care logistical information on supplies or hospital beds available in the area, and vastly more capabilities.

EA and BPM are already transforming Emergency Preparedness and Disaster Recovery from a local to an international basis. This EA and BPM approach, focused here on health care, influenced Congressional legislation and funding and influenced Federal Government procurements at FEMA for critical-mission Emergency Preparedness and Disaster Recovery. The same thought processes and techniques for matching technology enablers to health care processes required for normal operation as discussed here can exponentially facilitate health care activities required for Emergency Preparedness and Disaster Recovery from a local to international level. The following illustration shows a screen shot from an emergency response scenario involving inter-governmental health authorities built with EA using BPMS, all with COTS software using this EA and BPMS approach.

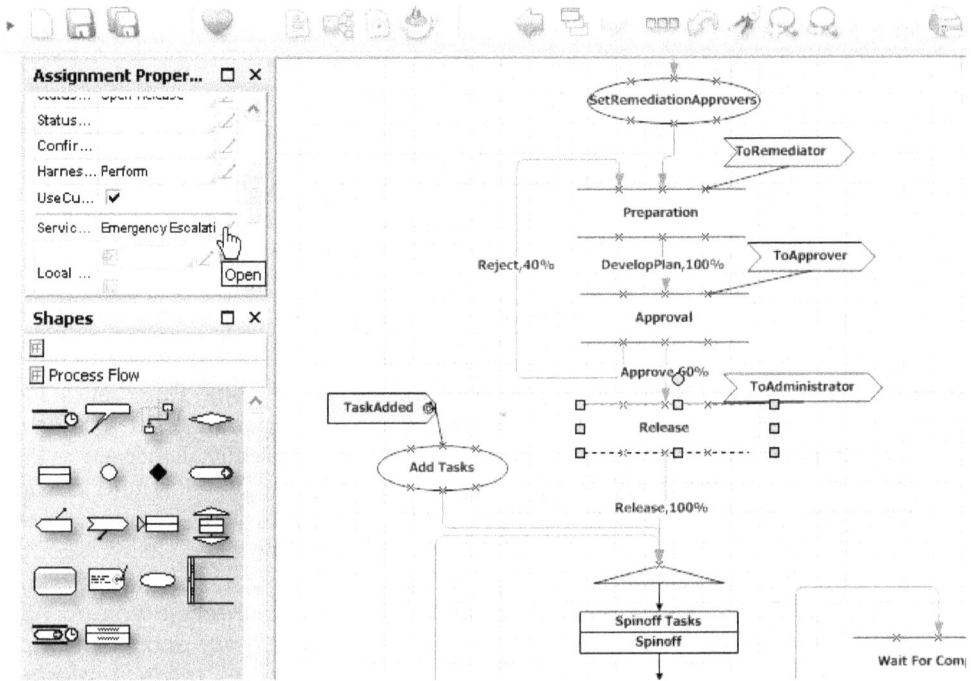

Figure 1: Process diagram and approvals for chemical spill response

Figure 2: BPMS emergency response for a chemical spill work list

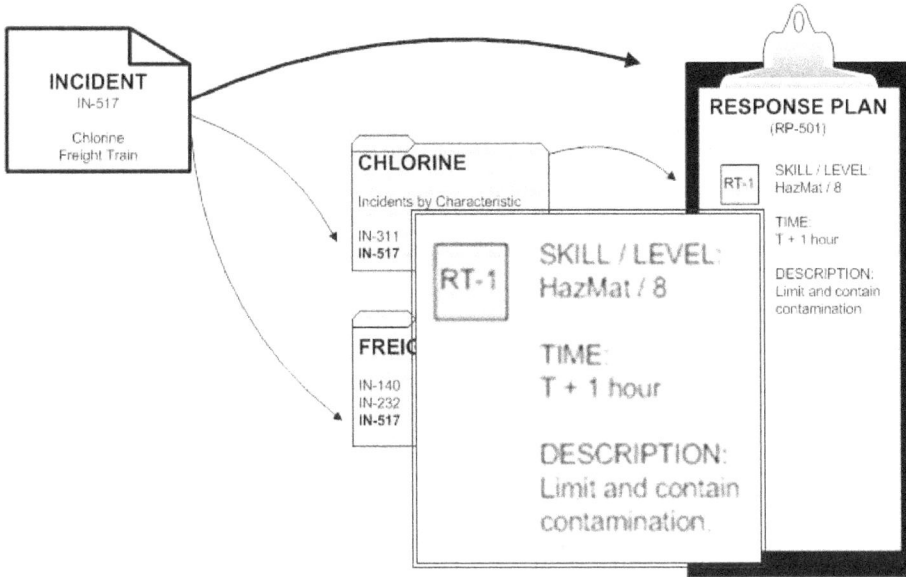

Figure 3: BPMS sequences for chemical spill emergency response

The health care community also addresses Special Needs Populations with this EA and BPMS approach. The members of this population are least able to fend for themselves during emergencies and far more dependent on others for their well-being. The vulnerable Special Needs Populations include the elderly, people with disabilities, children, those without transportation or do not speak English well enough to communicate with emergency workers. Some nursing home occupants were abandoned by their health care providers during Hurricane Katrina, illustrating one of the most tragic and highly visible results of inadequate planning for emergencies and the devastating consequences for Special Needs Populations.

Information Security and HIPAA

Health care providers often find HIPAA compliance exceptionally daunting and understanding this regulation has become a discipline unto itself. Health care providers must protect patient data while providing accessibility and helping to promote health care affordability. On top of HIPAA, Federal agencies have to comply with Federal Information Management Security Act (FISMA) requirements, create and test a Continuity of Operations Plan and IT Contingency Plan for all production systems, and other compliance requirements. HIPAA and other Federal governance require that agencies test their Disaster Recovery and other plans once per year.

Information security also falls into the realm of EA and BPM process and technology design improvements. EA incorporates the detailed security design requirements from highly skilled professionals who have the aptitude and skills to build the processes and design the systems that can provide defense-in-depth security on a multi-layered basis to protect the agencies themselves as well as patient data. These professionals design, monitor, and maintain the load balancers, intrusion detection and prevention systems, firewalls, obtain patches and upgrades, and manage authorized role-based access to health care and other. They also perform Business Continuity and Disaster Recovery planning and testing required to satisfy Federal Information Management Act, HSPD 20 and HIPAA requirements.

Information Sharing Environments

Health care information sharing is critical on so many levels to promote health care accessibility and affordability, protect the nation against disease and other health threats, and to participate in Emergency Preparedness and Disaster Recovery. Unless different organizations are able to share information on potential health care threats, available treatments, and other available services, many will miss out on the potential benefits that can mean life and death to individuals, communities, affect our health as a nation, and that of the international community as well.

The Federal Government's Federal Enterprise Architecture and other frameworks vastly facilitate the planning of the Federal Health Information Sharing Environment (FHISE) and other information sharing Federal and international environments right down to state and local governments. These environments encourage collaboration among government and private partners; each contributing to the knowledge base. Facilitating this environment requires translating extensive information of how agencies such as the Centers for Medicaid and Medicare, the Centers for Disease Control, the FDA, the USDA, DOD and others need to share information into the BPMS and enabling technologies with the appropriate information security protections necessary to protect patient and other sensitive data.

Health care providers thus focus on what data they need to share and the Enterprise Architects and Business Architects focus on designing the business processes, provide the information security, and design and implement the systems to ensure their ability to deliver health care. EA and BPM essentially encapsulate all the health care processes and supporting technologies to ultimately enhance the health care providers' abilities to do their jobs even better.

Electronic health care records are fundamental to the future of improving health care and key to patient accessibility and affordability of health care. Promoting the health information-sharing environment benefits both patients and providers on an individual, local, national, and global basis. This gives patients more control over their own health care by allowing them access to their own records with authorized access by health care professionals reviewing an individual's current health, medical history or means of paying for medical services.

The Global Community

We share a responsibility to protect global health as well. The Federal Government performs as our guardians of global health and first line of defense, creating checks and balances to encourage open borders, provide protections against health threats, and to help protect the world's population. Through EA and BPM we thus view the global health community. DOD, HHS, USDA, HHS and others play key roles in the critical infrastructure of the US and have an international impact as well on health care. Applying systematic process improvement and enabling technologies vastly accelerates our ability to participate in and continue our leadership role in global health while extending greater health care protection to the American public.

Because BPMS and other technologies enable Federal, state, local officials, and international parties to share information about health care, study data, and take action to prevent and contain potential threats on every level, the world community must invest in these capabilities far more extensively than today.

The currently tools in use certainly allow health care practitioners and decision-makers to assimilate data enabling them to conduct thorough analysis and make critical decisions about our health care on one screen versus accessing multiple terminals. An example of combined technologies incorporating networking, storage, and computing requirements and powerful databases and BPMS is shown in the following figure. This specific example shows how these systems can be used for local and international health care and are currently in use.

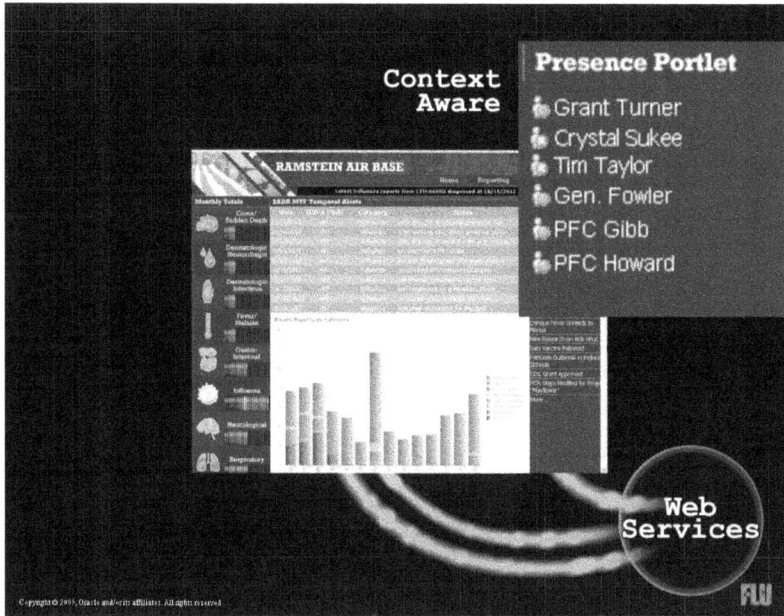

Figure 4: Collaboration for international outreach

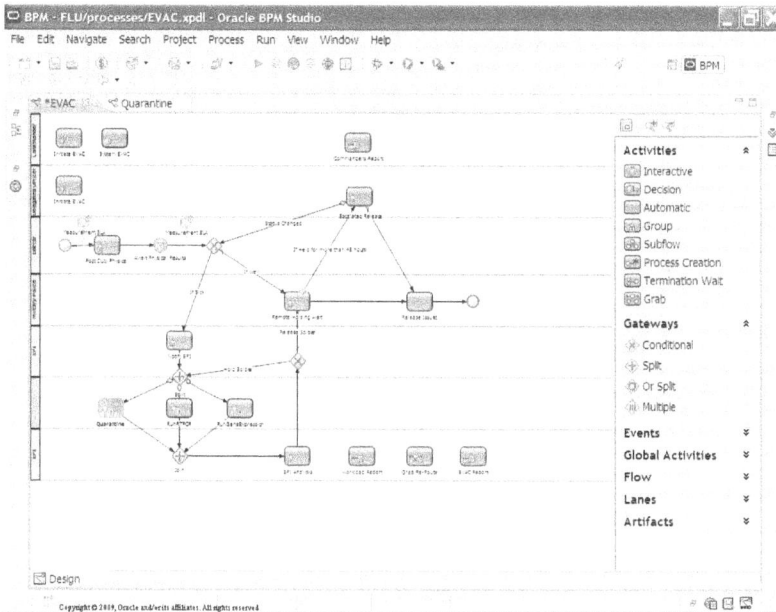

Figure 5: Process diagram—international Information Sharing Environment

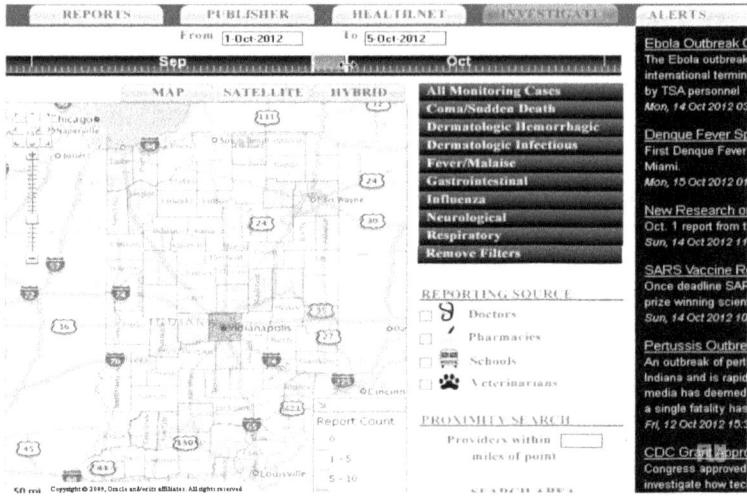

Fig 6: Information from international Information Sharing Environment

SUMMARY

EA and BPM vastly improve health care from a Federal Government, state, local, to an international perspective using EA and BPM frameworks and an array of technology-enablers tailored to the specific requirements of the health care providers. We need only tap the EA and BPM bodies of knowledge and existing technologies and invite "architecture to have a seat at the table" with the health care leaders and decision-makers. We can help achieve greater affordability and accessibility of health care, protect patient data more efficiently, and provide far greater capabilities in providing Emergency Preparedness and Disaster Recovery.

Acknowledgements

CSC's Dr. Chander Ramchandani, John Dodd, Karlton Kim, and William Branch of Fox Systems, Inc. worked with CMS to develop the MITA model now used as the IT architecture model for all 51 Medicaid entities. CSC's thought leaders particularly in the fields of EA and BPM include many internationally renowned authors, key leaders who are instrumental in helping the new administration from the federal budget to EA and BPM, and as a corporation CSC is known for its world leadership in industry and government. www.csc.com

Oracle, whose screenshots appear in Figures 4, 5, and 6, is one of the world's largest software companies whose software solutions are used extensively across the Federal Government and health care sectors, supporting customers in 145 countries around the world. Oracle and CSC worked together on the first government procurement, based on CSC's concept that it shared with the Federal Government, using BPMS for an enterprise-wide Emergency Preparedness and Disaster Recovery implementation for FEMA, although they did not formally bid on this procurement. CSC and Oracle are strategic partners in many initiatives around the world. www.oracle.com

Pegasystems, the world BPMS leader contributed to this paper in two ways. Pegasystems and system-integrator CSC collaborated to create a proof-of-concept of which three screens are illustrated in Figures 1, 2, and 3. This proof-of concept using EA and BPMS illustrates how to exponentially facilitate an emergency response for a chemical spill was shown to several audiences of senior Federal Government officials, industry analysts, Capital Hill, and many conferences. Pegasystems also agreed to include the description for the "Blue" insurance company story of EA and BPMS. www.pega.com

Delivering Strategy through Process: SAPO Case Study

Marietjie Lancaster and Carien Venter,
South African Post Office, Dr. Michélle Booysen, Pétanque
Business Specialists, South Africa

ABSTRACT

This chapter presents the case study of how the South African Post Office (SAPO) applied a process approach to create a fit for purpose organizational structure which would effectively roll out its new business model. An innovative methodology of interactive, people focused process mapping created the platform where institutional knowledge was offered by staff, shared, captured, improved on and transferred, engaging the entire organization (twitter effect) to review and develop those processes needed to roll out the new business model; to debate duplications and agree the actions that will address those; to identify gaps and agree on ways to eliminate gaps; and to agree on innovation and change.

This resulted in organization wide buy-in of broad spectrum change in processes and roles aimed at improved customer service, efficiencies and resource utilization. It further improved processes that would support the achievement of strategic goals, and delivered an organogram that would support the future growth of the SA Post Office with business model aligned processes.

INTRODUCTION

The South African Post Office (SAPO) delivers almost eight million letters to 12 million addresses in South Africa on a daily basis. It has more than 2 600 outlets covering the length and breadth of South Africa, aimed to provide postal services inside and outside South Africa.

As part of its growth strategy, SAPO developed a streamlined business model that required a new organizational support structure. In an organization of this size, the question was how to effectively position roles that would drive growth through the new business model and more importantly; how to avoid resistance against change that results from such an organizational overhaul?

Through an innovative, low cost, high impact approach, SAPO used enterprise-wide process mapping to identify gaps and duplications to improve processes, to identify roles in these processes, and to ensure buy-in of change by making internal resources the drivers and owners of innovation and change.

CONTEXT OF THE PROJECT

SAPO reached a turnaround point in 2004 (figure 1), turning years of loss into profit. In 2007, however, the company was reaching the proverbial 'glass ceiling': cost cutting had reached its plateau and growth was urgently required to fund capital investment programs (infrastructure and technology). In addition, innovation and creativity was required to respond to the changing environment and therefore SAPO needed to revitalize and refocus the total business to be more responsive to the needs of shareholders, employees and customers.

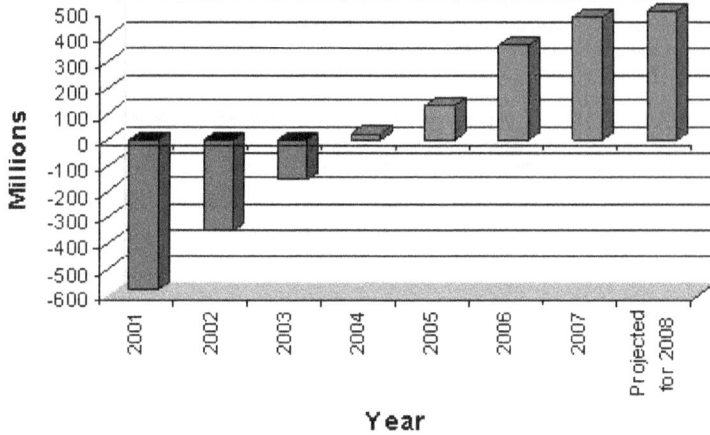

Figure 1: SAPO's Financial Performance 2001-2008

In 2007 it became clear that the total business needed to re-position itself in terms of less focus on cost cutting, with growth based on new product, services, markets and customer needs, through more innovation and creativity.

In support thereof a new Business Model was developed, based on principles of income generation, innovation, and increased support of, and alignment to, the Universal Service Obligations.

A focus on income generation while embracing the triple bottom line, being economic, social and environmental sustainability. In addition, innovation was required to drive business growth and this needed to be enhanced.

Each Business Unit needed to define, own and focus on their respective unique products, services and customers; operate within the framework of a holistic view; adopt to focused marketing for each respective unit; be supported by the Shared Services (Corporate and Business Support); and be prepared for possible Deregulation and Corporatization.

SAPO's vision was clear, but difficult to measure because of the diversity of the business. Besides, the strategy was sound but execution was very difficult. Once the new business model was approved, an effective structure (organogram) was required for roll-out of the business model. In addition, the business model principles were well defined, but the processes per business and per support unit were not.

The decision was made to engage an external supplier, for an out of the box approach. Pétanque Business Specialists—using their in-house developed Business Process Architecture methodology VizPro®—was selected, proposing a process approach in which the processes would define roles which in turn would result in a SAPO structure that is based on what the business requires. The processes in the business model would be documented and reviewed to bring about improved practices focusing on delivery of outcomes within the revised business model. Valuable institutional knowledge would be captured and applied for various purposes, including ISO accreditation, job descriptions, continuity planning and management, risk management, audit, performance management and change management.

The overall project consisted of two phases. In this chapter the second phase is highlighted. For background, the first phase consisted of the high level process positioning and detailing the key processes in delivering outcomes for the business model and documenting these processes, documenting the tasks to be performed to effect change, and the development of three optional organizational structures to drive these high level processes.

Three options for a new high level organogram were presented to, and discussed with the CEO. The three options were fully informed by what the processes required and was the result of extracting process requirements into a structure.

The CEO presented the preferred high-level organogram to the Board of Directors, who approved it in March 2008. When this was presented to the Executives as the approved structure, buy-in was instant. Why—because the Executive, having been part of the process mapping, knew the motivation for the structure and the decisions were made in an environment of transparency. They also understood what was expected from them as role players, ensuring that change could be implemented by an informed team.

The second phase focused on operational processes, within the framework of the processes that were defined in Phase 1. During this phase participation included General Managers, Senior Managers and Managers, as well as operational employees. Organograms for each Business Unit along with Action Lists containing actions that would ensure change and detailed and step-by-step process maps showing who does what when, was the output. This Phase 2 project is the topic of this chapter.

ON THE CONCEPT OF VIZPRO® PROCESS MAPPING

Business Process Architecture includes understanding (analysis), developing, modeling, documenting and improving business processes end-to-end. VizPro® is a process analysis and documentation methodology; a structured and interactive approach to Business Process Architecture. It is a methodology that applies the power of pictures, compared to words to show how processes support the enterprise goals, step by step and process by process. VizPro® facilitates workshops that engage highly interactively with role-players and capture knowledge real-time in process maps, making use of a laptop and a data projector. The visual display during the work session creates understanding and enhances the discussion between participants. Process positioning and flows as well as changes are reflected immediately since the process architecture team records and displays information real time.

In this project the following elements were cornerstones that resulted in multiple benefits:

1. *The Change Controller*

To ensure that processes support strategic goals, the VizPro® Change Controller lists the elements that must be addressed.

CHANGE CONTROLLER

		NOT CLEAR HOW TO ACHIEVE IT	IN ACTION LIST FOR LATER IMPLEMENTATION	IN PROGRESS	CONCLUDED	NOT APPLICABLE	CATEGORY
G	Growth						
C	Consumer Focused						
OS	Organisational Structuring						
OM	Organisational Management						
Are business units clearly segmented?		○	○	○	●	○	C
Is financial services clearly defined?		○	○	○	○	●	C
Are there financial KPI's for each business unit?		○	○	○	●	○	G
Is there adequate corporate governance?		○	○	○	●	○	G
Are services customer focused?		○	○	○	●	○	C
Do we reflect the various systems for shared services?		○	○	○	○	●	G
Are roles unpacked?		○	○	○	●	○	OM
Did we address employee satisfaction?		○	○	○	○	●	OS

Figure 2: SAPO Change Controller

In the case of SAPO, strategic goals were identified in the categories Growth, Consumer Focus, Organizational Structuring, or Organizational Management.

After the work session, participants work through the goals, and indicate for the process whether it is not clear how to achieve the goal, it is in Action List for implementation; it is in progress, it's concluded, or it is not applicable.

If an element received a "Not clear how to achieve it", it means that there is a gap that needs to be addressed. If it is "In Action list for implementation" it means that change actions have been defined, scheduled and assigned. If it is "In progress", it means that it is incorporated in the "as is" or "to be" process, i.e. it forms part of what needs to be done and outcomes will reflect the process impact on the particular element. If it is marked as "Concluded" it means that the process outcomes are supporting the relevant element. Finally, "Not applicable" means that the process is not intended to address the element.

Each SAPO process map contained the same Change Controller against which the process was tested to make sure the process contributes towards strategic goals. A process would only be signed off once aligned to the Change Controller.

2. The Positioning Map

SAPO's Positioning Map (figure 3) was developed to show what the enterprise is about and which processes are needed to achieve its goals. This Positioning Map session took nine hours with 18 people participating. In this instance, the Positioning Map was scoped at high level, covering the entire organization (16,000 employees). The 10 most important executive level processes needed to bring about the changes required by the new business model, were selected, Those processes for example, needed to ensure that SAPO become more consumer orientated and more accessible to more people nationally (these are two of the SAPO strategic goals).

The Positioning Map was "unpacked" so that the relevant functions and processes would be effectively positioned to support the attainment of all strategic goals.

The relevance of these processes was checked by asking for each: does this contribute to strategic outcomes and how? Where there was a gap or duplications, processes were marked: as duplicates—to later merge in further workshops; or as a gap—to develop new processes to fill the gaps.

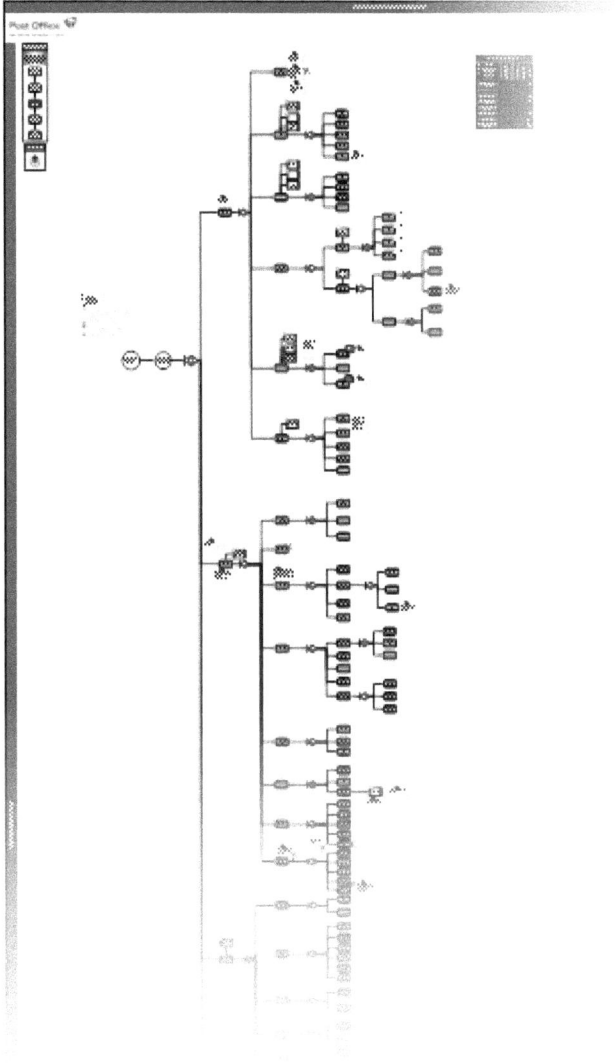

Figure 3: SAPO Positioning Map

Zooming in on the top section of the map, the detail becomes clearer in figure 4.

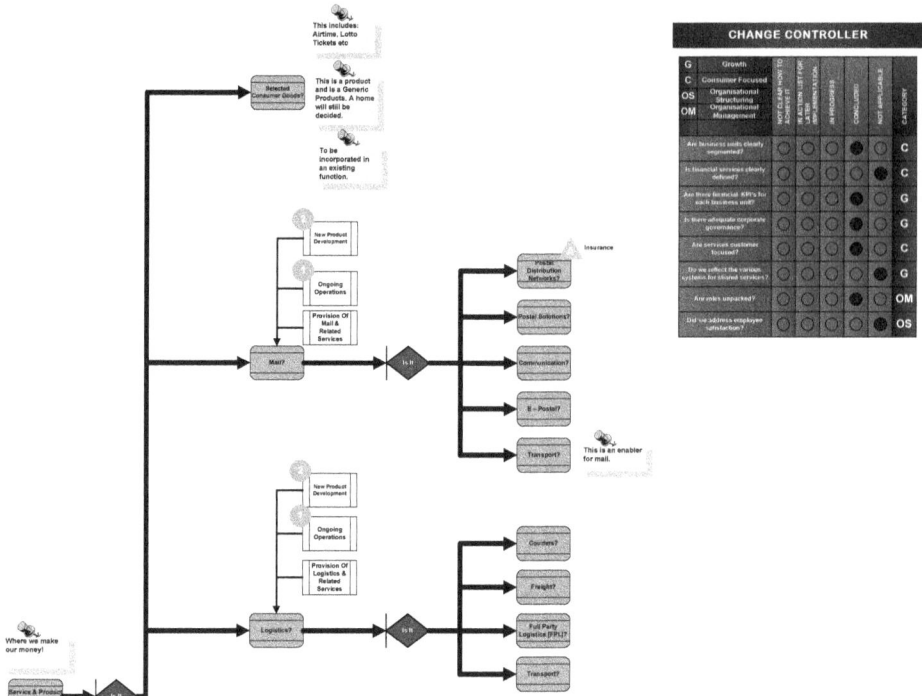

Figure 4: SAPO Positioning Map: close up of a section

To the right is the Change Controller. The icons with the horizontal lines represent the functions that need to be performed and the with icons vertical lines represent the processes that will deliver the functions' outcomes. By prioritizing the top 10 processes that will achieve the elements in the Change Controller, the project was scoped.

3. The Process Maps

For each process the work session started with a blank screen. After agreeing the name of the map, the purpose and scope of the process was defined, discussed and recorded. From here on each process would be recorded, developed and improved on: step by step. The Process Maps contained SAPO customized icons, documenting processes to show who does what, and when; identifying risks, controls, management information, accounting points, quality assurance, and key performance indicators.

Process Maps were developed in different versions:

Version 1: depending on the process seven up to 25 people were unpacking the "as is", adding changes when needed. For new processes, the same approach of step by step definition was followed. Time spent per Version 1 process: 4-8 hours.

Version 2: other role players joined in this version to challenge, debate and agree on the process, adding improvements. In this session Management Information, KPIs, Risks, Controls, Quality Control Points, Financial Impact Points, Burning Points, Escalations, Checks and Governances were added. Average time per Version 2: 3-8 hours.

Version 3: evaluation where related processes were presented and cross referenced. All role players, including management reviewed this session and continue to add to the Action List. Average time:1.5 hour per process; for 5-6 processes to cross reference, required a full day.

Figure 5 reflects an extract of a Version 3 process.

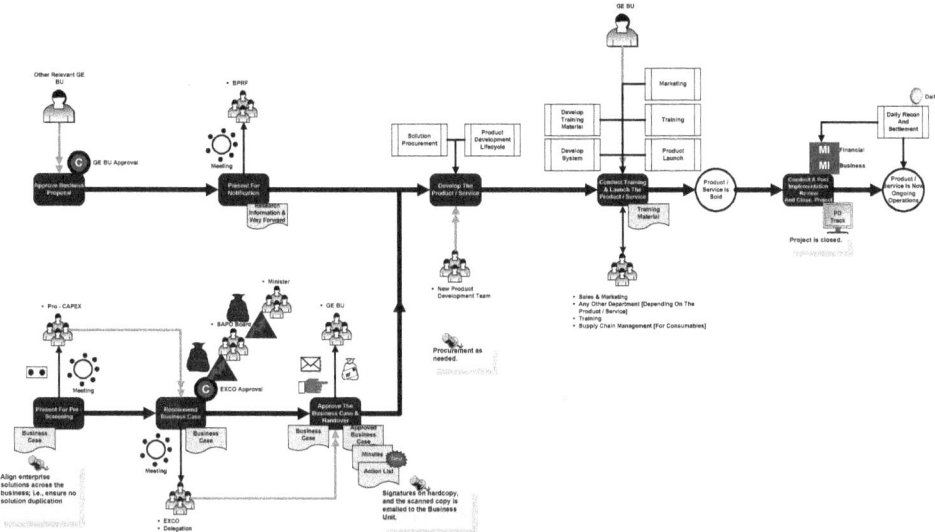

Figure 5: An extract of a high level process map that delivers outcomes in support of the Strategic Goals

4. The Action Lists

The Action Lists record the drivers for change. During every workshop, whenever an item needed to be addressed, it was added to the Action List. The 'who and when' was then agreed to by the participants.

Task No	Category	The Issue	What must be done	Outcome	Who
073	BU FinServ	Each Branch curently files customer docs around money orders and transfers. This is not a good system as important documentation is local, should be in a central DMS	Develop a Robust Documentation Management System.	A Robust Documentation Management System	
074	BU FinServ	Postal Orders as a Stock Is treated differently than other stock procured by SCM. Instead it is done by the processing team.	The Postal Order Procurement Process needs to be mapped as a seperate leg in the Procurement process.	Refer to this new process as FinServ Stock Ordering & Acknowledgment.	
075	BU FinServ	Best practice systems to be shared	The Process used by Fin Serve Processing Team should be investigated and adopted by Post Sales FinServe.	One process that serves 2 operational environments	

Figure 6: Extract from an Action List

THE PROJECT

Based on the benefits derived from the Phase 1, the second phase followed the same approach, in order to define, per Business Unit, the roles at General Manager, Senior Manager and Manager Level, by reviewing all processes to bring about improved practices; sharing and capturing knowledge via an inclusive and transparent process; and using information rich process maps to derive the enterprise organogram that would provide the appropriate structure for successful roll out of the business model.

This project, with the same project brief as for the high level project, resulted in a companywide organogram, informed by the business processes.

Every mapping session started with identifying each Business Unit's purpose and scope. This was followed by a Positioning Map for each Business Unit, with participating teams identifying at high level the activities of the Unit along with what processes are deployed.

Over 500 interactive workshops extracted information from process role players (operators) through a forum for share and challenge, evaluation and improved or best practice development opportunities. The knowledge was captured in 117 Process Maps reflecting 184 processes in a step-by-step what to do format.

Every process map shows graphical, easy to understand information, as in figure 7.

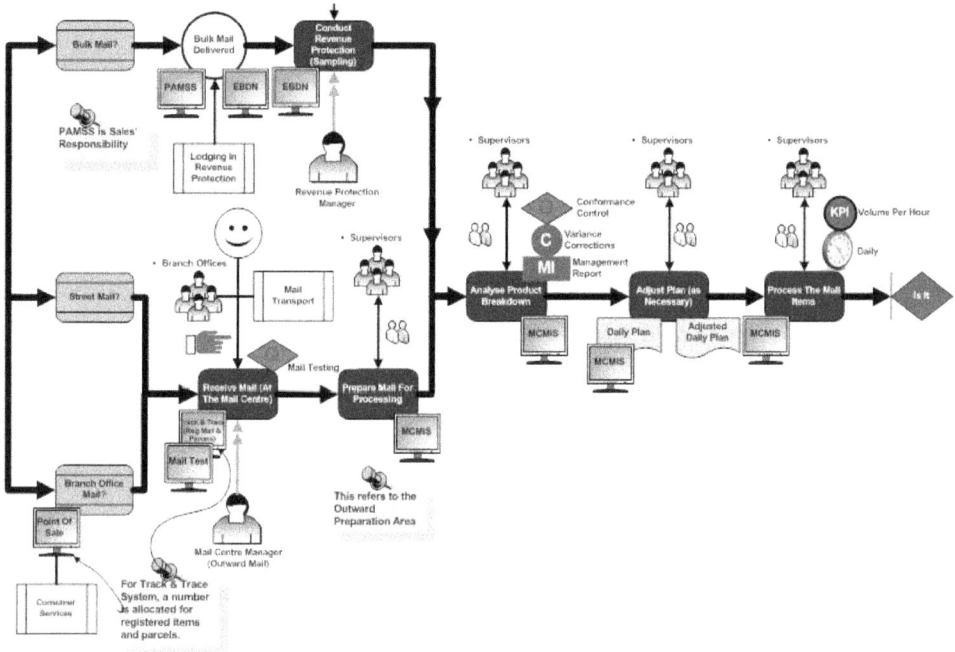

Figure 7: Snapshot of a VizPro® Process Map

Figure 7 demonstrates the output of part of a process where process role players and work-session participants agree on the step by step activities of the process, the responsible person of each activity and the other role players in a step, the timing or frequency of a step, the management information that is being created at specific steps, the risks to the process and what these risks are, the controls, the means of communication, the input and output per step, the supporting systems in the process and what the system function is per step, the interfacing processes, the key performance indicators per process, the steps where metrics are generated through MI and how KPIs input into scorecards, and notes to enhance information if needed.

Key success factors to this project were:
- Role-players from various organizational levels participated, resulting in vertical communication and knowledge share;
- Discussing end-to-end processes and projection of the visual map resulted in comprehensive understanding of the entire process to people who were only part of a specific part, and didn't understand their impact on the remainder of the process;

- Facilitation offers a platform of knowledge share: input from experienced employees was now captured and documented as part of SAPO's intellectual property;
- Offering an open, neutral, non-threatening environment, created an innovation platform, debating gaps and duplications to improve current practices;
- During the process mapping sessions all issues impacting on process efficiency were identified, prioritized and actions for change scheduled;
- After the work sessions, maps were printed and displayed in the offices and passages, for everybody to comment on and debate around the process. Handwritten notes were made on the maps, as input for the next version.

The transparency, and accessibility for everyone, made this project impact on the entire organization, and was therefore not only a top-down directed initiative, but instead top-down and bottom-up driven. This was critical for buy-in of change. People were invited to give their input, and became the drivers of change.

Once the first version of the processes was mapped, it was made available to the Business Units, who exposed their other team members to it over an approximate two week period. During this time period maps could be challenged by any employee. After two weeks second level processes were done and it usually reflected numerous process improvements. A third version was also done in most processes, where employees from other units were invited and the process was challenged in terms of efficiencies, resource utilization, dependencies, risks, gaps, and its contribution to strategic goals.

CHANGE AND IMPROVEMENTS RESULTING FROM THE PROJECT

The mapped processes enabled the effective implementation of the new business model. The key element, however, is how employees and management buy-in was achieved through the process mapping workshops. The change was brought about by employees through participation in and collaboration around process review, design and improvement. The processes further defined roles, which mean that employees agreed on what roles are needed to perform what steps in each process. Change is therefore driven by employees, with a pull from management who oversaw Action Lists being carried out. Consultation, collaboration, buy-in, and accountability for change and implementation were all built into the project.

The processes were mapped to operational level and organograms that were derived from what roles each of the process needed, reflecting the resourcing needed in respect of Group Executive (level 2), General Manager (level 3), Senior Management (level 4) and Management (level 5/6).

Deliverables of the project were:
- The complete SAPO positioning map which reflected:
  - All processes developed/documented and improved on per Unit;
  - Processes, identified during the project, that need to be developed in a next project;
  - A short summary of the participation in each unit, which impacts on the quality of the work (participation is tracked through a tracker in which every participant per project is registered and signs their name to);
  - A summary of burning points in each unit, as observed and recorded in the work-sessions;

- The SAPO structure map;
- All process maps and Action Lists on soft copy;
- A wrap-up of project actions, the project cost profile;
- In-house training to maintain the processes.

TECHNICAL ELEMENTS OF THE PROJECT

VizPro® is a software independent methodology, but Pétanque prefers Microsoft Visio® to apply the methodology. The process maps are storyboards created thought the intelligent use of customized icons. Additional benefit for SAPO was that it didn't require an additional investment in expensive software.

During Process Mapping sessions the information captured in Microsoft Visio® is shown on a screen and all changes and additions are done electronically.

Maps were saved in both Microsoft Visio®-format and as a PDF document. The PDF documents were saved to ensure version control and for easy distribution to stakeholders. Prints (though not encouraged) were made from the JPG versions on a HP Designjet 400 printer. The maximum size of a possible map is 0.84 meters by 25 meters, though SAPO only printed maps up to six meters.

IMPACT ON REVENUE GROWTH

The Process Maps hold a vast amount of information which has served the South African Post Office well in other applications.

A number of the Process Maps were used to explain processes during new business propositions. In offering new, innovative services to potential SAPO clients, the process of offering those solutions could be collaborated on, and agreed on with the new client. In other words, process solutions are explained to third parties by using the relevant map. This has already assisted in the start-up of three successful new business ventures.

Through process enhancements, new products and solutions can be market ready, more speedily. An example can be found in the process improvements that were made in the "new product development" processes. The processes found in three different business units were standardized and resulted in quicker approval and development time, providing for quicker "go to market" readiness.

IMPACT ON COST REDUCTION

Cost reduction following on the identification and addressing of process inefficiencies is a principal benefit of the project, as duplicated processes within and across business units were identified and eliminated; opportunities for automation were identified; more cost-effective resource structures were identified, linking roles to what was needed to be done in processes; and the old versus new way of doing tasks were identified.

IMPACT ON CUSTOMERS

The main customers in the project were all the Business and Corporate Support Units. The following benefits were derived:

5. **Process Benefits**
    - Documentation of all processes that support the new Business Model;
    - Identification of process improvement areas or where total process reengineering needs to happen;
    - Identification and elimination of process duplications;
    - Identification of process gaps which usually impact on efficiency and cost;

- Identification of interfacing processing and identification of end-to-end responsibilities, for example, how the Transport and Mail Delivery processes fit into and complement each other and where "handshakes" take place;
- Serves as input into business continuity, as the impact of risk factors are easily identifiable and mitigation, management or risk transfer is then built into the process;
- Provides detail required for ISO accreditation by identifying which steps require what level and what specification of quality to comply to standards;
- Input into Risk Management as all risks are identified and marked on the step or stage where the risk occurs. Controls are defined and agreed to, ensuring that controls are assigned to role players and stakeholders agree on who is accountable for which risk and how those are managed.

6. **Business Unit benefits**
- By listing unaddressed process issues in the Action Lists, areas for improvement are identified, including new solutions and systems development;
- Breaking of the silo mentality as units see the process impact which their deliverable has on other Business Units;
- Easily identifiable key performance areas and key performance indicators, along with what information needs to be captured where to provide the metrics for measurement. These are used in balanced scorecards and performance appraisals.

7. **Structure / Organogram formulation**
- Communication lines are identified, discussed and agreed to;
- All structures are aligned to business needs and new business model.

8. **Governance**
- All elements that need to be complied to per process are identified and indicated on the maps;
- The maps serve as input into Internal Audit as all processes to be audited are defined, transparent and easy to audit;
- Time saving for Internal Audit as processes and issues are defined.

9. **Management Information and Key Performance Indicators**
- Performance measurement points are identified and linked to metrics in the workshops. This means that role players are quite aware of what needs to be measured when, why and how.
- Alignment of all processes with the company strategic objectives, deliverables and the corporate balance scorecard through the Change Controller, Key Performance Indicators and Key Performance Areas.
- Linking all process KPIs with the company knowledge management system.

10. **People**
- Interactive, cross functional, fun and high energy workshops;
- Provided a forum for problem and issue discussion and resolution in a non threatening environment;
- Transparency, as all maps were made available to all team members, of particular benefit to those who did not take part in the work sessions and whom were invited (inclusion) to comment and provide input;
- All roles are defined, discussed and clarified;

- Provided input into unit specific job profiles, allowing for inclusion and bottom up participation in organization structures;
- Knowledge sharing and skills transfer took place;
- The maps are applied to train new employees as the maps provide for the "big picture" and the detail needed for induction and quick understanding of roles;
- Buy-in and a sense of participation in creating a new, improved enterprise.

11. IT Systems

Process Maps were applied by the IT department for Enterprise Architecture, Business Continuity including disaster recovery processes.

12. Finance

Process maps are also used to verify and define activities for the company's costing model, Therefore each activity in a process or the complete process can be estimated to measure the value of the process. This again leads to comparison and elimination of unnecessary activities that adds no value, forcing more cost-effective processes throughout the company.

For the South African Post Office, these multiple benefits impact on successful repositioning as an employer, service provider and role player in the South African economy, while ensuring the most effective way of supporting the USO (universal service obligation).

TRANSFERABILITY OF THE PROJECT DELIVERABLES

SA Post Office continues to benefit from additional outcomes not directly related to the objectives of the project.

13. Documented Knowledge

All maps are electronically available to all employees in the company, creating continuous knowledge sharing.

14. Ownership

Every Business Unit Head takes ownership of their maps, the accuracy thereof and Action Lists to continue the process of improvement and change.

15. Process Facilitation, Mapping and Version Control
- Resources from the Post Offices Group Strategy unit have been trained in the methodology, process mapping and facilitation of the VizPro® methodology;
- Training has allowed SAPO to take responsibility for version control.

16. Early Users / Usage of the Process Maps
- To develop new company wide organograms based on what the processes defined needed to be done and what roles were needed to perform those functions;
- To adjust, improve and / or develop processes to support the roll out of the new business model;
- To introduce new employees where both unit specific and company process are used to fast track newcomers into productivity;
- For application in Internal Audits, where the process maps form the basis of all audits;
- For application in risk management, where risk areas are highlighted and can be monitored, managed and reported on quickly and effectively;

- To create a performance culture that flows through the enterprise as each process has a set of KPIs that link to the Profit, People, Planet, KPAs of the Corporate Balanced Scorecard;
- For application in IT where the information is used for Enterprise Architecture, systems development and data management.
- To communicate processes to external consultants, for example for the development of IT disaster recovery and business continuity as every process step indicates what system supports both for inputs and outputs.

IN CONCLUSION

The South African Post Office displayed the foresight of applying a process architecture methodology that went beyond structuring the organization in support of their new business model, and that in particular benefitted the people in the organization, creating a solid foundation for future growth.

ACKNOWLEDGEMENTS

Gratitude for making this project a success goes out to everyone who contributed:

Ms Motshoanetsi Lefoka (CEO), Louise van der Bank (CIO), Nick Buick (CFO), Totsie.Memela-Khambula (COO), and the Group Executives: Janras Kotsi, Molefe Mathibe, Ndala Mnisi, Ray Mkhize, Malesela Sekhasimbe, Abner Marabe Mofokeng, Selvia Mahlangu, Project Coordinator and the Pétanque team members: Justin Siljeur, Jeanne Fredericks, Fhatuwani Netshiavha, MJ Fick, Paulla Primich, Elisabeth Stavenga, Banzi Nkosi, Derrick Ntoampe, Kgape Tlhaleroe, and Varinia Ladbrooke.

Managing Change with Re-Usable Assets for Government Agencies

Dr. Setrag Khoshafian, Pegasystems Inc., USA

ABSTRACT

Business Process Management (BPM) suites automate policies and procedures. The policies and procedures are captured in executable process flows, different types of business rules, case data, user interactions and service integration—all in the context of organizational access controls. These are the operational BPM assets of government agencies.

This chapter will show how BPM can realize change and agility through re-usable government BPM assets. Dynamic BPM repositories allow each government agency to use common practices, while specializing for their particular agency extensions and needs. Thus re-usable assets can be organized in different collections pertaining to shared as well as specialized solutions for various sectors such as healthcare, financial management, education, and national security. The chapter will discuss dynamic BPM repositories for the public sector. These repositories organize the re-usable assets for specific agency needs.

Agility has often been elusive in government initiatives. IT-focused government projects have tended to be "bottom up" —large, long, and expensive technology architecture projects with little business value. The alternative is an agile BPM focused "top down" approach that starts with prioritized business objectives and provides quick and tangible returns to government stakeholders.

Government solutions have many similarities with their commercial counterparts. But there are also significant differences. Revenue generation is not the primary driving force of government agencies. Instead government objectives span cutting unnecessary waste, reuse of assets, agility in responsiveness, transparency, resiliency, security, and overall efficiency of processes. This chapter will conclude with a summary of the main advantages of the BPM approach to these critical objectives of government agencies: especially in managing change through re-use.

INTRODUCTION

With the recent economic meltdown, government agencies are facing almost insurmountable challenges. Government is accountable to the citizenry. The lack of popularity of the last administration *and* congress demonstrate that the citizens were not happy with the government's performance. In 2008-2009 a large portion of the population lost their jobs and most saw the eradication of their retirement savings. The Obama-Biden campaign ran on a platform of change [1]. With this new administration, the leadership in government agencies is facing a conundrum: how to reorganize, modernize, and restructure, while at the same time becoming agile, efficient, transparent, lean, and responsive to the citizenry in the midst of unprecedented economic challenges, regulatory governance, and security threats that constantly change. How can agencies manage change organizationally *and* be agile operationally?

Change and agility need to be managed. When change is not managed, it can lead to increased costs, degradation of agility, and to general business chaos. One impact of the chaos is the "gap" that gets created between the objectives of the agency and the underlying systems or solutions that are attempting to realize these objectives. Many times agencies (and also private sector enterprises) have tried to address this change challenge through bottom-up IT SOA initiatives. As we shall discuss below, these have not worked very well. The better approach is to go top-down, starting with agencies' objectives and the automation of the policies and procedures that realize the objectives.

Policies and Procedures

An agency is a collection of policies and procedures. All categories of agency operations involve policies and procedures, be they citizen-facing (e.g. E-Government [2]), inter-agency, or internal operations.

Take a typical agency and you will find at least six areas that contain the organization's policies and procedures:

- *Policy and Procedure Manuals:* The most obvious of these are the policy and procedure manuals: how do things get done in the agency. We will most likely witness an increase in regulations through policies and procedure. Compliance to codes and procedures need to govern the agency as well as the public sector(s) under the jurisdiction of the agency.

- *People:* Almost invariably there are designated and well recognized "heroes" who know how to get things done. Government agencies are facing increasingly an aging workforce that is going to be retiring in the next few years. They know the written and often the unwritten policies and procedures. They have the policies and procedures in their "heads." These are the go-to people for specific tasks or procedures—and every organization has them. People are also the source of innovation. The innovation spans new products and services as well as process innovation, in any business unit or domain.

- *Legacy Code:* The counterpart to the aging workforce is the aging IT infrastructure and the aging transaction or operational systems in government agencies. There is embedded policy and procedure logic within legacy systems. Government agencies are attempting to modernize, digitize and transform. Sometimes these IT focused modernization initiatives have either failed or had very little to show for in terms of tangible benefits. Legacy systems span ERP application code, database stored procedures, and "raw" programs in languages such as COBOL, Java, or C/C++/C#. So government agencies attempt to go through legacy transformations toward modernization—through enterprise architecture (especially SOA) initiatives. The transformation often entails harvesting the policies and procedures and porting them to modern platforms, especially BPM Suites.

- *Enterprise Architecture (EA) Modeling Artifacts*: The other option is to launch EA and modeling initiatives and generate numerous modeling artifacts, often organized in an EA repository. The models could represent "as-is" and "to-be" process, organization, information, or infrastructure models. The goal is to have an "architecture" that modernizes the agency. The problem with the modeling and EA artifact approaches is that what you end up with is a collation—often volumes—of artifacts. Documentation that eventually gathers dust with little to show for in terms of concrete business benefits. Sometimes different tools are used for capturing EA artifacts, business process analysis (primarily generating models) and business process management suites that execute policies and procedures. The proliferation of different tools creates problems and semantic gaps [3] between modeling and execution. This is the antithesis of agility, especially when considering continuous improvement changes to the policies and procedures.

- *Databases: Operational as well as data warehouses:* Government agencies often analyze and model (predictive) operational or intelligence data to harvest business rules that can then be operationalized. Both transactional as well as historical data in data warehouses and data-marts provide tremendous opportunities to discover patterns: associations, dependencies, tree models. These business rules can then execute in the context of BPM cases. Most government agencies can benefit from the discovery and especially the execution of discovered policy patterns in BPM solutions. For instance, a predictive model that is discovered through the fusion of several intelligence sources and is operationalized for military processes is one example of such an application. Both policies and procedures can be discovered from data and then automated through the BPM solution.
- *Automation:* This is the key. As noted above, it is not sufficient just to model—explicitly or through discovery—the policies and procedures. What is modeled need to be executed; hopefully with little or no further mappings or transformations. The best approach is to directly capture and automate the policies and procedures. The more direct the execution from requirements or models to automation, the better. BPM Suite automates the work through processes. Work can be assigned to specific agency workers, roles, skills, work-queues, or the assignment can be done via policies or business rules. The BPM Suite automation also involves many types of business rules that "drive" the processes. Examples include decision trees, expressions, event rules, and constraints. Processes execute in the context of cases. Case management typically involves multiple flows and case content. The BPM engine also keeps track of all cases and allows stakeholders monitor, control and execute business performance reports on the process instances or case data.

BPM SUITE: THE RE-USABLE ASSETS

Policies and procedures can be captured through business process management suite assets. These assets include:

- *Process Flow:* This is perhaps the most visible asset in a BPM suite application. The process diagrams typically include swim-lanes, tasks or activities and the overall flow of the process. Processes can have sub-processes and you can also specify simulation parameters and simulate the process. Figure 1 illustrates a typical flow diagram with swim-lanes:

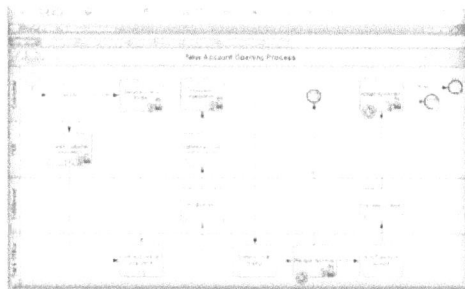

Figure 1: Account opening Flow (BPMN notation)

- *Business Rules:* The processes provide the procedural flow models of work, involving human participants, systems, and trading partners. You also need to model the business policies and decision rules. Rules such as risk level determinations, service level agreements and approval levels are examples of business policies and decision rules. These can be associated with processes or can pertain to the application or even the enterprise as a whole. Figure 2 illustrates different types of business rules: Decision rules, Expressions, Event Rules, and Constraints.

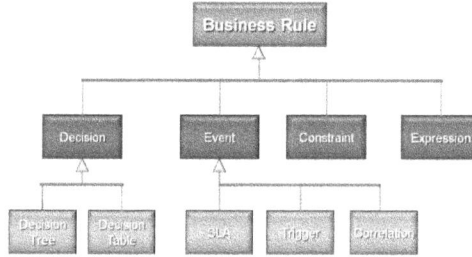

Figure 2: Some examples of rule types

Business rules *drive* business processes: policies for assigning tasks, policies behind deciding on alternative choices (e.g. level of risk), calculations of process attributes, event generation or correlations etc. are all examples of business rules that "drive" or the flow. So there are business rules behind every assignment, decision, calculation, branch, service call, or user interaction.

These are not the only assets; there are many more—including the process information, user interactions, and service integration. As illustrated in Figure 3, even though process flows are sometimes the most visible assets in a BPM suite solution, there are other assets that are supporting, driving, and executing the process application in a unified and complete BPM Suite engine.

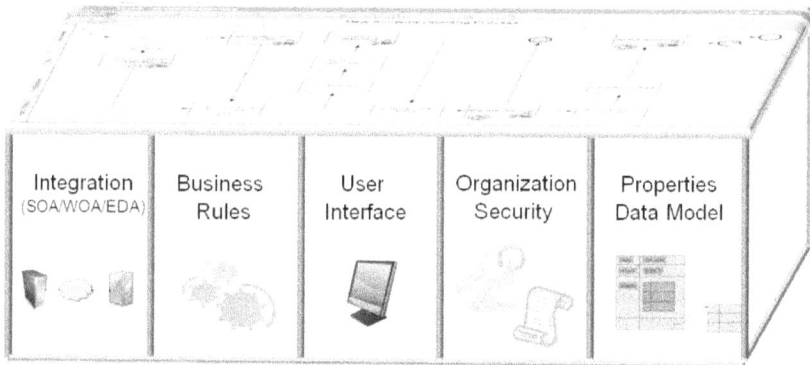

Figure 3: Business Rules and other assets "drive" business processes

ORGANIZING THE RE-USABLE ASSETS: THE DYNAMIC REPOSITORY

The re-usable executable BPM assets need to be organized and managed in a dynamic and agile repository. The objective of having re-usability within and across agencies has well been recognized by the federal government. For example, the following illustration (Figure 4) of segments and services is from *FEA Practice Guidance* [4] from the Office of Management and Budget (OMB):

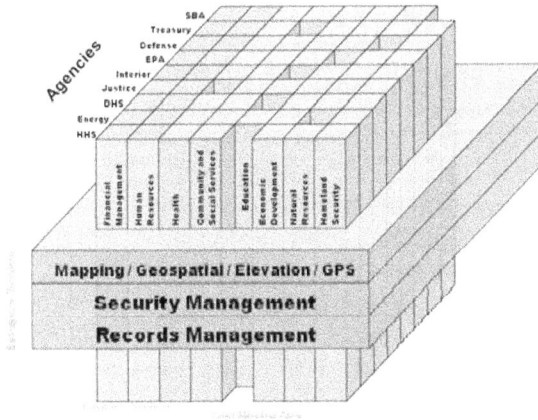

Figure 4: Segments and Services Within and Across Agencies [4], [7]

As stated in the guide: "A single agency contains both core mission area segments and business service segments. Enterprise services are those cross-cutting services spanning multiple segments. Segments can be leveraged within an agency, across several agencies, or the entire federal government."

The main conclusion to glean from this high level illustration is the sharing of solutions (segments / services) within and across agencies. Contrast this with siloed, expensive, and inefficient replication of similar solutions (e.g. procurement) within or between agencies. It is not uncommon to find private and public sector organizations with replicated applications, with applications or solutions that are difficult to maintain or extend with changes.

The following (Figure 5) illustrates the organization of the BPM assets in re-usable layers. Each layer contains flows, different types of business rules, properties, UI, reports, integration etc.: elements that make up executable BPM solutions. The foundation is the BPM Suite. On top you can have multiple cross-agency layers.

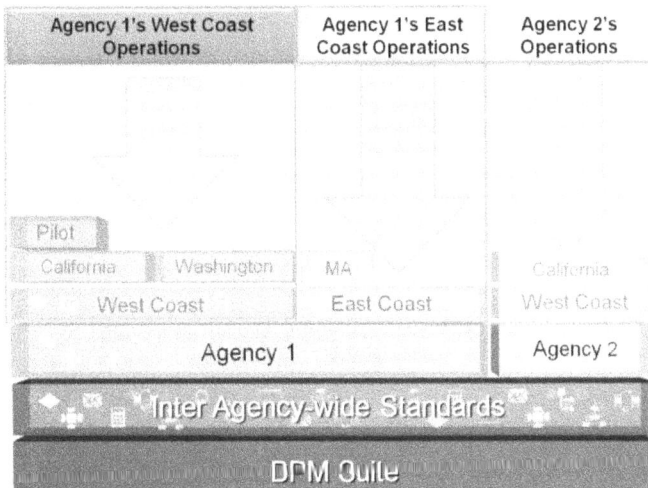

Figure 5: BPM Suite Layers Across and Within Agencies

Figure 5 shows basically *two* dimensions: Agencies and Geographical locations at the granule of states. The organization of the layers can in fact involve many dimensions. Examples of dimensions include the type of the citizen, the state or location of the interaction, the version, the access control security, the version of the asset that is applicable, the type of the BPM solution (the equivalent of "Product" in the commercial world), the time of the interaction, and other customizable dimensions. At run-time the underlying BPM suite will pick the best asset to apply for the give values of the dimensions. This the *dynamic* attribute of the repository. The repository is used to organize the assets along multiple dimensions *and* dynamically select the best asset to apply for a given situation that is captured in the values of the dimensions.

Though not recommended, it is important to note that the various dimensions (such as location, type of the citizen or requestor, time, version, type of the solution, access control, etc.), *could* be embedded within the application or solution.

In Figure 6(a), the decision to grant the visa is preceded by the selection of risks including age group, country of origin, and prior visa denial. Then depending upon these criteria, you will have the policy of granting the visa such as:

IF Application Verified AND Reference Checked THEN Grant Visa

It is of course a simplified rule. There will be many more details in the grant (e.g. duration and type). In fact the actual rule that needs to be executed is the decision rule to grant the visa.

The other criteria are used to determine which rule to apply: they are selecting the appropriate business logic. If we take a different branch, there will be a different rule logic, with the same purpose (Granting Visa):

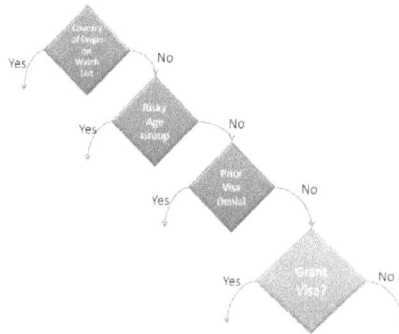

(a) Flow logic to select the appropriate decision the Grant Visa purpose

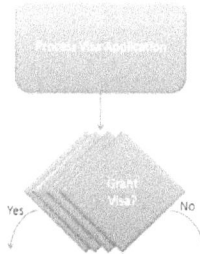

(b) Directly Capture business decision intent (Grant Visa): with multiple options

Figure 6: Alternative Decision Representations

Clearly Figure 6(a) is cluttered. Even if this is done in a sequence of IF … THEN IF… THEN IF … logic, it will be difficult to maintain or make changes in all segments where similar "selection" logic or decision is needed. Mixing selection logic to the intent of the decision (as illustrated in Figure 6(a)) creates maintenance nightmares and makes it very difficult to manage change. This option of embedding the selection logic within process or business rule decisions is the anti-thesis of agility and change.

In contrast, with Figure 6(b), rather than cluttering either the process map or the business decision rule to select the business logic for granting the visa, the BPM suite organizes assets such as decision rules along a number of dimensions and then given a particular situation (often expressed through values of properties in the application) it dynamically picks the most appropriate policy or procedure. Thus the flow will be similar to the one in Figure 6(b). The "shadow" effect is a visual hint, implying there are potential multiple decision rule in the repository with the same intent or purpose (Grant Visa) and the underlying BPM Suite will pick the most appropriate one dynamically.

This same concept of dynamic selection and application applies to all the elements in the BPM Suite: process flows, SOA integration (which service to invoke based on a given situation), user interface (which language or type of interface to use based on, for instance, the type of the worker, language proficiency, 508 accessibility considerations, skills etc.), decision rules (as illustrated above), event policies, calculations, and constraints.

Dynamic BPM Suite Repository

The following are the salient features and requirements of the Dynamic BPM Suite repository that helps agencies manage change:

- *Flexible and Dynamic Multi-dimensional organization of assets*: the repository should be multi-dimensional. This means many dimensions such as the type of the solution, time, location, category of the citizen, etc. are used to organize and subsequently at run-time select the most appropriate policy, procedure, service, or user interaction. More importantly, the dimensions should be flexible. For instance one policy could be decided based on geographical location; another, say, service selection could be based on security and availability; yet a third expression evaluation could depend on the type of the citizen and the product. The repository should allow addition and deprecation of dimensions at will.

- *Built-In Versioning:* The repository should make versioning one of the dimensions in organizing the assets. The repository should support rolling backward (deprecation) of versions. This means the underlying BPM Suite could potentially execute an application as it executed in a particular point in history, prior to the changes or the deployment of the newer versions.

- *Change History:* The repository should maintain the change history of assets with the same intent or purpose as well as specific assets.

- *Ease of Support of "Delta" updates or changes:* This sounds obvious, but incremental changes should be easy to make. The trend in BPM Suites is to allow business users own and make changes to the policies and procedures. In contrast to major application versions or updates these typically tend to be minor or incremental changes, often of particular policies or procedures that they own.

- *Promote intra and inter-agency reuse*: With a rich security and access control support, the dynamic enterprise repository should support and promote inter and intra agency reuse. Often the re-use initiatives have focused on SOA component or web services based re-use. While of some value, BPM assets are much richer: including process flows, rich collection of rule types, user interaction/interface assets, and also integration (SOA or otherwise).

For the last bullet, the following example in Figure 7 illustrates how the federal government can have common healthcare provisioning standards that can potentially be shared across all agencies that provide healthcare. The figure shows specializations of Center of Medicare and Medicaid Services (CMS) [5], further specialized for Part D and Part C enrollment. Briefly, Part D provides prescription drug coverage. Part C provides medical services and hospital care through approved private insurance companies. These companies tend to operate in geographical areas—such as the many companies of Blue Cross Blue Shield Association. There are specializations for the policies of specific states or private companies. The figure also shows the Veterans Health Administration's [6] specialization of the common cross-agency healthcare practices. These are the extensions or specializations of benefits and patient programs for veterans. This is a conceptual organization of assets, reflecting what could be achieved for managing healthcare across agencies or for specific programs within the same agency.

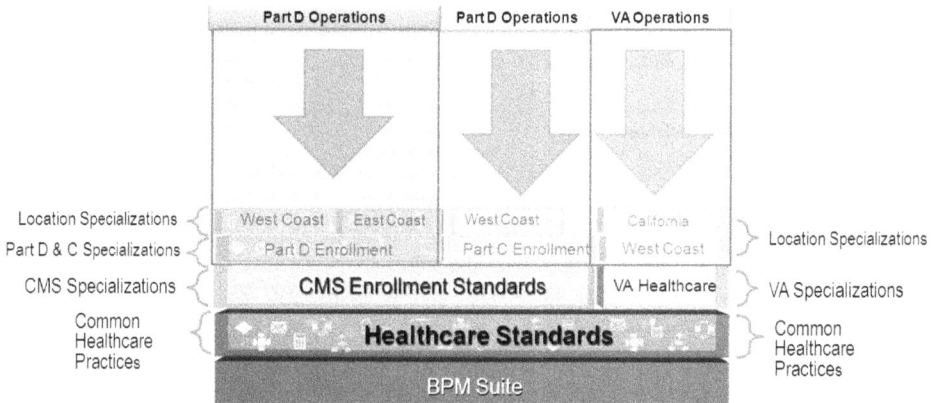

Figure 7: Healthcare enrollment and provisioning in Federal Agencies

BOTTOM-UP VS. TOP-DOWN IMPROVEMENT INITIATIVES

The following sections illustrate and contrast two alternative approaches in modernizing government. Bottom-Up initiatives tend to come from the IT side. These initiatives typically focus on the lower two layers of the Federal Enterprise Architecture [7] (Data Reference Model and Technology Reference Model). More specifically, often government IT initiatives are Service Oriented Architecture (SOA) efforts. In contrast, increasingly agencies are discovering the benefits of top-down business performance approaches: especially through BPM Suites. The top-down approach is iterative: it identifies quick-win opportunities.

Bottom-Up (SOA) Initiatives

Both IT and business agree on the general objectives of agile approaches that support change. The objectives of change and improvement are not new. But the specific approaches are quite different. There are, of course, many nuances, but overall two approaches have been vying for following in enterprise computing. The Top Down business process management suite approach discussed below and the more IT popular bottom-up approach in building re-usable "assets" (which tend to be services and software components). One bottom-up alternative is to lay down a strong infrastructure foundation and then build upon it the layers for business requests (see Figure 8 and [10]). This is the approach that is sometimes pursued by large and complex SOA initiatives; in both the private and public sector. At the risk of over-generalizing, the bottom-up SOA approach has some salient features:

- *Major IT transformational (modernization) projects*: with often no clear return on investment benefits. The claim of course is the "future" benefit of a more modern and scalable architecture. For example, SOA is an architectural discipline that supports standards based integration (especially Web Services WS-* standards), loose coupling, service bus, and component or service re-use organized in a registry/repository. Sometimes, SOA initiatives attempt to completely restructure the technical foundations with common re-usable information, architecture, and service infrastructures. While these are desirable goals on the long term, they make it difficult to demonstrate the tangible ROIs; especially for the business stakeholders.

- *Technology purchases with no clear business vision or benefit*: Bottom-up initiatives often start with purchasing an Enterprise Service Bus (ESB). ESBs do offer some benefits (such as message transformation, message routing, protocol mapping, service registry, etc.). However, an ESB purchase does not automatically deliver tangible benefits. Having an ESB does not guarantee the success of the bottom-up technology focused transformational initiative.
- *Enterprise Architecture Artifact-focused*: often there is almost a given conviction that agencies need to have enterprise architectures with numerous artifacts. The challenge is not really in generating numerous artifacts, either in documentation or via an EA or business process analysis tool.
- *Re-Use Of Composite Services:* Many organizations have applications or functions that are replicated in a variety of solutions. It is not uncommon to find enterprises that have tens of, say, procurement applications. Sometime the bottom-up approach attempts to create an inventory of these applications and goes about extracting the common "services" to promote cost savings, component/application sharing, and overall governance.

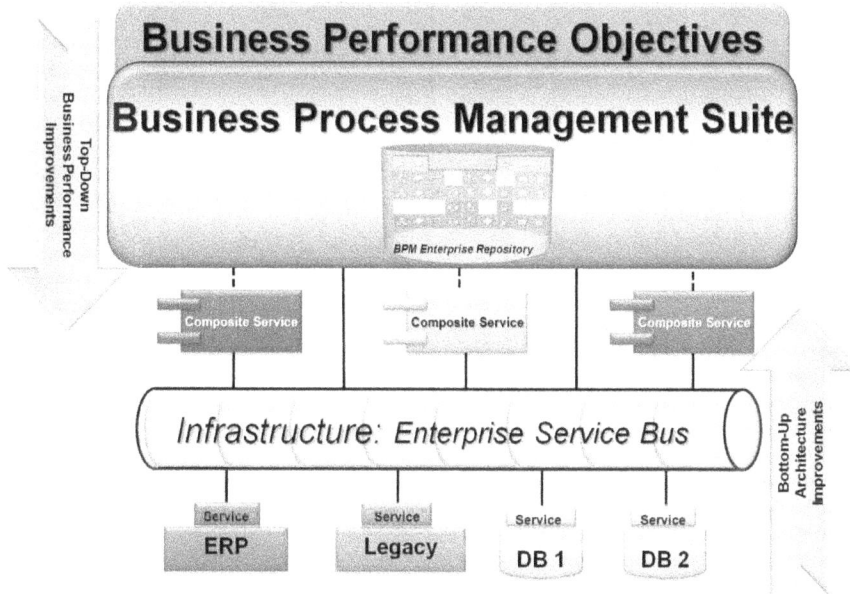

Figure 8: Bottom-UP and Top Down Improvement

Top Down Continuous Improvement

The top-down approach starts with the business requirements. Often these requirements are expressed in key performance indicators (KPIs). These requirements then translate into use cases that are directly supported by the policies and procedures that are automated in the BPM Suite. Large and complex transformational projects are abandoned in favor of iterative continuous improvement initiatives. Agencies have specific key performance indicators that measure the performance of citizen-facing, mid-office, or back-office processes. As illustrated in Figure 8, you start from the business performance objectives and map those directly to BPM Suite applications organized in the repository of the BPM suite re-usable assets.

With the top down approach, each solution is linked to specific business objectives. Business performance objectives drive building the assets. Thus process flows, policies captured in different business rules, and service invocations to back-end systems are linked to business performance indicators. Legacies are accessed or transformed based on what is needed in the BPM solution. Each change will have an impact and the impacts will be visible to the stakeholders. Ideally, through a management dashboard the stakeholders will be able to view the performance of their BPM solutions at different levels of details.

How about "continuous improvement"? There are at least three iteration cycles in continuously improving agency projects, through BPM.

- The first iteration cycle deals with selecting the next project for automation. Typically an agency will have many projects or "processes" that need improvement. The agency can organize these projects along two dimensions: business value and implementation risk. The goal here is to iteratively choose measurable, high impact, highly motivating, and highly visible projects while minimizing the technology (e.g. integration with legacy systems) and complexity risk. Figure 9 illustrates an impact/risk matrix, with iterations.

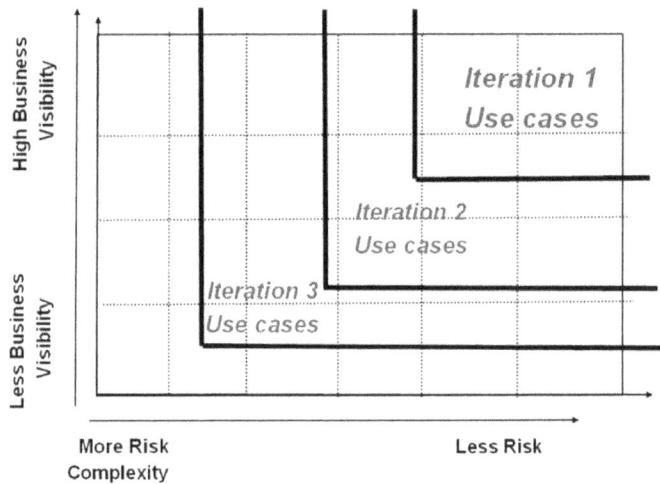

Figure 9: Impact/Risk Matrix

- The second iteration cycle deals with the iterative methodology that quickly goes to automation with demonstrable values. The iteration goes through inception, elaboration, construction, and transfer phases [8].
- The third continuous improvement cycle focuses on improvements to achieve process performance objectives. Through automation, the process data is readily available for analysis. Typically these continuous measurement approaches go hand in hand with analytical process improvement methodologies, such as Six Sigma [9].

CONCLUSION: THE BENEFITS

BPM Suites provide major advantages, all aligned with government agencies' objectives to support change while being efficient and transparent. Governments across the globe are embarking upon modernization and transformation initiatives. The 2008-2009 recessions resulted in a resurgence of regulatory compliance initiatives. To add to the challenge, government is also facing an aging work force that will be retiring in the next few years. Governments need to harvest their know-how while remaining agile and cutting costs.

When change is supported and managed through the BPM Suites and its robust organization of policy and procedure assets, government agencies can keep up with the increasingly demanding objectives of their stakeholders. Conventional solutions —such as point solutions or in-house development or maintenance of legacy systems—will not be able to keep up with the changing government needs. This is illustrated in Figure 10.

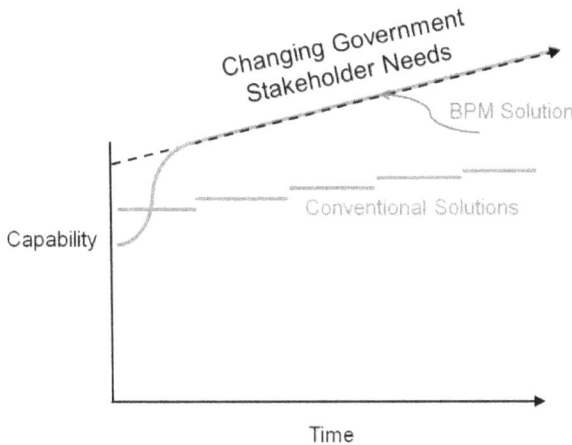

Figure 10: BPM solutions can keep with changing government needs

The advantages of BPM Suites could be summarized as follows:

Government Objectives	BPM Suite Advantage
Manage Change	It is relatively easy to introduce changes in BPM solutions. BPM can also organize the changes in repositories that maintain not only services but also complete BPM solutions. Typically changes are realized with zero coding—through changing executable forms or models— which are the re-usable assets of BPM solutions.
Intra and Inter Agency Re-Use	The dynamic repository of policies and procedures and the specialization directly supports this requirement and allows agencies to share common practices and then specialize for their particular objectives.
Cost Savings	BPM Suites can be used to avoid waste and increase process efficiency. Waste can be reduced in building solutions, while executing automated processes, and in monitoring executing processes for continuous improvement. BPM Suites capture business objectives and requirements directly: substantially reducing the cost of building solutions. BPM Suites automate work: substantially reducing the cost of operating agency services. BPM Suites continuously monitor and control work: substantially reducing the cost of keeping processes in control.
Regulatory Com-	BPM Suites can directly capture and automate all the policies of regu-

pliance	latory compliance in any domain, including financial. The controls for compliance can be automated. In addition, since the dynamic BPM repository keeps an audit trail of all the changes, agencies can easily find out the exact policies and procedures executed at a particular point in time.
Transparency	Policies and procedures are not "black boxes." Through the appropriate access controls and secure filtering, agency stakeholders can find out clearly and explicitly exactly what is being executed in providing services either internally or to the citizenry. Transparency of government policies and procedures could best be achieved through browsing the dynamic BPM suite repository. Transparency of government operations could best be achieved through the business activity monitoring of executing processes.
Retiring Work Force	Most government agencies have skilled workers who, as part of the baby boomer generation, will be retiring in the next few years. These are knowledge workers. Through BPM suites and proper discipline, government agencies can harvest the knowledge of these workers and incorporate them into business process solutions.
IT Modernization	BPM suites provide an agile business friendly process case management platform to extend, expand, and modernize legacy solutions. This means new policies and procedures are built in the BPM Suite, while accessing and leveraging legacy systems of records, via service calls. The extension and integration can be bi-directional. This means new policies and procedures can be captured in the BPM Suite and be invoked from legacy systems: via service calls [10].

REFERENCES

1. http://www.change.gov/ now directed to: http://www.whitehouse.gov/ The technology agenda: http://www.whitehouse.gov/agenda/technology/
2. http://www.usa.gov/Topics/Includes/Reference/egov_strategy.pdf for the US strategy. Most developed and developing countries have E-Government initiatives.
3. Khoshafian, S. (2005). "Narrowing the Semantic Gap between Business Process Analysis and Business Process Execution." *The Workflow Handbook 2005*, Published in association with the Workflow Management Coalition (WfMC). Future Strategies Inc., Lighthouse Point, FL. Edited by Layna Fischer.
4. Office of Management and Budget (2007). *FEA Practice Guide*
5. http://www.whitehouse.gov/omb/assets/fea_docs/FEA_Practice_Guidance_Nov_2007.pdf
6. Centers for Medicare & Medicaid Services http://www.cms.hhs.gov/
7. Veterans Health Administration http://www1.va.gov/health/index.asp
8. FEA Web Site: http://www.whitehouse.gov/omb/e-gov/fea/
9. Khoshafian, S. (2007). "BPM Center of Excellence Manifesto." Published in *The Workflow Handbook 2007* Published in association with the Workflow Management Coalition (WfMC). Future Strategies Inc., Lighthouse Point, FL. Edited by Layna Fischer.
10. Khoshafian, S. (2006). "Business Process Management for Six Sigma Projects." *The Workflow Handbook 2006*, Published in association with the Workflow Management Coalition (WfMC). Edited by Layna Fischer.
11. Khoshafian, S. (2006). *Service Oriented Enterprises.* Auerbach Publications, Boca Raton: FL.

Streamlining the Congress of the Republic of Peru e-Government

Rocio Angelica Sanchez, Congress of the Republic of Peru, and Amy Wyron, Colosa, Inc., Peru

ABSTRACT

In late 2008, the Congress of the Republic of Peru began the pilot phase of an initiative to automate and streamline governmental processes through application of a Business Process Management (BPM) System. After a competitive bid process, the Congress chose ProcessMaker, a leading Open Source BPM Solution, as its BPM Vendor. This case study examines the factors that drove the Congress of Peru to implement a BPM system, the expected outcomes of this BPM initiative, and suggestions of best practices for e-governments when transitioning to a BPM system.

INTRODUCTION

Peru is a rapidly-developing South American nation, with more than 15 million cell phone subscribers and nearly eight million Internet users among its 28 million inhabitants. One of the principle missions of the Congress of Peru is to support the economic and political development of the country[1]. The Congress of Peru has made e-government a priority in recent years, and is working toward a comprehensive modernization of all congressional areas.

E-government is an important part of the Congress of Peru's development strategy. A 2008 e-government study conducted by the Brookings Institution gave Peru a score of 35 out of a possible 100 points[2]. This score shows a marked improvement from 2007, when Peru received a score of 24, and reflects the ongoing commitment by the government of Peru to invest in e-government technology.

In 2008, the Congress of Peru embarked on an ambitious plan to implement a BPM system by the year's end. The BPM system forms a fundamental part of the future e-government strategy of the Congress. Through the implementation of a BPM system, the Congress hopes to achieve agility in information sharing across departments and systems. The BPM creates a centralized process information hub, serving as an integrator for various critical systems and increasing transparency and efficiency in congressional operations.

At the time of this article, the Congress of Peru has implemented the BPM system, and is in the early stages of running the first round of automated processes. This paper will examine the importance of e-government to the Congress of the Republic of Peru, the context in which the BPM system is being introduced to the Congress, as well as lessons learned from the Congress that could be applied to other governments transitioning to a BPM system

---

1 Congress of the Republic of Peru Official Website. http://www.congreso.gob.pe Accessed February 27, 2009.
2 West, Darrell M. "Improving Technology Utilization in Electronic Government around the World" Governance Studies at Brookings Institute, 2008. p.15

I. Why include BPM in an e-Government strategy?

E-government is widely considered the key to modernizing government operations, increasing efficiency, and eliminating waste. In its most basic definition, e-government involves the use of information and communication technology (ICT) in government operations, regarding both internal operations and external relationships with citizen constituents. The transformation and modernization of those relationships through e-government is precisely the goal of the Congress of Peru in choosing to implement a BPM system.

MODERNIZATION THROUGH TARGETED E-GOVERNMENT INITIATIVES

Modernization of government through technology can help a government to better meet today's challenges. As globalization and technology transform all levels of society, government must also transform itself, or risk becoming outdated and ineffective. Due to the growing demands of a globalized world, government services must be delivered ever more rapidly yet with increased capacity. The demands on government have never been greater, and the need for modernization has never been so necessary.

As part of a larger integrated modernization strategy, ICT provides tools that can help governments to respond to these demands. ICT can help a government to "gain speed, precision, simplicity, outreach, and networking capacity,"[3] and thus improve the efficiency and capacity of government operations and services. The idea behind e-government projects is that well-applied technological interventions can enable a government to do its job faster, better, and with more accuracy. And this in turn results in better outcomes for the citizen constituents that rely on the government, both directly and indirectly, for quality services.

It is too often taken for granted that technology is the best solution to the modernization and globalization issues facing government. It is important to note, however, that ICT is not a modernization solution in and of itself; the solution lies in the way that technology is applied. Just as in the private sector, any new technology adoption implies resources and costs; thus, costs and benefits must be weighed, and concrete goals must be established and met in order to demonstrate success. The BPM implementation in the Congress of Peru is an excellent example of a targeted initiative that directly addresses a specific pain point.

Technology must also be applied to improve a tangible problem and increase the satisfaction of the clients, or in this case, the citizens. An e-government solution should improve the status quo in a measurable way in order to justify its existence. As the UN notes, "the mere existence of e-government says practically nothing about the quality of life in a society."[4] So the technological interventions must be adopted in a way that, directly or indirectly, produces positive impacts for citizens.

Much like clients, citizens pay for government through taxes and express their preferences through democratic elections. However, unlike a private customer, citizens of a nation cannot easily choose another provider, or quit consuming government services. Furthermore, government also serves constituents who are unable to express preferences, such as children. Thus the responsibility of the Congress of Peru to its clients is even greater than that of a private entity, and the

---

3 "E-Government at the Crossroads: World Public Sector Report" United Nations, New York, 2003. p.7

4 "E-Government at the Crossroads: World Public Sector Report" United Nations, New York, 2003. p.6

benefit to the citizen clients must always be at the forefront when implementing an e-government project.

A successful e-government strategy, in the Congress of Peru or in any government entity, must be about more than just increasing efficiency. As IDEA UK notes, successful e-government "is about making sure you make technology available in the right places to streamline the business but also to genuinely help the customer," or in this case improve the provision of public services to the citizens through the modernization of government[5]. Efficiency, automation, and technology are all important components of a modernization strategy, but only when considering the intended benefit to the consumer.

Keeping the benefits to citizens at the forefront, initiatives must be chosen that will be effective, directly improve internal and external operations, and most importantly, make concrete improvements to the status quo that can be felt by the consumer. E-government is a powerful tool that can be used to help the government modernize the services that people count on, while also streamlining the government's own ability to provide them. The goal of better serving the constituency is very important to the Congress of Peru and has helped guide the course of its e-government BPM project.

E-government is a very broad term, however, that covers all types of technology adopted by public institutions. There are an endless number of systems and strategies that fall under the ICT umbrella and choosing among them can be a challenging prospect. So when the Congress of Peru embarked on a comprehensive e-government project, care was taken to select technological interventions that directly address the pain points felt by the internal staff and external constituents, specifically, through the adoption of a BPM system.

BUSINESS PROCESS MANAGEMENT—AN INTEGRAL PART OF E-GOVERNMENT STRATEGY

The Congress of Peru selected a Business Process Management (BPM) system as a fundamental piece of its e-government initiative. Business process management refers to the automation and optimization of workflow. A BPM system can help an organization to streamline processes, essentially reducing waste and virtually eliminating the need for physical paperwork.

A BPM system can help a government to streamline and modernize its operations by maximizing transparency and efficiency and minimizing waste. Through the automation of paper-based processes, a BPM system closes the gaps among people, systems, and information throughout a department or agency. BPM makes it easier for people across offices and in distinct locations to share information with each other, and with systems and databases, in a streamlined way.

Transparency, efficiency, and enhanced coordination fall right in line with the broader of e-government; thus, a BPM system is a logical component for a government pursuing an integrated e-government strategy. A BPM system, especially an open source system like the one implemented in the Congress of Peru, can help move a government towards open standards and provide increased accountability to citizens, thus providing a great advantage to an integrated e-government project.

---

5 Foley, Paul, Ximena Alfonso, John Fisher, Gail Bradbrook "eGovernment: Reaching Socially Excluded Groups?" Improvement and Development Agency for Local Government, UK, 2005. p.16

No two governments are the same, and each agency or department has its own specific manner of doing business. BPM systems can save a government valuable time and money through the development of customized applications. The ability to design personalized workflow applications is a great advantage to a BPM system like the one implemented in the Congress of Peru. Rather than the Congress adapting to a rigid system, the system itself can adapt to reflect the unique reality of the Congress. Each workflow then functions as a distinct custom-built IT application, robust enough to support critical processes yet flexible enough to respond to ever-changing demands.

Business process management and e-government are a natural match. Both aim to reduce waste, maximize efficiency, increase transparency, and simplify operations through the intelligent application of technology. For precisely these reasons, the Congress of Peru selected a BPM system as a fundamental part of its e-government project in 2008.

II. BPM implementation in the Congress of the Republic of Peru

Initially, the Congress of Peru chose to implement a BPM system in order to address concerns about information sharing, customer service, and transparency of results among the 1500 Congressional employees. With the introduction of a BPM system to the Congress of Peru, the mission was to create a more agile system for sharing information and getting approvals. At the time of this paper, the BPM project is currently in the pilot phase; four processes have been automated and are up and running electronically in the Congress through a BPM system.

PAIN POINTS IN THE CONGRESS OF PERU

After examining the operations of the Congress of Peru, an excess of paperwork was identified as a principle problem, creating delays and bottlenecks in the Congress' internal processes.

Before the BPM implementation, the Congress of Peru was running an integral administrative management system known as Sistema Integral de Gestion Administrativa (SIGA). This system was designed to store information, share news, and offer a web portal; however, it did not address the need for approval-related process automation and therefore did not fully meet the workflow management needs of the Congress.

The paperwork situation had become very difficult to manage in various departments of the Congress of Peru. Daily operations consisted of piles of paper files without coherent indexing or ability to prioritize their urgency. At times, papers were difficult or impossible to locate in an efficient manner. The policy for dealing with paperwork was essentially a "first in – first out" policy, meaning that the oldest paperwork was attended to first, and the rest were left waiting for attention. With this system, it was very easy to lose track of urgent or pressing paperwork, and it was nearly impossible to delegate priorities.

With the introduction of a BPM system, the Congress of Peru has specifically targeted increasing paperwork agility throughout the institution. The goal in embarking on a BPM project is to create a centralized, integrated system that could encompass all of the approval-related processes of the Congress, without the need to manually re-enter data into a second system. A BPM system seemed like a very appropriate solution to this requirement, and the BPM system implementation began in 2008.

PILOT PROJECT VISION AND IMPLEMENTATION

Rather than try to implement a BPM system throughout the entire Congress at once, the e-government BPM project began with a pilot phase in a single department. The department selected for the BPM pilot project was the Office of Information Technology, or Oficina de Tecnología de Información (OTI). The members of the OTI department are responsible for the implementation of the BPM system in the rest of the Congress following the completion of the pilot phase in their own area.

The BPM pilot phase involved the automation of four processes within the OTI department. These processes were specifically chosen for the pilot phrase because of their involvement in the daily operations of the OTI, and for their clear and mature process documentation. Process automation began with the "Documentation Process of the Congressional Office of Information Technology," the process by which the Congress officially receives documents. This first process was identified because it is extensively documented, approval-based, and paperwork-intensive. Thus, it was an ideal candidate for automation through a BPM system.

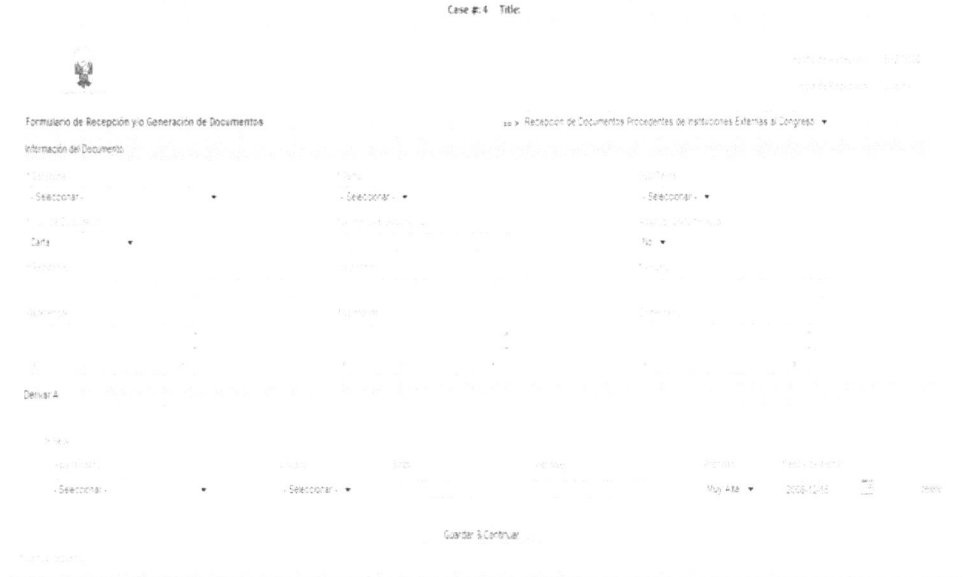

Fig. 1: Documentation Process Dynaform

The process itself includes three branches for three different types of documents: those originating in external institutions, those originating inside the Congress but outside of the OTI department, and those generated by the OTI department itself. Each case includes different forms, actors, supervisors, notifications, and necessary approvals. Through the BPM system, the Congress is able to upload the received documents, route them to the correct secretaries, area heads, and directors, receive the appropriate approvals, and verify the documents using an electronic signature, thus eliminating the need for a paper-based document reception process.

The BPM system adds transparency to this process in a number of ways. At any time a user can track the status of a given document using its case number. The system also eliminates the possibility of losing or misplacing a document, as everything is centralized within the BPM system itself. In addition, the BPM system allows for the prioritization of documents as "urgent", allowing the operators to organize their work and respond to the most pressing needs first.

Furthermore, the BPM system allows for the creation of customized reports, a vital tool for OTI supervisors. Reports can be based on selected criteria, including area of document origin, type of document, and date of submission, among others. Through reports, supervisors are able to track the progress of documents, monitor employee efficiency, identify bottlenecks, and make appropriate adjustments in order to optimize process performance. The BPM system reports provide a useful management tool by shedding light on detailed aspects of process operations.

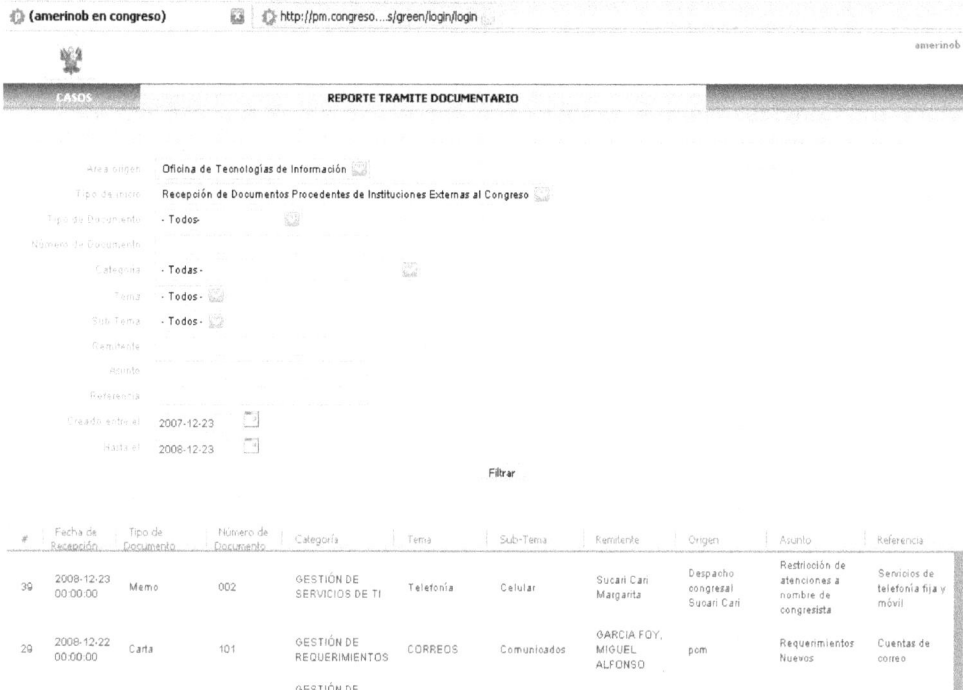

Fig. 2: Documentation Process Reports and Filters

Following the first process automation, three more processes were automated using the BPM system during the pilot phase. The second round of processes included the Request for Equipment and Services Process, the Request for Network and Telephone Services Process, and the Request for Hardware and Software Process. These processes all form a crucial part of the daily operations of the OIT department, and just as with the Documentation Process, require various approvals among different actors. Thus, by automating the processes using the BPM system, a significant amount of paperwork is saved.

PILOT PROJECT RESULTS

The pilot project has been particularly important in the planning and projection of the e-government project in the Congress of Peru. By starting small, the idea is that any and all kinks will be resolved before moving to the entire Congress. This strategy is very important to the success of the overall e-government project.

"Particularly in the developing world, where resources are scarce, e-government must target areas with high chances for success and produce 'winners'" in order to achieve success throughout an institution[6]." In order to get the project off on the right foot, the pilot phase was specifically designed to target the Office of Information Technology (OTI), where success was likely and enthusiasm for the project was high.

The OTI office began running the first round of processes in the first trimester of 2009, and at the time of this paper was beginning to analyze the results from the BPM system implementation. While the implementation of these four processes is complete, the BPM system has only been running for a short time, and as details continue to be adjusted it is difficult to measure the results thus far.

It is estimated that by the second trimester after implementation, there will be measurable indicators to compare with the baselines taken before the project was implemented. However, thus far the outcome has exceeded expectations. In other Peruvian institutions, the implementation of process automation software has taken more than one year; in the Congress of Peru this implementation took only one trimester. This fact bodes well for the efficiency of the Congress of Peru in implementing and successfully adopting a BPM system.

Following the successful completion of the pilot phase, the BPM and e-government project in the Congress of Peru will be expanded beyond the OTI department. Having already implemented the BPM in their own department, the OTI officers will be better prepared to move forward with the Congress-wide implementation in the project phase.

Based on the results of the pilot project, the plan is to extend the project to the entire Congress not only as paperwork automation software, but also as the software to model and automate all of the Congress' complex and interdepartmental processes. Some of the critical processes identified for automation through the BPM system include the Organization Process of the Law, the Official Visits Process, and an Electronic Constituent Services Counter, among others. The pilot phase will provide valuable experience and lessons that will guide the future Congress-wide implementation.

III. Lessons Learned and Suggested Best Practices

In examining the experience of the Congress of Peru in implementing a BPM system, it is useful to reflect and consider the lessons that can be drawn and offered to others considering an e-government BPM project. As the UN reminds, "For a public administration, there is no single established way, no 'best practice' that would lead to successful e-government".[7] Nor do the following recommendations seek to establish firm rules for a government BPM implementation.

While these guidelines are by no means binding, they do reflect the best practices that the Congress of Peru has identified in its pilot implementation, and will continue to follow in the implementation of its Congress-wide BPM project:

Do a pilot project. Pilot projects can provide a valuable experience for organizations, and a chance to work out issues early and on a smaller scale before they are introduced to the entire organization. A pilot phase will also help achieve success that will propel the project forward. The UN Sector Report, citing the OECD, maintains that when it comes to e-government, "the risk of failure is proportional to the size of the project" and "expensive, long-term, and complex initiatives often

---

6 The Working Group on e-Government in the Developing World, "Roadmap for e-Government in the Developing World." Pacific Council on International Policy, 2002. p.1
7 "E-Government at the Crossroads: World Public Sector Report" United Nations, New York, 2003. p.7

fail".[8] Thus, a pilot project is a concrete and less complicated trial phase that can demonstrate the feasibility of an e-government initiative.

Take it step-by-step. While a BPM system can help eliminate paperwork, it will not produce an overnight change. BPM is best described as evolution, not revolution, especially in a government setting. The project should be taken phase-by-phase, and implemented in concrete stages. Users may reject an implementation when it is too abrupt.

Start with mature, well-documented processes. Though tedious, Process Discovery is a vital phase, and should be given considerable time and attention at the beginning of a BPM project. The organization must have standardized processes; otherwise it can be a very long road to standardize them in tandem with a BPM implementation. In the case of an institution where processes are immature or poorly defined, it is important to choose a BPM tool that is flexible enough to adapt to a changing environment. A flexible workflow tool makes it easier to process documents according to the needs that may arise and, little by little, incorporate the necessary routing rules for the common cases and exceptions.

Train both on-the-job and in the classroom. It's no coincidence that the OTI department that will be responsible for implementing the BPM system in the entire Congress of Peru is the first department to use the system internally. This ensures first-hand experience and knowledge about the system. But hands-on experience is not always enough. Train the people who will be directly involved in the implementation before the project begins to create in-house experts. If users do not have enough training to take advantage of the potential of the system, they will lose significant benefits. Conversely, "if they understand the methods, they are less likely to resist them".[9]

Create a BPM implementation team. Regardless of external consultants, there must be an internal project manager and designated BPM implementation team. Capacitate the team so they are prepared to fulfill this important role, and create regular meetings to facilitate communication within the team and between the team and management. It is wise to work with experienced external consultants, but to also foster those capacities and abilities internally. In-house experts provide a better guarantee of project success.

Set measurable and concrete benchmark indicators. Benchmarks will help to measure and demonstrate the success of a BPM implementation, or of any e-government initiative. Be sure to take a baseline indicator before the start of the project, for example average completion time, average number of errors per month, average number of official complaints, average number of cases processed per day, etc. Retake these measurements at periodic intervals. Measurable indicators will not only help demonstrate the BPM system's impact, but will also help justify the e-government initiative.

Leave time for optimization. In the case of Peru, the goal was set to transition to a BPM system by January 2009. While this goal was met in part, it did not leave enough time for evaluation and system optimization. When implementing a BPM system, it is critical to leave time for revision and improvement (hence, the optimization and not just automation of workflow.)

---

8 "E-Government at the Crossroads: World Public Sector Report" United Nations, New York, 2003. p.59

9 The Working Group on e-Government in the Developing World, "Roadmap for e-Government in the Developing World." Pacific Council on International Policy, 2002. p.18

Invest in the development of local capacities. In the case of the Congress of Peru, after a competitive bid process that included both local and multinational companies, a local BPM partner was selected. This partnership turned out to be a great strength for the project, in that the Congress had a direct relationship with the software developer and that developer was able to respond quickly and clearly to the Congress' needs. As noted by the Pacific Council on International Policy, "In the short term, the most viable (and perhaps most desired) e-government partners may be multinational companies that have proven experience and capacities to deliver. However, the long-term development of local ICT companies can, and often should, be part of e-government planning".[10]

Choose a BPM system wisely. When selecting a BPM system, the committee should investigate the advantages that each tool can offer. In some cases the most sophisticated system may not be the best or most practical for addressing the specific pain points felt by the organization. Additionally, select a system that will grow with the government in the long-term. Will the system facilitate integrations with other systems? Or will the system present challenges and become itself an obstacle down the road? BPM systems offer different features and functions, and it is important to research both proprietary and open source tools to determine which best meets the needs and resources of the particular institution.

In conclusion, as the Congress of the Republic of Peru continues with its organization-wide BPM implementation, it will continue to apply the lessons learned from the pilot phase in order to best implement a modernized, comprehensive e-government. Through the introduction of a BPM system, the Congress is steadily moving towards more openness, efficiency, and responsiveness in government operations. In order to respond to the ever-growing demand for faster and more effective services, the Congress of Peru will continue to develop its e-government capacities in order to streamline internal processes and provide enhanced services that will directly benefit the citizens of Peru.

ACKNOWLEDGMENTS

The authors would like to thank Victor Diaz Canchy, Jose Fernando Leon, Julio Cesar Laura Avendano, Patricia Cabero Tapia, and Brian Reale for their contributions to the preparation of this paper. In addition, the authors would like to express their deep gratitude to the Congress of the Republic of Peru and the Department of Information Technology for allowing us to share and reflect on the BPM implementation experience.

PROCESSMAKER OPEN SOURCE BUSINESS MANAGEMENT SOFTWARE

ProcessMaker is Open Source business process management (BPM) software that enables organizations, SMEs, and government agencies to automate document intensive, approval-based processes across systems including finance, HR and operations. ProcessMaker is an AJAX-enabled, SOA, web-based application that allows users across single and multiple sites to create and share workflows, customize forms, manage processes, and enhance reporting. ProcessMaker has been implemented in organizations including financial institutions, insurance companies, and governments. ProcessMaker is developed by Colosa, Inc., and has offices in Brooklyn, NY, Lima, Peru, and La Paz, Bolivia. For more information, visit http://www.processmaker.com

---

10 The Working Group on e-Government in the Developing World, "Roadmap for e-Government in the Developing World." Pacific Council on International Policy, 2002. p.23

REFERENCES

1. Congress of the Republic of Peru Official Website. http://www.congreso.gob.pe Accessed February 27, 2009.
2. "E-Government at the Crossroads: World Public Sector Report" United Nations, New York, 2003.
3. Fingar, Peter. "Government's BPM Imperative," 2005, CIO.com, http://www.cio.com.au/article/144136/government_bpm_imperative?fp =4&fpid=21, Accessed February 27, 2009.
4. Foley, Paul, Ximena Alfonso, John Fisher, Gail Bradbrook "eGovernment: Reaching Socially Excluded Groups?" Improvement and Development Agency for Local Government, UK, 2005.
5. Gupta, Piyush and Pranav Kumar Vashista. "An Approach for e-Government Project Assessment." Foundations of E-Government, 2007.
6. Lau, Edwin, "E-Government and the Drive for Growth and Equity". Organization for Economic Cooperation and Development, 2005.
7. OECD Background Paper: Implementing E-Government in OECD Countries: Experiences and Challenges. OECD, 2005.
8. Riley, Thomas B. and Cathia Gilbert Riley. "E-Government to E-Democracy: Examining the Evolution" Commonwealth Centre for E-Governance, Ontario, Canada, 2003.
9. SocItm, "Managing e-Government – a discussion paper". SocItm, 2003.
10. "UN E-Government Survey 2008 – From E-Governance to Connected Governance" United Nations, 2008.
11. West, Darrell M. "Improving Technology Utilization in Electronic Government around the World" Governance Studies at Brookings Institute, 2008.
12. The Working Group on e-Government in the Developing World, "Roadmap for e-Government in the Developing World." Pacific Council on International Policy, 2002.

Process Systematization of the High Court of Justice, Mexico

Juan Chacón, Vanina Marcote, PECTRA Technology, USA and Luis Ramirez, ACERTI, Mexico

ABSTRACT

In this chapter, we analyze the implementation carried out by the High Court of Justice (Mexico) developed within the framework of e-governance strategy. The project included the integration of tasks of 51 first instance courts and their second instance courts, each one of them with numerous individual, complex, and manual processes. In addition, all the value chain participants—both internal and external—were integrated: Organization (Courts, Courtrooms); citizens (Lawyers, parties involved in the trial), and the Government.

INTRODUCTION: THE ORGANIZATIONAL CONTEXT

In an effort to offer an answer to the citizens' needs of having transparent public management and, with the purpose of being protagonists in the knowledge society, the Mexican government has developed an e-government strategy which frames its actions. To do this, it was crucial to make a change in mentality, in methodology and in perspective, which is translated into a change of the public service concept for citizens. Mexican public institutions have been forced to reformulate their guidelines and their methods to apply in service provision as well as in the costs administration derived from them and to improve communication with the citizens in a simple and effective way.

In this context, the High Court of Justice developed the Integral Program of Processes Systematization (BPM), offering a faster, more dynamic and more transparent legal management.

In this sense, the implementation of a work platform based in Processes (BPM) was not limited to certain courts nor to any areas considered strategic by the Judicial Power, but it was conceived as an ***Integral Program*** which unifies the jurisdictional and administrative processes to integrate them in an unique language to follow the activities applicable to each Court, Lower Court and Administrative Areas.

To do this, it was necessary to integrate the tasks of the following areas which make up the organization: 51 first instance courts and second instance courts, each one with numerous individual, complex, and manual processes.

- **Courts of first instance:** Their function is to administer and solve lawsuits in civil, family, business and criminal matters. This function includes analyzing the claims and statements of the parties, receiving the evidence presented for the case and passing sentence. The project includes 51 courts distributed as follows: 15 for criminal matters, eight mixed, two lower mixed, three for family matters, six for civil matters, 15 for civil and family courts and two specialized in justice for teenagers.

- **Second instance courts:** their function is to learn and solve the appeals, which allows making a new revision of the court resolutions challenged.

The project was started with the goal of guiding the actions of the Judicial Power of the State of Hidalgo, assigning people in charge, times and short, medium and long term goals to offer a more effective public service and to strengthen the Judicial Power at the institutional level.

THREE KEY INNOVATIONS: BUSINESS, PROCESS AND ORGANIZATION

During the implementation carried out, we identify three main levels of innovation: a business level, where different actors were integrated; a process level, which shows the best practices in BPM; and an organizational level, which shows the changes the High Court of Justice has gone through.

Business level: how the value chain is integrated

The development of the project has a strong impact on the main participants of the value chain, linking internal and external participants to the organization, geographically distributed throughout the State of Hidalgo, Mexico, including: Organization (Courts, Courtrooms); citizens (Lawyers, parties involved in the trial), and the Government.

To illustrate the relationship of the value chain through the solution, the graphic below is shown. Every process starts with a "promotion" at the Filing Office. At this stage, the type of trial (matter), court and location is distributed according to criteria. Once the court receives the requirement, all the activities linked to the First Instance processes are activated and—in case of appeal—the Second Instance court activities are started. All this is controlled by the government and by an online follow-up by the citizens.

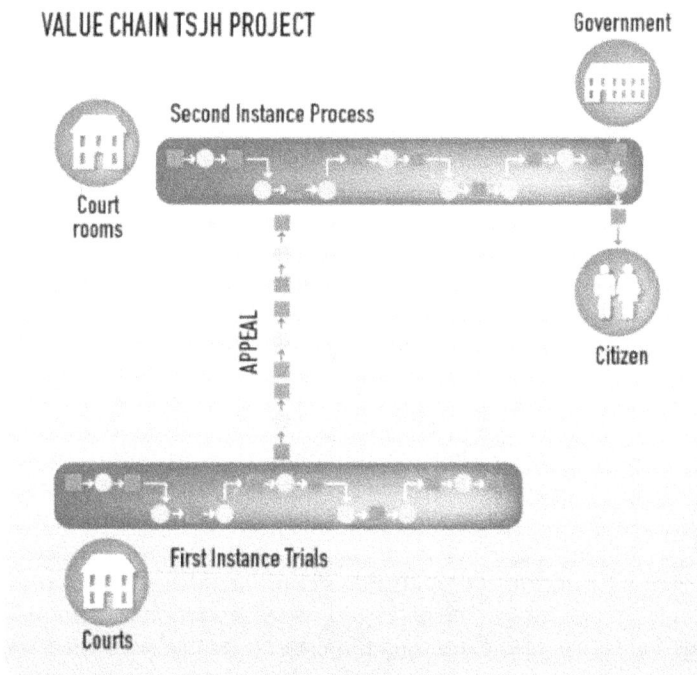

VALUE CHAIN TSJH PROJECT

Organization's participants

At the level of the organization's participants, three main functionalities are presented: traceability and on-line follow-up, judicial funds management, information security with access in accordance to profiles, and *Business Intelligence* tools.

Traceability and online follow-up.

After implementing the project, public officers can have detailed information of the process stage in which the legal action is, as regards the status and physical location of the file. Sentences corresponding to each event can also be accessed to on-line.

Judicial funds management:

The process also includes the Judicial funds management, which consists of handling values on consignment to the court when, in some cases, one of the parties makes payment deposits. This is so; for example, when a father pays alimony for his children to the court while the trial is in process and until the legal custody is determined. The judicial fund gives the money to the mother when the process is finished and it ensures law enforcement.

Value-handling by the judicial fund is an extremely careful and priority task. Through the BPM solution inclusion, it was possible to establish clearly the value handling within the court, which also allowed tracking its location both in the courts and in the fund itself, offering total transparency in the process.

Access to information in accordance with profiles.

The third key point that manifests the impact of the implementation at business level in the internal participants of the organization is the access to information in accordance with user profiles, which ensures its security and confidentiality. Profiles internally considered are the following:

At the court
- Judge (1st instance) / Magistrate (2nd instance)
- Agreement secretary.
- Clerk of the court.
- Commissioner.

At the institution
- Judicial Fund.
- Administration.
- Accounts office.
- Presidency.

Business Intelligence Tools.

Having access to centralized management information to make decisions and to plan the public administration is another of the central contributions of the solution. This allows having quantitative and qualitative information of the execution of defined processes, bottle necks and budget execution. It also allows the total control of the management with clear, accurate and objective metrics.

Citizens:

In the other hand, the solution also allows providing a high added value service for citizens: control and on-line follow-up of legal actions and files statuses.

It is done by the list notification system published on the Internet in the portal: http://148.245.145.212/notificaciones/frm_busqueda_notificaciones.aspx, where an information service which benefits lawyers involved in the trials and the parties is offered.

The notification is published automatically once a resolution in relation to an event is achieved, and it allows informing the parties about the "process status" and "the result". This notification is automated for all the courts participating in the project: 17 courts in 17 cities geographically distributed in judicial districts.

In the portal, the main functionalities offered to the citizens are:
- To consult the notifications by entity
- To consult the court to which he/she was assigned
- To assign several search filters (e.g. file number or date on which the notification was issued)
- The notification system can be accessed from Internet 24/7.

State and Federal Government.

There are two main contributions offered by the solution in the integration of participants belonging to the government: transparency in management and information security.

Transparency portal.

At government level, the main benefit offered by the solution is the transparency portal, which can be accessed by the following URL: http://www.pjhidalgo.gob.mx/trans/index.php. Transparency, apart from being the core of the Program for Institutional Strengthening, is an obligation on the part of the Federal and State Government and all their institutions.

This transparency portal allows users to:
- Review all the documentation related to transparency regulations.
- Consult information request statistics in real time.
- Review the transparency publications in all the corresponding instances.
- Request detailed information about salaries, wages, commissions, legal operation, among others.
- Link with INFOMEX system through the website to request non-restricted information for the citizens (http://infomex.hidalgo.gob.mx/infomexhidalgo/).
- Settle an accountability culture.

Apart from accountability and information transparency, the system is linked through the process to the publication of sentences of each matter dealt both in the first and second instance processes and for civil, criminal and family matters.

Information security: access by profiles.

Also in the case of external users belonging to National and State Government, the solution proposes an information access scheme through profiles, which ensures confidential information security. Profiles considered are the following:

The Government:
- Instituto Federal de acceso a la información Pública (Federal Institute of Access to Public information).
- State Government.
- Record, statistics and universities institutions.
- Process level: a technical view

The process implemented consists of an automated administration model, as a solution of process integration for the management and justice administration of the Judicial Power of the State of Hidalgo. One innovation of the project was the creation of a **unique process of civil, criminal and family matters**; this is why all the courts of the 17 judicial districts must comply with these processes, reducing the discrepancy of criteria and procedures in each one of the courts.

The implementation of the project was based in the following architecture:

Computer Networks and wireless networks implemented in each judicial building allow computer systems to store information directly in the server, so that the local server data are validated and consulted in real time.

The BPM Solution functioned as the basis on which all the processes are executed, integrating databases and intranet applications for different functionalities, such as file traceability.

And at **integration** level, vertical applications have been developed (web applications) in Microsoft .Net 2003 (Visual Basic) and a Microsoft SQL 2000 database is used, developed under the guidelines of the implemented processes and internal policies of the organization.

Organization level: change in management & external recognition

For the development, implementation and maintenance of the project a special area in the System Department has been created; this area is aligned with and specialized in the Process Management philosophy. It includes different profiles, which go from project leaders to functional analysts and developers.

This team works in a transdisciplinary manner with the teams of the "owner" areas of the processes which were automated, including judges specialized in criminal and civil-family matters and officers involved in the tasks to be developed.

Impact at the organization level has been really important since it implied changing substantially the organizational culture, with strong actions by Change Management and areas and departments integration.

The impact in the organization: competitive advantages

The implementation the BPM solution allows the High Court of Justice of the State of Hidalgo to count with the main competitive advantages described below:

Efficient management processes: They integrate workflows to create fast, productive and highly organized management processes.

Service quality: It provides the tools necessary to become an administration oriented towards providing quality services to the citizens.

Strategic information: The solution provides key information to make crucial decisions, allowing planning and accurate control of resources and costs.

Advanced functionalities: They allow managing the strategy, investments, human resources, records and relations with the citizens, providing the necessary technology to create modern and simple services.

Policies and government plans measurement: It allows having quantifiable results for a responsible use of budgets.

Security: To facilitate the compliance of legal issues in relation to information security and protection.

In the framework of the best practices and competitive advantages, the institution was granted the award to Innovation and Quality in 2007 by the Government of the State of Hidalgo to the most innovative institutions of the Public Sector. Thanks to this award, the organization was positioned both at social and political level for its innovation and quality.

BEST PRACTICES: CERTIFIED QUALITY METHODOLOGY

The development and implementation of the project was based on the quality methodology certified under **ISO 9000:2000 standards.** From the implementation of this successful solution, we can highlight as Best Practices and Learning Points:

- Follow-up of implementation methodology certified by global standards.
- Thorough evaluation of the business context and the customer's needs, both current and future.
- Thorough documentation of processes and data gathering.
- Execution and monitoring of the project together with the customer, with milestones and deliverables defined at the beginning of the implementation.
- Use of risk and diverts management methodology.
- Satisfaction of all needs presented by value chain participants in the market to which the solution aims.
- Thorough market studies for the detailed gathering of these needs.
- Methodological framework:

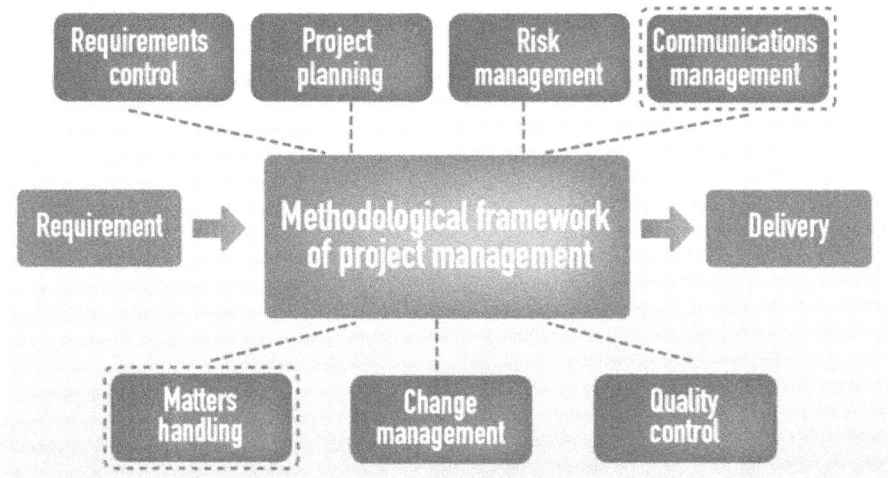

Implementation:

To plan the development and application of this technological platform made necessary the prioritization of those areas which require immediate implementation of this information management scheme. To this end, a 6-month work scheme was defined. Its goal was to gather the civil, family and criminal trial processes, connectivity, training and release of five pilot applications in the same number of courts corresponding to civil, criminal, family, and mixed and lower mixed legal matters.

Once the functionality goals and expectations were achieved, after the first 6 months, a three-month period of program repetition in the rest of the Judicial Districts was started to operate in all the courts.

THE RESULTS: MULTIPLE BENEFITS

We can identify several levels of benefits of this implementation: cost savings, time reductions, better service for citizens and productivity increases. The solutions administer an annual average of 40,000 legal actions and lead to the following main results:

- Time saving of administrative paperwork: 90 percent.
- Time saving of jurisdictional paperwork: 60 percent.
- Reduction in the average length of a trial. Before the process implementation, trials lasted two years or more; after the process automation and unification, this period was reduced to 1 year.
- Time reduction when submitting records; from 30 seconds before the implementation to one second after the implementation.
- This time saving as regards downtime goes up to 10,000 hours per year for citizens and staff. This is a consequence of the online traceability of files and status which considerably reduces the visits to the places where the documents are found.
- Goal fulfillment of management transparency, through government indicators which measure technological innovation and quality.
- Traceability of the process and employee control.

Section 2

The Business Value of BPM and Workflow

Application Provisioning in the Cloud

Jon Pyke, Cordys, Netherlands

EVERYONE'S HAVING CLOUDY THOUGHTS!

The economic turmoil, globalization and the changes in the New World Order means that organizations cannot afford to waste time, human and financial resources on processes that can rapidly and easily be automated and managed. Businesses need to transform themselves into agile operations capable of turning a constantly-changing business environment into opportunities. Process innovation and speed of change are the key opportunities for competitive differentiation moving forwards. Traditional IT solutions are finding themselves under stress as the struggle to meet the demands of the business leaders and customers they serve.

Unfortunately the IT organization, responsible for facilitating changes demanded by the business, often falls short of being able to do just that. Many studies and surveys show that changes to IT infrastructure and applications are fraught with complexity, costing much more and taking much longer than initially anticipated. It is not uncommon for an IT organization to take five or more years to make significant enterprise-wide changes; this pace just doesn't support the business initiatives required in today's business climate.

So it is inevitable the businesses leaders are looking for new ways to use computing power to meet their needs and fortuitously two trends are beginning coalesce to provide a new way of delivering applications as services. These two are:

1. The Cloud
2. Process Centric Situational Applications.

THE CLOUD

The entire field of computing is fast becoming a "cloud"—a collection of disembodied services accessible from anywhere and detached from the underlying hardware.

There will be many ways in which the cloud will change businesses and the economy, most of them hard to predict, but one theme is already emerging. Businesses are becoming more like the technology itself: more adaptable, more interwoven and more specialized. These developments may not be new, but the advent of cloud computing will speed them up.

A recent analysis of cloud computing in the Economist[1] stated that there were a plethora of data centers worldwide and estimated that 7,000 data centers existed in America alone. Most of these data centers were one-off designs that had grown over the years. Many surveys show that these data centers are highly inefficient. According to a study by McKinsey, a consultancy, and the Uptime Institute, a think-tank, on average only six percent of server capacity is used. Nearly 30 percent are no longer in use at all and many organizations are unaware of which ap-

---

[1] Let it Rise. A special report on corporate IT. 25th October 2008.

plication is running on which server. What a waste and think of the impact on the environment.

According to IDC a quarter of corporate data centers in America have run out of space for more servers. For others cooling has become a big constraint and often utilities cannot provide the extra power needed for an expansion. IDC believed that many data centers will be consolidated and overhauled. Hewlett-Packard used to have 85 data centers with 19,000 IT workers worldwide, but expected to cut this down to six facilities in America with just 8,000 employees by the end of this year, reducing its IT budget from four percent to two percent of revenue. HP is not alone and the financial "Perfect Storm" will speed up this trend as companies strive to become more efficient.

This cloud of computing resources will not only effect the number of data centers and the number of people employed in them—it will have profound implications for the organization. On one level the cloud will be a huge collection of electronic services based on standards. Many web-based services are built to be integrated into existing business processes. IT systems will permit organizations to become more modular and flexible and this will lead to further specialization. In the cloud it will become even easier to outsource business processes, or at least those parts of them where firms do not enjoy a competitive advantage. This also means that companies will rely more on services provided by others.

Furthermore, there will be not just one cloud but a number of different sorts: private ones and public ones, which themselves will divide into general-purpose and specialized ones. People are already using the term "intercloud" to mean a federation of all kinds of clouds, in the same way that the internet is a network of networks. And all of those clouds will be full of applications and services.

There will be many ways in which the cloud will change businesses and the economy, most of them hard to predict, but one theme is already emerging. In the current economic environment businesses will have to become more like the technology itself: more adaptable, more interwoven and more specialized.

SITUATIONAL APPLICATION PROVISIONING

Situational Application Provisioning is a very different proposition from what we think of as an application; it therefore represents a very different opportunity and is a mechanism whereby a user can put together an "application" based around normal working patterns, using readily available services.

This means that is possible to handle any sort of business problem usually tackled by enterprise solutions by being able to leverage the capability to associate virtually any number of web services within the context of an application. Process Provisioning is effectively an application generator within a process and is inherently more flexible, easier to provide, easier to manage and easier to use than traditional ERP-type products.

BUT WHAT DO WE MEAN BY "SITUATIONAL APPLICATIONS"?

According to Wikipedia, a situational application is software created for a small group of users with specific needs. The application typically has a short life span, and is often created within the group where it is used, sometimes by the users themselves. As the requirements of a small team using the application change, the situational application often also continues to evolve to accommodate these changes. Significant changes in requirements may lead to an abandonment of the situational application altogether—in some cases it is just easier to develop a new one than to evolve the one in use.

According to IBM[2] *situational applications* (SA) describe applications built to address a particular situation, problem, or challenge. The development life cycle of these types of applications is quite different from the traditional IT-developed application. SAs are usually built by power users using short, iterative development life cycles that are measured in days or weeks, not months or years. As the requirements change, the SA often continues to evolve to accommodate these changes. Significant changes in requirements may lead to an abandonment of the used application altogether; in some cases it's just easier to develop a new one than to update the one in use.

The idea of end-user computing in the enterprise is not new. Development of applications by amateur programmers using IBM Lotus® Notes®, Microsoft® Excel spreadsheets in conjunction with Microsoft Access, or other tools is widespread. What's new in this mix is the impressive growth of community-based computing coupled with an overall increase in computer skills, the introduction of new technologies, and an increased need for business agility.

WHY IS THIS APPROACH DIFFERENT?

Treb Ryan said in an opinion piece back in March 07[3] that, "Most software companies think on-demand applications (SaaS) are a replacement for traditional business software. They couldn't be more wrong.

"Sure, these software-as-a-service (SaaS) applications are sold as a service and paid for per-transaction, but they are developed, sold and delivered in the same manner as traditional licensed software.

"The most successful software-as-a-service (SaaS) companies do not think of themselves as software companies selling software on-demand, but as Web companies with business users accessing a service over the Internet. These companies realize that to effectively start and grow a SaaS business, they need to act more like a consumer-based Web company than a traditional enterprise software company."

WHY DO WE NEED PROCESS TECHNOLOGY TO DELIVER SITUATIONAL APPLICATIONS?

There are two clear reasons for needing process technology to underpin the provision of these applications:

1. Rapid Innovation—Ra-In Clouds4
   The cloud is, as discussed above, the ideal mechanism for utilizing extensive computing power; be that storage or specific applications such as SalesForce.com. As it stands it saves you money. It doesn't help you innovate; the cloud does not enable you to simply build applications to meet the needs. Process technology, in its broadest sense, lets you do this in a easy and flexible way; the processes orchestrate the interaction and integration of services.
2. Compliance
   Situational Applications can be very disruptive and lead to anarchy and a breakdown of corporate governance and compliance. Think of all those Excel spreadsheets—Situational Applications—that are used to run most businesses; no control, no compliance, no ownership.

---

2 The rise of Web-based situational applications
http://www.ibm.com/developerworks/webservices/library/ws-soa-situational1/
3 Treb Ryan, OpSource http://www.sandhill.com/opinion/editorial.php?id=125&page=1
4 RA-IN is a Capgemini initiative

Process enablement of these types of applications will provide ownership, control and auditability; making the compliant with the corporate demands without stifling innovation and change.

THE APPLICATION TARGET

The initial thrust for the cloud is data center and "standard" applications such as SalesForce.com and Google Apps. But this is just the start; the cloud has significantly more potential than simply being able to provide specialized applications and flexible data storage.

Gartner defines cloud computing as a style of computing where massively scalable IT-related capabilities are provided "as a service" using Internet technologies to multiple external customers.

"During the past 15 years, a continuing trend toward IT industrialization has grown in popularity as IT services delivered via hardware, software and people are becoming repeatable and usable by a wide range of customers and service providers," said Daryl Plummer, managing vice president and Gartner Fellow. "This is due, in part to the commoditization and standardization of technologies, in part to virtualization and the rise of service-oriented software architectures, and most importantly, to the dramatic growth in popularity of the Internet."

Plummer said that taken together, these three major trends constitute the basis of a discontinuity that will create a new opportunity to shape the relationship between those who use IT services and those who sell them.

As we have seen, business process management has a key role in enabling the cloud to deliver applications; more importantly situational applications, in a new, flexible and cost effective way, and we call this Application Service Provisioning. The cloud then has the potential radically change the way the small to medium sized business market operates and at the same time disrupt the enterprise software market making it redundant and obsolete—almost overnight.

THE CLOUD AS A DELIVERY MECHANISM

According to Gartner, The types of IT services that can be provided through a cloud are wide-reaching. And include:

- Compute facilities to provide computational services that use central processing unit (CPU) cycles without buying computers.
- Storage services to store data and documents without having to continually grow farms of storage networks and servers.
- SaaS such as CRM services through multitenant shared facilities so clients can manage their customers without buying software.

The advent of the cloud means that the focus has moved up from the infrastructure implementations to mechanisms that access to the capabilities provided. This means that the ultimate measure of success will be how the services are consumed and whether that leads to new business opportunities.

Gartner predicts that the impact of cloud computing on IT vendors will be huge. Established vendors have a great presence in traditional software markets, and as new Web 2.0 and cloud business models evolve and expand outside of consumer markets, a great deal could change.

"The vendors are at very different levels of maturity," said David Cearley, vice president and Gartner Fellow. "The consumer-focused vendors are the most mature in delivering what Gartner calls a 'cloud/web platform' from technology and community perspectives, but the business-focused vendors have rich business services and, at times, are very adept at selling business services."

How do business take advantage of low cost, on demand, computing power to drive their business growth, make them more efficient and better able to compete in a global market economy?

This is where SaaS-enabled BPM platforms come into play by providing an environment where business users and developers can work together to build new applications from scratch or by mashing up services that are widely and readily available in the cloud.

1. These applications will almost certainly start out as situational or *ad-hoc* applications.
2. These applications are important to the company but are not ones that are strategic line of business requirements.
3. These applications are ideal for process centric deployment in the cloud.

WHY IS THIS SO?

Despite the fact that these Situational Applications are not strategic, they do have to be properly controlled. That means they have to be compliant, auditable, recorded and controlled. Furthermore there is every possibility that they will have to be fully integrated into some "on premise" applications, or even outsourced processes, therefore they need to show proper and full corporate governance. For most, deploying these applications in the cloud is too radical unless they can be properly controlled and managed. Furthermore even though they do not involve large IT investment or involvement they cannot be allowed to flaunt corporate standards; building situational applications based on proper process control in the cloud is by far and away the only way to do it.

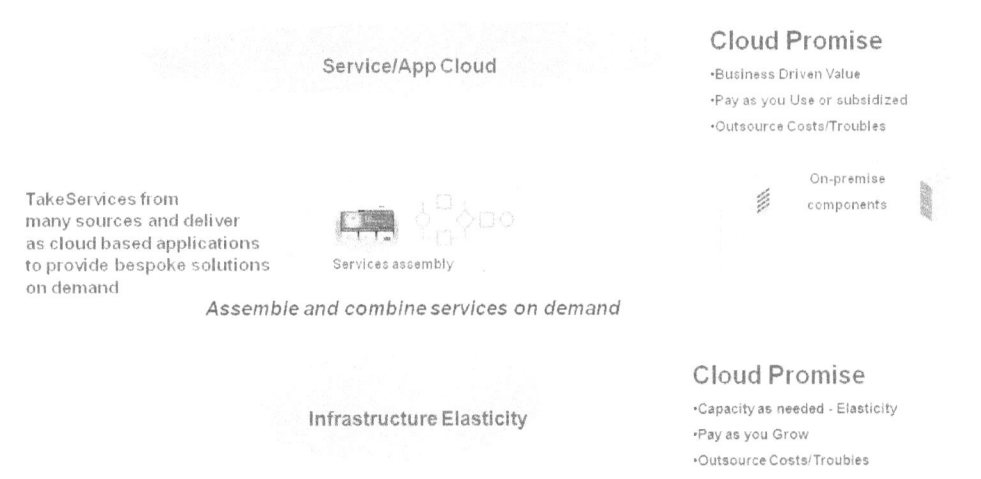

Service/App Cloud

Cloud Promise
•Business Driven Value
•Pay as you Use or subsidized
•Outsource Costs/Troubles

TakeServices from many sources and deliver as cloud based applications to provide bespoke solutions on demand

Services assembly

On-premise components

Assemble and combine services on demand

Infrastructure Elasticity

Cloud Promise
•Capacity as needed - Elasticity
•Pay as you Grow
•Outsource Costs/Troubles

Fig 1. Typical Cloud/On Premise set up

The above diagram illustrates the promise of the cloud in two areas; Service/App Cloud and the Infrastructure Elasticity Cloud. At the Service /App Cloud the promise is that the Cloud will deliver Business Driven Value, a subscription model based on either "Pay as you Use" or through subsidy and the ability to outsource costs and or troubles. At the Infrastructure Cloud the promise is that the

151

cloud will deliver capacity as needed, a usage model based on "Pay as you Grow" and the ability to outsource costs and or troubles.

In addition the organization will require access to On-premise Enterprise applications such as SAP, Oracle etc and these will be accessed through both Private and Public Business Application Clouds.

The combination of the high availability of cloud infrastructure at a low cost and innovative cloud services means that the organization needs an Assembly and Orchestration layer in the Cloud to fully deliver useful business advantages.

Benefits of this approach to the business users:

1. No significant IT investment
2. Low start up cost
3. Addresses annoying needs in a controlled way
4. All Operational expenditure – no capital outlay
5. Solutions are compliant with corporate standards of governance
6. Easy to change
7. Pay per use – no idle investments laying around
8. Provides real and tangible cloud benefit without the risk

APPLICATION PROVISIONING IN THE CLOUD

The following situational applications might be considered to be the minimum requirement for true office administration type services that one might expect Application Provisioning to deliver.

- Help Desk management
- Project Management
- Travel Approval
- Requirements Management
- Expense reporting
- Payment requests
- Budget Approval
- New Hire Setup
- Training

WHAT DO WE DO DIFFERENTLY?

In order to truly leverage the power of the SaaS model, we need to reconsider the SaaS BPM proposition; we shouldn't think of this as BPM as a Service, more a *platform as a service*, a redefined application server if you will.

SaaS applications that emulate consumer Web sites in the way they are developed and sold tend to achieve much more success than those that emulate traditional enterprise software. Therefore we need to put the application in the hands of the consumer not the technician.

Software companies that cast a blind eye to the Web-based model, whether originating online, migrating to SaaS or taking a hybrid approach, will find that the ever-winding road to success will be a frustrating excursion on the road to nowhere.

Business Transformation Blueprint—BPM as Key Enabler

Vinaykumar S. Mummigatti, IBM Global Business Services and Tom Bobrowski, Capgemini, USA

ABSTRACT

Economic uncertainties put executive management under increased pressure to react to changing market conditions, protect revenues and deliver cost efficiencies quickly. Management needs to transform how the business operates without major new investments. This paper addresses how Business Process Management (BPM) can play a key role in enabling an effective business transformation (BT), driving measurable results while maximizing value from existing technology investments. This paper is an effort to provide an holistic look at Business Transformation and to provide a methodical approach to evaluate, implement and measure the outcome from BT.

INTRODUCTION

Global companies are constantly rediscovering themselves in order to keep pace with changing business dynamics, specifically the emergence of new product and service offerings, business models, organizational structures, technology adoptions, and customer service metrics. The main determinant of success is the ability to **adapt**. Winners succeed because of leadership style, organizational culture, and the ability to identify, measure and constantly optimize key performance parameters.

"Business Transformation" has become a buzzword, if not a major trend, in the plotting of every CEO's strategic roadmap. While many companies have been able to achieve success in one-off BT initiatives, it isn't really **transformation** until outcomes are measured and the results built into a repeatable, improvable model.

The focus of this paper is to demonstrate how enterprise investments in Business Process Management enable the cost-effective initiation, implementation, and measurement of successful BT initiatives.

We are seeing some very significant and universal trends in the global business arena:

1. The rate of **Change** is accelerating
2. The pressures on **Capital** are intensifying
3. There is increasing demand for more transparent **Compliance and Control**
4. Extreme competition is enforcing the need for **Global Sourcing**

What do these trends mean for business leaders? *The ability to innovate is the key to survival.* Companies like Apple, Google and Cisco, who have made *innovation and transformation* a serious part of their cultures, prove the point. Especially in global markets where competitors have similar access to capital, technology, and talent, the winners all display vision, innovation-friendly cultures, superior talent management, financial discipline, and the intelligent deployment of technologies.

What differentiates any two competitive companies with similar strengths? Based on proprietary case studies and daily interactions with clients, we believe *winning companies leverage their processes to create competitive advantage*. A quote from Cisco's John Chambers, from an interview published in *Harvard Business Review*, substantiates the point:

"From a business-model and leadership perspective, we're seeing a massive shift from management by command and control to management by collaboration and teamwork. You could almost say this shift is as revolutionary as the assembly line. Business processes are being turned upside down to better compete in a global environment. The truth is that each time a market is in transition, you can either gain or lose market share. If there was a time that we lost market share, it was because we moved too slowly so we've had to build speed and scale into all of our processes. Spotting a market transition only counts if you can capture it and execute on it."

Many companies have invested in BPM initiatives and technologies without larger transformational goals in mind. As this paper focuses on providing an implementable and measurable blueprint for BT, it will demonstrate how BPM is an inherent component of the BT framework. The essence is that one cannot exist without the other and demonstrating returns from BT without leveraging BPM is next to impossible.

DEFINING THE TURFS

Business Transformation is about driving fundamental change in the way an enterprise conducts its business. This change could be driven by customers, investors or competitors. Transformation is a "lifestyle change," not just a one-time activity. It's about how a company manages itself through the various stages of the business life-cycle and adapts to change in real time. Everything a company does, or delivers, is defined and governed by its processes. Business processes are the underlying linkages between people, systems, and external entities like suppliers and customers. BT programs need to integrate strategy, organizational structure, people, processes, and technology in a holistic approach.

Business Process Management is a set of concepts, methods and tools used to define, measure and automate processes for continual improvement in operational performance. BPM provides an orchestration layer between people, processes and systems, thus providing the ability to measure performance and continually optimize any business process.

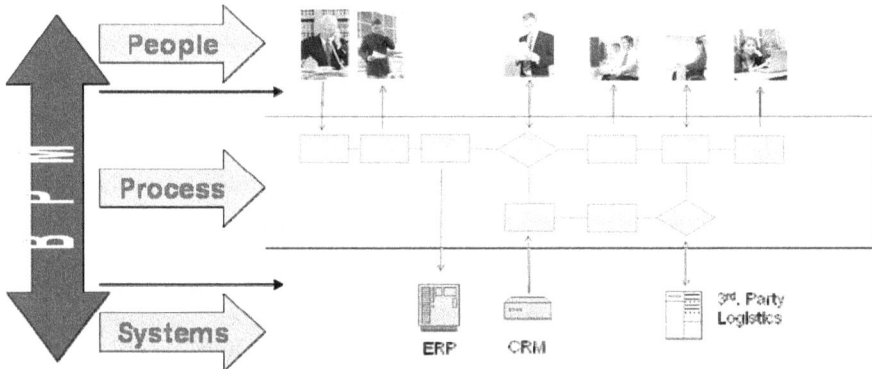

Figure 1: BPM Provides an Orchestration layer across People, Process and Systems

The words *Innovation* and *Invention* are often used synonymously. Any invention which brings about a betterment or improvement of a product, service or process is considered an innovation. Innovation refers to a company's ability to succeed by continually rediscovering itself. There are elements of process and method in innovation, hence making it measurable. There is innovation in process and a process of innovation, and here we look at with innovation in process and everything an organization does to create ongoing value.

Quoting Peter F. Drucker, "Innovation is the specific instrument of entrepreneurship. Innovation is the act that endows resources with a new capacity to create wealth."

Driving business transformation through continuous innovation using the measurable and repeatable approaches offered exclusively by BPM is the theme of this paper.

SCOPE FOR BT AND ASSOCIATED CHALLENGES

As organizations grow larger and more complex, silos are created separating layers of management, lines of business and operating geographies. The main problem with silos is that they hinder implementation of corporate strategy across lines of business and geographies and the alignment of capital investments to corporate directives.

Annual reports published by companies basically aggregate financial numbers in a standard format accepted by statutory bodies. We have globally accepted standards such as GAAP (Generally Accepted Accounting Principles). But as we move towards real-time control of performance, it's important that we start measuring the process metrics which govern the financial numbers. In addition to standard financial ratios, we can publish process metrics as a part of quarterly and annual reporting, which would be of keen interest to analysts in comparing and benchmarking performers versus non performers. While the financial numbers say something implicit about operational efficiencies, if we could establish **"Generally Accepted Process Metrics (GAPM)"** by industry vertical, we would be able to directly and explicitly compare and contrast peer company operations. Also, bringing uniformity to performance standards through process metrics would drive a greater degree of alignment (cross-silo) between corporate strategy and down stream investments.

It is in this context that the role of **"Chief Transformation Officer"** becomes very critical. The need for a BT blueprint becomes evident as we try to bring common process measures and develop a culture of innovation to bridge the gaps between process benchmarks and actual performance.

BT has garnered lot of hype but it has also been met with apprehension for its lack of ability to deliver true results. It's important that we address the challenges before getting into any discussions on implementation.

- The basic challenge arises from lack of ownership for any BT initiative.
- There is no methodology or process for implementing and measuring BT initiatives, hence a new path must be walked every time a new BT initiative is undertaken.
- BT is usually looked upon as a one-time activity. Whereas, BT is a round-trip endeavor in which outputs are measured and follow-on phases identified to continually improve overall outcomes.
- Most organizations do not align Technology and BT initiatives. Technology is a great enabler for BT as it helps ensure outcomes are measured and constantly improved.

HOW DOES BPM ENABLED TRANSFORMATION DRIVE MEASURABLE BOTTOM-LINE RESULTS?

Here are some real-life examples of BPM-enabled business transformation initiatives which have resulted in tangible metrics and ongoing performance improvements:

- An engineering services company transforms its customer management, invoicing and accounts receivable processes to shorten its revenue collection cycle, use working capital more effectively, and improve profitability.
- A retail or manufacturing company radically reduces its capital requirements and improves operating results by streamlining its supply chain processes – closely monitoring supplier performance and payment terms, streamlining material processing, improving shipping performance and gaining real-time inventory visibility.
- An insurance or financial services company transforms its account opening, loan origination and underwriting processes to become faster and cheaper while delivering best-in class customer service.

These examples illustrate how in most cases we can and should link the Business Transformation initiatives with the Technology Transformation initiatives.

The following diagram paints a clearer picture:

Business Transformation Initiatives			Technology Transformation Initiatives	
Product Innovation	Managed Processes, collaboration and seamless flow of ideas and content, foster Innovation	"Process Management" The common theme	Legacy Modernization	Abstract process and Rules into an agile layer to Modernize Legacy apps to deliver time to market & cost goals
Business Transformation Outsourcing (BTO)	Strategic Partnering to reengineer and optimize prior to outsourcing		Service Oriented Architecture	Process driven applications call services and enable faster time to market
Eliminate Costs, supply chain optimization, Zero Touch	Reduce manual touch points - Self Service and end-end automation		Straight Through Processing	Eliminates most of human decision making and data entry in a process
Managing Customers for growth	Customer value creation to growing revenue per customer; next generation Customer management		Business activity monitoring (BAM), Event Driven Processing	Real Time process monitoring and exceptions management

Figure 2: Alignment between Business and Technology Transformation Initiatives

As we can see from each of these initiatives, it's clear that process is the common theme across both streams. Tying business and IT initiatives through process goals is the best way to achieve measurable returns from BT. Many of the challenges in achieving measurable success through BT get addressed through this alignment.

The following table presents different industries and relevant Key performance indicators (KPI's) relevant to their core business models. This should help in further elaboration of the above table.

Industry→ Samples KPI's	Manufacturing	Financial services	Retail	Healthcare
Supply Chain Optimization	High	Low	High	High
Time-To-Market	High	High	High	High
New Product development	High	High	Low	High
Customer service/ Contact center	Medium	High	High	High
New Business origination	Low	High	Low	Low
Governance and compliance	Medium	High	Low	High

Figure 3: Relevance of KPI's to industry business models

BRINGING ALL ELEMENTS TOGETHER – A FRAMEWORK FOR BT

How to get started: The Business Transformation Blueprint.

Even before recent economic developments, the role of the CIO was changing from an IT executive to a Chief Process Officer, responsible for accelerating business transformation via technology. In this evolving role, CIOs are challenged with a steeper set of expectations:

- Investors are demanding more tangible business value for IT investments.
- Given volatile business dynamics, how well can any given IT solution map to rapidly changing requirements, adapt to the needs of users, and produce anticipated returns?
- How can IT reduce cost and risk, while accelerating the delivery of new business capabilities?

In order for CIOs and IT departments to reliably answer these questions and drive business transformation, they need to understand the business ***value chain*** and the potential for specific process changes.

As a first step, a **"Business Transformation Blueprint"** should be developed to identify high-payback process improvement opportunities.

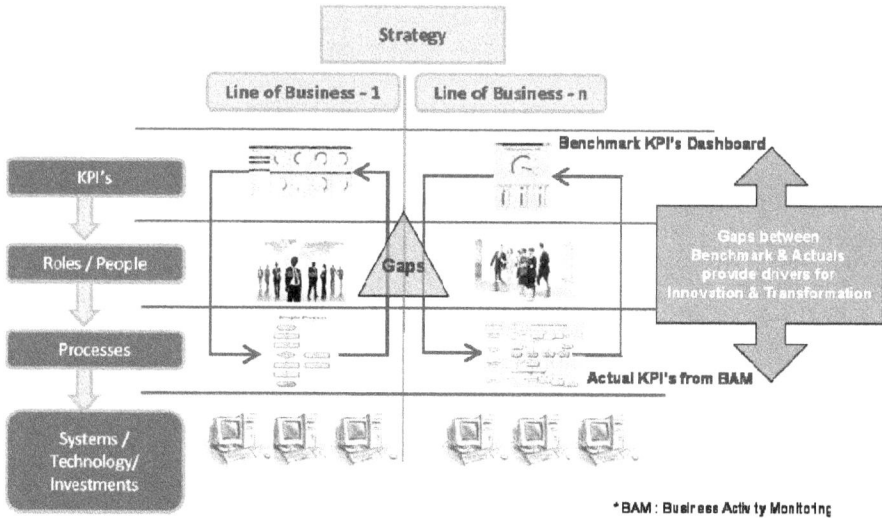

Figure 4: Components of a BT Blueprint and their linkages

Strategic planning involves visioning, goal setting, and the development of organizational objectives for the near and long term. Once the direction is decided, it's important to conduct a SWOT (strengths, weaknesses, opportunities and threats) analysis to evaluate the relative position of the firm, i.e. the firm's starting point. Strategies typically evolve around pricing, market share, global footprint, mergers and acquisitions, new products, restructuring, and re-engineering.

As chosen strategies are implemented through specific initiatives, it becomes important for returns to be measured in terms of their impact on key metrics such as revenue, profitability, and delivery (on-time) performance.

Each financial measure is controlled by different levers. Companies that know how to use these levers to achieve desired performance will be able to manage change and win in a dynamic environment. These levers are familiarly known as "Key Performance Indicators (KPIs)."

Defining KPIs is the first step towards the practical measurement of any strategic initiative. As part of each KPI metric we also need to drill down to define:

- Who is accountable for each KPI?
- What processes drive each KPI?
- What systems enable or contribute to these processes and, in turn, enable and contribute to each KPI?

A clear articulation of the value chain governs the alignment of strategy to investments in technology or other assets.

Let us explore how innovation becomes a part of this value chain and examine the triggers of innovation. Interestingly, the linkage between KPIs, people and processes is what drives innovation. The gaps between KPI benchmarks and actual metrics, drive people within an organization to find a better way to close those gaps. ***KPIs are the tools, process innovation is the means, and business transformation is the desirable end***.

This concept of a blueprint tries to form a linkage between key variables, such as strategy, goals, KPIs, people, processes and technology (systems). Because we can tie the highest level of strategy to lower levels of investments, a good blueprint enables a company to remain aligned to business objectives via tangible metrics.

BT JOURNEY AND LIFE CYCLE

As indicated earlier, BT is a journey and not an end in itself. Hence we need to keep an evolutionary mindset and phased approach when embarking on enterprise-wide BT initiatives. The key variables which define maturity are related to cultural change, process orientation, metrics-driven performance, education and adoption of BT methods, demonstration of early and measurable success, repeatable methods, technology enablers, and a governance model.

This section addresses the stages of the typical BT journey. Although by no means the only or even optimal path, it helps by suggesting a framework for charting progress. To make this chart more practical, the next section provides the key variables.

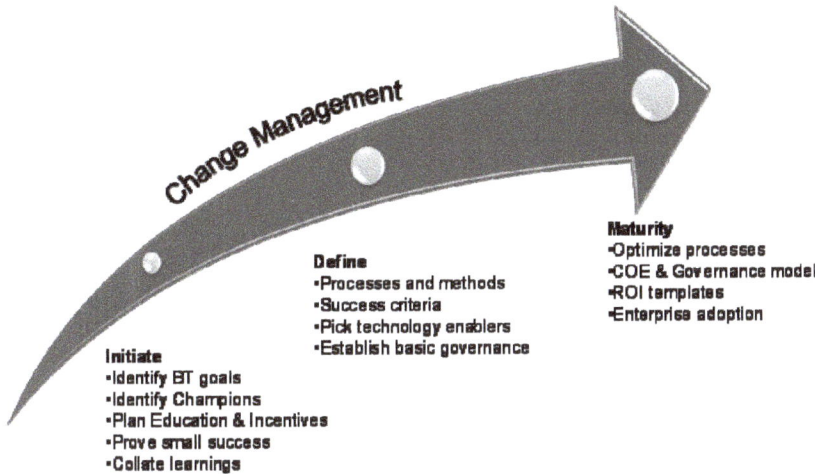

Figure 5. Maturity Phases in BT journey

We have tried to focus on ten variables, in defining the maturity phase of an organization with respect to its stage in the BT lifecycle. Each of these parameters is easily identifiable and any organization can, in turn, measure them through the following analysis.

Parameter	Initiate	Define	Maturity
1. Clear definition of stakeholders and management commitment to BT	***	***	***
2. Leadership Roles are aligned to process and KPIs	***	***	***
3. BT Education and incentives to innovate, are in place	***	***	***
4. Clear definition of success criteria and goals of BT	***	***	***
5. KPIs are well defined, measured and compared with benchmark KPIs		***	***
6. Investments in technology are aligned to BT initiatives		***	***
7. Governance model established with business and IT stakeholders		***	***
8. Role of CIO involves process and transformation focus			***
9. BT Center of Excellence established with repeatable methods and tools			***
10. Enterprise adoption of BT methods and tools			***

Figure 6: BT Maturity Index Criteria

The baseline for this maturity index lies in the following facts:

- Early definition of success criteria, stakeholders and goals, is critical to long term success
- Creating reusable methods, tools and educational frameworks is essential for enterprise adoption
- As adoption takes off, the governance model becomes increasingly relevant

TECHNOLOGY ENABLERS FOR BUSINESS TRANSFORMATION

Technology has become an inherent part of organizational strategy. In some sectors, investments in technology mark competitive differentiation. That said, many organizations still do not align technology investments with their transformational blueprint. Let's look at the qualifications for any given technology to be classified as a **"transformation enabler":**

1. Technologies and systems that provide business users with real-time visibility of process and business performance are key to making sound business decisions. Also, as market conditions change or the socio-economic-political-technological landscape changes, processes must be updatable in real time.
2. Real-time change brings its own challenges in terms of learning, usability and adoptability. Hence the technology enablers of BT must possess these characteristics. *No tool is transformational that can't be transformed itself.*
3. The heart of change in any business lies in its policies, procedures and processes. Hence any technology that can abstract and infer business rules and processes from core transactions is best suited to be a transformation enabler.
4. Many technologies create silos and as investments in technology and systems proliferate, the silos grow more rigid and resistant to change. Systems that handle processes, content management, portals and eCommerce, enterprise resource planning, customer relationship management and data, analytics, and supply chain, all impact the ability of an organization to transform itself. Business Transformation demands that future technologies be built and bought with an eye toward convergence and the orchestration of multiple functions.
5. The days of multi-year implementations and non-quantifiable ROIs are over. Business conditions demand an average payback period on any IT investment of less than one year. Making process-oriented IT investments with an eye toward Business Transformation, ultimately delivers consistently shorter development and delivery times.

RECOMMENDATIONS AND ACTION PLAN

We hope this paper was thought-provoking and we were able to introduce some new concepts which can be incorporated in your organization's planning. A good starting point would be drawing up a high level blue print, which requires analysis of your organization's BT maturity and definition of key focus areas. Identifying initiatives which are low cost, measurable, and offer a quick pay-back period will help spark business buy-in. The long journey toward the cultural adaption of Business Transformation, and the innovation it promises, begins with small steps and a high degree of commitment".

Financial Crisis Front Line: SNS Bank

Eric D. Schabell and Stijn Hoppenbrouwers, SNS Bank and Radboud University Nijmegen, Netherlands

ABSTRACT

SNS Bank, Netherlands, has made a strategic decision to empower its customers on-line by fully automating its business processes. The ability to automate these service channels is achieved by applying Business Process Management (BPM) techniques to existing selling channels. Both the publicly available and internal processes are being revamped into full scale Straight Through Processing (STP) services. This extreme use of online STP is the trigger in a shift that is of crucial importance to cost-effective banking in an ever turbulent and changing financial world. The key elements used in implementing these goals continue to be Free Open Source Software (FOSS), Service oriented architecture (SOA), and BPM. In this paper we will present an industrial application describing the efforts of the SNS Bank to make the change from traditional banking services to a full scale STP and BPM driven bank that can survive on the Financial Crisis front lines.

INTRODUCTION

The Dutch SNS Bank is making a strategic move to automate its support and selling channels to provide its customers with modern on-line services. Realizing that it will take more than just an on-line web shop to excel in the financial world, the bank has also moved to automate many internal processes. The key elements used in implementing these goals are full scale Straight Through Processing (STP) [1] and Business Process Management (BPM) [2].

In this paper we present the efforts made to change from traditional banking services to a full scale STP and BPM driven financial institution during the current world wide Financial Crisis. We begin in *Full Scale STP* by clarifying what the various concepts mean to us and why they are of importance to the future of SNS Bank. In the section *A case study* we take a closer look at the STP Purchasing project. We will provide some insights into the application of STP with BPM within an open source development environment, discuss the component architecture, take a look at our process modeling steps, examine how we utilized customer testing, and conclude with an overview of some general empirical data. We will present our experiences, both good and bad, in dealing with a large BPM implementation. As can be expected, there will always be challenges to be met when such an expansive shift in strategy is being implemented, and in *Observations* we start our tour of the issues encountered in the project. The *benefits* section will discuss the brighter side, outlining the positive impact that this project has had in the technical realm. This will leave the reader with a good idea of the challenges involved, hopefully helping in implementing other industry BPM applications. Finally, in *Moving ahead* we will look at applying the lessons we have learned to survival on the Financial Crisis front lines.

FULL SCALE STP

The application of STP with BPM is not a new phenomenon in the financial industry, with other banks having reported some success with relatively straight forward on-line financial solutions [3, 4]. Some are even dreaming of taking on the more challenging processes within the banking industry, such as mortgage processes [5]. The difference between these types of solutions and the one presented here concerns complexity. We offer the following definitions:

Definition 1 (Business Process Management) Business Process Management concerns aligning business processes to the customers want and needs by applying relevant methods, tools and solutions.

This is a simple and straight-forward look at how we intend to apply BPM within our organization.

Definition 2 (Straight Through Processing) Processing a business transaction automatically, without requiring people to be involved in the process. The purpose of STP is to create efficiencies, eliminate mistakes, and reduce costs by having machines instead of people process business transactions.

This definition is in line with most of the definitions we have encountered in the financial world [6, 7, 8]. It will work fine as a beginning definition of how we construct our processes, but we need to refine it a bit for real world financial business processing.

Definition 3 (Full Scale STP) A straight through process (STP) implementation that requires the solution to encompass a wide range of system integration and will include human tasks which embody the complex decision making that automation either cannot legally implement, or is precluded by technical limitations.

We exclude cost as a factor to determining if an implementation is full scale STP or not. We feel that cost, in terms of time, money, or other value risk, is a business concern that is not related to complexity, but rather to some current operational or environmental situation (i.e. budgets, deadline pressures, politics, environment, etc.).

The drive to push for full scale STP with BPM is multifaceted. The leading goals are cost reduction, manpower reduction in business processes, removing potential (human) mistakes, and channel independent processing. Users should experience such processes as transparent, quick, simple, directly usable, and should be able to complete their task in one attempt.

SNS Bank is targeting effective and efficient processing where as much human intervention as possible has been removed. The customer will be kept informed at crucial process steps, communication always being an important factor in customer experience. For the cases that are exceptions or fall out of STP processing, there will be clear and predefined processes to ensure expeditious handling. Last but not least, the entire communication process is as paperless as can be. This encapsulates the SNS Bank's idea of full scale STP processing.

As Heckl and Moormaan [9] concluded "…long term success cannot be achieved without the development of new business ideas, innovative products and services, and customer retention." We believe that such success can only be achieved if BPM techniques are fully integrated. Full scale STP with BPM will continue to be expanded on and implemented throughout the range of products, sales channels, and business processes that affect both customer and customer support. We believe that the time for full scale STP with BPM is now.

A CASE STUDY

In the beginning of 2007 the first full scale STP project at SNS was launched, with the goal of putting four new savings products on-line at the start of 2008. This project is known as *STP Purchasing* and will provide us with a case for closer examination of full scale STP with BPM. This section will present the component architecture, take a look at how the process was modeled, show how customer testing was used to verify the solution, and provide some empirical data of the results.

Overview

The goals for this project were for a customer to be asked as few questions as possible during the purchasing process, that the entire process would be completed within a maximum of five clicks in the on-line website, and that the customer would be kept informed during all crucial steps in the process with clear, directed communication relevant to a specific purchasing process. A further desire was to maximize paperless communication with the customer. It was essential to maintain as short a processing time as possible, with processes involving human action stages causing no more than one-day delay. It should be volume independent, deliver reusable processes, reusable services, be multi-label, and multi-channel. Above all, the project should provide a full scale STP solution with a maximum degree of automation.

With our definition of full scale STP [definition 3] in mind, we already assume that the process is not free from human tasks. There are several instances in which we could not avoid having human interaction as part of this process. The resulting challenges will be discussed in more detail later on in this section. The project resulted in a general end-to-end purchasing process, initially for savings products, and a new process for document scanning and storage. A purchasing request database implementing the data model for each processing request was delivered along with a BPM process flow; a web front end was created for the initial savings products and the relevant SOA services. A new department was created, called *Process Management Evaluation and Processing*. Total project IT investment was 14,000 hours.

Architecture

The SNS implementation environment for full scale STP with BPM is one of pure Java [10]. The emphasis is on building solutions within the bank's own IT department, making use of Free Open Source Software (FOSS) where possible, achieving reusability of existing applied solution components, and using best of breed components when forced to shop outside of our existing code base.

There was a shift in component strategy in 2004 from three main commercial suppliers to one where FOSS components are preferred when possible. Open source is now quite pervasive throughout the solution architecture of all SNS projects. Furthermore, the development environment and tooling used to implement the solution consists of almost only FOSS. This is outside the scope of this paper and will therefore be excluded from further discussion. The component architecture as shown in Figure 1 (UML package-style visualization) is a very generic and high-level view. We will discuss the components as shown, from left to right.

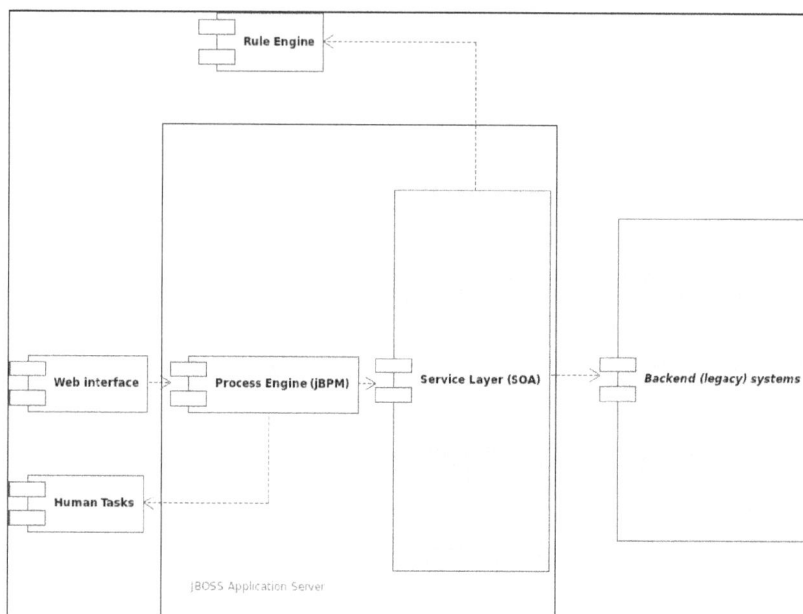

Figure 1: STP Purchasing architecture

Web interface

The entry point for any full scale STP application is the web interface as seen by the customer in the on-line banking website. This is a Java based website that makes use of a content management system. In the STP Purchasing project it provides the user with the option to apply for one of four saving products. If placed, a request is gathered together with user information, verified through various web services, and then using a web service it is deposited into the *Request Database*.

One might expect that a request is submitted directly to the jBPM process engine, but each request is put into a database to ensure that no single customer request is every lost due to the process engine begin unavailable. This is required by a banking regulation that ensures that no risks are taken with customer-submitted information. We must and will always be able to trace and audit every single step in the chain of events from customer request to product delivery. This small design step has been left out of the component diagram as it happens underwater and is of little importance to industries where intensive risk protection is not needed; we mention this in the interest of completeness.

Human tasks

A human action interface was implemented to provide functional administrators with the ability to deal with tasks as they drop out of the automated process for various reasons. Furthermore, Service Centre employees provide input to the system through another interface with the document monitoring section of the process flow. Communication with the customer can require for a human task to be performed, such as customer's reply to questions which needs to be judged on completeness, correctness, and validity. This input to the jBPM process flow causes pending processes to be triggered into their next stages, to be stopped, or to be restarted. The interfaces have been created in-house by the project development team.

Within the project process definition it is always possible to encounter problems, planned or not, that need human intervention to be solved. This intervention is called a human task, where the process is dumped into a task bucket for further action by an authorized person. We refer to the need to invoke human tasks as having the process *fall out* of the process flow. This fall out can then classified as either technical or functional. The first is often related to some error in processing a request within a process step, the latter is related to a problem in the application flow logic. When we look at full scale STP we are concerned with processes that by definition contain planned functional fall out points in their process descriptions.

STP Purchasing supplies a web-based Java interface that enables humans to manipulate the tasks that they have been authorized to view. This component makes use of web services in the SOA layer to retrieve and manipulate process data located in various locations. It is mostly concerned with the *Request Database* where we find the complete request data structure that is maintained during the process life-cycle. One example of a functional fall out is a planned review of the applying customer credit rating results. This process might legally require that more than one person must review the customer's rating results before approving them as new bank customers.

Rule engine

This is a non-FOSS component supplied by a third party which we access from STP with BPM projects for business rules. This allows the business entity to maintain their own rule set regarding their businesses unit within the financial organization. For example, within a savings product you will have various rules and regulations as to the various conditions that must be met before a customer can be allowed to purchase that specific product. These rules and regulations can change over time or due to a special offer on that product during a specific time frame. It is often a wish from the contracting business unit to be able to manipulate these rules and regulations without having to contact the software vendor (i.e. project team).

JBOSS: jBPM and Service Layer (SOA)

The application server is an open source component called JBOSS [11], from the JBOSS component family we have adopted the jBPM engine [12] and its process definition language (PDL) implemented in jPDL [13]. These are the main FOSS components in our project solution and are considered core components in the enterprise architecture.

The jBPM process engine is used for all BPM projects, so component selection was not an issue. The BPM process flows are defined by the information analyst together with the business customer for the application. It is a process involving workshops and use cases. It provides the lead developer of the project with a starting point, in the form of a process flow. This is mapped almost one-to-one into the process definition language, which delivers a jPDL file. The resulting process definition is used for matching nodes to business services. In most cases this again is a one-to-one mapping and the design of the services is the most time consuming part of the implementation. Should there be any technical details that call for adjustment to the flow, consultation ensues with the information analyst, and eventually with the business customer. Individual developers are then given technical designs based on use case realizations that allow them to integrate their implementations into the proper process steps.

The project was completed using only simple nodes that contain all business logic in plain Java. Basic service calls were combined in the Java code to achieve what later could be implemented as a more complex business service. There were no nodes implemented as actual wait states, where the process can wait for action from an external system. Our backend systems are not yet set up to trigger jBPM process instances to allow for real wait states. To facilitate wait states, a polling mechanism was used at points in the process were external systems need to be checked for completion of a task. For example, while waiting for a customer to correctly identify herself by returning a signed contract with a copy of a valid identification, the process will use a scheduler to periodically poll the backend system via a web service to determine if the identification has been completed. Once completion is detected, the scheduler triggers the process via a web service. Furthermore, there are the standard decision nodes, transitions, and human task nodes within the project's process implementation.

We have implemented a standard Service Oriented Architecture (SOA) [14], referred to in-house as our Service Oriented Architecture Layer (SOAL). Granularities of the services in this layer have been defined as basic services, business services, and some very simple composite business services (CBS) [15]. A basic service brings the existing transaction out of the backend system and makes it available through a web service. For example, to validate a postcode, the basic service *postcodeCheck* has been created to expose the backend mainframe transaction that checks if a given postcode is valid. The business services handle more complex processing that may consist of one or more basic services. One of the more complicated issues is that of allowing the existence of CBS's in our SOA layer. These are business services that can contain not only calls to basic services, but to other business services, if the business service being called is in the same classification category as the caller.

The SOA layer deploys web services with versions. If a new release of the SOA layer contains services with interface changes, then the version of the release will be increased. To support backwards compatibility, a total of three versions are maintained for production applications to use. This allows for applications to upgrade to the newer versions over time.

Backend systems

These systems can be anything in the wide variety that exists within our banking infrastructure: banking applications that provide and interface, external third party services, legacy systems, or some form of data storage like a data warehousing solution. It should be noted that these systems are always approached from our projects via the SOA layer in the form of a web service. We will provide the three most important backend systems that are used in STP Purchasing.

A *request database* was implemented for tracking each purchasing request as it migrates through the BPM process flow. This was the direct implementation of our purchasing request data model. As stated in context of the *web interface* and *human task* components, this database is filled with the initial request data, manipulated by the process as it migrates through the various steps, and directly affected when technical or functional fall out occurs. Access is arranged by a very specific service dedicated to accessing, reporting, and updating data in the database works for the web interface, the human task interface, and from inside the process itself.

Another important component in the backend is the *customer information system*, used to maintain all customer and prospect contact information. This is a marketing data pool and there is a specific service dedicated to accessing and updating the information kept here.

A central system in our backend network is a legacy COBOL mainframe. This is where the bank customers are managed and it is accessed via web services that make use of a Java communication layer. This layer bridges the gap between Java and COBOL mainframe functions which are provided when functionality is exposed from the mainframe.

Customer testing

From the very beginning of the project, customer input was sought. An initial prototype was created for which four customers and four internal customer support personnel were invited to conduct usability testing in a controlled environment. These eight sessions were 90 minutes long, each dealing with a single respondent and a task assignment walk-through. The walk-through was done by the respondent with verbal communication accompanying all actions which were recorded by an observer sitting in a different room with a hidden view.

Even though it was a small usability test, it did provide relevant details which led to advice for the development team in the areas of information structure, interaction, navigation, content, graphical information, style, layout, and features. Our view is that any steps taken to improve customer satisfaction should be exploited to the fullest.

Another customer test took place before the project was released into production. It was a last test that the business users took to examine the entire project. The testing users were guided by a test leader during the earlier project iterations to develop functional stories. These were then set up in the databases to allow them to test actions on submitting new requests, handling functional fall out, schedulers, and other such actions as deemed necessary for project acceptance. This is a standard practice in our project release cycle and it remains a valuable feedback loop for finding functional problems before the project hits production status.

The running process

Empirical data providing results concerning running STP Purchasing in production since February 2008 is presented in Table 1. The numbers represent the total number of processes per month, with a rather large spike in the months starting in September 2008. This was the beginning of the worldwide Financial Crisis, which lead many Dutch citizens to spread their savings to different financial institutions.

Table 1: Production process overview – 2008/2009 monthly

Month	Requests
Feb	750
Mar	2750
Apr	2000
May	1200
Jun	1100
Jul	1500
Aug	850
Sep	4250
Oct	2250
Nov	1000
Dec	2340
Jan	3715
Feb	3210

Taking a look at Table 1, we can clarify some of the dips and peaks in the numbers. In February 2008 the project was released half way through the month, resulting in a low start number. It picked up steam and was pretty steady until August 2008, which we believe is due to the vacation period when most Dutch people tend to be on their holidays and away from computers. In September we see the explosion of interest due to the Financial Crisis, followed by a leveling of interest. At the end of

November 2008 the second set of five *deposito products* hit production. Logging shows us that the number gains for December 2008 to Feb 17th 2009 can indeed be attributed to the new *deposito products*, which were almost exclusively purchased. It should be noted that at the time of this publication, the numbers were climbing steadily each month. This could be attributed to the competitive interest rates being offered, by the worsening of the Financial Crisis, or a combination of both. More time will be needed to evaluate the eventual results and we plan to continue to track them during the remainder of the Financial Crisis.

Table 2: Status overview of customer processes

Status	Percentage
Completed on time	52%
Rejected for various reasons	8%
Human action (functional)	0.7%
Human action (technical)	0.3%
Currently in a fall out status	4%
In Document Monitoring	12%
Taken out of STP flow, completed by hand	23%

Another view of results is given in Table 2, which shows us percentages of the various statuses a process can be in. We must take into consideration that our metrics are limited and that we are only able to report on process totals. Even so, it is encouraging that the amount of functional and technical fallout that needs attention is both less than one percent of the total. Also encouraging is that over 50 percent of all processes are completing on time. The ones that do not complete on time and are listed in *Document Monitoring* tend to be waiting for customer response to documentation problems as previously discussed. We have a timer running that ensures a customer receives reminders several times. Should the customer not reply at all, we eventually abort the request. The category listing 23 percent of processes taken out of the engine and completed by hand needs more explanation. This feature was added to allow special cases to be handled in the original manner, by hand.

With only eight percent being rejected due to various reasons, it appears we are hitting the target audience and providing a process that is effective.

OBSERVATIONS

Not everything is as pretty as it seems and there are some technical issues remaining, at which we will take a closer look at here.

Technical challenges

There are some interesting technical challenges that need to be watched for future projects. They cover issues concerning BPM, business logic, and (business) service releases. A currently completing BPM reference implementation project [16] has taken a closer look at these challenges and has come up with a few solutions and suggested ways of dealing with them.

Starting with the BPM issues, we have spent much effort to move the business logic out of the BPM process engine and down into the architecture to the SOA layer. This keeps the BPM engine lean and mean, requiring a lot less testing during the deployment phases of a project. Once the BPM flow is working, tests are passing, handlers call the correct services, and the infrastructure to support all of this is available, then there is not really much looking back. The main focus is on searching out application problems that are contained in the SOA layer. Developers spend their time testing and maintaining the business logic in the services, where it be-longs. The delivered BPM flow should be almost maintenance free.

Many of the problems that the developers encountered with BPM process definition designs as described by Brahe [3] were avoided in our process by keeping the process flow definition, creation, and modification out of the hands of the develop-ers. Modeling took place at a higher level, with a small group containing informa-tion analysts, business representatives and the lead developer. This process led to a completed BPM process definition in the selected process definition language, but expression in that language happened only at the end of the modeling process. In future we would like to look into ways of more directly generating actual BPM process designs close to the chosen process definition language, together with the business.

Individual developers were able to concentrate more on working out the individual process steps (nodes and handlers) the given initial business service designs, test coverage, and documentation. This has worked well for us and we will continue to use this approach in the future.

Although there has been some literature on the use of SOA [17, 18], we have found that most of the issues it discussed were of little help when dealing with our own service construction. It seems that issues are often related to local conditions and infrastructure limitations. One complex issue arose in our environment: unreliable services due to all web service calls being implemented over the HTTP protocol [19]. The problem becomes even more complicated when the basic services, themselves mapping to single backend transactions, are unreliable. It is conceivable that a ser-vice call is made to some complex business service that makes use of several basic services, and that it fails somewhere in the processes of executing basic services. We have no ability to implement anything other than a functional rollback and of-ten are not sure what state the backend systems are left in.

There are potential problems with any service releases in the SOA layer that mi-grate to a major version number. For example, all minor version number releases from v1.0 to v1.1 of a given service contain no interface changes. These are there-fore backwards compatible and should continue to work with all previously written consumers of the service. For major version changes, such as v1.1 to v2.0, we are confronted with a service containing an interface change that might break existing consumers of that service.

Service granularity has started to become a problem with more and more projects attempting to make use of basic, business, and composite business services that they find in the SOA layer. We hope to spend more time on looking into composite business service issues and do some ground work with regard to guidelines for fu-ture projects.

A very sticky problem that has raised its ugly head is what to do with BPM process instances that are running when the new service release is planned. We are looking at our options at this time but have come up with the following strategy to provide a choice depending on the given situation:

1. Phase out older service versions as old process instances have completed
2. Build service converters that translate calls between different versions
3. Activate a new BPM process instance for each existing old process instance
4. Build a process converter that translates old processes into the new process definition (one time)
5. Human interaction to guide the process or complete the process flow

This is an integral part of our current SOA service release strategy and can be found in the internal SOA documentation.

A solution is currently being tested that provides a custom class loader for each individual jBPM process engine. This allows each deployed process definition to provide the exact service version for each service it uses. Different deployed processes can thus access any of the SOA layer deployed service versions, independent of each other. This will have a positive effect on testing phases when multiple processes can be deployed on a single jBPM process engine, thereby saving extra hardware resources. This solution will also allow older instances of a process to be run next to newer ones so that they can be phased out as mentioned above.

All contact between the process and internal systems is realized via web services. These calls are synchronous, but many of the backend systems are not. Many systems run in batch, which means that the web services provide transactions to functionality that can only report that the request has been received correctly. For example, a fictitious account is opened via a web service call, but this actually happens in a night batch run on the backend mainframe. The web service call will get the mainframe reply, *Account Opened*, but this process will not actually be completed until later. This indirectly means that web services can not be transactional or atomic in nature and a great effort is made in business service implementations to create as much of a functional roll back as can be achieved. More often than not, it means having to fall out of the process with a technical problem to be fixed by human hands.

At the time of this writing, a *state-proxy* is being implemented to allow for real wait states in the process definitions. When using a wait state, the business service call is done through our state-proxy. The process is then put into a wait state and the proxy handles the web service call, returning either an exception or the results. The state-proxy can then be expanded with extra plug-in like functions, such as dealing with service windows for known down time on backend systems running a batch, allowing for technical retires to services that can be offline for short periods of time, and dealing with standard exceptions. These plug-ins are on the drawing board for future implementation.

The scheduler discussed in above in the *Architecture* section is a point of concern. It does not scale well and in the future we will need to look into getting our backend systems to trigger on certain events. This should be possible in principle; the discussion is underway.

Another nice-to-have would be to remove the non-FOSS rule engine discussed in the *Architecture* section. We want to spend some time looking into the JBOSS rule engine in the coming year which seems to provide a solution that is integrated in our existing development tooling.

THE BENEFITS

As we have seen, the benefits of BPM are promising, based on the generic data collected in the deployed production process. A closer look at customer and development benefits will make it clear that much has been gained already.

Improving the customer experience

A key concept in the vision of this solution is that the customer must be central to the process. A customer centric business model is not new [9], but we feel that aligning the entire strategy to empower one's customers is breaking the mould. As strategic products are made available through full scale STP with BPM we are able to adjust easily to customer needs. Products and product lines can be introduced into existing business processes in a cost effective manner. The flexibility to combine extends beyond products, product lines, and selling channels to become a very effective tool to reach customer bases in a timely and personalized fashion.

Customer communication can be personalized and tailored to specific processes, products, and customers' personal needs as the data generated by their behavior within the processes is documented. There have been very positive reactions from customers with regards to the speed, quality, and the level of detail in communications.

Development process improvements

The initial STP Purchasing project has provided a starting point for the IT department to build on for future full scale STP with BPM projects. Lessons learned and best practices are being applied, resulting in some interesting improvements to the process.

To our initial surprise, BPM process definitions can be easily changed with a minimal impact on the development time. The work is not in the process definition, but in the business services and basic services in the underlying structure.

A standard way of implementing process nodes and testing has made this part of the development process much less critical. It is important to focus on what we call the *Happy Flow* during initial development. This is the backbone of the process flow which represents a positive test case that processes as expected. For example, we would focus in the STP Purchasing project on a single savings product being requested by a verified and known customer of the bank. This means that you do not have to deal with any exceptions during the initial run through your process implementation. The focus of the first iteration of development is to get this Happy Flow working. By providing a quick working Happy Flow, the business can be shown tangible progress in the project at an early stage.

With an ever growing base of BPM process definitions it is clear that the time to market for similar products is much quicker. We have projects with estimates ranging from one third to one half of the initial development hours put into STP Purchasing. This is quite a big improvement. One thing of note here would be that the development of business services should always be carefully considered, as they tend to be the focus point of complexity.

The initial process definitions as provided by the information analysts and business analysts are not in our process definition language. Much depends on the quality of this process flow model, but with some care and attention to this step it is not too much trouble to map the process flow model to our process definition language. The generated image of the flow is a very good communication tool with the business. No better way to let them see the business services and understand where the development time is spent. Bringing the business closer to the development team with regards to communication about the process flow has been a positive experience that we would like to see continued.

MOVING AHEAD

In this paper we presented the efforts of a Dutch bank at migrating from traditional banking services to a full scale STP with BPM driven financial institution during the current world-wide Financial Crisis. The components being used to realize the STP Purchasing project were described and some basic resulting empirical data were presented for evaluation. The issues and benefits were covered along with the challenges yet faced by the IT organization. The large shift in strategy has started to deliver the desired results and we expect these will continue to roll in as future full-scale STP with BPM projects are implemented.

The positive effects on customer interaction, improvements on accelerating product deployment, and more flexible product/customer support channels have energized some internal ideas about becoming a facilitator to external third party enterprises. Imagine a future where individual entrepreneurs would be able to open a banking store with complete full scale STP with BPM selling channels for products and services.

We hope that our experiences, lessons, and observations will be of value to the industry as a whole. This is a financial industry story as we experience it on the front lines, but it could be applied to many different situations to help you survive the current Financial Crisis.

REFERENCES

1. Khanna, A.: Straight Through Processing For Financial Services: The Complete Guide. Academic Press, Burlington, MA. (Nov 2007)
2. van der Aalst, W.M.P., Hofstede, and A.H.M, Weske,M: Business Process Management: A Survey. In: van der Aalst, W.M.P., Hofstede, A.H.M., and Weske, M. (eds) BPM 2003, LNCS, vol. 2678, pp. 1–12. Springer, Heidelberg (2003)
3. Brahe, S.: BPM on Top of SOA: Experiences from the Financial Industry. In: Alonso, G., Dadam, P., and M.Rosemaan (eds) BPM 2007, LNCS 4714, pp. 96–111, Springer, Heidelberg (2007)
4. Guerra, A.: Bloomberg Aims To Simplify Straight-Through Processing. On: Information-Week, On http://www.informationweek.com/817/bloomberg.htm (18 Dec 2000)
5. Strickland, R., Aach, D.: Getting to straight-through processing: in theory, there is a way to deliver faster and better service in the mortgage lending business. On: BNet Business Network, http://findarticles.com/p/articles/mi_hb5246/is_/ai_n29277448 (Feb 2006)
6. The Free Dictionary, http://encyclopedia2.thefreedictionary.com/Straight+Through+Processing (10 Feb 2009)
7. Answers.com, http://www.answers.com/topic/straight–through–processing (10 Feb 2009)
8. Investopedia, http://www.investopedia.com/terms/s/straightthroughprocessing.asp (10 Feb 2009)
9. Heckl, D., Moormann, J.: Matching Customer Process with Business Processes of Banks: The Example of Small and Medium-Sized Enterprises as Bank Customers. In: Alonso, G., Dadam, P., and M.Rosemaan (eds) BPM 2007, LNCS 4714, pp. 112–124, Springer, Heidelberg (2007)
10. Java Technology. 18 March 2008, http://java.sun.com (19 March 2008)
11. Jboss.org: Community Driven. http://labs.jboss.com (19 March 2008)
12. jBPM Overview. http://labs.jboss.com/jbossjbpm/jbpm overview (19 March 2008)
13. Welcome to jBPM jPDL. http://labs.jboss.com/jbossjbpm/jpdl (19 March 2008)
14. Erl, T.: Service Oriented Architecture: Concepts, Technology and Design. Prentice-Hall, Englewood Cliffs (2005)
15. Neuman, S.: Composite Business Services. IBM Global Business Services, http://www–935.ibm.com/services/us/index.wss/offering/gbs/a1027243 (25 October 2008)
16. Schabell, E., Benckhuizen, J.: Software Architecture Document – jBPM Reference Project. SNS Bank IT, s-Hertogenbosch (2008)
17. Mahajan, R.: SOA and the Enterprise – Lessons from the City. In: IEEE International Conference on Web Services (ICWS'06), pp. 939–944, IEEE Computer Society, Los Alamitos (2006)
18. Acharya, M., Kulkarni, A., Kuppili, R., Mani, R., More, N., Narayanan, S., Patel, P., Schuelke, K.W., Subramanian, S.N.: SOA in the Real World - Experiences. In: Benatallah, B., Casati, F., Traverso, P. (eds) ICSOC 2005, LNCS, vol. 3826, pp. 437–4449, Springer, Heidelberg (2005)
19. HTTP – Hypertext Transfer Protocol. 27 Feb 2008, http://www.w3.org/Protocols (19 March 2008)

Leveraging Best Practices through a Human Process Management System

Jacob P. Ukelson D.Sc., ActionBase Inc., USA

Human processes are business processes which are heavily dependent on interactions among people. These are also called "tacit interactions" (Beardsley, Johnson, & Manyika, 2006) by economists, which is an attempt to differentiate among routine, predefined transactions and interactions that rely heavily on human judgment and context. Other terms used to describe these types of processes include unstructured processes, ad-hoc processes, knowledge work and office work. No matter what the name, both analysts and organizations are coming to the realization that these tacit interactions make up most of the processes in organizations (Beardsley, Johnson, & Manyika, 2006) (Haag, 2006). Even more importantly, as tools and applications for managing structured processes (e.g. CRM, BPM) become more prevalent in organizations, people are coming to the realization that these tools can't, by themselves, provide a complete end-to-end solution to the processes they manage. This is because no matter how good the model, there is always the need for human intervention for exceptional cases—and as time goes by and the business environment changes, the number of exceptions grow. Unless a process is 100 percent defined for all possible cases (with no exceptions) it can't be completely managed without addressing the unstructured, ad-hoc human processes surrounding it.

Most of the work involved in executing these human processes is in managing the communication, coordination and data collection aspects of the process. Knowledge workers everywhere execute these human processes using standard productivity tools (e.g. Microsoft Office) and email (e.g. Microsoft Outlook)—excellent tools in themselves, but sorely lacking in the basics needed for actually managing these processes; causing missed deadlines, lost opportunities and general feelings of email overload. For most users, the only other route for managing these processes is to get IT involved, but that is too time-consuming, costly and inflexible to meet their needs. Lacking a better choice, people continue to use standard email and document tools to execute their ad-hoc, unstructured processes since that is really the only way to get the job done.

The Business Process Management community has started to pay attention to this issue, and many BPM tools are coming to the realization that they need to explicitly include people as part of the process. Most BPM tools either add extensions aimed specifically at managing humans, or view humans as just another resource that needs to be managed (e.g. BPEL4People). In short they view humans as part of the assembly line of services needed to complete a business process. This view works only for the portion of human tasks that fit the assembly line metaphor and certainly doesn't hold for the large, and growing, amount of unstructured processes handled by knowledge workers (Adams, Edmond, & H.M. ter Hofstede, 2003, Pyke 2007).

What is needed are Human Process Management Systems (HPMS) for managing this interplay between people, giving just enough structure and management so the process can be managed, but not so much as to strangle it. For knowledge workers, the communication, coordination and data collection tasks needed for participation in, and management of, human processes is the crux of their jobs. The most time-consuming and critical components in these processes are gathering the appropriate process and data context along with communication and coordination; and email is the primary tool used for this task, both by knowledge workers and management. The pervasive use of email for these tasks is, while understandable, especially onerous during long-running interdependent tasks, exacerbating user perception of email overload and user frustration with email systems (Kushmerick, Victoria Bellotti n.d.).

Given all the drawbacks, why is email is so widely adopted as the preferred tool for these processes? Mainly because email is really the only tool under user control that is appropriate for the basic interactive structure of human processes. Human processes are based on the back and forth of human communication and coordination. The most basic example of a business communication pattern is made up of the *order phase* that is used by a person to initiate a request for someone to execute a work task, an *execution phase* where the work is done and work product produced, and finally a *response phase* where the executor notifies the initiator that the task has been completed and the result is accepted by the initiator (T Winograd 1986) (Dietz n.d.) (Hans Mulder n.d.). It sounds simple, but the order and response phases are actually a negotiation between the two parties and can generate a flood of communication and coordination activity.

Looking at human processes in this light explains why email is so heavily used (overused?) in business—it is the general purpose tool of choice for asynchronous human-to-human communication, coordination and data collection and fills the gap left by the structured business process enablement tools (e.g. BPM, CRM, ERP) which focus on the execution phase. Email also naturally supports agility and ad-hoc processes; you can always send an email to anyone and get them into the loop when needed.

Human Process Management Systems are needed to manage this interplay among people, giving just enough structure and management so the process can be managed, but not so much as to strangle it. It is different, though complementary, to BPM and WfM systems that focus on predefined flows and the execution phase of the process, and don't really support the critical communication and coordination phases that generate much of the work in human processes.

THE DEFINING ATTRIBUTES OF HUMAN PROCESSES

Human processes have a number of inherent attributes that any system attempting to manage them must support. Human processes are:

1. Unstructured or loosely structured—there may be a standard framework for the process (or best practice) that guides people towards the intended result, but each instance is handled separately and requires human understanding (for both decisions and flow) as part of the process. There isn't enough standardization between instances of the process that allows for a formal, complete and rigorous description of the process end-to-end.
2. Dynamic—the people participating in the process instance can modify the flow of a process instance.
3. Interdependent—the activities of the humans in the process are interdependent and cannot be done completely in parallel.

4. Extended and extensible—require more than a single interaction among humans to be completed, and any participant can decide to pull more people into the loop as needed.
5. Borderless—human processes can involve anyone that is relevant; be it within or outside the group/team/project or even organizational borders.
6. Exceptional—in the sense that many instances of the process are "exceptions" and need to be handled based on experience and judgement.

THE BASIC COMPONENTS OF A HUMAN PROCESS MANAGEMENT SYSTEM

The goal of a HPMS is to provide knowledge workers with a tool that they will actually use that provides just enough structure and management so that human processes can be managed, but not so much as to strangle them. A complete solution to human process management should support recommended (e.g. guidelines) and ad-hoc user interactions, as well as standard knowledge worker coordination and communication mechanisms, feedback and reporting both for the individual worker and management. It should also provide mechanisms for the understanding and analysis of the evolving human processes to support learning from exceptions as the way for best practices to evolve.

The basic components of an HPMS are:

Executable Guideline Documents—Documents are a natural way for people to describe guidelines, best practices and procedures. An HPMS needs a way to augment these documents so that they are "live documents" that can be used to kick off the first step in all the related processes, recommend possible next steps and continue to track the initiated processes as they evolve. This ensures that process guidelines are both used and kept up to date, since it allows guideline documents to drive the processes they describe.

Managed Human Communication and Coordination Infrastructure—for most organizations that means email, but if your organization uses something else, choose that (for example if wikis are the primary mechanism for human-to-human communication and coordination in your organization). There are a number of key requirements for this component:
- The messaging system needs to be available to everyone since you won't know with 100 percent certainty who will become part of a process. For the system to work, every process communication among people needs to be managed by the HPMS. This means that even if the communication goes outside the boundaries of your organization the HPMS needs to make sure that these communications are managed.
- It needs to be usable with no formal training.
- It needs to be flexible; it can be connected to a guideline describing a recommended next step, but the participants own the flow. It must be simple and natural for people to change and modify the flow and content of the process as needed.

Analytics and Reporting Infrastructure—needs to provide both personal reporting mechanisms (where do I stand with respect to the processes I participate in?) and organizational overview mechanisms (where does my department stand with respect to its processes, both on-going and historically?).

System of Record Repository—a repository of all the documents, messages and interactions (either storing them directly, or through links to the organization's document repository) that are part of every process instance. This is a critically important component since human processes tend to change from instance to instance and there needs to be a centralized mechanism to allow the tracking and management of the different instances. The system of record enables the HPMS to ensure follow-up to completion and proper reporting. This component also enables continuous learning from actual process instances so that exceptions can be understood and incorporated into best practices as needed.

DEFINING A HUMAN PROCESS MANAGEMENT SYSTEM

As the process unfolds a Human Process Management System takes care of:

1. tracking and management of the actual communications flows of the process and recommending next steps when appropriate
2. management of status, related documents and user input
3. keeping participants updated and notified of the evolving status of the process (including deadlines)

The most natural user paradigm for an HPMS would be an integrated system of *"process email"* (for coordination and communication flows) and executable *"process docs"* (for executable best practices and guidelines). Enhancing standard email and documents, which means building on the de-facto existing mechanisms for handling human processes today, is the easiest way for most organizations to get started. Another way to implement an HPMS is through wikis, but for most organizations that requires a new mode of work and change in methodology increasing the learning curve and cost of integration.

Enhancing Email for Human Processes Management

A *"process email"* is like a standard email in many respects, but with a few enhancements that would make it more appropriate for handling human processes, rather than just general correspondence. These *process emails* should reside side-by-side with regular email, allowing the user the ability to decide which type of email to use. *Process email* is like an email template, specially tailored for human process management with the following capabilities:

1. Shared templates appropriate for different organizational processes. These templates define possible process statuses and recommend participants, attachments and next steps. These recommendations can be as simple as a suggested next step as part of the template, or a next step calculated through computation (e.g. a decision table such as those described in Nicola Boffoli 2008). This allows users to explicitly kick-off a specific process in a very simple and familiar way— essentially selecting a template, adding content and sending the email.
2. A way to associate specific states from a set of standard states, both general purpose process state information (e.g. accepted, in-process, overdue) and status specific to the process. Usually state (or status) transition is handled by the user, though in specific cases it could be useful to be able to calculate state transition algorithmically.
3. A way for the participants to see a shared context for the process as it evolves, along with a way to link the evolving chain of interactions and relate them back to the original process. Users can freely launch subprocesses directly from within the *process email*, which retain a link back to the parent process. Ideally, complete chain of process related interactions should show up as a single process email in the user's

inbox, which visible status changes to reflect how the process is evolving.

4. A complete audit trail of the process, including process status changes, participants, attachments, and related sub-process.

5. All the information about *process email* and its flow is stored in a system of record and can be used to generate both personal and departmental reports about process execution. It can also be used to aggregate information of how process instances for specific process are actually executed.

Using this *process email* based approach allows the end-to-end flow to be defined incrementally, rather than requiring a rigorous definition of the complete process flow from the start. The *process email* evolves based on the process and is monitored throughout the flow of the process as it executes. As tasks flow back and forth as part of the process, each step executed is summarized as part of the audit trail of the *process email* itself, and the status of a *process email* reflects the current status of the process. The flurry of emails that would usually be associated with a process becomes a single *process email* mailbox entry in each participant's inbox that is continually updated with the current status of the process.

Process templates can either be predefined within the organizations email system, or can be created by a participant in the process to create an ad-hoc next step, or sub-task for a process. In both cases these templates should be easy for anyone to define and use. A user that "owns" a specific process step can define a simple template for the task, which contains a due date, task related content, task participants and standard status. A more complex template can add process-specific status information types and recommendations for next steps. These *process email* templates can later be linked and reused, as one method toward creating a best practice. As a human process progresses through each step, the next step is defined by the participants dispatching sub-tasks to other people, or by dispatching next steps as part of a recommended sequence. As a result, the complete process flow is incrementally built as the actual process flow progresses. Of course, users are always free to use their own judgment to decide what to do and how to continue at any step, and the system will continue to keep track and monitor the new flow as it is defined. As we'll see later, this has interesting consequences for the bottom-up definition of best practices and adaptive benchmarks for human processes.

Human Processes, Documents and Meetings

Documents and meetings are an important part of human processes. For example, meetings often end in an agreed-upon and documented set of decisions and action items. In many cases these actions items are like a guideline; a way to kick-off a set of human processes with the goal of gathering more information, or implementing the meeting's decisions. Process guidelines and best practices are also often described in standard documents that are shared in the organization. These guidelines often grow stale quickly, since there is no incentive to keep them up to date.

Rather than let these work items just wither away from lack of attention, the use of an executable *process doc* would allow users a mechanism for augmenting action oriented documents with the ability to initiate and manage human processes through *process email*. *Process docs* are regular documents related to *process email* templates for each process to be initiated as a result of a work item. Each process that is to be initiated as a result of an action described in the document is linked and related to a specific section of the document. This allows these action oriented documents to become living documents, monitoring and tracking the implementation of the work items described in the document. Examples of documents that lend themselves to become *process documents* are guidelines, review documents, work plans, 1:1 sessions and of course meeting minutes.

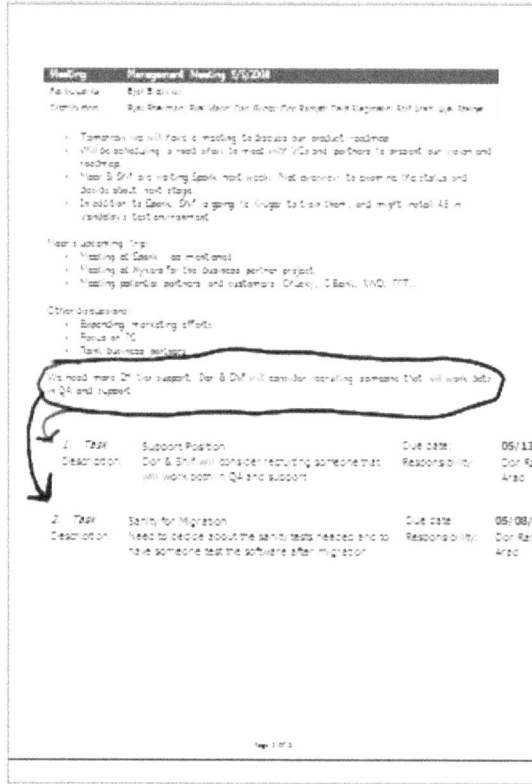

Figure 1. Schematic "process doc" meeting summary with two process email related items

Figure 1 shows a schematic *process doc* meeting summary where there are two action items associated with the last part of the summary. These two action items initiate processes through *process email* sent to the participants (Dor and Shif) and will be tracked and monitored.

Documents (either as reference documents or as a work product) are a natural part of human processes and in both *process email* and *process docs* any document can be added as an attachment. While these attachments can be stored anywhere (e.g. a document management system) the relation to a specific human process instance ensures the connection of the documents to their specific business context.

HUMAN PROCESSES AND BEST PRACTICES

Best practices are closely related to human processes. Best practices are a way for an organization to codify "how things are done around here." Sometimes they are based on industry best practices, and sometimes they are specific to a company, division or department. Best practices are lightweight descriptions of a how a certain type of problem is solved or specific human process is implemented. To remain viable over time best practices need to be dynamic; evolving both based on the needs of the business and on incremental learning of how the process is actually executed.

Process docs and *process email* enable the linking of a best practice description of a human process and its actual execution through the *process email* flow. Users initiate a best practice by selecting and instantiating a best practice *process doc*. The instantiated *process doc* generates the appropriate *process emails* that kickoff and manage the process.

Using *process docs* for best practice documentation enables live, executable descriptions of a best practice process which can be easily initiated, updated, tracked and monitored. One added benefit is that the actual execution of best practices implemented through *process emails* and *process docs* can become part of the organizations system of record, and the definition of the best practice is incrementally refined based on how the process is actually executed, rather than based on some theory of how it should be executed. This information can then be measured against internal, or industry, benchmarks to enable continuous process improvement.

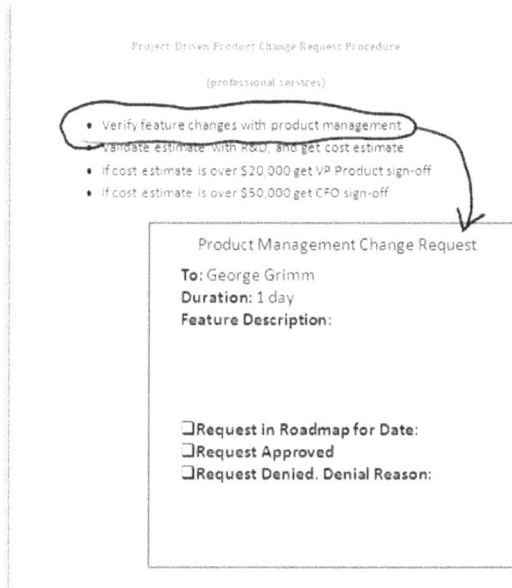

Figure 2. Schematic best practices "process doc" with one immediate next step template

BRIDGING HUMAN PROCESS MANAGEMENT AND STRUCTURED PROCESS MANAGEMENT

So how do you bridge between your structured processes and your human processes? Combined reporting through a common dashboard is the easiest way to get a bird's eye view of an organization's processes, assuming the different process are exclusively unstructured processes or exclusively structured process.

However if a structured process (e.g. one implemented in a BPMS) needs to invoke a human process (e.g. exception handling, investigations) the processes themselves need to be linked. In that case the easiest way to link the two processes is to have the structured process initiate the human process via a *process email* with the appropriate template. The *process email* is sent to the appropriate user and the process flows as needed. The final step in the human process should be a *process email* back to an automated agent that notifies the structured system that the human process is complete (along with a link to the process instance in the human process system of record).

By using *process email* to enable loose coupling between human processes and structured processes, what used to be completely unmanaged exceptions to structured processes can now be managed and monitored, but be as ad-hoc and fluid as before. This methodology allows for true end-to-end process management; using a BPM system to handle the structured portion of the process and using an HPM system for the lightweight ad-hoc human part of the process that has been ignored until now.

It also allows for structured systems to evolve incrementally, using the learning that occurs as a result of humans handling the exception to the structured process. As exceptions are handled, over time, the HPMS system of record can be used to mine and analyze these exceptions, and enhance enrich the structured process model.

PROCESS DISCOVERY AND ANALYSIS THROUGH HUMAN PROCESS MANAGEMENT

Another use for an HPMS is to enable iterative bottom-up discovery and analysis of an organization's actual processes and how they are executed. By enabling people to use process email instead of regular email for process management, not only do they gain control over their processes, they are providing the organization with important information on the actual flow and use of processes. Over time certain processes may be found to be used enough, and structured enough, to be optimized and implemented via a structured process management system (e.g. BPMS).

This bottom-up approach to capturing processes allows process automation to be based on actual process execution information, and evolve along with the process as it changes over time. By making the actual execution of the process the basis of process automation, this goes a long way towards solving the problem of out-of-date, unused best practices and guidelines.

HUMAN PROCESS MANAGEMENT IN ACTION

HPMS has been used in quite a variety of business verticals and business scenarios. Here is a (non-exhaustive) list of how companies have benefitted from an HPMS:

- Audit and Compliance—Audits and Compliance processes require lots of collaboration and coordination between the participants (e.g. auditors, auditees, management) throughout all phases of the audit process. Most organizations use email and documents, making visibility into the overall process as it progresses non-existent. This lack of visibility and control practically ensures missed deadlines and lack of follow-up, which can lead to non-compliance and fines. Using an email and document based HPMS enables collaboration, coordination and follow-up throughout all phases of an audit as a natural part of the audit process itself. The HPMS provides visibility to both the participants and process owners into the exact state of the audit process, enabling end-to-end tracking and ensuring follow-up to completion; all within their standard email and document environment. Companies have used HPMSs in a variety of audit and compliance scenarios—including HSE (Health, Safety and Environment), ISO, SOX and other regulatory compliance audits.
- Incident Reports—Be it a personal injury, or environmental incident, getting the right information to the right people at the right time, and ensur-

ing follow-up are the essence of proper incident reporting. Using an HPMS enables organizations to know the status of incidents throughout the organization, ensuring proper (and auditable) reporting and investigation. This allows organizations to take a real-time holistic view of incidents and to recommend corrective and preventative actions, ensuring follow-up on these actions till completion.

- Executive Management, Committee Governance and Board of Directors Meetings—Using an email and document based HPMS, strategic decisions and their associated work items can be documented and kicked-off as processes that can be tracked and managed to completion. This enables the linking of the decision documentation to the processes needed to implement the decisions. Owners of the processes can see the status any time, and resolve any issues or roadblocks quickly and efficiently.

- Fraud Escalation—There are numerous systems used to detect fraud in different industries. However, once fraud is suspected, there is usually a very human intensive process of investigating the specifics of the fraud. Different expertise is used based on the type of fraud, and the process changes quite often as new evidence is found. HPM systems can provide a framework for the fraud escalation process, and provide a mechanism to manage and audit the unstructured fraud escalation process, while providing the flexibility to include different experts and process flows as needed.

- Exception Handling—No matter what the process, there always needs to be a mechanism for getting people involved for handling process exceptions. These exceptions generate a huge cost in resources, time and customer satisfaction. Extending standard process management tools (e.g. CRM, BPM) with an HPMS for handling exceptions solves these problems and allows true end-to-end process management.

SUMMARY

Human processes make up the vast bulk of actual processes for most businesses, but standard business process technologies aren't appropriate for the lightweight ad-hoc nature of human processes, which is why email is the de-facto, but clumsy, mechanism used by most businesses (Butler Group, December 2007). This is true both in the private and public sector.

The BPM approach of managing humans as just another system in the process doesn't work for these unstructured ad-hoc processes. Human processes are dynamic and fluid, relying on human judgment and best practices while structured processes are more regimented and require exact specification. Human processes also require a lot of communication and coordination, while structured processes emphasize straight through processing and automated execution. Today, users bridge this gap through an email "back-channel" of shadow processes unmanaged by the business, leading to lost productivity and email overload. This paper outlines a different approach, defining an approach to human process management that provides a natural way to manage these ad-hoc, unstructured processes.

BIBLIOGRAPHY

Adams, M., Edmond, D., & H.M. ter Hofstede, A. (2003). The Application of ActvitiyTheory to Dynamic Workflow Adaptatin Issues. *7th Pacific Asia Conference on Information Systems*, (pp. 1-17). Adelaide, Australia.

Beardsley, S. C., Johnson, B. C., & Manyika, J. M. (2006). Competitive advantage from better interaction. *McKinsey Quarterly* , 53-63.

Butler Group, T. (December 2007). *Business Process Management: Building End-to-end Process Solutions for the Agile Business.* Butler Group.

Dietz, J. L. *Generic Recurrent Patterns in Business Processes.* www.demo.nl.

Haag, S. C. (2006). *Management Information Systems For the Information Age (3rd Canadian Ed.).* Canada: McGraw Hill Ryerson .

Hans Mulder, V. v. (n.d.). Three Ways of Talking Business and IT Design. *www.demo.nl* .

James M. Manyika, R. P. (2007). Eight business technology trends to watch. *McKinsey Quarterly* .

Kushmerick, R. K. (n.d.). Email Task Management: An Iterative Relational Learning Approach. *School of Computer Science and Informatics, University College Dublin, Ireland* .

Michael zur Muehlen, J. R. (2008). How Much Language is Enough? Theoretical and Practical Use of the Business Process Modeling Notation. 20th International Conference on Advanced Information Systems Engineering (CAiSE 2008), Montpellier, France, June 16-20, 2008., Springer LNCS.

Nicola Boffoli, D. C. (2008). FLEXIBLE PROCESS MODELING THROUGH DECISION TABLES. *IASTED International Conference on Software Engineering*, (pp. 280-285). Innsbruck, Austria.

Pyke, J. (2007). Knowledge Intensive BPM. In L. Fischer, *2007 BPM and Workflow Handbook.* Future Strategies Inc.

T Winograd, F. F. (1986). Understanding Computers and Cognition: A New Foundation for Design. *Ablex.* Norwood,NJ.

Victoria Bellotti, N. D. Quality Versus Quantity: E-Mail-Centric Task Management and Its Relation With Overload. HUMAN-COMPUTER INTERACTION, 2005, Volume 20, pp. 89–138.

People Relationship Management: Completing the BPM Value Proposition

Roy Altman, Peopleserv, Inc., USA

ABSTRACT

Introduction

Today's business environment is challenging and complex. Layoffs are rampant and employees who remain are being asked to do more with less. The best way to remain competitive in this environment is to streamline your business processes, linking the touch points through automated workflow. As a result, software products with a workflow component have become ubiquitous in the enterprise, yet their true value has not been realized. The reason is that workflow software depends on worker relationships in order to automate the business processes effectively. Yet there is no source of worker relationship information available that is robust enough for all applications, guaranteed to be accurate, and a complete model of the organization to enable an automated process to scale across the enterprise.

The BPM Value Proposition

Business Process Management (BPM) allows effective automation of business processes, by getting the *right* information to the *right* person at the *right* time. Service-oriented architectures address the content issue by integrating disparate repositories as appropriate for the end-to-end business process. Automated workflow is the transport mechanism allowing the information to be available when needed. People Relationship Management (PRM) completes the picture, by ensuring that the correct person receives the information, in order to make an informed decision. The BPM value proposition involves the per-transaction cost savings gained by reducing the "white space" between touch points in a business process, and the consistency provided by imposing order on organically-occurring processes. BPM falls short if the recipient of a workflow item is the wrong person, or if the automated business process is limited in scope.

Changing nature of work and the worker

The nature of work and the worker are changing. Just as the industrial age put an end to physical labor, the automation age is putting an end to the administrative tasks of the knowledge worker. Companies are relying more heavily on the knowledge worker with very specialized skills to use their knowledge and skills to create value for the company. It is essential that automated workflow be employed to manage the tasks effectively and allow the worker to concentrate on the types of tasks where human decision making is required. Formalizing all of the relationships in an organization is essential to effectively automate critical business processes. Increasingly, companies are realizing that the key to optimizing output is acknowledging and leveraging important human interactions in the workplace.

THE PROBLEM

Single hierarchy

Enterprise wide software such as Enterprise Resource Planning (ERP), Human Capital Management (HCM), Org Charting, etc. usually stores only a single hierarchy to represent the organization structure. This is inadequate since each software application or BPM installation may require different types of relationships in order to route a workflow item to the correct person.

Only hierarchies

Many relationships in a company are not hierarchical at all, but rather matrix or network structures. This management organization originated in the early 1970s and has rapidly gained popularity[1]. It allows for more agile resource allocation, since a resource can be used by several business areas to maximize their effectiveness. The strict hierarchical structure requires redundancy of resources, which deliver suboptimal effectiveness. It is essential that matrix management structures be reflected in organization models.

Relationships not validated

Some hierarchical structures are deemed "mission critical." However, sometimes a worker has no supervisor assigned to her in the organization system of record, because it is often not a required field. Sometimes that supervisor's reporting structure ends in a circular reference: she reports to someone who, in turn reports to her. Sometimes the reporting chain does not go all the way to the top of the company. A valid structure of this type is called a "fully articulated tree structure." If an automated business process relies on a supervisor who is defined as someone who can approve a transaction, and that supervisor cannot be found, the business process is broken. Additionally, there are circumstances where if a critical structure is not fully articulated, the company runs a regulatory compliance risk.

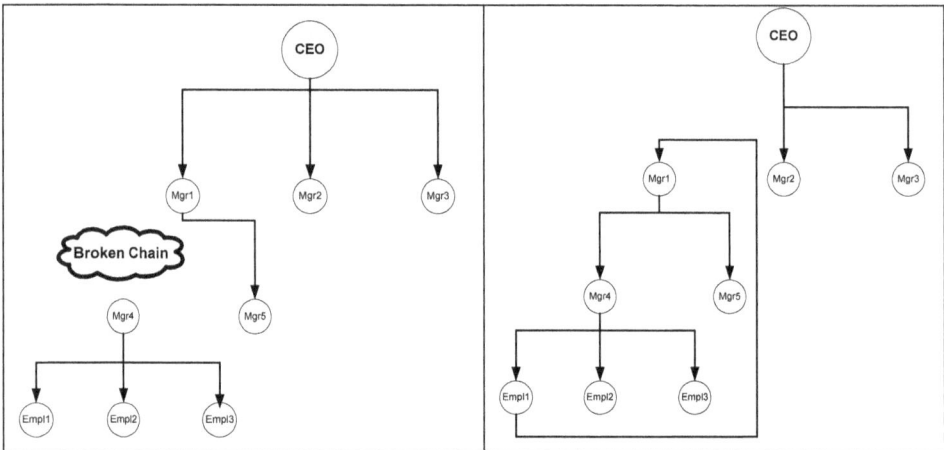

Broken chain (L) & circular reference

Person to person only

For large companies, indicating all reporting relationships on a person-to-person basis is tedious, and not really reflective of the true organizing principles of the company. Organizing principles are often rule based, which can allow them to be self-maintaining. For example, suppose you are the supervisor of all accountants in the Prague office, and an accountant transfers to the Zurich office. The reporting relationships must be hand-maintained, whereas applying the rule based on the employee indicative data would make the relationship self-maintaining.

No central repository

Since the system of record for organization structure information is inadequate to serve the needs of all software applications with workflow, what often happens is that each application stores the relevant structure information in its own "silo." This is an undesirable practice because there is often no procedure in place to keep the information up to date—and it's changing all the time! Thus, reporting structure information becomes invalid and automated business processes fail to work correctly.

Scalability

Suppose a BPM solution is in place, and the implementer has successfully modeled the business process and correctly identified the actors. This will work well if it is confined to the limited scope that was analyzed. However, if the company would like to standardize the process enterprise-wide, the process will not scale because the actors identified were individuals and not a full contextual organization model.

THE PEOPLE RELATIONSHIP MANAGEMENT SOLUTION

Contexts

A People Relationship Management solution should be able to maintain relationships in multiple *contexts*. This effectively creates a multi-dimensional organizational model.

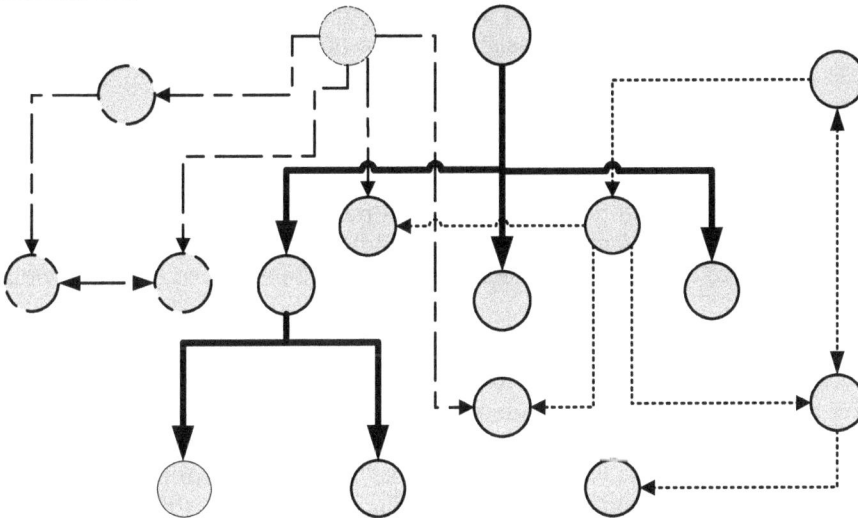

A multi-dimensional organizational model (line types indicate contexts)

Multiple structure types

A People Relationship Management solution should be able to represent relationships in hierarchical, matrix and peer-to-peer structures.

Validates relationships

A People Relationship Management solution should validate that critical contexts are compliant as a fully articulated tree structure. It should be sensitive to daily HR transactions (new hires, terminations, transfers, etc.) that would break the fully articulated tree structure, a process should move all nodes up in order to remain compliant, and notify a responsible party to make the proper adjustments in a timely manner. This process has been referred to as "self-healing."

Organization Modeling

A People Relationship Management solution should be able to apply rule-based criteria for assembling workers into groups that have similar reporting relationships. This way, movement within the organization would be self-maintaining by consistently applying the rules. In order to accomplish this, it is helpful to leverage the meta-data layer of the Human Capital Management system in order to dynamically construct and enforce the rules.

To achieve the above, there are two other concepts in addition to the one of multiple contexts, stated above.

Spheres

A sphere is a collection of assets, most commonly: workers. The most elemental is the employee. Each employee is, by default, its own sphere. However, spheres can be ad hoc groups of individual employees (such as a project team), or it could have an organizing principle enforced by rules (i.e., all salesmen in the Düsseldorf office). These rules leverage the meta-data layer of the data model in order to have maximum flexibility. For instance, if I have a rule that says that all managers within a particular location belong to the same sphere, or all non-exempt employees in the same department, I can enforce that by dynamically creating the criteria using the data items and operators needed. If a sphere is rule based, it is self-maintaining. Spheres can be nested to create complex macro-structures, as a company's maturity with the process grows. Spheres don't necessarily need to refer to human assets. The elemental sphere can be, let's say, a server in an IT support desk function. You could assign a sphere of servers to the IT technician assigned to support them, so that outage requests are directly routed to the correct person for the server that needs attention.

Business Rules

Business rules can be assigned to spheres, for instance, to require that the rules in a collective bargaining agreement apply to all members of the sphere containing those union members. A business rule could be applied to a context also, for instance: require that a fully-articulated tree structure be enforced for a particular context.

Contexts/Spheres/Business Rules

This application is brought to life by combining Contexts, Spheres, and Business Rules. The basic structure is two spheres connected in a context, with the business rules of each enforced. However, spheres can filter contexts as well. For instance, the context of "Union Reporting Structure" is only relevant to people in the Union sphere, so this context will only be available to those within that sphere. Business rules from contexts or spheres are inherited when spheres and contexts are combined. When they conflict, the user will be given the choice as to how to resolve. Through the interaction of contexts, spheres, and business rules, very flexible models of the organization are achievable in very dynamic ways.

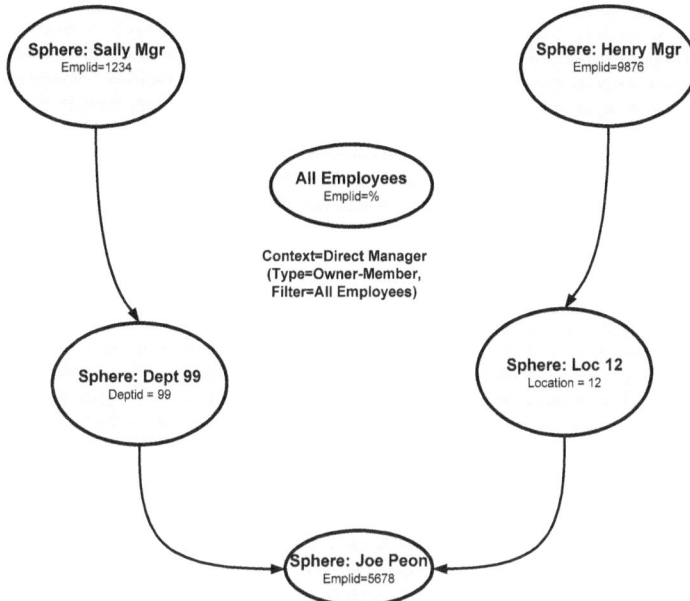

Simple Sphere-Context example

BENEFITS OF SOLUTION

Workflow software

Any software that has a workflow component will benefit from a People Relationship Management solution. This includes, but is not limited to, BPM systems. Workflow-based software applications have become ubiquitous in the workplace. Some examples are:

- Human Resource application, such as:
  - **Workforce management**—a timesheet is often routed to a direct manager for approval. However, oftentimes a manager will designate a subordinate to approve timesheets for her. A People Relationship Management solution is essential to categorize the timesheet approver, and formalize that role in the business process.
  - **Talent management**—360° reviews often require the input of one's peers. In addition, if the employee is working on a project in a matrix environment, feedback from the matrix project manager is essential for an accurate review. These relationships are not captured in a traditional organization structure.
  - **Employee/Manager Self-Service**—the recipient of a self-service workflow item is usually the employee's direct report…but not always. Often, the second-level approver is a senior manager. That's when the business process gets tricky. It's not good practice to bother senior managers with approval routings that are not relevant to them. Routing the transaction to the correct manager is essential to its quick approval, and staying in the good graces of senior managers who don't want to be bothered with approvals that are not their responsibility.
- **Help desk applications**—most help desk applications have an escalation structure for dealing with issues that arise in the organization. Often, the trouble ticket comes to a "dispatcher," who then routes it to the appropriate resource (based on colloquial knowledge). If the responsibility and es-

calation structure was encoded in the PRM solution, the ticket could be automatically routed to the right person, saving a step in the process and better serving the company. After the issue is resolved, the users could be automatically notified by the application. Notice here that a robust PRM solution can store relationships between people *as well as* other entities, such as servers or networks.

- **Procurement**—a budget approver is often required to ok purchases. Purchases outside of guidelines often require a second level of approval. The financial approval structure of an organization is often different than the supervisor reporting structure. A PRM solution is needed to capture and maintain these relationships.
- **Financials**—the financial reporting structure of an organization is often different than the HR structure. This often leads to manual "work-arounds" to get the financial reporting correct.

Regulatory compliance

Compliance Reporting—Sarbanes-Oxley requires managers to sign-off on the financial statements of all managers who report to them. If the organization structure stored is incorrect, incomplete or not within the "financial responsibility" structure that is required, the company is out of compliance.

Identity/Entitlement Management—large companies often audit employees' entitlements by management level. Unless that information is maintained accurately, and validated, the company may be out of compliance.

Audit trail—all transactions in a workflow system can record who approved each transaction and when it was approved; and report on that information.

Reorganizations

Companies periodically reorganize to meet the ever-changing challenges of the business environment, or to respond to an acquisition or divestiture. Reorganizations can be disruptive, so it is essential that they are effective in addressing the needs that prompted them. To do so quickly and effectively, the company must (a) understand its current multidimensional structure, (b) have a method of restructuring that doesn't require moving people on an individual basis, and (c) have the ability to do "what-if" modeling and analysis.

Scaling Business Processes

If the organization structure is effectively modeled within a context, automated business processes can scale to the enterprise level. Thus, if a company has improved a business process by automating it, it can apply the new model as a "best practice" company-wide.

SYNCHRONIZING THE INFORMATION

The biggest challenge to getting the most out of your People Relationship Management solution is keeping the information up to date. A company is like a living organism, with cells constantly dying, reproducing and mutating. As soon as the multi-dimensional organization structure is complete, one can be sure that it's no longer valid. This challenge is mitigated using the techniques articulated below.

Aligning with Human Capital Management System

The Human Capital Management system is the system of record for employee indicative information. An HR generalist is typically the person who processes transactions involving the movement of a person through the company. When a person is hired, promoted, or transferred, the HR generalist can adjust reporting relationships, in multiple contexts, while modifying other job-related information.

In addition, a robust People Relationship Management solution will contain rules that apply to the reporting contexts in which the person participates. For instance, let's refer back to the example cited earlier. A manager is designated as the supervisor of all accountants in the Prague office. Processing the transfer of an accountant from the Prague office to the Zurich office will generate a warning, indicating to the HR generalist that the transfer action will have an impact on the employee's reporting relationships. Thus, rule-based enforcement is in effect, but the HR generalist is prompted to ensure that the automated enforcement is valid, and can manually adjust if necessary.

Self-Service Model

Who is better equipped to maintain a worker's reporting relationships than the people closest to them? Each employee should have visibility to all of the reporting contexts in which they participate. If they notice a discrepancy, they can initiate a change. The change will have to be approved by both the "losing" and "gaining" managers. Once approved by both, the change becomes part of the employee's record.

If a manager wants to "pull" an employee from a different manager, or "push" one to another manager, she can initiate such a transaction, which would have to be approved by the other manager to take effect.

Mass Change

During reorganizations, it is essential that executives and HR have a mass change capability to support quick and effective organizational restructurings. This involves the grouping of workers based on rules. Utilizing a "what if" capability, HR can model the change before applying it. The rules can evolve as companies become more mature with the process, and begin to understand the true organizing principles of the company.

PUBLISHING THE INFORMATION

The People Relationship Management solution is intended to be the system of record and a central repository for all relationship information for the enterprise. It is intended to feed all application software that requires relationship information for workflow recipients, or any other purpose.

Web service

A web service will be the primary method for disseminating relationship information to the company. Using a web service, the company can easily enforce its security policy with regard to who can see what information. Also, whichever application is accessing the information can be assured that it is current. In a real-time situation, if an application wants to access the recipient of a workflow item, it needs to specify the following information:

- **Starting point**—the employee who is the subject of the transaction
- **Context**—the type of relationship relevant to the application (i.e., direct manager, HR responsible, financial approver, etc.)
- **Direction**—whether you are ascending a hierarchy (supervisor), descending a hierarchy (subordinate), or accessing a peer
- **Scope**—this is an optional parameter. Scope refers to how many levels you want to retrieve. The application may require the service return a full path up, down or sideways along a context

There are applications, however, that are not designed to access a web service for workflow recipient information, but rather look inward to its own relationship structure. Currently, the vast majority of workflow applications work this way, but hopefully, with the penetration of People Relationship Management solutions, more and more will be designed around a central repository to enable the concept of multi-dimensional relationships. These applications rely on a periodic batch feed to populate relationship information in their internal structure, or expect the structure to be populated manually by the user. In this circumstance, an additional service will be provided which will return an entire context. For instance, a time and attendance product would update its reporting structure during a nightly batch feed, based on the entire time & attendance context from the PRM repository. The obvious disadvantage to this is that you are limited to start of day information.

Despite the penetration of web services to support service oriented architectures, for the most part the world still works on individual interfaces (at the time of this writing). From a procedural point of view, one should be careful not to get bogged down in the business of constructing a plethora of one-off interfaces. The publication model should therefore be the "pull" model, rather than the "push" model, where it is incumbent on the support team of each application to access the information they need in order to get that application to effectively automate its business process.

Visualization

The multi-dimensional organizational model can be complex. Therefore, it is essential that a tool be leveraged to allow employees to view the relationship structures in a simple and understandable way. This tool should allow the ability to change focus among the various contexts, just as an artist would perceive negative and positive space when viewing a subject.

The tool should allow the user to drill down to lower levels or up to higher levels in order to obtain a birds-eye view of a context. The tool should allow an authorized user to invoke the web service to return information when selected. It should allow the user to drag sections and attach to different nodes in "what-if" mode. This is essentially the mass change and modeling function discussed previously.

LEVERAGING SOCIAL NETWORKS

Social networks have become and irresistible force in society, fundamentally changing the way we interact. Networks geared toward professionals, such as LinkedIn, allow people with similar interests to form discussion groups and share ideas. Informal social networks, such as MySpace and Facebook, allow friends to connect and communicate.

Many major companies are using corporate social networking solutions to aid in areas such as recruiting; however there are many other opportunities to leverage this information. If people are given the opportunity to form connections with others, they will...because that's what people do. People form relationships that are mutually beneficial. For instance, a global technology provider has a corporate social network where software architects from around the world can connect, share ideas and experiences, and help each other solve problems. An interesting phenomenon occurs when people voluntarily connect: they have a stake in each other's outcome. This author has anecdotally observed that if one follows the "official" path for information and assistance, there is less incentive to provide assistance, since that relationship is not formalized and won't be reflected in the person's evaluation. However, the "unofficial" connection, which was made voluntarily, will more readily provide assistance despite the lack of tangible benefit. Essentially what is happening is "self-management" where workers find their own avenues of problem solving rather than those directed by management (if management were even to provide such direction). The challenge is for management to tap into this groundswell and leverage it to achieve management's goals, rather than continue to let it be haphazard, while still encouraging spontaneity and creativity. Essentially, to impose structure on something that is inherently un-structured.

A social network (or any network structure) is essentially a set of peer-to-peer relationships, which People Relationship Management natively supports. Since a corporate social network is under the auspices of the company, the company has access to all of the information captured within it. Rather than let happen whatever happens within the network, the company can define rules that encourage behaviors that are beneficial to the company. Following are examples of how a company can leverage social media to achieve its objectives:

- The company can monitor and reward (by integrating with the Talent Management application) mentoring that occurs between a senior and more junior employee.
- Tasks can be assigned to collaborative groups, and the entire group evaluated based on the outcome.
- A collaborative group can be defined as a recipient in a workflow application. For instance, a manager is asked to make a decision based on complex information. The manager can route the information to a collaborative group, asking them for a consensus recommendation. Thus the manager is leveraging the social network to make more informed decisions. Since the process is controlled by a workflow application, it is much more structured than if the same thing was attempted in an informal manner.
- Social networks grow organically. The organizing principles behind them are not readily apparent. Yet, as a PRM context, all transactions and states are stored and available for analysis. One can tap into them to analyze trends and patterns, and be able to scale beneficial structures throughout the organization.
- Social interactions are intrinsic. If we can understand the underlying logic behind social interactions, we have a great insight into solving just about any problem. The study of man-machine interactions has always been an important aspect to successful technology design. Thus having insight into social interactions will become more valuable as technology evolves.

CASE STUDY

Major Financial Services Provider

In the earlier part of this decade, a major financial services provider found itself in regulatory hot water. Through acquisitions and growth, it had evolved into one of the largest multinational financial services "supermarkets" in the world. However, managing this growth had proven to be an issue. Under intense pressure for prof itability, there had recently been incidents where the bank's employees had not acted in an above-board manner. The CEO had committed to the SEC that controls would improve.

To do this, the CEO outlined a multi point plan where managers at each level would undergo training so that they fully understood their commitments to their clients and stockholders. New accountability procedures were enacted.

Although the CEO's plan appeared well-meaning, the company lacked the information requirements to enact it. The company was truly global: in dozens of countries on six continents, speaking multiple languages. The total employee base was in the hundreds of thousands. Through the acquisitions, it was difficult integrating the HR systems of the various companies. The company had eventually settled on a common provider (PeopleSoft), but still had several HCM system instances, arranged geographically, with different business rules, and managed by different business units. All information eventually made it to a global data warehouse.

The problem was that, even though the company was global, each HCM instance had its own organization structure. So if a manager in Singapore was supervised by someone in New York, the New York manager had to exist in both HCM systems! The company had a full suite of HR applications (eRecruiting, Time & Attendance, Manager Self-Service, procurement, compensation, etc.), all of whom had workflow components.

A Problem and an Opportunity

However, the main business driver for the system was an Identity and Entitlement initiative. The company was required to carry out periodic entitlement reviews, to determine which assets each employee had access to, based on her position. To implement this, it was imperative that the company have a handle on its fully articulated tree structure. The company needed its primary reporting structure to be fully articulated at all times or else it was out of compliance. There was a "drop-dead" deadline imposed, by which date the system *had* to be implemented.

The company also recognized that it had several contextual managerial roles, and had a matrix management structure. The decision for the initial roll out was to support three management contexts, although the system was designed to support an unlimited number of contexts. Representatives from the business felt that additional managerial contexts would require additional training and a cultural change, so it was deferred to a later phase. The cultural change to implement three managerial contexts was significant in its own right. Each regional HCM had its own business rules and processes. The "direct manager" in one region meant something different than "direct manager" in another. Also, one region's HR generalists were used to updating the reporting structure from the HCM and didn't want to change the process—so the system had to be designed to propagate a context from the HCM, but only in certain circumstances. Coordinating the implementation and testing efforts among the regional HCMs and the global data warehouse presented management challenges.

Planned Functionality

The system was to support employee and manager self-service in order to keep the information in sync. A mass change function allowed executives and HR to respond to reorganizations quickly. A real-time edit during updates to the critical structure ensured that a fully-articulated tree structure would be maintained. A batch process would run every night which would capture HR transactions that would break the fully articulated tree structure resulted in moving all affected nodes up a level, to ensure that the structure was compliant at all times. The users called this a "self-healing" function. The stakeholders recognized a need to "filter" contexts for particular groups of individuals. For instance, the European Union has strict laws governing information privacy. Therefore, the company needed to make certain reporting relationships visible only to authorized parties.

As with many projects, the ambitious functionality came into conflict with the strict deadline. The deadline was paramount, so scope was pared to make the date. The self-service and filtering functionality fell victim to these realities.

Despite some tense moments, the system went live on the required date, and has since provided a real-time view of the true organizational structure across hundreds of thousands of employees, in dozens of countries, whose information resides in several HCM systems. One of the stakeholders summed up the benefits: "The People Tree allows the services to reliably present to the Direct Managers their direct reports for manager-allowed updates to worker records, entitlement reviews for: 1) applications; 2) building space access; and 3) provisioning/de-provisioning of worker services...The tree now is 'self-healing' in that if a Direct Manager is terminated one day the tree will move their former direct reports (and rollup reports) up the tree to the first active Direct Manager[2]."

At this writing, the system has been in production for three years, serving the needs of the company. However, due to economic conditions, deployment of subsequent phase functionality has been deferred.

CONCLUSION

As practitioners of Business Process Management, we strive to make work easier, by automating the administrative tasks involved with a business process, therefore allowing the workers to focus on the tasks that require a human touch. Through effective automation, we are therefore promoting the human capacity, by allowing people to focus on tasks that only a human being can accomplish. Many of the jobs that have recently been lost will never return. Companies will rely more heavily on automation and workflow to eliminate tasks formerly handled by administrators, and even some knowledge workers. The nature of work and the skills that will be more highly valued are changing irrevocably. MIT's Frank Levy and Harvard's Richard Murnane argue that the automation of business processes has heightened the value of two categories of human skills: "expert thinking— solving new problems for which there are no routine solutions; and complex communication—persuading, explaining, and in other ways conveying a particular interpretation of information[3]."

Through effective automation, we can reduce the administrative and burdensome tasks that get in the way of people doing the creative work that humans do best. People Relationship Management completes the Business Process Management value proposition by acknowledging the value of worker relationships in a business process. Only once the mundane tasks are reduced or eliminated can we leverage the insights that PRM delivers into the way humans interact. If properly implemented, PRM will contribute to improvements in the way organizations are managed, and take the automation of business processes to the next level.

Endnotes:

[1] Galbraith, J.R. Matrix Organization Designs: How to combine functional and project forms. Business Horizons, February, 1971

[2] Email from project stakeholder, January 17, 2007

[3] Levy, Frank and Murnane, Richard. The New Division of Labor: How Computers Are Creating the Next Job Market, April, 2004

Section 3

BPM in Technology and Standards

Two Strategies for Handling Models: Preserving vs. Transforming

Keith D Swenson, Fujitsu America, Inc., USA

ABSTRACT

This chapter defines two key concepts: the "Model Preserving Strategy" and the "Model Transforming Strategy." It then compares the effectiveness of these two strategies in a number of different situations and assesses their effectiveness in meeting different goals. BPM systems tend to implement one of these two strategies. These strategies represent two fundamentally different approaches to providing Business Process Management (BPM). By identifying which strategy the product takes, we can identify which goals the product is more adept at achieving. Neither strategy is superior to the other in all cases. Instead, it is important to identify the goals of the solution you are implementing. Organizations wishing to have business people in control of processes and optimizing processes for business goals are likely to find the Model Preserving Strategy most effective. Organization wishing to empower the system engineers and allow for optimization of system resources may find the Model Transforming Strategy most effective. The most important thing is that we all need to be aware of these two strategies and understand that there is no single approach that works best for all BPM solutions.

During a casual conversation at the October 2008 BPM Tech Show in DC that quickly turned into a debate on "What are advantages/disadvantages of either preserving or transforming a BPM model?" we found that most existing systems tend to follow one of two possible strategies. Existing BPM Systems (and their associated methodologies) can be categorized as supporting either a "Model Transforming Strategy" or a "Model Preserving Strategy."

Some of the debaters insisted that preserving the model through the process development lifecycle was the critical ingredient that makes agility possible. Others argued strongly that transforming the model into other forms is the correct and most effective way to implement processes. After the event, we held a number of conference calls in the attempt to fully understand the distinction, and most importantly, when each of these strategies is best used.

It was remarkable how passionate people were about their position, and equally remarkable how oblivious many were to the existence of differing positions. This blindness to the two different strategies for using models convinced us of the importance of this topic for the Workflow Handbook, and for helping the industry resolve some long debated issues on process modeling. This chapter does not discuss what elements are needed for process modeling. By staying clear of model specifics, we can discuss instead how models are treated during the business process lifecycle, and gain a clear understanding of these two different goals of modeling.

COMMON GROUND

In part, both strategies make similar assumptions about the process of creating a process. All agree that we want to make a model of a business process so that this expression of the business process can be used to support the organization in actually running the business process. There is also broad agreement that once implemented, this process will not be fixed forever, but that we will engage in Business Process Management which is the continual incremental improvement of the process to optimize the resources of the organization.

There are many different business modeling formalisms. Many claim to be loosely based on Business Process Modeling Notation (BPMN), but there are many alternate formalisms available as well and should not be discounted out of hand. Many of the modeling formalisms are based on a visual, graphical approach, but some are not, and it is important to remember that when talking about a model we are not necessarily talking about a visual diagram. This chapter will not discuss what a model is but will instead focus exclusively on how models are handled, and specifically on how different handling strategies will provide different kinds of benefits.

In the world of BPM, nothing is static. We need to understand that there are at least three different kinds of dynamics, and these terms will help us distinguish them:

- Business Process Enactment: The process itself has a dynamic component as it moves from the beginning to the end of the handling of a single case. The process definition does not normally change here. Only the context of the process instance that records the state of a particular case changes.
- Business Process Lifecycle: These are the changes that a business process goes through from initial concept, to modeling, to integration, and finally to deployment into an enactment environment.
- Business Process Improvement: This is the change to a business process that occurs over time through repeated use of the business process lifecycle followed by analysis of how well that version of the business process worked. This is the TQM or continual improvement aspect of BPM.

There is broad agreement that a process definition passes through a lifecycle that will involve different people with different specializations along the way. The original concept for a business process will probably start with a "pure" business owner. There may be a "business process analyst" who has insight into the business itself, and also has skill in being able to model that process. There may be a "systems engineer" who performs the work of integrating the process with the other systems in the organization. Finally in the enactment environment, there are administrators and users who interact with the running processes.

Business Process Analyst	Systems Engineer	Administrator & End Users
MODEL	**MODEL**	**MODEL**

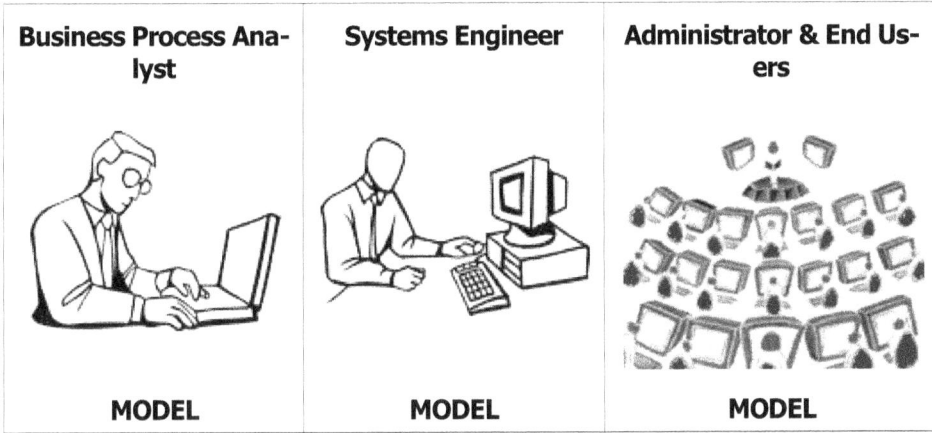

This is a common example lifecycle, but in some cases much more elaborate lifecycles exist that pass through four or more different specializations. For discussion, we should stick primarily to this three-step lifecycle.

A Model Preserving Strategy is distinguished from a Model Transforming Strategy only within the process development lifecycle. Both strategies support process enactment. Both strategies support process improvement. Both strategies have a process lifecycle, but the way that the model is handled within the lifecycle is very different.

MODEL TRANSFORMING STRATEGY—DEFINITION

Proponents of the Model Transforming Strategy hold that the model should be transformed into different forms as it steps through the stages of the process lifecycle. Each form of the model is designed to be most appropriate for the specialized domain at that stage in the lifecycle.

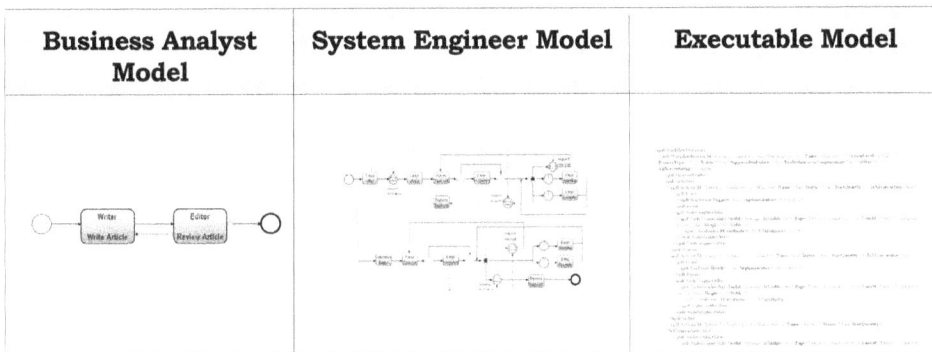

Business Analyst Model	System Engineer Model	Executable Model

The business process analyst designs a high-level model in the business domain. This business person/process analyst is not expected to be a programmer. The high-level model is then transformed into something suitable for a programmer for the second stage in the lifecycle. This is done by translating a "business domain" model to a "system domain" model, either by adding in extra nodes that handle integration activities, or by transforming the diagram into a completely new diagram that represents the system-level interactions that have to go on in order to cause the business-level interactions to take place. The systems engineer then works with this form of the model to integrate the process with the other systems. Later, this is transformed again for the enactment environment.

The model transforming strategy comes from a long tradition of programming and system development. In the software engineering field, the high-level model is often expressed in a visual language known as Unified Modeling Language (UML). This might then be translated into a programming language like C++. The intended program is there, but the form is entirely changed and bears no resemblance to the original UML. Some would say that the UML is "destroyed" and then replaced by the other form. Meaningful aspects of the original are expressed in the new form, but in an entirely different way. Often the transformation is "lossy," which is to say that there are some aspects of the original which are simply not included in the transformed version. Perhaps the transformed version does not need those aspects of the former model. For example when C++ is transformed to machine code, the variable names are lost because the machine code has no need for the variable names. These kinds of transformations are routine in the software development world.

Coming back to a BPM example, the business analyst might put an activity describing a document review in the business view. This would be transformed to the following set of activities

1. An activity which sends email informing the person
2. An activity to check the document out of a repository
3. An activity to send a reminder message if the response is getting late
4. An activity that waits for the response to come back.

The programmer might extend this to include notations for handling exceptions and other timeouts that the business person did not include. Later, this might be transformed again to obtain the executable code.

Being accustomed to this approach, it is easy to imagine how software engineering experts viewed BPM as just another case of the translation of a high-level model into executable code. Conventional wisdom says that we should stay with the successful approach from the past, and this is strongly encouraged by vendors that have tools designed to support the Model Transforming Strategy.

MODEL PRESERVING STRATEGY—DEFINITION

An alternate strategy exists that retains the same form of the model through the process lifecycle. This strategy is actually quite common among the Human BPM products. The lifecycle is essentially the same:

First, the business person draws up a high-level model of the process that represents the business view of what has to happen in the process. It has all of the major activities in a way that is meaningful to the people in the organization.

Second, the process model is given to a programmer, who implements the integration of this process with other information systems. The difference is that this is done without changing the form of the original model. Instead of transforming the model, the original visual nodes are left in place. Additional settings are made on those existing nodes to make them capable to do the integration tasks. This embellishes the nodes in the model, but does not change its form.

Third, the model is installed into the process execution engine, again without any transformation. The number of activities nodes in the engine is exactly the same number of activity nodes that the business person drew. The connections between them are exactly the same as the business person drew. This is the principle of "What You Draw is What You Execute" (WYDIWYE).

Business Analyst Model	System Engineer Model	Executable Model

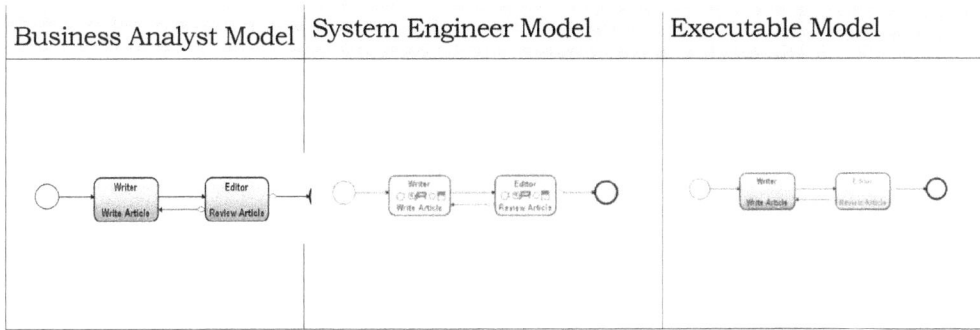

This model travels through the entire system without any change of form. At least there is no change required by the lifecycle. It is possible that the developer will see a way to improve the original model, but such a change is done in collaboration with a business analyst because both are working on the same model and both are seeing the same form.

THE ESSENCE OF TRANSFORMATION

The above pictorial representations of the models used in three different stages are designed to illustrate what it means for a model to change form, but you should not take these illustrations as literal pictures of actual models. The pictures are somewhat exaggerated to emphasize the sameness that a model preserving strategy gives and the change that a transforming strategy brings.

A model preserving strategy does not change the form of the model, but that does not mean that the model cannot be exported into other basic formats. There are many formats that can be used to represent a model. These formats often preserve the fundamental form of the model. Thus, just because a product exports the model to another format, you should not assume that it is necessarily implementing a model transformation strategy. Model transformation employs a fairly fundamental change to the form of the model with the emphasis on consuming and digesting the original model, then generating a new model in a new form which is optimized for the current step of the lifecycle, without any regard to preserving the original model. While it is difficult to put a formal definition on what is preserving and what is transforming, in practice existing implementation tend to fall very clearly into one strategy or the other.

COMPARISONS SCENARIOS / GOALS

There are many different goals and benefits that one might expect when employing BPM in an organization. The two different model strategies will have an effect on the amount of return in these different areas. We can compare the two strategies in the following areas:

- Analytics—A by-product of automating work is the records made that indicate precisely when each task is started and completed. Analytic information about how your organization is working can actually be far more valuable than the cost savings derived from the automation. A lot can be learned from this analysis that can help you improve your organization. Some claim that this is the principle benefit of BPM.
- Round Trip Engineering—The process lifecycle is explicitly about moving the process through different people with different specializations. The business analyst draws a high-level model and the systems engineer in-

cludes details for connecting the systems. Round Trip is the ability to bring that back to the business analyst to make modifications without losing the work that the system engineer did.

- Agile Development and Continual Improvement—The ability to quickly respond to changes in the business environment is an advantage of an Agile approach to the development of a business process. One aspect of Agile development is the idea that changes are made as small, incremental improvements, and this fits well with the idea that BPM is about continual improvement of business processes.

- Performance—The main reason for transforming a model into another form is to realize performance improvements and to be able to make use of specific capabilities that are available in one domain and not in others.

- Simulation—Most BPM systems offer some form of simulation capability. Simulation capabilities range from the very simple ability to walk through a process, to very sophisticated case-arrival/activity performance models, and even to goal-seeking optimization capabilities.

- Diagnosing Process Problems—No process is perfect, and regardless of how well a process is designed, cases will occur that were not anticipated and not handled correctly. When these problems occur, the people working on the process must recognize this situation, and be able to recognize what is wrong with the process, so that future instances of the process will not have that problem.

All of these areas are affected by the model strategy.

ANALYTICS

The purpose of analytics is to provide information about how well your organization is performing, and to help to find areas that might be improved.

The raw analytical data consists of records that document when an activity within a process changes state. For example, a record is made when an activity starts, and another when the activity ends. There can be other records if the activity goes through other internal states. Business managers want to know how long an activity typically takes. This is calculated as the difference between the start time and the end time.

In the Model Transforming Strategy, the activities within a process are replaced with activities that are appropriate for another domain. In the business domain you may want an activity to represent the review and approval of a document. In the system domain there is an activity for retrieving the document, an activity for sending an alert message, an activity for a possible reminder message, and an activity to sit and wait for the response. In other cases, multiple steps at the business level may be consolidated into a single step at the system domain.

The transformation is not trivial because there are logic constraints in each domain that may not be compatible. The business level may allow unbounded loops, while the system level requires strict nesting. There may be logic patterns allowed in one domain, but not in the other.

The analytic information collected by the runtime engine tells when activities started, when they completed, how long they took, and how often different branches are taken. However this information is not useful to the business analyst because it does not match the model with which the business person is familiar. There will be statistics about activities that the business person has never seen, and information about activities that exist only in the business domain will be completely missing.

In the Model Preserving Strategy, the model in the business domain retains the same form in the system domain as it is when installed in the enactment engine. The analytic information about when an activity starts and completes, how long activities take, and how often a given branch is taken is all useful in a discussion with the business person because the form of the model is the same. A business person can point to a particular activity in a model, and mine the Analytics records to find out how long that activity typically takes. The Analytic information is meaningful to the business analyst, as well as to the users and system integrators.

The Model Preserving Strategy has an advantage when your goal is to provide good analytic information that is useful to business people.

ROUND TRIP ENGINEERING

We often talk about the process "Round Trip." The process lifecycle is explicitly about moving the process through different people with different specializations. The business analyst draws a high-level model and the systems integrator includes details for connecting the systems. Round Trip capability is a way to allow the business analyst to be able to make further changes to the model, without forcing the system engineer to start from scratch with the integration work. The basic Round-trip concept is that all the changes made by the programmer during integration are somehow brought back to the original model. If Round Trip is well supported, then the business analyst can make a small change, and the system engineer only needs to make the associated small change. The earlier engineering work has been preserved throughout the cycle.

The Model Transforming Strategy presents a significant challenge to an effective round trip. When transforming from business domain to system domain, certain aspects of the model that are not needed for the integration or enactment are typically left behind. Then the systems engineer starts to modify the transformed model. When done, it is not always clear how those changes should fit with the things in the original business domain model.

It is not always the case that information must be left behind when transforming between domains. Some systems encode those things needed only in the business domain into passive elements of the system domain model. This works if the two models are only slightly different, but transformation is often more significant. Without a one-to-one correlation between objects in the two domains, there is often no place to put this information.

A second approach to allowing round trip is to simply put identifying numbers into the generated elements that indicate the parts of the business domain model from which they came. The business domain model is retained by the business analyst. Later the modified integration domain model can be re-imported into the retained business model. If any of the identifiers match at import time, then that integration information is associated in such a way that it can be re-exported again next time.

While it is a significant challenge, it is possible for a Model Transforming Strategy to support round trip capabilities even though they transform the model to other forms.

The Model Preserving Strategy has a much easier time carrying all the information by all roles through a complete round trip. Each domain may have specialized information for its use, but because the model retains the same form through the lifecycle, it is fairly easy to provide a single model that can carry all information from all domains. Preserving the form of the model guarantees a correspondence between the work done in the business domain with the work done in the system domain. Additions in one domain will necessitate corresponding additions in another domain, while removals in one domain will automatically remove the corresponding information from the other domains.

There is almost nothing to do. Since the model is preserved in the same form, it is simply a matter of making sure that the business analyst uses the latest copy with all the integration embellishments.

Because the Model Preserving Strategy supports round-trip engineering so well, it is actually possible for the business analyst and the system integrator to work simultaneously on the same model. (By simultaneously I don't mean keystroke-for-keystroke simultaneousness, but rather that one opens, changes, and saves; then, the other opens, changes, and saves.) All you need is a standard resource management system to allow each person to lock the model while they edit. This enables true collaboration between the various domains.

While it is not impossible for a Model Transformation Strategy to provide round trip engineering, it is technically very difficult, and only the most sophisticated systems support it. In contrast, round trip engineering is so easy for a Model Preserving Strategy that virtually all such systems offer strong round trip support, and even go further to offer very fast cycle times and near-simultaneous collaboration.

AGILE DEVELOPMENT & CONTINUOUS IMPROVEMENT

"Agile BPM Development" is not just about implementing quickly, but also about implementing iteratively. The Agile method is to implement part of a solution, try that out, maybe measure how well that works, implement a bit more, try that out, and so on. There are many small changes, with each change being implemented and released in a very short time. In each cycle you want to start with the results of the last cycle. In this way, you avoid a significant amount of rework on every cycle.

The ability to support round trips is directly proportional to the ability to support Agile. Any limitation in carrying integration changes back to the business domain adds significant effort on every cycle because some parts of the integration work must be done again. The more work that is required to perform an iteration, the less net value you get from making a small change. In order to prevent waste, an organization in this situation will wait longer and save up more changes before executing the iteration.

The Model Preserving Strategy holds a clear advantage for those interested in Agile development. Because the form of the model remains the same, it is possible for different parts of the lifecycle to be working on the same copy of the model at (nearly) the same time. A business person can make a five percent change to a model. The programmer can make a five percent change to the same copy of the model. The modified process can be installed into the enactment engine without significant rework. A Model Transformation Strategy can get close to this, but the fast pace in which the model is transformed prevents people from working simultaneously.

PERFORMANCE

Transforming for Execution Performance

Processes and programs are written by people, but execute in a machine. Those machines (or execution environments) have certain capabilities, either limitations or affordances for doing specific things. Transforming the model can allow you to take advantage of those capabilities, or work around the limitations, to have a faster running program. This is like an optimizing compiler that will take a third generation language and convert it to machine code that uses specific capabilities of the target machine to run faster.

The alternative to compiling a program to machine code is to interpret the program. Interpreted languages such as LISP, PERL, PHP, Ruby, and JavaScript come to mind. Sometimes a "just in time" compiler is used to compile the code just before it is run, but the environment does it transparently so that the transformed version is never seen by anyone. Java is a language that is compiled to an intermediate form that is then interpreted. The trade-off between using a compiled language and an interpreted language is much debated, and still depends upon how much performance you need. The core of a database server is a performance critical component that clearly requires a highly optimized language. Many web application development environments use an interpreted language, because CPU performance is not a critical aspect of these types of applications.

The model transforming strategy can do the same for business processes by taking in a diagram that is meaningful to a business analyst and producing an optimized output that runs faster in the execution environment.

Transforming for Developer Optimization

Another reason for transforming a model is to put it in a form that is comfortable for a system integrator. If you have Java developers on staff, then transforming the BPMN model to Java would allow those developers to be more effective with less training than if they were forced to learn about the constraints of BPMN.

This transformation will not necessarily be from BPMN to a programming language. In some cases the transformation will be from one style of BPMN to another style of BPMN. The difference being that the business domain model is a BPMN diagram representing flow of responsibility, while the system domain model is a BPMN representation of the flow of data.

The point is that the transformation is from a form that is best for a business analyst to use, to a form that is best for the system integrator to use. If your business process requires a lot of system integration work, then optimizing developer time might be significant.

Strategy Comparison for Performance

The entire reason for preserving the model across the process lifecycle is to make end-to-end coordination easy at the expense of the intermediate steps. System engineers are not prevented from doing the system integration, but they simply must do the work directly in the same model that the business person used. The execution of the model is not prevented, it simply must execute from the same form that the business person used. This is the trade off.

If you have a BPM project that involves a lot of programming work to integrate systems, relatively less work from the business domain, and a low likelihood of a need to evolve the business model over time, then a Model Transforming Strategy will allow you to optimize the use of the systems engineers. They can work in a familiar way using tools and skills they already have.

If you anticipate a large rate of transaction processing, you may need to consider the Model Transformation Strategy for high performance, but how large is large? You can determine your rate of processing as follows:

1. Count the cases per month.
2. Multiply by the average number of activities per case.
3. Divide by the number of hours per month to find the approximate number of activity executions per hour.

If this works out to be more than one million activity executions per hour, then you must consider carefully whether a compiled approach is required. If you anticipate 10,000 activity executions per hour or less, then there will be no problem using an interpreted approach, even on a very modest server. These are just ballpark figures, and between these two you will have to consider the specifics of the implementation and the type of transactions being invoked. It is worth noting that many important business critical processes involve less than 10,000 activity executions per hour, and performance is simply not an issue.

Performance experts know that programs spend most of their time in five percent of the code. If you can optimize that five percent of the code, you can often attain 99 percent of the performance that would have been gained from optimizing all of the code. This explains why interpreted BPM diagrams working at a high level by calling into functions that are themselves optimized often perform just about as fast as compiled programs. Thus, overall performance is less related to whether the code is compiled or not, and more related to whether the supporting functionality is a good fit for the need.

The rise in popularity of interpreted languages for web applications is an indication that CPU performance is no longer a limiting factor in many web applications. Experience shows that servers are more limited by IO bandwidth now, than they are by CPU usage, so overall performance can often be enhanced by spending CPU time on interpreting a language if in return you can reduce the data transfer requirements.

If most of the project effort is going to be in system integration, or you have an extremely high rate of activity execution, then the Model Transforming Strategy allows you the flexibility to be able to optimize for the programmer and the specific requirements of the execution environment.

SIMULATION

Most BPM systems offer some form of simulation capability. Simulation capabilities range from the very simple ability to walk through a process, to very sophisticated case-arrival/activity performance models, and even to goal-seeking optimization capabilities. The usefulness of simulation is often debated, but let me categorize people into two camps: simulation optimists and simulation pessimists.

The simulation optimist probably expects a little too much detailed insight into how future cases will flow through the process. The optimist expects precise quantitative measures of what everyone in the process will be doing. Simulation can provide this information, but in order to do so, the simulator must be provided with precise quantitative measures of the cases that will be coming, the amount of time it will take to handle every activity, and precise models of the workers who will be doing their jobs. This works passably only in cases where you have extremely large numbers of essentially identical cases and for jobs where the individual differences in the workers' skill, knowledge, or background makes no difference at all. Even in these cases, tracking down accurate information on activity time and case distributions can take more effort than the information gained from the simulation is worth. While the optimist has inflated expectations, there is no denying that simulation can give you good information on relatively straightforward scenarios, like "What if my case load increases 20 percent, where will I have to increase resources?" or "if I can eliminate one step for 90 percent of least-risk cases, how do the time savings compare to the expected cost of the low probability problem?"

The pessimists don't expect a rabbit that was not already there to come out of a hat, but even a pessimist can see that running a simulation provides an ability to see the dynamics inherent in the model as an aid to understanding the process as it is modeled. Formal graphical models are things that are not entirely natural to most people, and we can all use help understanding the model. This is a kind of "debug" capability that allows the business analyst to find basic problems before they get into the next step of development.

Simulation and Transforming Strategy

For the pessimist, simulation is very important because it allows the business person to work the problems of the model out at the business level, before it is transformed into a model for the system domain. Since mistakes at one level are magnified after transformation, it is important to use whatever techniques are available in order to debug before going to the next level.

For the optimist, the problem is that simulation of the business domain model may, or may not, be relevant in the system domain or the enactment domain. Spending a tremendous amount of time building a precise model of the workers and the caseload may be for nothing if the model is transformed for actual execution. Finding that a particular resource level produces optimum flow through the business model may not turn out to be the optimum solution once the model is transformed. Simulating in the system or enactment domain will give you a better optimum, but these models don't have meaning for the business analysts, and it may not be obvious how to translate the optimum situation back into the business domain. Simulation optimist are finding that simulations are significantly complicated by the model is transformation.

Simulation and Preserving Strategy

Clearly the optimists are on better ground when the model designed by the business analysts is represented in a one-for-one way with the process that is executed in the enactment engine. An optimum setting is more likely to represent reality.

For the pessimist, the situation is about the same between the two strategies. Simulation can help one understand the dynamics of the situation, and that will be the case whether the model is transformed later or not. Although one might point out that since the model is never transformed, there is no urgency to complete the simulation before progressing to the next stage. If the model keeps the same form through the lifecycle, the business analyst and the system integrator can cooperate on running simulation models with increasing precision.

In summary, the pessimist sees a basic benefit from simulation regardless of whether the model is transformed or not, but the optimist who is really trying to get quantitative results from the simulation will see much better results in a system that preserves the model's form through the BPM lifecycle.

Problem Diagnosis

Process definitions are designed to support a process, and usually have built into them assumptions about what to do in the case of an exception to the normal rules. But there are two types of exceptions: those that you anticipate and those that you do not anticipate. If an exceptional situation can be anticipated, then the business process can have a way of handling that exception built into it. An example might be a deadline: if an applicant does not respond within a specified time period, then the application is automatically canceled. The exceptional situation is handled by the process and there is no problem.

But there are exceptions that cannot be anticipated. Of course, the process cannot be designed to handle unanticipated exception. If this exceptional situation occurs, then the process may go off in a direction that is entirely inappropriate. Clearly when a business process is initially implemented, there will be more of these unanticipated exceptional situations. One might assume that over time the process will become more complete. There will be a decrease in the number of unanticipated exceptional situations. Because the world is changing, the business environment is continually changing, and the organization is continually changing, there is no way to completely eliminate unanticipated exceptional situations.

When an exception occurs, members within the organization must somehow notice that the process is somehow wrong for the exceptional situation. Noticing that something is wrong is normally not difficult. The next step is to diagnose what it is about the process that is incorrect and propose a change that will fix it. This is a practice known well to programmers as "debugging." Debugging a business process is a little different than debugging a standalone application because when many people are using a system it is not easy to identify the exact set of input which led to the failure situation.

The Model Transforming Strategy produces an executable model that is different from the one drawn by the business people. The business person who designed the process may not recognize the state into which it has gotten. It may not be clear how to change the process to avoid this situation in the executable model. The systems engineer, who is familiar with a model that is presumably closer to the executable model may have a much better chance of identifying the cause of the problem, but may not be able to relate this back to the business situation that ultimately causes the problem.

The Model Preserving Strategy offers a much greater chance of diagnosing problems in the business domain because the form of the model has remained the same. When the process goes down the wrong branch, that branch is the same branch that the business person put in place, and will be more recognizable. The execution of the model follows the same form as the original business model, so if there is a problem, it is far easier to identify the location of the problem. The program execution moves through the same states that the business person designed. The business person presumably is knowledgeable about the people who perform tasks in a process, and since there is a one to one mapping between those activities and the activities designed by the business analyst, there can be better and more effective communications between these people. It is more likely that the business person will understand the problem situation, and more likely to be in a position to offer a change that is appropriate.

So the Model Preserving Strategy offers an advantage when debugging a process. It is not impossible for a Model Transforming Strategy to offer similar level of support for debugging the process, but it is significantly harder to do so, and many such systems lack sufficient support for this.

CONCLUSIONS

Software engineers have a lot of success with the Model Transforming Strategy in producing software of all types. An elaboration of this strategy is called Model Driven Architecture. MDA is defined as "a style of enterprise application development and integration, based on using automated tools to build system independent models and transform them into efficient implementations."[1] It is important to emphasize that this approach is not only well accepted, but that there is plenty of evidence that it works very well.

Yet in most of the cases above (all except for performance) the Model Preserving Strategy provides a clear advantage for BPM. This apparent contradiction is explained once you understand that BPM is not software engineering.

One major difference between producing an application and supporting a business process is that a typical user has no need to know the internal state of a running application. For example, the user has no interest in knowing how many times a particular branch is taken inside a typical word processor. The users of an application are not engaged in continual improvement of the application. While an application program can be a black box to the people who use it, Business Process Management requires some amount of visibility into how well the processes are being enacted so that the organization can enter into a cycle of continual improvement. A business manager needs to know what the people are doing in the business processes. A business process is fundamentally different from a program that is executing on a computer CPU because it involves people doing work.

Analytics is really just visibility into the running environment, so it comes as no surprise that coherence between the execution environment and the business domain design environment is a fundamental requirement for retrieving information, and allowing the business person to understand it. The same is true with simulation, which is similarly enabled by keeping the form of execution to be the same as the form used by the person who knows the business. Analytics, simulation, and visibility into internal running states are simply not as great a concern when writing a traditional application.

BPM must respond to changes in the business environment, and as such there is a greater need for change. Since the business environmental change is a business domain change, it is much more critical to have round trip support, Agile, and continual improvement than it is for changes in traditional application development. Problem diagnosis is an area that requires both the internal visibility as well as the ability to make changes. Traditional applications also must change and improve, but those doing the changing use a different time scale and have a different level of technical expertise.

What it really comes down to is: "Who is in the driver's seat?"

- Business Analyst: A system that is designed to allow the business analyst to be in control of process definitions will find that the Model Preserving Strategy gives the business analyst better information and a better ability to control the process. A business analyst will find that a Model Transforming Strategy is less comfortable because it is harder to understand what is happening in the process at run-time and that there is a bigger barrier to making changes.

- System Engineer: A system engineer will tend to prefer a Model Transforming Strategy because it provides a more optimized output and allows the engineer to make use of the specific capabilities of each domain. A system engineer will find the Model Preserving Strategy less comfortable because the integration work must be accomplished in a form that fits, literally, with the model designed by the business analyst.

The conclusion is that there is no single choice of a better strategy. Each strategy offers benefits for different situations. It is important, then, for each purchaser of BPM technology to understand what their goals are, and then ultimately to select a system that implements the strategy that allows them to best achieve their goals.

ACKNOWLEDGMENTS

A great number of people were involved in discussions around model transforming and model preserving strategies, and all of their input was greatly appreciated.

I am grateful to Fujitsu Computer Systems for supporting my research into these topics, as well as my time to participate in the Workflow Management Coalition. Fujitsu produces a wide range of middleware technology under the brand Interstage. Fujitsu has offerings that support the Model Transformation Strategy (Interstage Integration Manager) as well as offerings which support Model Preservation Strategy (Interstage BPM). More information can be found at http://www.fujitsu.com/interstage.

REFERENCES

[1] Grady Booch et al, "An MDA Manifesto," MDA Journal, May 2004, http://www.bptrends.com/publicationfiles/05-04%20COL%20IBM%20Manifesto%20-%20Frankel%20-3.pdf

A Design Methodology for BPMN

Michele Chinosi and Alberto Trombetta
University of Insubria, Varese, Italy

ABSTRACT

We present our contributions to business process design. Our starting point has been a thorough analysis of the OMG standard BPMN. While uncovering several of BPMN's weak points, our analysis has brought in a novel three-phase design methodology for BPMN.

INTRODUCTION

Having a business processes notation and a corresponding conceptual model is not enough when dealing with the modeling of large, complex business processes. As already done in several other contexts [6, 7], we provide a modeling methodology to support users design and represent business processes. Often, in real scenarios business processes are described using (more or less formalized) graphical languages and/or models. During the last few years, several efforts have been made in order to provide tools to accomplish this requirement, the more notable being WS-BPEL [4], XPDL [5], UML [7], BPMN [1]. As another active line of work, there have been several attempts to provide a formalization.

Our design methodology proposal fills a gap in the business processes modeling scenario, since there is no mention about BP design and/or modeling methodologies inside the most recent specifications published or submitted to be published (as for example in the case of BPMN 2.0 proposals). Nonetheless, it is acknowledged that design methodologies for business process will be intensively investigate in the next coming years [9].

By a business process design methodology we mean a set of transformation rules specifying how a business process element can be modeled and a set of (possibly semi-formal) rules addressing how such transformation rules should be applied in order to derive a correct and complete business process, with respect to the initial specifications.

In this chapter, we present our proposal which consists in a three-phase methodology. Each phase takes care of relevant features of every design methodology: the first phase deals with the conceptual modeling of BPs, intended as a way—through so-called *design rules*—of identifying the relevant tasks and information flows that contribute to the business process to be modeled, as inferred from the (usually natural language-based) requirements.

The second phase takes the resulting BP diagram from the 1st phase and refines it using *reduction* and *refinement rules*. Such rules are applied in order to bring a diagram satisfying criteria like correctness and economy (to be explained later).

Finally, the third phase serializes the resulting diagram from the 2nd phase using a self-developed XML-based representation of BPMN 1.1 called BPeX (Business Process eXtensions). The conceptual model behind such serialization is a very relevant piece of our approach but due to space constraints, we will focus on just the first two phases, which are more relevant from a design point of view. Furthermore, we will motivate and discuss our approach with an example taken from a classical customer/supplier scenario. A more extensive description of such work as well as the motivating example is found in the Ph.D. Thesis of the first author [3].

RELATED WORK

To the best of knowledge there are no other works defining a design methodology for business processes, using in particular BPMN as the reference notation.

Several efforts has been made to develop business processes modeling notations and languages, starting from the more classical approaches like UML and workflows and passing through Petri Nets, π-calculus, Event-driven Process Chain (EPC). Also several serialization formats have been published in the last few years, as for the WfMC XPDL and WS-BPEL. Many works have thoroughly discussed on the capabilities and advantages as well as on weak points of using each of those notations and languages [10, 11, 12, 13, 14]. Muehlen et al. have provide a thorough analysis of BPMN elements set usage [30] emphasizing some properties a good business process modeling technique should have [29].

Our definition of business processes design methodology draws inspiration from several contributions on workflows patterns analysis (among others, the well-knows contribution of van der Aalst work [2] and new works as for [21]), reduction rules (even if applied as stand-alone approaches) [25,26] as well as engineering approaches [27,22]. These frameworks were applied to other processes modeling representations [19], like EPC or Petri Nets.

There are some works regarding a query language for BPMN, as in [18, 19] with BPMN-Q and in [15, 16, 17] with BP-QL, but they are still at an early stage of formalization.

As the Object Management Group (OMG) published in 2007 a Request For Proposals for a new version of BPMN named BPMN 2.0, which should encompass the BP modeling notation, its metamodel and a serialization format, there are two main submission teams, one led by BEA, IBM, Oracle [31] and the other by Adaptive, Axway Software, Hewlett-Packard, Lombardi Software, Fujitsu [32]. This motivated us not to provide an implementation tied to a specific model of the design methodology but to give a more general, high-level description of it.

BUSINESS PROCESS DESIGN METHODOLOGY

As already said, we propose a *three-phase* methodology to support modelers design processes starting from natural language-based specifications. Each phase comprises a set of *rules* which act as guidelines for the modeler to obtain a well-formed and valid business process model starting from natural language specifications. Here, *valid* and *well-formed* mean having result diagrams which are compliant to BPMN specifications under several aspects as, for example, graphical representation, syntax and semantics. We remark that the application of the rules to a process description in natural language may yield different valid diagrams—assuming that the resulting diagrams fulfill the requirements, correctly describing the original process features and behavior. This is because there are several ways to model a process depending on different factors, not least the varying skill levels of modelers.

Instead of starting from scratch, in order to develop our methodology we chose to start with a well-known modeling methodology (the E-R modeling methodology for databases, but also the more general ANSI definition [8]), adapting it to our needs. The significance of this approach, according to ANSI, is that it allows the three phases to be relatively independent of each other. Hence, this design methodology could be applied independently from a BPMN specific element set, from the underlying model or, even, from the chosen serialization language (with the adequate changes if needed).

PHASE 1: CONCEPTUAL MODELING

Natural language specifications are very often the starting point of the design phase. Most enterprises have lots of documentation describing internal processes and their relationships with other stakeholders (e.g., customers, suppliers). It is difficult to understand the behavior of a set of (often interacting) processes and only few employees can accomplish this task successfully. Few attempts to adopt a standardized lexicon for writing specifications have been made [33]. But up to now they are not very well known. Thus, the lexical analysis upon which the first phase is centered is still a first necessary step. The output of this phase is a first version of the process modeled with BPMN, using especially its core elements set [30]. As already stated, the goal is to obtain one *correct*, *complete* and *compliant* graphical representation of the process to be further refined.

Rule 1.1: Participants identification.

Participants are all the actors, services, people, employees involved in the processes' execution. Participants are those entities or roles which perform actions, activities and tasks. Every Participant in BPMN is represented with a *Pool* (from the BPMN specification: "A Pool represents a Participant"). Thus, for each Participant a different Pool must be graphically drawn. The Pool name is the same of the Participant's. If one ore more actors are in hierarchical relationship with one other, it is safe to represent them partitioning the Pool with corresponding Lanes.

There are no semantic rules to determine when two or more actors' names are the same. One well-described process should follows a fixed and shared taxonomy, at least inside the company boundaries. Without a predefined taxonomy or glossary, we have to recognize synonyms, technical or standard terms. In the customer/supplier example process we can easily found four different actors: one Customer (someone, customer), one Store, one Sale Assistant (sale assistant, cashier) and one Warehouseman (warehouse clerk, warehouseman, warehouse). We can infer from the context that the Warehouseman and the Sale Assistant work for the Store and, thus, we can conclude that we have to deal with two processes: one for the Customer and one for the Store. The Store will have two Lanes, one for each employee.

Rule 1.2: Activities identification.

For each Participant, the main activities set is to be identified. If one action taken from one of the Participants has a simple structure and does not have relevant associated properties, it can be represented with an Activity Task. During the first phase, it is possible to define all tasks as of type *None*. If one action performed by one of the Participants is a complex action, which could be specified more in detail, it can be represented using Sub-Processes.

It is necessary to make a semantic analysis of the actions performed by the Participants to state if an action has to become a Task or a Sub-Process. Typically, atomic actions are to be represented with Tasks, while complex actions with Sub-Processes. Modeling a Sub-Process does not necessary mean that it is required to specify also the content of the process. BPMN allows to represent collapsed Sub-Processes making feasible to indicate that an activity is composed from simple tasks up to an entire whole process. Sometimes the textual description of the activities gives no detailed information pertaining the behavior or the content of such elements. It is likewise possible to model them. During the second phase there will be the possibility to substitute Sub-Processes with Tasks and vice-versa. Since Activities are the most expensive elements in terms of processes execution inside a process, a careful implementation of this step is very important. As an aside observation, modeling tasks with different granularity layers could be useful to represent also different views of the same process as well.

A guiding principle is to define all the actions as Tasks, refining the diagram during the second phase. This is because is more simple to group activities together obtaining a Sub-Process (e.g., an Ad-Hoc Sub-Process) than extracting information form a Sub-Process splitting it into several different Tasks. The latter way is not recommended because, as consequence, the overall complexity of the process rapidly increases. Finally, it is also important to give attention in distinguishing between something that "happens" during the process (Events) and work that participants perform (Activities).

Rule 1.3: Events identification.

An event is something that "happens" during the course of a process, affecting its flow. Depending on when an event occurs, events could be classified as Start Events (when they occurs at the beginning, causing the start of a process), End Events (when they indicate the end of a process) or Intermediate Events (when they occur between the start and the end of a process).

Without using a formalized language it could be difficult to distinguish between some kind of activities and events. Actually, there could be activities that may be modeled as events, saving the number of activities (more complex to model and to serialize) and simplifying the diagram. Moreover, some events are not clearly specified inside the process description. This could be a problem in the case of Start or End events. BPMN specifications provide the possibility not to draw Start or End Events starting and ending the process with Tasks (but if at least one Start (End) Event is designed, there must be at least a corresponding End (Start) Event for the same process).

Rule 1.4: Choices identification.

It is possible to identify choices every time a single flow could be splitted in more than one different path. Choices are often introduced by conditional or boolean expressions, like, for example, *if ... then [... else], while/meanwhile, or/otherwise*, and so forth. Choices could also be identified through conditional form of such verbs, like sentences containing the verbs *can*, *may* or the conditional forms *could*, *should*, *would*, and so on. Some of these constructs suggest which type of choices we are dealing with. For example, terms like *while/meanwhile* clearly indicate the possibility to have parallel flows (activities executed at the same time) while terms like *or/otherwise* suggest the use of alternate paths. Choices in BPMN are represented using Gateways. Gateways affect the flow of the process forking, branching, joining or merging different paths.

As said, inside a process, there can be different kinds of Gateways. There could be the need to split a flow in multiple, parallel flows or to choose which path to follow depending on the result of a condition or exceptions handling if particular conditions occur. Every splitting Gateway must have a merging Gateway (which may be implicit) or End Events to end all the paths. Simply follow each outgoing path until its termination is reached. BPMN specifications provide the *Token* notion to simulate the flows. There should not be left processes with non-terminating paths. Also, loops could imply some non-termination conditions.

Rule 1.5: Adding Relationships.

There are two different kind of relationships affecting flows: Sequence Flow and Message Flow. The easiest way to distinguish among them is to consider Sequence Flows as the representation of the order that activities will be performed *within* a process, while Message Flows are used to show the messages exchanged *among* different processes.

Sequence Flows. Following the order given by the process specifications, connect all the activities, events and gateways, beginning from Start Events and finishing with End Events. This step is to be separately performed for every participant.

Message Flows. Every information exchanged between different participants has to be represented with a Message Flow arising from the sender towards the recipient. Notice that the content of the Message exchanged could be a textual message or a nonspecific object, such as a paper document as well as an email.

It is a non-trivial work (especially if we have to deal with complex processes having an huge amount of elements) to list all the Sequence Flows needed to connect all the diagram shapes. Toward this point, it is useful to report in a table the list of the established relationships among processes.

Rule 1.6: Documentation of the processes.

If the process description provides some other information which has not been yet represented using the BPMN core elements set, it is possible to add them using BPMN Artifacts.

The outline of the example process at the end of 1st phase can be seen in Figure 1.

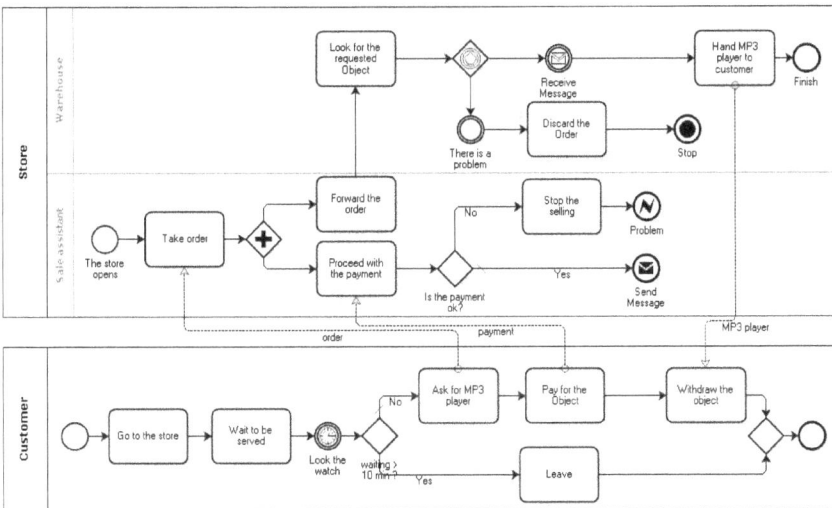

Figure 1: The first phase output process, ready to be refined

PHASE 2: LOGICAL MODELING

During the second phase of the design methodology we start reasoning about the diagram we outlined during the first phase. The first phase rules provided some simple means in order to perform the first necessary steps towards the design of a business process by graphical means. Now we present refinement rules to improve the business process diagram. At first, some preliminary assumptions have to be stated. BPMN specifications provide a large variety of symbols, to allow modelers to describe a high variety of processes. However, only a small set of symbols are commonly used. Muehlen and Recker in [30] present the result of a very large survey on the use of BPMN in different contexts (Web, Consulting, Seminar). The three different contexts are quite aligned on the results. They discovered that the six most used BPMN elements are: Normal Flows, Task, End Event, Start Event / Event, Pool, Data-Based XOR Gateway. They call this set the *common core of BPMN*. To the contrary, there are elements that are not considered at all, like Compensation Association, Multiple End Event, Cancel Intermediate Event, Intermediate Exception, Multiple Start Event, Compensation End Event. Looking at the number of the elements used for a diagram, they found that none of the diagrams used more than 15 different BPMN constructs, and none used less than 3. The models themselves could contain more elements, but a model with, e.g., 5 Tasks connected by Sequence Flows uses in practice only the Task symbol and the Sequence Flow symbol (only 2 symbols). The average subset of BPMN elements used in these models consisted of 9 different symbols, meaning that the average BPMN model uses less than 20% of the available vocabulary. The diagram we depicted at the end of the first phase of the methodology uses about 15 different elements, and, thus, we can argue that it could be positioned between the most complex processes (in terms of number of BPMN elements used). This analysis leads us to make some assumptions about the process we drawn in the first phase.

For a model to be *relevant,* it has to describe as better as possible the related processes. Here, we have to deal with two different points of view. First, we have to discover if we have described all the aspects of the process using the most appropriate elements (as BPMN provides a lot of choice in this respect). Second, we have to decide whether to change or delete not (strictly) necessary elements or represent the same object with less (and more appropriate) elements.

Before proceeding with the definition of the rules, it is important to consider that there are many ways to reduce a business process. Reduction rules have been successfully used as a stand alone approach [25, 26], as well as an engineering approach used to reduce the complexity of the process models [27, 22] to verify correctness of process models. These approaches where applied to other processes modeling representations [19], like EPC or Petri Nets. All these tools could be easily adopted to accomplish the rules of this second phase.

Rule 2.1: Participant dependencies.

An actor, a service, or an entity/role can be identified as a Participant when it does not have functional or hierarchical dependencies with other entities or roles. Looking at the diagram, it is to be considered the opportunity to identify Lanes which could be merged together and turned into a Pool or Pools that could be splitted in more than one Lanes.

Looking at the example, we have one Sale Assistant and one Warehouseman who are employed to the same store. Thus, we have represented them with two Lanes belonging to one single Pool called "Store". The Customer and the Store are independent each other, so, they are two different Pools. This is a very basic example, but sometimes could be very hard to state if two or more participants have not strict relationships. If we model a company with more than one office, we probably have to design one single Pool splitted in several Lanes. To the contrary, one process representing a patient who asks his doctor for an exam to be taken at the hospital would be modeled with three different Pools (e.g., Patient, Hospital and Doctor).

Rule 2.2: Transform the Activities.

Having in mind the intended abstraction level, it could be useful to transform Tasks in Sub-Processes (which correspond to reach an higher level of description) and/or Sub-Processes in Tasks (lower details level). Then, it becomes possible to consider the following guidance:

Activities ordering. Considering one Participant at a time, Activities should be ordered following some semantic precedence rules.

Activities types. According to the semantic of the work performed, each Activity should have been set the right type.

Activities substitution. This is a bi-directions rule. Both directions give as result a simplified version of the process. The first direction consists in substituting an activity (namely, in most cases, a Task) with an Event with the same behaviour or another Event which can perform the same work: Events do not count in the process total cost counting. The second direction pertains in grouping a set of Tasks in a Sub-Process, making the process more understandable [28]. Moreover, it could be the case that the process abstraction level (and, thus, its granularity) changes from the first phase. We could deal with the necessity to replace one Task with one Sub-Process or, on the other way, one Sub-Process with one Task. We suggest to make these changes sparingly to avoid an excessive difference between the first phase diagram and the second phase model. Finally, consider if the ordering and types selection should be applied again.

We now pass to a detailed description of these rules. During the first phase we have positioned all the activities inside the diagram, paying attention to assign an activity to the right participant. Now we pass to check activities precedences. Such precedences could be provided explicitly inside the process description text or, implicitly, looking at the process semantics. Basing the structuring of one process only on content-dependent rules makes the adoption of a clear and shared taxonomy a very important asset for organizations. A number of activities without precedence rules is a set, but we want to obtain a sequence (the concept of *sequence* is distinct from that of a *set*, in that the elements of a sequence appear in some order). The strategy we choose to adopt in this case is to create a system of precedence rules (quite similar to the system of linear equations concept) where variables are the process activities. Without any precedence rule, if a process has n_A activities, they could origin $n_A!$ different permutations. Using our example process, consider the Customer process. There are six different activities (in this case they are all Tasks, but this does not effect the strategy). To simplify the example readability we apply a letter from A to F to each activity. So we are in the condition depicted in Figure 2.

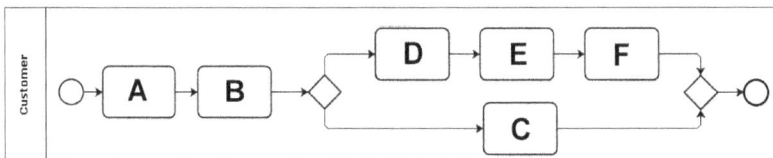

Figure 2: Process activities to be inferred

From the text description we can infer the following precedence rules, either implicit or explicit, temporal or functional:

- A must be the first activity
- C and F are the last two activities
- D and C come after B
- C and {D, E, F} should not be positioned on the same path

- E and F come after D
- B comes after A and before C and D

As for a classical equations system, if we can collect many (useful) rules as the number of the variables we can precisely arrange actions following the process flow. Collecting less than needed rules prevents the possibility to clearly model the process flow. The most suitable goal is to have no degrees of freedom in activities positioning. Another risk is to collect more rules than those requested. If there are equivalent rules, it is possible to simplify the system. Otherwise there could be inconsistencies or errors in the process description or in the first phase model. There are works (as, for example, [23]) which clearly state this problem providing some methodology to accomplish this task. This procedure can be applied also in the case we have to describe an Ad-Hoc Sub-Process showing also its tasks. Starting from a collapsed Ad-Hoc Sub-Process, expand and transform it in one Sub-Process showing its internal Tasks. Than apply the procedure tracing the Sequence Flows to connect the activities. At last add, if needed, all the other elements like Events or Gateways. The resulting Sub-Process will become no more an Ad-Hoc Sub-Process but an Embedded Sub-Process holding a complete business process.

Let us discuss now the other two rules. To apply the correct type to Tasks and Sub-Processes should be an easy step. BPMN specifications provide different activities types especially for Tasks. There could be present inside the model Service, User, Send, Receive, Script, Manual and Reference Tasks, depending on the Tasks behavior. Every type extends the common attribute set for activities adding particular features. Be careful to consider also general loop, compensation and multi-instance types, as provided by BPMN specifications for both Tasks and Sub-Processes. Assigning the correct type will increase the readability of the diagram making it easier to be understood by different persons and shared between offices, services, companies.

Finally, consider the two directions defined above for the third rule. The use of sub-processes in large process models is an important step for handling complexity in modeling practice. While there are several advantages attributed to such a modular design, the lack of precise guidelines turns out to be a major impediment for applying modularity in a systematic way. A systematic and principled approach to find the optimal modularization of a process model is still missing [24]. Therefore, looking at the process detect sections which could be replaced by Sub-Processes. This makes the process more understandable [28]. Following the opposite direction, instead, analyze the process looking for all those activities (in this case, they should be Tasks) which could be replaced by Events. For example, if the aim of a Task is only to wait for an incoming message, the Task can be replaced by an Intermediate Event of type Message. In our running example the "Send Message" Activity can be modeled using an Event rather than a Task.

Rule 2.3: Events.

The Events use, positioning and types have to be checked every time an Event has been identified inside the process diagram or the text description, keeping in mind the goal to build a relevant and economical model, easily readable and understandable.

BPMN specifications provide some guidelines about when and how Events should be used. For example, a Start Event is optional, but if there is an End Event in the Process, then one Start Event must be explicitly defined. To the contrary, End Events are optional, but if there is a Start Event, then there must be at least one

End Event. It is reasonable to choose a modeling style opting for to use Start and End Events if they are meaningful for the process. In fact, if a Start (End) Event is not used, it does not have any trigger (result). There may be multiple Start (End) Events within a single level of a process, but the behavior of the process may be harder to understand if there are multiple Start (End) Events. It is recommended that this feature be used sparingly and that the modeler be aware that other readers of the diagram may have difficulty understanding the intent of the diagram. But, while reading a process with one Start Event and more than one End Event is a common scenario (very often a process has one starting condition but may have multiple ends depending on the complexity of the process—the number of parallel or conditional paths that may be followed), dealing with a process which may start in several ways is disorienting. In [20], Decker and Mendling considered six different process notations and syntax: open workflow nets, YAWL, event-driven process chains, BPEL (the code, not a graphical representation), UML activity diagrams, and BPMN. They determined how an entry point is represented in each of these notations: start places (such as in open workflow nets), start events (such as in BPMN) and start conditions (such as in event-driven process chains). Having multiple start events in a process causes all sorts of problems in terms of understandability and soundness, and, endorsing the BPMN specifications suggestion, they do not recommend this in general; however, since the notations support it and therefore it can be done in practice, it is reasonable to use multiple Start Events only if the process is complex and/or the starting conditions are not obvious.

Rule 2.4: Gateways.

Gateways that are not relevant for the model should be replaced with implicit Gateways or with Events attached to the Activities boundaries. Splitting Gateways should have their (sometimes implicitly defined) corresponding merge Gateways.

Look at the process diagram in Figure 3, which represents the result process at the end of the Rule 2.3. The emphasized Gateways can be replaced by implicit ones or by intermediate events attached to activities boundaries. BPMN specifications provide some rule to express implicit splitting, branching, joining and merging paths. If multiple paths exit from an activity or from an event, they have to be considered as they were the output paths of a parallel (AND) gateway, meaning that all the paths will be executed at the same time. If one activity has conditional outgoing Sequence Flows, instead of common uncontrolled Sequence Flows, the branching point is represented by an Inclusive Gateway. To replace explicit elements with their implicit form is very useful if the diagram of the process has too much symbols, making it not so easily understandable.

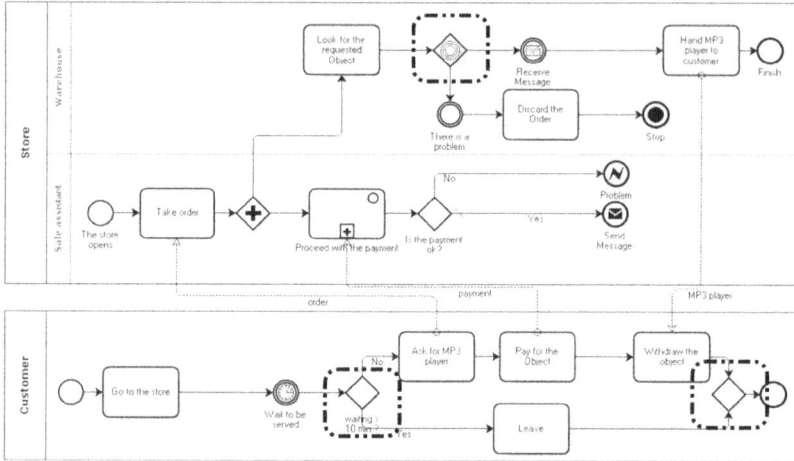

Figure 3: The example process with useless Gateways emphasized

Sometimes a Gateway could be changed with an Intermediate Event. It depends quite exclusively from the semantics and the behavior of the Gateway. Very often in these cases Gateways are used to model choices which generate exception flows. In the example, the Customer process has one Gateway which can be modeled attaching a Timer Intermediate Event to the boundary of the previous activity. Also in the Warehouseman workflow the selected Gateway can be substituted by an Intermediate Event placed on the boundary of the previous Task and generating an exception flow.

Rule 2.5: Patterns analysis.

Once all the elements of the model have been refined, flows are to be considered in order to reduce them, wherever possible, to well known patterns.

The most spread work on patterns is the workflow patterns definition by van der Aalst [2], used also to develop the flow patterns for BPMN. It is not feasible to change a pattern at the end of the second phase. This rule is positioned here because during the application of the other rules the diagram configuration could have been changed. Applying patterns from the beginning is a very useful way to model flows. Another help come from some really new works (among the other, [21] by Gschwind et al. is remarkable) on applying patterns during modeling or to already modeled processes. Although the business process community has put a major emphasis on patterns, only limited support for using patterns in today's business process modeling tools can be found. There is a lack of support for the users to correctly applying these patterns to many incorrectly modeled business processes. We decided to integrate in this rule this topic to give our contribution with this design methodology. In their work, Gschwind, Koehler and Wong describe an extension of a business process modeling tool with patterns. They distinguish three scenarios of pattern application: refinement of a single control-flow edge by applying a block-oriented pattern compound, application of a pattern compound to a pair of selected control-flow edges, application of a basic pattern to a set of selected control-flow edges. The result of their work is an extension which supports users to apply patterns to incorrectly modeled diagrams. While it is still better to apply patterns during the first phase, using some strategies or guidance like the one developed by Gschwind, Koehler and Wong it is still possible to correct old process designs or diagrams incorrectly modeled during the first phase, as well as to add/remove elements. We remark how it is important this rule after the model is changed because of the effects of the other second phase rules execution.

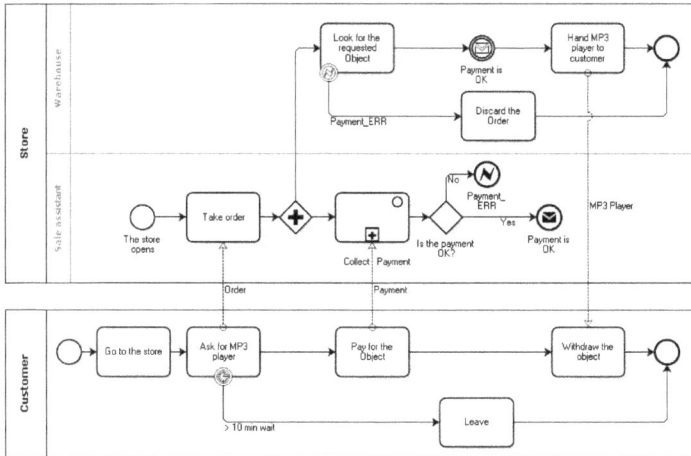

Figure 4: Final version of the example process

Second Phase Concluding Remarks.

At the end of this phase (the final version of the example process is depicted in Figure 4) the process should be still correct, complete and compliant as at the end of the first phase. Moreover, it should be *relevant* (all the symbols used are meaningful and appropriate) and *economical* (there are not useless elements). If all the rules have been correctly applied, the resulting model will be more easily readable and understandable.

The process now is ready to be translated in a suitable way, such as our BPeX XML schema serialization.

PHASE 3: PHYSICAL MODELING AND BUSINESS PROCESS NORMAL FORM

During the 3rd and last phase, the process should not be further modified. The goal of this phase is to translate the second phase output model into a physical format. We choose to use BPeX XML-Schema because of its natural correspondence with the BPMN model. We remark that our serialization is simple and self-validating. This means that it is possible to natively check the syntax of a diagram, all the BPMN structural semantics rules and most of the behavioral semantics rules. To accomplish this task we use a mix of top-down and bottom-up methodologies. We use the top-down methodology to derive the XML-tree structure starting from the model diagram, while we apply the bottom-up methodology to enrich the elements definitions with all the constructs and attributes. The output XML instances should be *valid* with respect to the XML-Schema and *trustworthy* in the sense of presenting no differences from the second phase output process model.

BUSINESS PROCESS NORMAL FORM

Finally, we introduce a lightweight concept of *Normal Form* applied to a business process, meaning that the processes modeled following these three-phase sets of rules will have some characteristics which guarantee some basic properties (e.g., the process diagram is compliant with BPMN specifications, the business process diagram can model correctly the behavior of the business process, and so forth). We can define *Business Process Normal Form* (or BPNF) as the desired form a business process model (with 'model' we mean both the graphical representation and its serialization together) should have.

If the three-phase methodology we presented in this chapter is applied the modeled business process will be in BPNF. One business process model is said to be in BPNF if it complies with all of the requirements stated in the three phases of the design methodology. The more important requirements are resumed in Table 1. If one business process model satisfies the minimum requirements it should also be easily readable and understandable.

Table 1: Summary of minimal phases requirements

	Correct, Complete, Compliant	Relevant, Economical	Valid, Trustworthy
Phase 1	X		
Phase 2	X	X	
Phase 3	X	X	X

Inside either the two main purposes for BPMN 2.0 specifications there is the definition of BPMN Complete Conformance or Full Compliance. We spend no space to describe these definitions because they are not yet approved and they may change. But it is interesting to notice how recently companies and organizations start to point their attention also on this topic. Their definition of BPMN Complete Conformance or Full Compliance does not overlap our definition of BPNF, because the aims are different. While we give a definition of the desired form for a business process model, the BPMN Complete Conformance / Full Compliance given for BPMN 2.0 describes what characteristics a software must have to claim BPMN 2.0 compliance or conformance.

CONCLUSIONS

The aim of the proposed design methodology is to provide a set of well-organized design steps to guide users represent their business processes in a form which owns some important properties and features. This is a novel and concrete answer to the lack of a design methodology for business processes which makes a massive use of BPMN and emerging related specifications. Of course, the example process used to illustrate the methodology is not complete and does not model all the process events should occur, but it was chosen to represent as better as possible the greater number of the most commons constructs used in business process modeling.

Promising plans for future works includes the review of such methodology to apply it to the BPMN 2.0 version and the development of an XML-based query language for business processes.

ACKNOWLEDGEMENTS

We wish to tank Vishal Saxena (Oracle) for his constant support and for his useful feedbacks and WfMC for hints and suggestions.

REFERENCES

1. White, S.A., Business Process Modeling Notation, V1.1 – OMG Available Specification. http://www.bpmn.org (last accessed February 26, 2009).
2. van der Aalst W.M.P. et al., Workflow Patterns. Distributed and Parallel Databases, Volume 14, Issue 1, pp. 5-51, 2003.

3. Chinosi M., "Representing Business Processes: Conceptual Model and Design Methodology", Ph.D. Thesis, University of Insubria, Varese, Italy, 2009.

4. OASIS Web Service Business Process Execution Language (WS-BPEL) TC, Web Service Business Process Execution Language Version 2.0. http://docs.oasis-open.org/wsbpel/2.0/OS/wsbpel-v2.0-OS.html (last accessed February 24, 2009).

5. Workflow Management Coalition, Final XPDL 2.1 Specification, Document number WFMC-TC-1025-Oct-10-08-A, 2008.

6. Chen, P.P.-S., The Entity-Relationship Model: Toward a Unified View of Data, ACM Transactions on Database Systems, 1, vol 1, pp 9-36, 1976.

7. Rumbaugh, J., Jacobson, I., Booch, G., The Unified Modeling language Reference Manual Addison Wesley 2004.

8. American National Standards Institute. 1975. ANSI/X3/SPARC Study Group on Data Base Management Systems; Interim Report. FDT (Bulletin of ACM SIGMOD) 7:2.

9. Rosemann2008 Rosemann M., Understanding and Impacting the Practice of Business Process Management, Dumas et al. (Eds), Business Process Management (BPM 2008), Lecture Notes in Computer Science (LNCS), vol. 5240, p. 2, Springer, 2008.

10. Dijkman, R.M., A Classification of Differences between Similar Business Processes, Proceedings of the 11th IEEE EDOC Conference (EDOC), pp. 37-47, 2007.

11. Dijkman, R.M., Dumas, M., Ouyang, C., Semantics and Analysis of Business Process Models in BPMN, Butterworth-Heinemann (Eds), Information and Software Technology, 12, vol. 50, pp. 1281-1994, 2008.

12. Dumas, M., Großkopf, A., Hettel, T., Wynn, M.T., Semantics of Standard Process Models with OR-joins, Meersman, R., Tari, Z. (Eds), OTM Conferences, Lecture Notes in Computer Science (LNCS), vol. 4803, pp. 41-58, Springer, 2007.

13. Recker, J., Indulska, M., Rosemann, M., Green, P., Do Process Modeling Techniques Get Better? A Comparative Ontological Analysis of BPMN, Campbell, B., Underwood, J., Bunker, D. (Eds), Proceedings of the 16th Australasian Conference on Information Systems, 2005.

14. Recker, J., Wohed, P., Rosemann, M., Representation Theory Versus Workflow Patterns—the Case of BPMN, In Embley, D.W., Olivé, A., Ram, S. (Eds), ER, Lecture Notes in Computer Science (LNCS), vol. 4215, pp. 68-83, Springer, 2006.

15. Beeri, C., Eyal, A., Kamenkovich, S., Milo, T., Querying Business Processes., In Dayal, U., Whang, K.Y., Lomet, D.B., Alonso, G., Lohman, G.M., Kersten, M.L., Cha, S.K., Kim, Y.K. (Eds), VLDB, ACM, pp.343-354, 2006.

16. Beeri, C., Eyal, A., Milo, T., Pilberg, A., Monitoring Business Processes with Queries, Koch, C., Gehrke, J., Garofalakis, M.N., Srivastava, D., Aberer, K., Deshpande, A., Florescu, D., Chan, C.Y., Ganti, V., Kanne, C.C., Klas, W., Neuhold, E.J. (Eds), VLDB, ACM, pp. 603-614, 2007.

17. Beeri, C., Eyal, A., Kamenkovich, S., Milo, T., Querying Business Processes with BP-QL. Information Systems, vol. 33, 477-507, 2008.

18. Awad, A., BPMN-Q: A Language to Query Business Processes. Reichert, M., Strecker, S., Turowski, K. (Eds), EMISA, Lecture Notes in Informatics (LNI), vol. P-119, pp. 115-128, GI, 2007.

19. Awad, A., Decker, G., and Weske, M., Efficient Compliance Checking Using BPMN-Q and Temporal Logic., Dumas et al. (Eds), Business Process Management (BPM 2008), Lecture Notes in Computer Science (LNCS), vol. 5240, p. 326-341, Springer, 2008.
20. Decker, G., Mendling, J., Instantiation Semantics for Process Models., Dumas et al. (Eds), Business Process Management (BPM 2008), Lecture Notes in Computer Science (LNCS), vol. 5240, p. 164-179, Springer, 2008.
21. Gschwind, T., Koehler, J., and Wong, J., Applying Patterns During Business Process Modeling. Dumas et al. (Eds), Business Process Management (BPM 2008), Lecture Notes in Computer Science (LNCS), vol. 5240, p. 4-19, Springer, 2008.
22. Mendling, J., Detection and Prediction of Errors in EPC Business Process Models., PhD thesis, Institute of Information Systems and New Media, Vienna University of Economics and Business Administration (WU Wien), May 2007.
23. Polyvyanyy, A., Weske, M., Hypergraph-based Modeling of Ad-Hoc Business Processes, Proceedings of the 1st PM4HDPS Workshop, 2008.
24. Reijers, H. A., Mendling, J., Modularity in Process Models: Review and Effects, Dumas et al. (Eds), Business Process Management (BPM 2008), Lecture Notes in Computer Science (LNCS), vol. 5240, p. 20-35, Springer, 2008.
25. Sadiq, W., and Orlowska, M. E., Applying Graph Reduction Techniques for Identifying Structural Conflicts in Process Models. Jarke, M., Oberweis, A. (Eds), CAiSE, Lecture Notes in Computer Science (LNCS), vol. 1626, pp. 195-209, Springer, 1999.
26. Sadiq, W., and Orlowska, M. E., Analyzing Process Models Using Graph Reduction Techniques, CAiSE, Information Systems, vol. 25, pp. 117-134, Elsevier Science Ltd., 2000.
27. van Dongen, B. F., van der Aalst, W. M. P., and Verbeek, H. M. W., Verification of EPCs: Using Reduction Rules and Petri Nets., O. Pastor and J. F. e Cunha (Eds), CAiSE, Lecture Notes in Computer Science, vol. 3520, pp. 372-386, Springer, 2005.
28. Vanhatalo, J., Völzer, H., Koehler, J., The Refined Process Structure Tree, Dumas et al. (Eds), Business Process Management (BPM 2008), Lecture Notes in Computer Science (LNCS), vol. 5240, p. 110-115, Springer, 2008.
29. zur Muehlen, M., Getting Started With Business Process Modeling. IIR BPM Conference, Orlando, Florida, May 2008.
30. zur Muehlen, M., Recker, J., How Much Language is Enough? Theoretical and Practical Use of the Business Process Modeling Notation, Bellahsene, Z., Léonard, M. (Eds), CAiSE, Lecture Notes in Computer Science (LNCS), vol. 5074, pp. 465-479, Springer, 2008.
31. Object Management Group, IOS Joint BPMN 2.0 revised submission, http://www.omg.org/cgi-bin/doc?bmi/09-02-01 (last accessed February, 26 2009).
32. Object Management Group, BPMN for Services submission team (BPMN-S) Revised submission to the BPMN 2.0 RFP, http://www.omg.org/cgi-bin/doc?bmi/09-02-04 (last accessed February 26, 2009).
33. SBVR Object Management Group, Semantics of Business Vocabulary and Business Rules (SBVR), Version 1.0, http://www.omg.org/spec/SBVR/1.0/ (last accessed February 26, 2009).

The Auto Optimizer

Robert M. Shapiro and Hartmann Genrich, Global 360, United States

ABSTRACT

Continuous Process Improvement is touted as a feature of many Business Process Management suites. Usually this means the provision of analytical techniques for measuring performance. These include Business Activity Monitoring, Balanced Score Cards, real-time measurement of Key Performance Indicators and the capture and analysis of event streams generated by the running system.

Some BPM suites provide a what-if simulation capability which allows the evaluation of changes to the system. This leaves the task of coming up with proposed solutions to the user, an often daunting task.

In this paper we describe an automated, goal-driven technology for process improvement. By focusing on the common characteristics of business processes in typical BPM applications, we have developed an integrated set of algorithms for generating and evaluating proposed solutions. The user specifies the desired goals in terms of performance or cost or KPIs. The algorithms run until the goal is achieved or no further improvement is found.

INTRODUCTION

Business Process Management Suites frequently include an analytics component for collecting and analyzing the log events generated by the process execution engine(s) and a simulation component that allows the exploration of alternative scenarios where the resourcing and/or the processes and/or the workload are altered in an effort to improve the overall performance of a complex business process.

The analytics offers a window in which one can explore what has happened or 'will' happen. Process improvement experiments are suggested by the analytics data and evaluated by the new data they generate. It is often the case that OLAP technology is employed to allow an analyst to rapidly explore the data and from the exploration come up with suggestions for improvement which can then be tried out (evaluated) using the simulator to generate new data.

The improvement process can be characterized as the following set of steps:
- Analyze the historical (or simulation) data to determine where improvements are needed. If the evaluation is satisfactory, stop.
- From the data, come up with an idea for improvement.
- Create a simulation scenario incorporating that idea and run a simulation.
- Evaluate the results to determine whether it has resulted in improvement and repeat the cycle.

Step 2 in the improvement process is typically a challenging manual step. In this paper we describe an approach to automating the entire cycle described above.

The optimization technology is intended to be used to improve the performance of a Business Process Management System. We provide a brief overview of the elements in such a system. Data collection and analysis is critical in Process improvement. We describe log events which are the source of the data and a brief overview of Analytics. Simulation plays a critical role in evaluating alternatives. We provide a brief overview of Simulation. We review the basic Optimizer. It provides methods for improving throughput, lowering costs and satisfying Service Level Agreement criteria. It uses critical path analysis, resource load balancing and shift assignments to accomplish this. We present an overview of the Auto Optimizer. It uses the technology in the optimizer to achieve goals provided by the user. The construction and evaluation of alternative scenarios is automated and the optimization cycle repeats until the user-stated goals are achieved or no further improvement can be found. We follow this with details of a particular analysis method that we employ in the Auto Optimizer: Critical Path Analysis

Finally we present a summary and outlook on future developments.

BPMS OVERVIEW

A Business Process Management Suite typically includes an analytics component for collecting and analyzing the log events generated by the process execution engine(s) and a simulation component that allows the exploration of alternative scenarios.

We have added an optimizer component to make recommendations for changes to business operations.

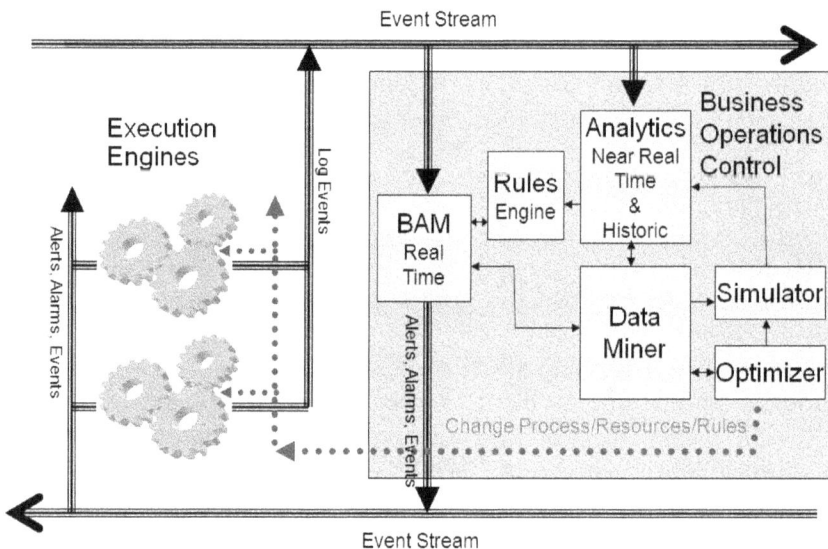

Figure 1: BPMS Modules

A stream of log events is generated by various execution engines, which include:
- Workflow enactment (BPM systems)
- BPEL
- Supply Chain Management
- ERP Systems (e.g. SAP)

The events are processed by:
- A BAM module to display KPI dashboards and generate alerts in real time. Makes use of a Rules Engine.
- An Analytics module which collects and organizes the event data.

An Optimizer module makes use of the analytics data, employing data mining and simulation, to improve the business operation:
- Resource schedules are altered and resources redeployed.

- Processes are modified to improve performance, control risk.
- Rules are changed to handle emergencies.

Elements

Analytics
- Storage and processing of operations data to provide useful business information.

BAM
- Business Activity Monitoring. Real time depiction of Key Performance Indicators (**KPI**s) and generation of alerts etc.

Data Miner
- Statistical processing of business information to extract patterns, detect trends and make predictions.

Event Stream
- Flow of information packets about meaningful state changes. The log events generated by currently running processes are an example.

Execution Engine
- Any business process enactment service, including workflow engines, BPEL executor, ERP system etc.

Optimizer
- A software tool that utilizes the Data Miner and/or Simulator to make recommendations for changes to business operations.

Rules Engine
- A software system that helps manage and automate business rules. Used to detect interesting business situations automatically.

Simulator
- Supports what-if analysis of current or planned operations.

Log Events

Process execution engine(s) and simulations generate a stream of log events to be collected and analyzed by the analytics component.
- Process events occur at the start and termination of a process instance.
- Activity events occur at various points in the execution of an activity. See next section for details.
- A timed sequence is associated with two activities, possibly in different processes, through which a work item passes

Figure 1 shows an example of a single log event, WORKFLOWCREATE. Figure 2 is a list of typical events, grouped by the event category. The timing data associated with log events are depicted in Figure 4.

```
<XPDLogEvent
System="MortgageDemo"
Scenario="Mortgage Lending AsIs"
Run="8/28/2006 6:29:01 PM"
InstanceId="6505"
        ParentInstanceId=""
        WorkflowInstanceId="6505"
        Timestamp="2006-08-01T07:00:00Z"
        SequenceId="281010"
        ProcessId="Mortgage Lending AsIs"
```

```
       ProcessVersion="1"
       EventType="WORKFLOWCREATE"
       ActivitySetId="1"
       ActivityId="15" QueueId="-1"
ElapsedTimeDays="0" ElapsedBusinessHours="0"
ElapsedBusinessDays="0" AccruedWaitDays="0"
       AccruedWaitBusinessDays="0"
       AccruedWaitBusinessHours="0"
       AccruedProcessingDays="0"
       AccruedProcessingBusinessDays="0"
       AccruedProcessingBusinessHours="0">
    <Participants>
       <Participant ParticipantId="System" />
    </Participants>
    <DataFields>
       <DataField Name="SIM_Cost" Type="FLOAT">0</DataField>
    </DataFields>
  </XPDLogEvent>
```

Figure 1: XML for a Single Log Event: WorkFlowCreate

Event	Event Group
WORKFLOWCREATE	
WORKFLOWTERMINATE	
CHILDCREATE	Process
CHILDTERMINATE	
ARRIVEACTIVITY	
BEGINACTIVITY	
COMPLETEACTIVITY	Activity
SUSPENDACTIVITY	
CANCELACTIVITY	
CONTINUEACTIVITY	
BEGINTIMEDSEQUENCE	Timed Sequence
COMPLETETIMEDSEQUENCE	
LOGGEDEVENT	Logged Event

Figure 2: Types of Log Events

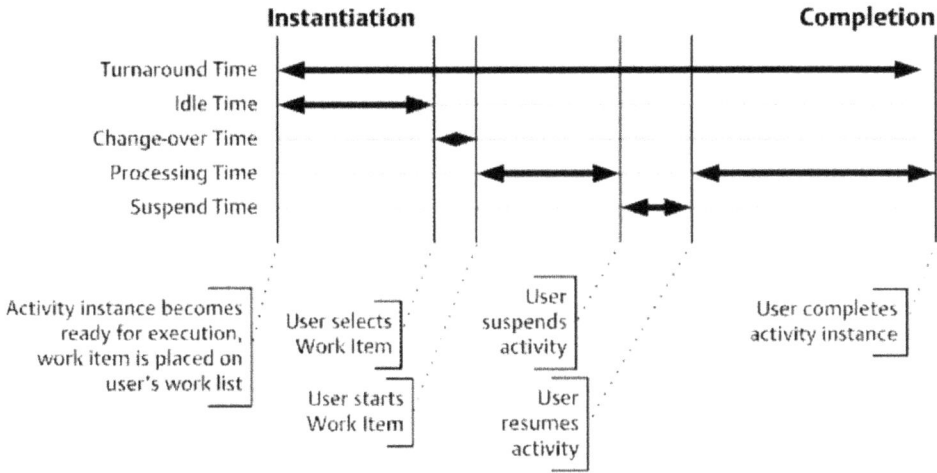

Figure 4: Timing Data from Log Events

Analytics

Figure 5 depicts a possible architecture for the analytics. The events generated by the process engine are collected in a relational data base and the data is used to populate the fact and dimension tables of OLAP cubes. Queries on the cubes support slice and dice charting and rapid reporting.

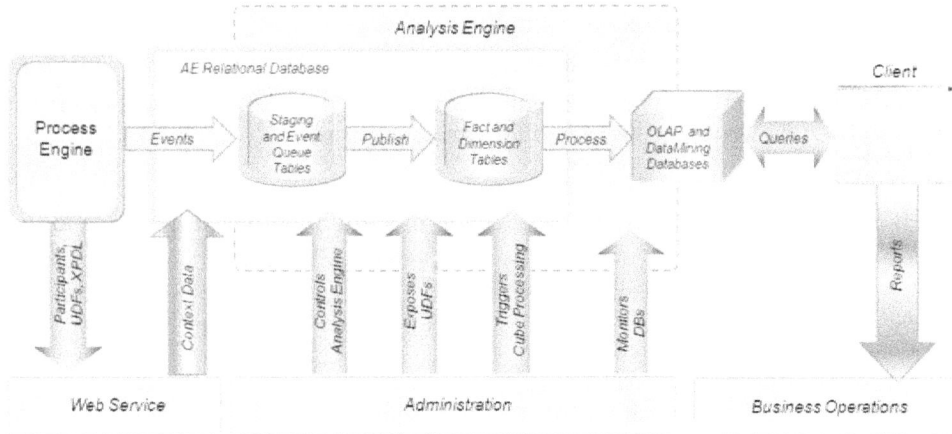

Figure 5: Analytics Overview

Simulator

The typical simulator for making predictions in a BPMS environment is a discrete event simulator. Preparation of a simulation run is commonly referred to as a scenario. The scenario consists of:

- The set of processes to be simulated. The process definitions may be represented in a format that supports process interchange, such as XPDL. Process definitions may be created by a diagram editor that is part of the BPM system, or by an independent tool such as a BPMN editor. Process definitions provide information about the activities performed, the routes taken, the rules impacting which routes and activities to perform, and the resources (human & automated) used to perform the activities. A scenario can include one or several processes for a simulation run.

- Incoming Work (Arrivals). Each scenario must involve work to be processed. The description includes information about when the work arrives, as well as all appropriate attributes of the work (e.g. region, amount, size) that may have an impact on processing.
- Resources, Roles and Shifts: As work is routed to activities in a process, resources are required to perform the activity. Resources may be human resources; they may be pieces of equipment; or they might simply be application systems. Roles are often used to describe the function performed and the skill required. Specific resources are then described as performing defined roles. The availability of Resources and Roles can also be controlled by using Shift information.
- Activity Details: In order for the simulator to reflect the real-world processing of a business process, additional information is often appended to the scenario. How long an activity takes to process is not defined in a Process Definition, but is included in the scenario information (historical data collected by the analytics may be the source of this information). This and many other details can be expressed as a single integer or a complex expression involving the attributes of the work and/or the use of statistical distribution functions for randomness. Other information appended for simulation might include routing information which tells the simulator under what conditions certain routes are taken. Routing information can come from rules that exist in the process definition, but it is often amended with percentages that, based on historical activity, reflect the likelihood of a certain outcome or path.

All scenario information is typically represented in an XML document.

A simulation run generates a log event stream – new data for the analytics engine. This can then be viewed or extracted for various purposes.

THE OPTIMIZER

The *Workflow Optimizer* contains a collection of simulation based methods to help in

- Improving throughput by reducing
- activity wait (idle) times
- activity perform times
- Lowering Costs by examining
- the effects of balancing resource utilization by cross training
- the effects of reducing staff or introducing part-time shifts
- Satisfying SLA criteria by
- assigning/changing priorities of certain work item classes

The *Optimizer's* functionality comprises three main areas:

- Activity wait time reduction through resource load balancing/cross training.
- Idle cost reduction through adjusting resource quantities and shift assignments; see section.
- Critical path/activity analysis: locates paths and activities that are 'critical' w.r.t. wait times, perform times and/or costs.

The *Optimizer* needs data to decide upon an action. The data come from two sources: the scenario document and the data base. An *Optimizer* action consists of making changes to one or more parts of the scenario document.

For example, wait time reduction by load balancing changes role assignments, and idle cost reduction changes shift assignments; both affect the resources section. Altering activity durations affects the activities section and setting work item priorities affects both the resources and the arrivals sections.

After each *Optimizer* action the altered scenario is simulated; the generated log event stream is analyzed and the results published to a set of database tables. From those tables the *Optimizer's* analysis part extracts the data structures that feed all *Optimizer* routines. There are mainly four kinds of data.

- Step data: accumulated wait and perform times (gross/net) and costs for each step per each significant work item attribute (workflow relevant data field of the work item).
- Execution path data: identifies the process paths for individual work items and accumulates step wait times, perform times and costs along those paths.
- Productivity data: utilization (busy, idle) for each resource accumulated during the core analysis period set by the Optimizer user.
- Timed Sequence (TS) data: durations, gross and net, for each Timed Sequence per work item.

The data may be averaged over several simulations to balance random effects. The following table shows which data the different *Optimizer* functions employ.

Table 1: Data Employment

Optimizer Function	Simulation Data Employed
Activity wait time reduction through resource load balancing	Accumulated wait times; (Critical) path analysis; Resource utilization (accumulated busy/idle times)
Adjusting of activity perform times	(Critical) path analysis
Idle cost reduction by adjusting resource quantities and shift assignments	Productivity (accumulated busy/idle time)
Monitoring	Timed Sequence durations

There is a special *Auto Optimizer* mode of operation that allows running the *Optimizer* on a given workflow scenario without user interaction. All the user has to do is to specify a *'strategy'*, a set of preferences and parameters, and then push the start button.

The *Auto Optimizer* puts the various components of the *Optimizer* into one, organized whole – a conceptual map that allows the user to get around in the maze of possibilities and approaches and to develop strategies for reaching specific goals.

In the sequel we use the *Auto Optimizer* as a vehicle for discussing the *Optimizer* functionality.

THE AUTO OPTIMIZER

The *Auto Optimizer* comprises most of the *Optimizer* features. There are two main groups or general goals that may well be in conflict with each other.

- Reducing activity wait times caused by workforce shortage (improving performance).
- Reducing unnecessary costs caused by workforce abundance (improving productivity).

Wait Time Reduction (Bottleneck Analysis / Critical Path Analysis)

Wait time reduction [2] is a core function of the *Optimizer*. Wait times at activities are caused by the lack of resources needed to perform an activity at the time a work item arrives at the activity. The *Optimizer* ranks the activities according to their accumulated wait times. The top one is considered the current *bottleneck* and its performer (*bottleneck role*) indicates the skill or resources of which there seems to be a shortage (*bottleneck resources*).

The search for bottlenecks may take place among all activities of the workflow or it may be restricted to a certain subset of activities: the current *critical path* or a timed sequence selected.

The *Optimizer* knows three ways of dealing with bottlenecks.

Role Removal (Specialization)

Bottleneck resources (i.e. resources that play the bottleneck role) may be set free to focus on this type of work by removing other roles of their role assignment as long as those roles can be played by other, less busy resources.

Role Addition

A bottleneck resource may be *complemented* by other, less busy resources that play roles 'similar' to the bottleneck role and may take over the bottleneck role, e.g. after some additional training of staff people. There are currently two ways to find such similar roles and their resources:

- The *Scenario Document* may list explicitly possible complements for the bottleneck role. For example, we say – for mere demonstration purposes – that

  <RoleComplements>
      <Complement **Name**="Registrar" **CanDo**="Discharge" />
      <Complement **Name**="Lab" **CanDo**="XRay" />
  </RoleComplements>

- There may be a systematic *similarity* between roles based on the syntax of their names.

For example, *NorthCal:Appraisal* and *SouthCal:Appraisal* are two roles of the *Bank Loan* workflow. They are similar in as far as the required skill – creating an *Appraisal Report* – is the same; the difference is only with respect to the region – *NorthCal* respectively *SouthCal* – from where the loan application originates.

Resource Addition

If load balancing between resources (role removal and role addition) can no longer help, there may still be 'critical' activities where the resources that perform those activities are unusually busy ('maxed-out'). Then it may be in order to add resources, i.e. hire additional workforce or buy more equipment.

Excess Idleness Reduction

While the first part of the *Auto Optimizer* tries to deal with the shortage of certain types of resources, the other part deals with resource abundance. There are in essence two ways of reducing excess resource idleness:

- adjusting resource quantities and shift assignments;
- increasing the arriving workload.

Availability Reduction

In the first phase the *Auto Optimizer* tries to make the best use of the available workforce in order to improve the performance of the workflow system. Except for adding new resources if absolutely necessary, the actions taken have no effects on costs. The second phase, however, explicitly addresses cost issues. It is concerned with reducing costs for excess resources.

The *Auto Optimizer* has a rather sophisticated algorithm for removing excess resource availability[3]. The degree of idleness of a resource is measured in terms of the time it is available for work and the time it is actually busy. The algorithm tries to reduce resource idleness (idle costs). It looks at resources in decreasing order of their *idle costs*. Depending on the quantity and the idleness (time) of the resource at hand, it tries one of the following reduction measures.

- Set resource quantity to the quantity really needed.
- Try *removal* either temporarily by giving it *Leave of Absence* or permanently, if it was added by the *Optimizer* itself in an earlier stage.
- Try *part-time work*, possibly combined with the idleness of some other resource that can perform the same work.

There are several details and particulars to the algorithm for reducing excess resource availability; for example: whether part-time work makes sense (is enabled), in what quantity a resource occurs, whether a resource is *replaceable*, whether a resource is on part-time already.

After each action the altered scenario is simulated again. If no action is performed the next resource (ranked by *idle costs*) is tried until the list is exhausted.

Workload Increase

Excess resource idleness may indicate the capacity of the workflow system for accomplishing more work. This may be tested by increasing the arriving workload.

Currently there is only one way of increasing the workload: the arrivals of one day are added and spread evenly over the period of arrivals.

Productivity Index

A simple productivity index and a fuzzy scale allow watching the progress of the *Auto Optimizer*. The index is the, possibly weighted, number of work items completed during the core period, divided by the sum of resource costs and fixed daily costs. The unit cost is defined in the *Scenario document*; default: $1000.

Auto Optimizer Strategies

Various parameters and preferences allow the *Auto Optimizer* user to define a specific strategy. Between sessions the settings are kept in the Scenario document. On the *Auto Optimizer* panel the fields are grouped in the following way:

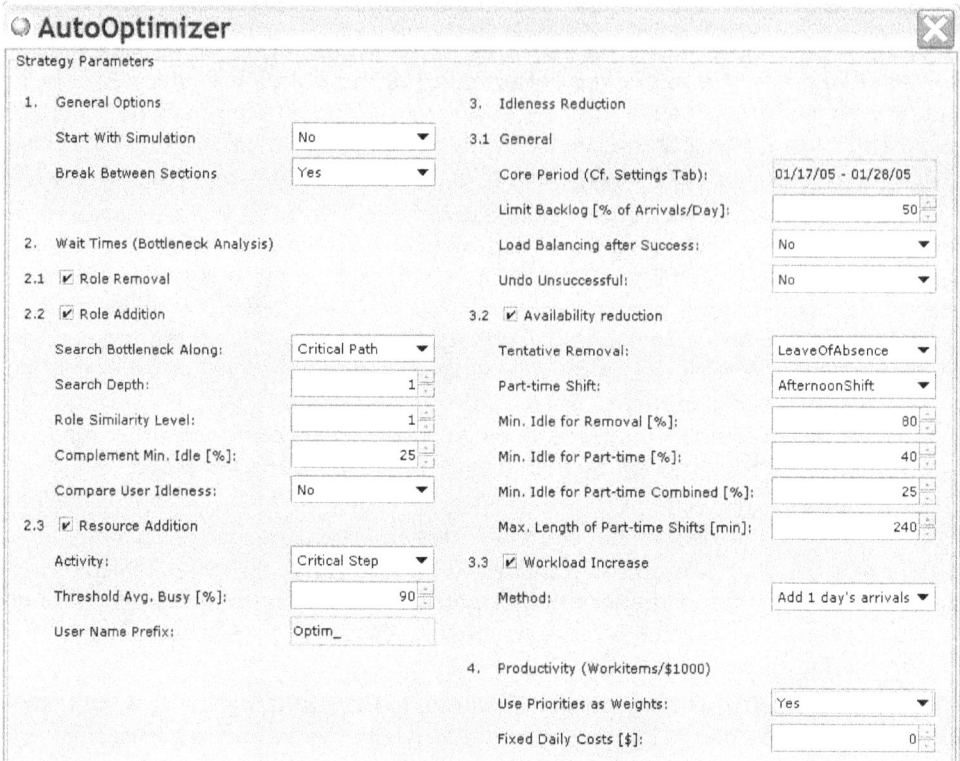

Figure 3: Auto Optimizer Settings

General Options

Between major sections the user can suspend the run and resume it later, after reviewing the results. If the current scenario has not been simulated/published after the last change the Auto Optimizer may start with simulation.

Wait Time Reduction

There are a number of options and thresholds that influence bottleneck analysis and critical path analysis and the subsequent actions.

A bottleneck can be searched within *'All Steps'*, a *'Critical Path'* or a *'Timed Sequence'*. If there is no complement for the current bottleneck role, role addition may stop or it may go on in the list of activities ranked by accumulated wait times.

The syntax of role names may distinguish several levels of similarity. As an example

- Level 2: identity (no difference must be ignored)
- Level 1: skill must be the same but the regions may differ (regional cross training)
- Level 0: ignore all differences, both in skill and in region

A resource that receives an additional role must show some amount of idleness.

If specializing and cross training don't help a new resource may be added to perform the most critical activity.

Idleness Reduction

After wait time reduction the remaining idleness can be reduced by either reducing the availability of resources or increasing the workload. Either method is applied only as long as the backlog of unfinished work objects is not greater than the given limit (in terms of the average number of work objects arriving each day). After each step the *Auto Optimizer* may return to the load balancing phase of the wait time reduction phase.

Reducing availability can be done by removing resources or assigning part-time shifts. Currently there is only one way of increasing the workload: the arrivals of one day are added and spread evenly over the period of arrivals.

Productivity Index

If priorities are defined for the work items, they may be used as weights in the number of work items completed. Fixed daily costs may be added for each work item.

CRITICAL PATH ANALYSIS

For Wait Time Reduction the Optimizer searches for 'critical' roles—skills required to perform 'critical' activities, i.e. activities that show large accrued wait times and hence indicate a shortage of corresponding resources. Here the term 'critical' is used in a rather loose, informal sense. In the realm of process and project management, however, there is also quite a powerful, formal meaning associated with the term.

Critical Paths

In project *mythodology*, the critical path is the sequence of work in all projects which, if identified and managed, always leads to success. Still, many seek the magical critical paths of their projects in hopes of making management simple.

The word critical seems to cause this misconception about the critical path. It implies pivotal importance, something crucial or indispensable.

In Critical Path Method (CPM), the critical path can be defined in two ways:
- The critical path in a project is the longest path relative to the time available to complete it.
- The critical path in a project is the path with the least project time reserves.

(Cited from [5], p.113.)

The kind of *projects* addressed by *Project Management* techniques like PERT and CPM differ in two major aspects from the *workflows* that appear in a BPMS.
- The project usually defines a single process like building a submarine or a power plant while a workflow defines a process that occurs many times, in parallel and in sequence.
- The project usually knows only sequencing and AND split/joins for structuring the set of basic tasks (steps). That makes it easy to define a *path* as a single start to end sequence of steps.

A workflow, however, may have—in addition to AND split/join—XOR split/join and loops. Each single instance/occurrence of a workflow, i.e. the processing of a single work item, when looking at it from hindsight, has the same simple structure as a project. All choices have been resolved, all loops have been unfolded. Only the AND split/joins remain and create a non-sequential course of action.

On the other side, it is the type of *Split* that affects the number of occurrences of the different paths in a larger set of work items being processed.

Loops may increase the number execution paths indefinitely and, if they contain AND clauses, quite rapidly. The path analysis component added to the analytics avoids such combinatorial explosion by overlaying occurrences of the same cycle. The details are outside the scope of this paper (see [4]).

The first definition above of being *critical* can be easily applied to the paths occurring in the processing of a single workflow object. For the purpose of analyzing/optimizing workflow processing, we generalize it to include different measures.

- The *X–critical* path in processing a work item is the path that is maximal with respect to measure *X* where
- *X* is the *wait time* at activities due to the resources not being available (*not* due to the synchronization at AND joins), accumulated along all activity occurrences of the paths;
- *X* is the accumulated *perform time* at activities;
- *X* is the accumulated sum of wait and perform times;
- *X* is the accumulated *perform costs* (resource costs) of activities.

Note that the third case captures the usual notion of *critical* in CPM.

(CRITICAL) PATHS OF WORKFLOWS

Based on data collected during simulation/analysis (by a special path analysis component, (see [4]), the *Optimizer* works with the following kind of tables. The screenshots are taken from the prototype implementation of our ideas. The example is based on the following simple business process.

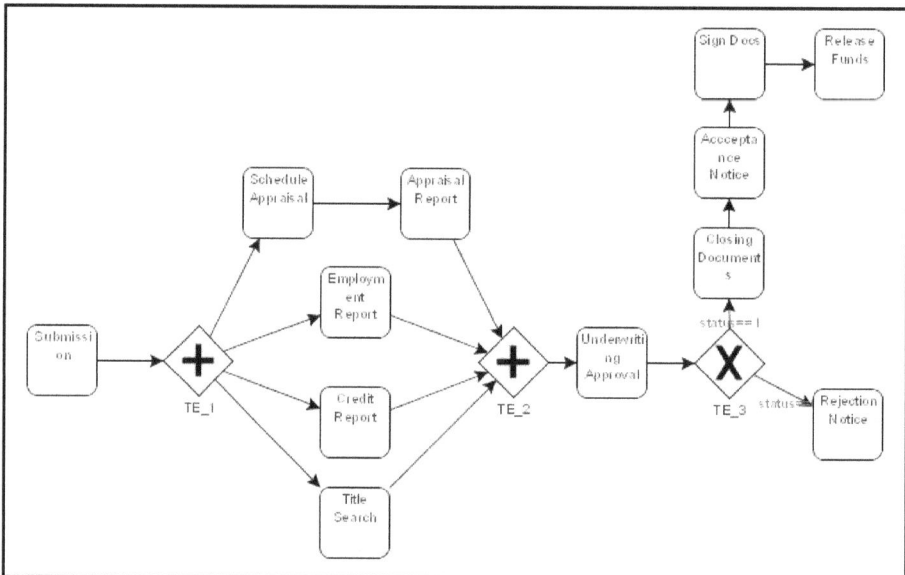

The workflow has both parallel (AND split/join) and alternative branches (XOR split). A loan application is sent along four parallel branches for preparing the reports needed for the underwriting decision. Then the applicant is informed accordingly.

The applications are processed in four regional centers, *Washington*, *Oregon*, *NorthCal* and *SouthCal*. This organization is reflected by the roles that the staff members may play. There are several discrepancies between the available staff and the needs induced by the actual (simulated) workload; they allow the *Optimizer* to show its power.

Optimizer: OPT_(dev)_BankLoan

Settings | Wait Times | Critical Paths | Utilization | Priorities

Critical Path Analysis

Execution Paths

Id	Descriptor	Total Wait [h:...	Prox. [%]	Freq. [%]	Crit. [%]
4	[Submi, TitSe, CloDo]	8715:38	100	83	46
6	[Submi, EmpRe, CloDo]	8035:15	92	83	21
7	[Submi, SchAp, CloDo]	7212:55	83	83	29
5	[Submi, CreRe, CloDo]	6680:58	77	83	3
0	[Submi, TitSe, RejNo]	935:45	11	17	41
2	[Submi, EmpRe, RejNo]	803:11	9	17	17
3	[Submi, SchAp, RejNo]	696:13	8	17	39
1	[Submi, CreRe, RejNo]	554:04	6	17	4

Accumulated Measures for Selected Steps (ordered by selected path measure)

Step	Path	Wait [h:mm]	Dur. [h:mm]	Cost [$]
Underwriting Approval	0,1,2,3,4*,5,6,7	3004:11	300:34	6011.28
Title Search	0,4*	2686:50	249:57	2499.49
Release Funds	4*,5,6,7	2304:46	103:28	1034.66
Sign Docs	4*,5,6,7	1183:25	307:06	3071.03
Closing Documents	4*,5,6,7	192:24	145:31	1455.16
Submission	0,1,2,3,4*,5,6,7	159:49	74:55	749.15
Accceptance Notice	4*,5,6,7	99:17	58:03	580.42

Settings

Workflow Selection

Dimension	Member
Region	
Category	

<all> ▼   600

Path Measure
● Wait ○ Dur
○ W+D ○ Cost

Aggregation
● Sum ○ Avg
○ Max

Step Selection
○ All ● Intersection ○ Difference

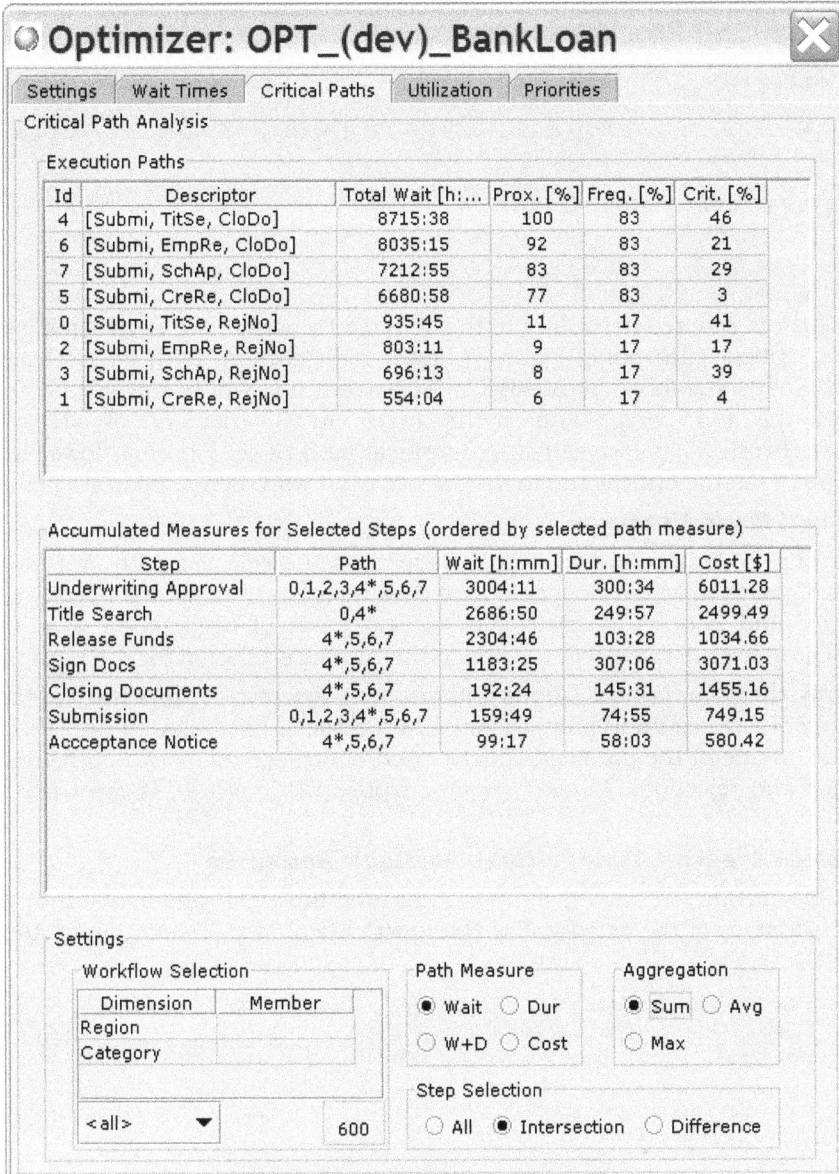

Figure 4: Critical Path Analysis

Execution Paths

The Execution Paths table above lists all paths that occur in one of the processes for the simulated set of work items. Each path is identified by the abbreviated names of the activities that mark the outcome of a split (initial activity, first activity after each split). So path #4 starts at *Submission* (as all paths do), at the first (AND) split *TE_1* it continues with *Title Search* and after the next and final (XOR) split *TE_3* it continues with *Closing Documents*.

A double-click on the path row brings up more detailed information about the path #4.

Global 360 Process Animator

Path Details #4:

[Submission, TE_1, Title Search, TE_2, Underwriting Approval, TE_3, Closing Documents, Accceptance Notice, Sign Docs, Release Funds]

[0, 17, 1, 12, 6, 13, 8, 9, 10, 11]

OK

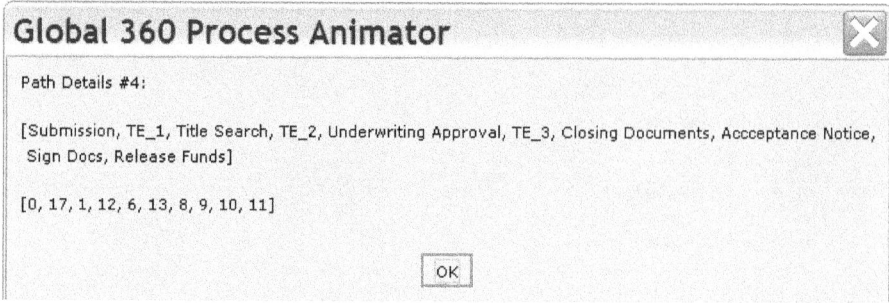

The paths are ordered according to the selected measure *total **wait time*** (see settings on critical path panel Figure 4, lower right corner). Path #4 is closely followed by path #6 whose 'proximity' is 92 percent, i.e. whose measure is 92 percent of the top path. Both paths occur in 83 percent of **all** selected processes/work items (see settings on critical path panel Figure 4, lower left corner). Path #4 is the critical one in 46 percent of all work items, #6 in 21 percent.

Steps and Basic Measures

The second table depicts the steps belonging to the selected path (#4). It shows the list of paths to which they belong and all their basic measures (*wait time, perform time* and *perform costs*) in the selected mode of aggregation (*sum* in this case). The steps are ranked according to the measure selected for the path table.

Currently the most critical step is *Underwriting Approval*; it has the largest total wait time and it occurs in all paths (in all processes). It is followed by *Title Search* which is on one of the parallel branches and hence occurs in two paths only (acceptance and rejection). Hence it is no surprise that path #4 is *the most critical* one.

Why Steps Are Wait Time Critical: Available Resources

By double clicking on an activity row of the step table one gets a look into the resource situation of the activity. For the most critical step, *Underwriting Approval*, we get:

CPA Selected Step (Total Measures)

Step	Path	Wait [h:mm]	Dur. [h:mm]	Cost [$]
Underwriting Approval	0,1,2,3,4*,5,6,7	3004:11	300:34	6011.28

Roles and Users (Average Measures)

Role	Wait [h:mm]	User	Avail. [h:mm/d]	Busy [%]	Cost [$/h]
*NorthCal:Underwriting	12:25	Gale	8:00	99	20
SouthCal:Underwriting	0:06	Pat	8:00	83	20
		Roger	8:00	64	20
Oregon:Underwriting	0:06	Penny	8:00	74	20
Washington:Underwriting	0:00	Yvon	8:00	61	20
		Dick	8:00	46	20

The lower part lists all performers (roles) that are required by some occurrence of *Underwriting Approval*. The * in front of the top most *NorthCal:Underwriting* indicates that this is also the current bottleneck role; it has an average wait time of 12.5 hours. The only resource to play that role is *Gale* who works 8 hours per day and is busy 99 percent of its time.

The situation shown is when no load balancing has happened yet. The table above suggests that Dick, who is the least busy resource doing *Underwriting Ap-*

proval in region *Washington,* is trained to do *Underwriting Approval* also in region *NorthCal.*

If all possible load balancing had been depleted already, a new resource *Optim_1_(Gale)*—a 'clone' of *Gale*—would be hired in the resource addition phase of the *Auto Optimizer,* as the average percentage of being busy of all resources that can do the most critical step is above the selected threshold of 90 percent (cf. optimizer settings, Figure 3).

When Steps Are Perform Time Critical

Currently the *Auto Optimizer* offers no way of automatically reducing the perform time of a critical activity. However, a simple right-click on the step row in the CPA step table opens a dialog for editing the activity's properties, e.g. the perform time or a participant reference to specially trained performer. And in the table showing the activity's resource situation, a right-click on a resource opens a dialog for editing its properties, e.g. its proficiency.

Another measure may be re-designing the workflow such that the critical activity is divided into two parts performed in parallel. Though conceivable in principle, no effort has been made to program this kind of change of a workflow definition.

SUMMARY, OUTLOOK

The *Auto Optimizer* puts the *Optimizer* components into one, organized whole—a conceptual map. It orients the user in the maze of possibilities and approaches for optimization and helps developing strategies for reaching specific goals.

There are a few unexplored possibilities worth mentioning.

Activity wait time reduction has come up with two competing notions: *bottleneck* and *critical.* It seems that all may be based on critical paths and activities alone. Bottleneck search can already be constrained to the respective wait-time critical path. In many cases the most critical role (i.e. the top role in the critical activities role/resource table) is also the bottleneck role. And if not, the bottleneck may not be that critical after all, i.e. on a parallel branch with a lot of slack (time reserve).

Currently the perform time of critical activities must be adjusted manually. This seems unsatisfactory, an unfinished business, and more research is needed. One option, for example, is to split a perform time critical activity into two parallel ones to allow for more work to be done in parallel.

The *Optimizer* uses statistics about timed sequence durations to monitor the effects of its actions. Watching/monitoring throughput in terms of TS durations may seem rather 'expensive' (complex); workload/backlog and cycle times, however, are not fine enough a measure. The TS statistics could serve as an alternative way of controlling the Auto Optimizer:
- High 'goal satisfaction' stops load balancing;
- Low 'goal satisfaction' stops idleness reduction.

Another unfinished yet quite promising business is the integration of some commercial workforce management system. With unlimited availability of resources/qualifications, a simulation run can create an ideal pattern of performer requirements. This pattern can be fed into a workforce management system to provide an optimal schedule for a given workforce. See [6] for an example of this.

REFERENCES

[1] *Automated optimization templates.* Discussion paper. Global 360, Sept 2004.

[2] *Reducing wait time.* Technical Report. Global 360, Aug 2005.

[3]   *The Workflow Process Optimizer.* Technical Report. Global 360, March 2006.

[4]   *Critical paths of workflows.* Technical Report. Global 360, Dec 2006.

[5]   Dennis H. Busch: *The new critical path method.* Chicago, Illinois. 1991

[6]   Robert Shapiro: Integration of Workforce Management with a Business
        Process Management Suite. *2008 BPM and Workflow Handbook,* published by
        Future Strategies Inc., FL, USA

Open Source Workflow Management Systems: A Concise Survey

Ricardo Garcês, Tony de Jesus, Jorge Cardoso*
and Pedro Valente, University of Madeira,
Portugal *SAP Research, Germany, *University of
Coimbra, Portugal

ABSTRACT

The use of open source Workflow Management Systems (WfMS) is appealing for organizations due to its low or inexistent cost and its customization capabilities. In this chapter we analyze ten different open source WfMS using a framework that offers decision makers a starting point for selecting a workflow solution. The framework is to be used as a basis for characterizing WfMS based on a set of 22 parameters.

INTRODUCTION

Nowadays, many organizations in the commercial, government and non-profit sectors benefit from the use of open source software [1]. Open source is having a growing impact on the software industry by becoming an important competitor to commercial software [2]. According to [3], the number of suppliers offering workflow management software is estimated to be two hundred. The selection of an open source WfMS solution may be quite a difficult and complex undertaking. A sound selection requires a complete analysis of the most popular solutions available. Otherwise, it may lead to the choice of an inadequate workflow product that will not support efficiently the business processes of an organization.

According to [4], the motivations for using and developing open source software are mixed, ranging from philosophical and ethical reasons to pure practical issues. Usually, the first perceived advantage of open source models is the fact that the software is made available gratis or at a low cost. But this characteristic is not exclusive to open source software [5]. What really distinguishes open source software from software available without a fee is the access to the source code and the right to modify it, the right to redistribute the modifications and to improve the code. Each organization has its particularities, so the characteristics of open source solutions allow the customization of open source workflow systems according to the functioning and the needs of organizations.

This chapter offers an overview and comparison of ten popular open source WfMS using a comprehensive framework for decision makers, providing a starting point to the complex process of selecting an open source WfMS. In fact, this document is intended to enable managers to better guide, justify and explain their decisions and choices.

WFMS COMPARISON FRAMEWORK

Several approaches have been proposed to compare information systems and information technologies. They have been provided by prestigious consulting companies such as Andersen Worldwide, Ernst & Young, Deloitte & Touche, Coopers & Lybrand, KPMG and Price Waterhouse. Since workflow technologies have specific characteristics, existing approaches do not address many important perspectives. Therefore, we propose a new and more complete approach. On the one hand, we want to determine what functionalities are provided by WfMS. On the other hand, we also want to evaluate the installation and usage of WfMS, as well as the definition of workflow processes. For this reason, and as showed in Table 1, we will focus our attention on the compliance of WfMS with the WfMC reference model [6] and on two functional perspectives: *runtime* and *design time*.

		Parameters
WfMC Reference Model		Process Definition Application (Interface 1)
		Workflow Client Application (Interface 2)
		Invoked Applications (Interface 3)
		Other Workflow Enactment Services (Interface 4)
		Administration and Monitoring tools (Interface 5)
Functional Perspectives	Runtime	Research Scope
		Installation Time
		Documentation
		Platform Independent
		Easiness of Installation and Utilization
		Web Based
		Other Software Required
		Middleware Platform
		DBMS Integration
		Transactions Support
	Design Time	Process Definition Time
		Documentation
		Easiness of the Process Definition
		Web Based
		Organizational Perspective
		Workflow Language

Table 1: Overview of the framework developed in our study

WfMC reference model

One of the many principles used by the WfMC (Workflow Management Coalition) is the so-called workflow reference model [6]. This model is a general description of the architecture of a workflow management system, in which the main components and the associated interfaces are described. In the workflow reference model, the tools for constructing and designing workflows are known as process definition applications (Interface 1). Work items are offered to the employees through workflow client applications (Interface 2). By selecting a work item, an employee can begin performing a specific task for a specific case. When carrying out a task it may be necessary to start an application. All the application software that can be started from the workflow system are known as invoked applications (Interface 3). According to the WfMC reference model, workflow systems may also be able to interact with other workflow engines (Interface 4). Workflow tracking, case control and staff management are supported by administration and monitoring tools (Interface 5).

Runtime and design time perspectives

According to [6], at the highest level, all WfMS may be characterized as providing support in three functional areas:

- *build time functions* are concerned with defining and modeling workflow processes and their activities;
- *runtime control functions* are concerned with managing workflow processes in an operational environment and sequencing activities;
- *runtime interactions* are concerned with human users and other application tools for processing the various activity steps.

As we can see, these three functional areas can be summarized in two core functional perspectives: design time (associated with build time functions) and runtime (gathering runtime control functions and their interactions).

The design time perspective, proposed by our framework, is associated with the task of designing a sample workflow process using the process editor. This functional perspective is also related to the ability of the process editor to easily, and in a small amount of time, help to define a relatively complete workflow process. Given the importance of these two functional perspectives, it only seems natural that they should be analyzed before choosing a workflow solution. The runtime perspective, proposed by our framework, is associated with the installation and the testing of the main functionalities of a workflow solution. It is also related to the analysis of the support that is offered by the workflow solution to workflow processes (e.g. support of transactions and treatment of exceptions).

COMPARISON ENVIRONMENT

We have chosen ten of the most popular and promising open source workflow systems available nowadays. The final set that we will analyze in this chapter is composed of the following WfMS: Bonita, Enhydra Shark, JawFlow, JBoss jBPM, JFolder, JOpera, OpenWFE, RUNA WFE, WfMOpen and YAWL. Before presenting the results of our comparison, it is crucial to clearly identify the environment on which the analysis of the WfMS was made. The installation and test of the workflow systems was made by two senior students in Computer Science within the scope of their final project. All the WfMS analyzed were installed and tested in a Intel Pentium M 2.00GHz computer with 1 GB memory, 100 GB disk space and running Windows XP. Since one way to quickly gain a good impression of a workflow management system is to work through a sample process chosen in advance, we have selected a sample workflow composed of 15 different tasks with multiple control structures (AND splits/joins and XOR splits/joins) and by nested workflow definitions. It also included 5 different participants.

COMPARISON OF THE 10 WFMS SELECTED

The framework specified in this chapter is now considered to compare the ten workflow systems. Table 2 offers an overview of our findings. Most of the systems are not completely compliant to the WfMC reference model. In fact, only Bonita, OpenWFE and YAWL are fully compliant. Moreover, most of the non compliant WfMS do not provide an interface to interact with other workflow enactment services. All solutions are platform independent. Two systems have been developed within the scope of a research project: YAWL and JOpera. Regarding installation and testing time, we have discovered a wide range of values that go from only 22 minutes, with OpenWFE, to 12 hours and 47 minutes with WfMOpen. One of the most important aspects that influenced the installation time was the documentation provided. We have reached the conclusion that most of the WfMS studied offer enough documentation in order to correctly install and use the system.

Regarding the installation easiness, JFolder's installation was straightforward, standing out from the all the other workflow systems. On the opposite end, we found Bonita, JawFlow and WfMOpen with a rather complicated installation procedure. We also discovered that only Enhydra Shark and JOpera do not offer a web based administration environment.

The process definition applications provided by five of the workflow systems analyzed offered mechanisms that allowed designing our sample process without major constraints. However, RUNA WFE, WfMOpen, Bonita, JFolder and JBoss jBPM process definition applications were quite limited and unpleasant to use.

The time spent to define our sample process assumed values that vary from almost 2 hours to approximately 6 hours. YAWL allowed the quickest process definition. Bonita was the one that required most time to design our sample process, 5 hours and 11 minutes.

Regarding the documentation provided, there is little or no documentation available about the process editor of several WfMS analyzed, like: JawFlow, JBoss jBPM, JFolder and WfMOpen. Finally, XPDL (XML Process Definition Language) is the process definition language most often used by the workflow systems analyzed.

In the following subsections we will discuss each workflow management system in greater detail according to our framework,

Bonita

Bonita was developed in 2003 by a team of 14 engineers, of which, Miguel Valdes Faura, Brice Revenant and François Charoy were the project leaders [7]. The current version is 2.0 and was released in June, 2006. Bonita is a complete workflow system that provides functionalities to handle long-running, user-oriented workflows and business processes. It allows to dynamically modifying the definition of a running process in order to take into account events that were not planned. This workflow solution also takes benefit from several services that the integration with a J2EE application server provides, such as transactions, role-based authentication and connection with external information systems.

1. WfMC reference model. Bonita is fully compliant to the WfMC reference model specification.

2. Runtime perspective. Bonita's installation and testing took 1 hour and 56 minutes. The documentation provided by the developers is comprehensive, allowing us to install the software without facing any major problem. However, its web-based user interface is unpleasant and not very user friendly. Bonita requires the installation of JDK, JOnAS Application Server with Tomcat, Jakarta Ant and a DBMS (database management system). It works upon the middleware platform, Java Message Service, in order to exchange data and events. Bonita offers an easy integration with most database management systems. It also supports exceptions treatment and rollback during process execution.

3. Design time perspective. In order to correctly define our sample workflow process we have spent approximately 5 hours. The graphical editor provided by Bonita is web-based. It is a Java Applet that allows us to design processes by dragging and dropping each activity. We have found a great amount of documentation about this process editor, but some details are not clearly explained. For instance, when defining a process, its sub processes should be defined first. For this reason the definition of our sample workflow process was quite complex. The Applet supports the definition of the organizational model, allowing for the specification of participants and roles. Bonita implements the Workflow Management Coalitions's XPDL.

	Bonita	Enhydra Shark	JawFlow	JBoss jBPM	JFolder	JOpera	OpenWFE	RUNA WFE	WfMOpen	YAWL
WfMC Reference Model										
Process Definition Application (Interface 1)	Yes	Yes	No	Yes	Yes	Yes	Yes	Yes	Yes	Yes
Workflow Client Application (Interface 2)	Yes	Yes	Yes	Yes	Yes	No	Yes	Yes	Yes	Yes
Invoked Applications (Interface 3)	Yes	Yes	No	Yes	No	Yes	Yes	Yes	Yes	Yes
Other Workflow Enactment Services (Interface 4)	Yes	Yes	No	No	No	No	Yes	No	No	Yes
Administration and Monitoring tools (Interface 5)	Yes	Yes	Yes	Yes	Yes	Yes	Yes	Yes	Yes	Yes
Research Scope	No	No	No	No	No	Yes	No	No	No	Yes
Runtime										
Installation Time	1h56m	6h11m	8h15m	1h09m	1h15m	1h56m	22 m	2h20m	12h47m	49 m
Amount of Documentation Found	Comprehensive	Basic	Inexistent	Comprehensive	Basic	Comprehensive	Comprehensive	Comprehensive	Basic	Comprehensive
Platform independent	Yes	Yes	Yes	Yes	Yes	Yes	Yes	Yes	Yes	Yes
Easiness of Installation	Simple	Simple	Complex	Simple	Trouble-free	Simple	Simple	Simple	Complex	Simple
Easiness of Utilization	Complex	Simple	Simple	Simple	Complex	Complex	Simple	Simple	Complex	Simple
Web Based	Yes	No	Yes	Yes	Yes	No	Yes	Yes	Yes	Yes
Other Software Required	Yes	Yes	Yes	Yes	Yes	Yes	Yes	Yes	Yes	Yes
Middleware Platform	Yes	Yes	Yes	Yes	Yes	Yes	Yes	Yes	Yes	Yes
DBMS Integration	Comprehensive	Comprehensive	Comprehensive	Comprehensive	Basic	Basic	Comprehensive	Comprehensive	Basic	Basic
Transactions Support	Exception Handling; Rollback	Exception Handling	None	Exception Handling; Rollback	Exception Handling	Exception Handling	Exception Handling; Rollback	Exception Handling; Rollback	Exception Handling	Exception Handling
Design Time										
Process Definition Time	5h11m	2h24m	3h03m	2h45m	4h25m	2h26m	5h15m	3h57m	3h03m	1h55m
Web Based	Yes	No	No	No	Yes	No	Yes	No	No	No
Amount of Documentation Found	Comprehensive	Comprehensive	Inexistent	Inexistent	Inexistent	Basic	Inexistent	Comprehensive	Inexistent	Comprehensive
Easiness of the Process Definition	Complex	Simple	Complex	Complex	Complex	Simple	Simple	Complex	Complex	Simple
Organizational Perspective	Yes	Yes	Yes	Yes	No	No	Yes	Yes	Yes	No
Workflow Language	XPDL	XPDL	XPDL	jPDL and BPEL	Developed its own XML Based Language	JOpera Visual Composition Language	Developed its own XML Based Language	jPDL language	XPDL	YAWL

Functional Perspectives

Table 2: Summary of our comparative study

Enhydra Shark

Enhydra Shark was developed by Enhydra.org community in 2003. It is an extendable and embeddable Java workflow engine completely based on WfMC specifications [8]. Shark can be used as a simple Java library in a servlet, a swing application, or in a J2EE container. The current version of Enhydra Shark is 2.3 which was released in November, 2008.

1. WfMC reference model. Shark is completely conformal to the WfMC reference model.

2. Runtime perspective. Enhydra Shark's installation and testing took 6 hours and 11 minutes. The documentation provided by the developers was quite straight forward, allowing for a relatively simple installation of the software. In order to properly administrate the workflow system, we should use a commercial administration tool. However, this is not mentioned in the documentation, and this application is not available to download in the project's homepage. This workflow system does not offer a web based environment. The administration/client application is very user friendly, allowing for a quite easy testing. This workflow system works upon a middleware platform (CORBA). Shark provides an easy integration with most database management systems and offers mechanisms that support exception treatment during a process execution.

3. Design time perspective. It took 2 hours and 24 minutes to define our sample workflow process. The documentation provided for the workflow process editor is quite comprehensive. This workflow solution provides, by default, a graphical editor very similar to JPEd (used with WfMOpen) called Together Workflow Editor (TWE). It is very practical and easy to use, assuming itself as a complete and interesting editor. TWE supports the design of the organizational perspective and the workflow language used is XPDL.

JawFlow

JawFlow was developed by Vincenzo Marchese in October 2006 and currently it is in version 3.0. JawFlow is a workflow engine partially conformal to WfMC directives and completely written in Java. It can be customized using activities written in Java or in any scripting language supported by the Bean Scripting Framework [9]. To deploy, test and run JawFlow, we have used the JBoss application server. However, there are no code dependencies to JBoss.

1. WfMC reference model. JawFlow only offers an embedded administration (interface 5) and client application (interface 2). It does not offer a process definition application (interface 1). This workflow system also does not offer interfaces to invoke other application (interface 3), or to interact with other workflow enactment services (interface 4).

2. Runtime perspective. It took 8 hours and 15 minutes in order to correctly install and test this WfMS. The documentation provided by the developer is very poor making the installation process quite complex. The process administration environment is web-based and relatively easy to use. JawFlow requires JDK, Jakarta Ant, JBoss and a DBMS. JawFlow can be integrated with any database management system and offers mechanisms that support error handling during the execution of a workflow process.

3. Design time perspective. This workflow engine does not provide a process editor. Any editor supporting XPDL can be used. In our case, we have used JPEd (used with WfMOpen). For this reason, the results presented it the Table 2 are identical to the ones that are described in the WfMOpen design perspective.

JBoss jBPM

JBoss jBPM is a flexible and extensible workflow management system. The JBoss jBPM' core component is the plain Java software for managing process definitions and the runtime environment for execution of process instances [10]. Its last release is version 3.2.3.

1. WfMC reference model. JBoss jBPM offers an administration/client application. JBoss jBPM is also able to interact with other applications. However, it is not able to interact with other workflow engines. This workflow system also offers a process definition application.

2. Runtime perspective. It took 1 hour and 9 minutes in order to correctly install and test a working version of jBPM. The documentation provided was comprehensive. This was the main factor for making the installation and usage of this workflow solution quite simple. Its web based administration/client application is poor in terms of features offered. For this reason, the use of this workflow solution should require the creation and implementation of a customized client and administration application. jBPM requires the installation of JDK and Eclipse with the JBoss IDE plugins. It offers mechanisms that make jBPM portable across the most popular databases and supports an effective treatment of transactions, allowing exceptions treatment and rollback during process execution.

3. Design time perspective. To correctly define our sample workflow process using the Eclipse-based tooling available for BPEL, we have spent 2 hours and 45 minutes. BPEL provides process orchestration which is the ability to combine web services into a process execution flow. The lack of documentation about JBoss jBPM' process editor reflected negatively upon the ease of the process definition. But this was not the only problem faced. In fact, another problem found was that the decision building block (XOR-split) had to be directly implemented in the code. Because JBoss jBPM uses BPEL in order to define processes, the definition of sub processes is not supported. This results complex workflow diagrams, which are difficult to analyze and understand. The definition of our sample process was therefore quite difficult. This process definition editor supports the specification of the organizational perspective. JBoss jBPM supports two process definition languages: jPDL and BPEL. jPDL is a process language to implement business processes and workflows in Java.

JFolder

JFolder (also known as PowerFolder) was developed by Gary Steinmetz in 2004 and is in version 1.1. It is a business application development studio and server that uses a XML based language in order to define workflow processes that run within a J2EE environment. Development and administration takes place through a web browser. JFolder contains features like security, persistence, email, file management and data access [11].

1. WfMC reference model. JFolder offers administration and monitoring tools as well as a workflow client application. However, it is not able to interact with other applications and with other workflow engines. This WfMS also offers a process definition application.

2. Runtime perspective. JFolder installation and testing took 1 hour and 25 minutes. The amount of documentation provided by the developers is sufficient, allowing us to install the software without facing any major problem. Its web-based administration environment is quite unpleasant, becoming very often confusing. This fact makes this workflow solution unattractive from an administration point of view. JFolder requires J2EE, Jakarta Ant and JBoss. This workflow system works upon the middleware platform. The documentation does not indicate if is possible to integrate JFolder with other than its default DBMS (hsqldb). JFolder offers mechanisms that support error handling during the execution of the workflow process.

3. Design time perspective. It took 4 hours and 25 minutes in order to design our sample workflow process. A poor documentation is available for this editor. This tool provides a very limited web-based process editor. It is not based on a "drag and drop" idea. This situation makes it harder to add or edit elements of the diagram. There is also no automated mechanism to save the process definition. All these aspects made the design of our workflow process quite hard and complex. It does not support the definition of roles and participants (organizational perspective). The JFolder process editor uses a XML-based proprietary language in order to define workflow processes. This language does not support the definition of sub processes.

JOpera

JOpera is built as a collection of plugins for Eclipse. It is a service composition tool that offers a visual language and an execution platform for building workflow processes. It includes a graphical modeling environment, a light-weight execution engine, and also a set of powerful debugging tools which natively supports the iterative nature of service composition. JOpera has a wide range of applications and implications: from rapid development of service-oriented business applications to classical workflow management and business process automation [12]. JOpera plugin for Eclipse 1.9.11 is the latest release of this system.

1. WfMC reference model. JOpera offers an administration and monitoring tool. It is able to interact with other applications. This workflow system also offers a process definition application.

2. Runtime perspective. The JOpera system was developed with research purposes. Its installation and testing took 1 hour and 56 minutes. The comprehensive documentation provided by the developers has allowed us to install the software without facing any major problem. However, the environment offered, based on Eclipse workbench, is not a practical and user friendly management environment. This poor management environment makes this workflow solution unattractive from a usage point of view. JOpera requires the installation of Java JDK and Eclipse. JOpera provides integration with the most popular DBMS and supports a simple exception handling model.

3. Design time perspective. In order to correctly define our sample workflow process we have spent 2 hours and 26 minutes. Enough documentation related with the graphical editor is provided. In spite the fact that the definition of the process is quite simple, JOpera process editor is quite repetitive, making the definition of our sample process longer. Another problem found is that the processes being designed quickly became confusing and it was difficult to analyze/identify the transitions between tasks. This limitation added to the fact that it does not support the organizational perspective allows us to say that this is a very unattractive process editor. The workflow language used by JOpera is JOpera visual composition language.

OpenWFE

OpenWFE is an open source workflow engine that has been developed by Lukas Eder and Nicolas Modryzk. It is a complete Business Process Management suite with four components: an engine, a worklist, a client application and a host for automatic agents. It is written in Java, but features access libraries for languages such as Python, Perl, and Ruby, C# (.NET), PHP and Pnuts [13]. OpenWFE is based on a distributed and web-friendly infrastructure. It offers mechanisms that allow persistence, automated form generation and workflow administration. In November 2006, OpenWFE 1.7.2 was released.

1. WfMC reference model. OpenWFE is completely conformal to the WfMC reference model.

2. Runtime perspective. OpenWFE' installation and testing took only 22 minutes mainly due to its intuitive and user friendly environment. The comprehensive documentation provided by the developers allows us to install the software without facing any major problems. The only problem found during the installation was that the documentation available mainly described the installation of the system for a Linux operating system. The web-based administration tool and client application were very user friendly and simple to use. OpenWFE installation requires JDK and JRE in order to work properly. This workflow system works upon a middleware platform (Java RMI). It is also able to be integrated with all of the most important database systems and it supports an effective treatment of transactions, allowing exceptions treatment and rollback during process execution.

3. Design time perspective. Using the graphical editor provided, we have spent 5 hours and 15 minutes in order to correctly define our sample workflow process. Workflow processes are designed in their own XML based language. The lack of documentation of the process editor made this definition process quite long. Droflo is a very limited web based process editor. In fact, it is not based on a "drag and drop" idea. This situation makes it harder to add or edit element of the flow diagram. Another problem found is that in order to save the XML code generated the user has to copy it and then paste it in a text document. In other words, the editor does not have any option to perform this action. This process editor is so unpractical that in most situations it is much easier to define the workflow process directly using XML. The definition of our sample process was, therefore, quite hard. It supports the definition of the organizational perspective.

RUNA WFE

The Runa Consulting Group has released RUNA WFE, an open source workflow/business process management environment for jBoss jBPM engine. It is an end user solution for business process management, written in Java, which provides a rich web interface containing a work list handler, a process monitor and a form player. It also supports the interaction with external applications [14]. This workflow solution most recent update is RUNA WFE 2.2 (November 2008).

1. WfMC reference model. RUNA WFE offers an administration/workflow client application and also supports the interaction with other applications. However it is not able to interact with other workflow engines. Moreover, this WfMS offers a process definition application. RUNA WFE is partially conformal to the WfMC model because it does not interact with other workflow enactment services.

2. Runtime perspective. The installation and testing of RUNA WFE took 2 hours and 20 minutes. The comprehensive documentation provided was sufficient to install and test this system without facing any major problem. The friendly web based administration/client application offered also contributed to an easy testing. RUNA WFE requires the installation of JDK. This workflow system works upon the middleware platform. It offers an easy integration with the most popular database management systems and also supports an effective treatment of transactions, allowing exceptions treatment and rollback during process execution.

3. Design time perspective. The definition of our sample workflow process, using RUNA GPD (a process editor for RUNA that sits upon Eclipse workbench), took 3 hour and 57 minutes. The documentation provided was comprehensive, describing several workflow process definition examples. This workflow system does not allow the definition of sub processes, which results in the creation of complex and confusing workflow diagrams. It also requires the direct implementation of the user forms; which may become quite hard for inexperienced users. For these reasons, the definition of our workflow process was quite complicated. It supports the definition of the organizational perspective. The workflow language used by RUNA WFE is jPDL.

WfMOpen

WfMOpen is a J2EE based implementation of a workflow engine. The workflow component is based on a set of Java interfaces that defines API for workflow management facility. It may be used as the core for any process based application implementation and is well suited in providing solutions for business process management related jobs [15]. In May 2008, the most recent update, WfMOpen 2.2, was released.

1. WfMC reference model. WfMOpen is only partially conformal to the WfMC model, because it does not interact with other workflow enactment services.

2. Runtime perspective. It took 12 hours and 47 minutes in order to correctly install and test a working version of WfMOpen. The information available in the documentation provided was confusing, dispersed over the document and in many aspects insufficient. This was the main reason for making the installation and testing of this workflow solution very complex. Moreover, besides the fact that it is poorly documented, the web-based management environment offered is in many aspects quite user unfriendly. WfMOpen requires the installation of JDK and JBoss. This workflow system works upon a middleware platform (Java RMI, CORBA and SOAP). The database integration is achieved only using the default DBMS of this workflow system. It offers build-in solutions for handling exceptions during a process execution.

3. Design time perspective. To correctly define our sample workflow process using JPEd, we spent 3 hours and 3 minutes. The lack of documentation about JPEd reflected negatively upon the ease of the process definition, making it quite complex. After understanding how it works, JPEd becomes very practical and easy to use. It supports the organizational perspective. WfMOpen uses XPDL with some extensions to define workflow processes.

YAWL

The YAWL system is an open source workflow solution based on the YAWL (Yet Another Workflow Language) language, designed by Wil van der Aalst, Lachlan Aldred, Marlon Dumas and Arthur ter Hofstede, members of the Faculty of Information Technology of Queensland University of Technology. The project designers developed this new language by taking Petri nets as a starting point and adding mechanisms to allow for a more direct and intuitive support of the workflow patterns identified [16]. YAWL provides direct support for all of the workflow patterns and offers mechanisms that allow persistence, automated form generation and workflow administration [17]. YAWL supports the control-flow perspective, data perspective, and is able to interact with web services. The last version of the system, version 2.2, was released in November 2008.

1. WfMC reference model. YAWL system is completely conformal to the WfMC reference model specifications.

2. Runtime perspective. The YAWL system was developed for research purposes. YAWL installation and testing took only 49 minutes. The documentation provided by the developers is comprehensive, describing in detail each step of the installation and allowing us to install the software without facing any major problems. In fact, the installation of the software was simple. This workflow system provides a web based administration/client application that is very user friendly and easy to use. In order to work properly, YAWL system installation requires JRE and Apache Tomcat. This system is compatible with a middleware platform: SOAP. The database integration provided does not support some of the most popular DBMS available. It only offers integration with PostrgreSQL as an alternative to Hypersonic. It allows exceptions treatment during process execution.

3. Design time perspective. Using the graphical editor provided, which is not web-based, we spent 1 hour and 55 minutes in order to correctly define our sample workflow process. The provided documentation related to the editor was comprehensive. The definition of our sample process was simple. In fact, the process definition editor uses a small set of elements to design a process, simplifying its analysis. It is also based on a "drag and drop" idea. This situation makes it easier to add or to edit elements of the flow diagram. However, one of the major drawbacks of this workflow solution is that it does not support the organizational perspective. For this reason, we are not able to associate participants or roles to a task.

RELATED WORK

Aalst et al. [16] offers a comparison of the functionality of 15 workflow languages based on a set of workflow patterns. We have a different objective since our aim is to evaluate the main features offered, the easiness of the installation and use of WfMS as well as the easiness of the definition of workflow processes. The research on runtime and design time perspectives of workflow systems is very limited. However, these two perspectives have been somewhat and indirectly addressed by academic papers. In [21], Murray offers a case study that analyses the implementation of a commercially available healthcare workflow system in two hospitals' settings. The framework proposed also includes a parameter with the same aim as our parameter named *organizational perspective*. It also proposes the parameter *ease of use of the WfMS* which is similar to our parameter *easiness of utilization*. The research developed by Stoilova and Stoilov [22] addresses problems related to the assessment and comparison of workflow management systems. The paper proposes an evaluation template composed by eight categories. The functional category is composed by some parameters equivalent to the ones that we have used. These parameters are: *modeling process definition, workflow client application, integration with other workflow engines (supported standards)* and *administration and monitoring*. The paper also proposes another evaluation category: *usability*. This category is related with our parameter: *easiness of utilization*.

RELEVANCE AND VALUE

The selection of an adequate workflow system to manage the business processes of an organization is an important and complex decision that depends on several aspects. The decision is significant due to the wide and heterogeneous set of WfMS available, either commercial or open source. The use of open source solutions may become very advantageous for organizations since source code as well as the right to modify it allows organizations to address specific requirements. Moreover, there are many success cases using this type of software. Nowadays, open source software is used extensively in the industry. The recent acceptance of Linux and the Apache project are excellent examples of this phenomenon. Due to the success of open source solutions, open source workflow systems have, therefore, become particularly interesting and appealing to IS and IT decision makers. From a set of open source WfMS currently available, we have chosen the most popular and, in our opinion, most interesting WfMS to be analyzed and compared. The framework proposed in this chapter for comparing open source WfMS is based on the WfMC reference model and on the runtime and design time perspective of workflow systems. This chapter offers an important study for industry decision makers by providing a starting point to the complex process of selecting an open source WfMS.

ACKNOWLEDGEMENTS

This work has been support by Foundation for Science and Technology (FCT), POCTI-219 and FEDER. The support of SAP Research, CEC Dresden, Germany, is also gratefully acknowledged.

REFERENCES

1. TDG, *Open Source Software: Case Studies Examining Its Use.* 2003, The Dravis Group.
2. Peeling, N. and J. Satchell, *Analysis of the Impact of Open Source Software.* 2001 QinetiQ.
3. Aalst, W.M.P.v.d. and K.v. Hee, *Workflow management: models, methods, and systems.* 1st edition ed. 2002: MIT Press Cambridge, MA, USA.
4. EWLS, Free Software / Open Source: Information Society Opportunities for Europe? 2000, European Working group on Libre Software.
5. Kenwood, C.A., *A Business Case Study of Open Source Software.* 2001, The MITRE Corporation.
6. Hollingsworth, D., *The Workflow Reference Model.* 1995, Workflow Management Coalition.
7. BONITA. *BONITA: Workflow Cooperative System.* 2007 [cited 21. May 2007]; Available from: http://bonita.objectweb.org.
8. Shark. *Enhydra Shark: Java Open Source workflow engine based on XPDL.* 2007 [cited 22.05.2007]; Available from: http://www.enhydra.org/ workflow/shark/index.html.
9. jawflow. *jawflow: Java Workflow Manager.* 2007 [cited 22.05.2007]; Available from: https://www-304.ibm.com/jct03004c/servers/solutions/ finder/solution/overview.jsp?solution_id=soq74085540080014002%7C30.
10. jBPM. *JBoss jBPM.* 2007 [cited 22.05.2007]; Available from: http://www.jbpm.org/.
11. JFolder. *JFolder - Application development and deployment platform.* 2006 [cited 22.05.2007]; 1.1 Alpha:[Available from: http://www.powerfolder.org.
12. JOpera. *JOpera Project: Process Support for more than Web Services.* 2004 [cited 22.05.2007]; Available from: http://www.iks.ethz.ch/jopcra.
13. OpenWFE. *OpenWFE - open source workflow engine.* 2007 [cited 22.05.2007]; Available from: http://www.openwfe.org/.
14. Runa. *RUNA WFE.* 2007 [cited 22.05.2007]; Available from: http://runawfe.sourceforge.net/.
15. WfMOpen. *WfMOpen.* 2005 [cited 22.05.2007]; Available from: http://wfmopen.sourceforge.net.
16. Aalst, W.M.P.v.d., et al., *Workflow Patterns.* Distributed and Parallel Databases, 2003. 14(1): p. 5-51.
17. YAWL. *YAWL: Yet Another Workflow Language.* 2007 [cited 22.05.2007]; Available from: http://yawlfoundation.org/product/index.php.
18. Fitzgerald, B. and T. Kenny. Open Source Software can Improve the Health of the Bank Balance - The Beaumont. in 24th International Conference on Information Systems (ICIS). 2003. Seattle.
19. Scacchi, W. OpenEC/B: electronic commerce and free/open source software development. in The 5th Workshop on Open Source Software Engineering, part of The 27th International Conference on Software Engineering (ICSE 2005). 2005. St. Louis, Missouri: ACM Press, New York, NY, USA.
20. Gurbani, V.K., A. Garvert, and J.D. Herbsleb, *A case study of open source tools and practices in a commercial setting.* SIGSOFT Softw. Eng. Notes, 2005. **30**(4): p. 1-6.
21. Murray, M. Strategies for the Successful Implementation of Workflow Systems within Healthcare: A Cross Case Comparison. in 36th Annual Hawaii International Conference on System Sciences (HICSS'03). 2003: IEEE Computer Society, Washington, DC, USA.
22. Stoilova, K. and T. Stoilo. Comparison of Workflow Software Products in International Conference on Computer Systems and Technologies—CompSysTech'2006. 2006. Veliko Tarnovo, Bulgaria.

Extending XPDL with the Temporal Perspective

Denis Gagné, Trisotech and André Trudel
Acadia University, Canada

ABSTRACT

We extend XPDL to capture the temporal perspective of business processes. This extension deals with the various temporal constraints and dependencies that may occur while characterizing real world business processes. We precisely describe each temporal construct, and provide an XML schema for each. These individual schemas are then integrated into the XPDL schema providing a simple extension. With this extension, XPDL becomes expressive enough to account for a large set of time dependent real world business processes.

INTRODUCTION

Every process and/or activity needs or consumes various types of resources. Examples are material goods, skills, capabilities, and time. Time is a critical dimension of a process model or workflow specification as it is directly related to customer satisfaction and cost reduction. The speedy delivery of goods or services has a direct impact on customer satisfaction.

Time is a contributing factor to both the definition and the enactment of a process model or workflow specification. When defining a workflow, the temporal perspective allows the modeler to explicitly specify temporal constraints and dependencies to ensure that all temporal requirements of the process are met. At enactment time, the temporal perspective of the workflow specification leads to the ability to precisely schedule a process and its resources.

Time management is important when specifying a process model or workflow. Keep in mind that time is a finite resource. We cannot change the amount of time in a day. Furthermore, time optimization is often an effective cost reduction strategy for an organization.

Surprisingly, time is currently poorly addressed by the various business process standards. Given the importance of time with respect to process definition and enactment, our current research direction is to introduce time as a first class citizen to some of the main business process standards. In this paper, we describe a proposal for extending the XML Process Definition Language (XPDL) with a temporal perspective schema.

XPDL is a widely accepted [6] XML process definition format from the Workflow Management Coalition (WfMC). The current XPDL version (XPDL 2.1) [3] is the result of many years of standards evolution towards process definition interchangeability [2]. The origins of XDPL can be traced to the Workflow Process Definition Language (WPDL) [5] which was a text-based process definition language created to specify the "Interface 1: Process Definition Interchange" of the WfMC's Workflow Reference Model [4]. With the emergence of XML as an extensible markup language for describing documents to be exchanged, the WfMC introduced a new XML-based Process Definition interchange Language (XPDL 1.0) [7] as the new specification for Interface1. At the time neither WPDL nor XPDL 1.0 proposed a specific graphical representation or notation for the definition of processes.

Some years later, with the growing adoption of the Business Process Modeling Notation (BPMN) [8], the WfMC extended XPDL to provide support for BPMN. With the advent of XPDL 2.0, not only was there a new specification for Interface1, but also a standard text-based representation language (serialization) for Business Process Diagrams (BPDs) drawn in BPMN. The latest version of XPDL, adopted in April 2008 by the WfMC, is XPDL 2.1[3]. According to WfMC, XPDL 2.1 provides for a system and platform independent process definition and diagram interchange.

In the next section, we summarize the various temporal constructs required to capture the temporal perspective. The following sections progressively introduce the extensions required of XPDL in order to capture these various temporal constructs. We then reflect on further work required to bring time forward as a first class citizen of business process standards, and offer some conclusions.

THE TEMPORAL PERSPECTIVE

The temporal perspective of process modeling was defined in [1] by providing a series of generic temporal constructs. This characterization, independent of any specific modeling formalism or approach, precisely defined each temporal construct and provided, when possible, a formal temporal account of these constructs based on Allen's interval algebra [9]. These constructs can be categorized into a few main categories: time points, intervals/durations, temporal constraints and, temporal dependencies.

When modeling a process, we often need to specify time points or intervals of interest to the model. Time points can be specified as *absolute* (e.g., Tuesday February 17 2009), *periodic* (e.g., every Monday) or *relative* (e.g., in 2 days).

Interval size can either be explicitly specified as a duration, or implicitly derived from the interval's endpoints. Given that the actual duration of a process or activity is only available after its actual occurrence, the *Estimated* duration of a process or activity is of interest while modeling a process or activity. Furthermore, two aspects of interval duration are of interest as constraints, namely the maximum and minimum duration.

Many other intervals are of interest to the temporal perspective: *Transfer Time, Queue Time, Wait Time, Set Up Time* (also known as *Changeover Time), Processing Time* (also known as *Working Time), Validation Time* (also known as *Inspecting Time), Rework Time,* and *Downtime.* We do not address these specific intervals in this paper. See [1] for a discussion and logical formalization.

Temporal constraints can be specified to control the start or finish time of a process or activity. These temporal constraints can be inflexible (i.e. tied to a specific time point) or flexible (i.e. not tied to a specific time point). The inflexible temporal constraints are:
- Must Start On (MSO) and
- Must Finish On (MFO).

A flexible temporal constraint does not specify a specific time point for a process or an activity, but rather imposes scheduling upper and/or lower bounds. The flexible temporal constraints are:
- As Soon As Possible (ASAP),
- As Late As Possible (ALAP),
- Finish No Later Than (FNLT),

- Start No Later Than (SNLT),
- Finish No Earlier Than (FNET), and
- Start No Earlier Than (SNET).

Flexible temporal constraints work in conjunction with temporal dependencies, which are described below, to make a process or activity occur as soon or as late as the process or activity dependency will allow.

A temporal dependency is a relationship between two processes or activities in which one process or activity depends on the start or finish of another process or activity in order to begin or end. There are four types of temporal dependencies between a predecessor and successor:

- Finish-to-start (FS),
- Start-to-start (SS),
- Finish-to-finish (FF), and
- Start-to-finish (SF).

Temporal dependencies can be further constrained with delays called *Lead* and *Lag Time*. A *Lag Time* is normally specified as a duration (e.g. 2 days). *Lead Time* is useful when the successor activity requires a head start. Usually, *Lead Time* is specified using a negative *Lag Time* (e.g. -1 day).

TEMPORAL PERSPECTIVE EXTENSION TO XPDL

Some temporal elements are native in XPDL (e.g. Limit, TimeEstimation, Waiting-Time, WorkingTime, Duration, Deadline, and TimeDate)[3], but most of these are simulation elements which are treated as second class citizens. Our goal is to incorporate the various temporal constructs of the temporal perspective while respecting the current syntax and semantics of XPDL, and the semantics of BPMN for which XPDL offers a serialization. An important feature of XPDL is that implementers can include their own extensions to describe new process constructs. We therefore present these new temporal elements using the namespace-qualified extension capability provided within XPDL. The particular namespace we are adding is called "temporal."

We opted for the namespace-qualified extension to XPDL, rather than a re-engineering of the standard, as this approach has a greater chance of being accepted and integrated by the business process community. Extensions are possible in XPDL because most elements contain an *"any"* element. The *any* element allows XPDL files to contain additional elements that are defined within another namespace. Our extension also further accounts for the depiction of the various temporal constraints and dependencies using a temporal perspective notation extension to BPMN, which is currently under development and not presented in this paper.

In the spirit of the current XPDL standard, we do not strongly type the elements of our extension schema with existing XML data types. Where appropriate, we identify and discuss data types that could be used.

Our proposed extension allows for the specification of the temporal perspective in a fully XPDL compliant fashion, while maintaining abstraction from any product specific details until execution.

TIME POINTS

During its enactment, a process or an activity is instantiated and takes place over a period of time. We often refer to a process instance as a *Case*. In this paper, we refer to the point in time when a process is instantiated and started with the constant *CaseStart*, and to the point in time when the particular instance of the process is completed as the *CaseEnd*. Note that these constants represent a concrete time point and not an interval.

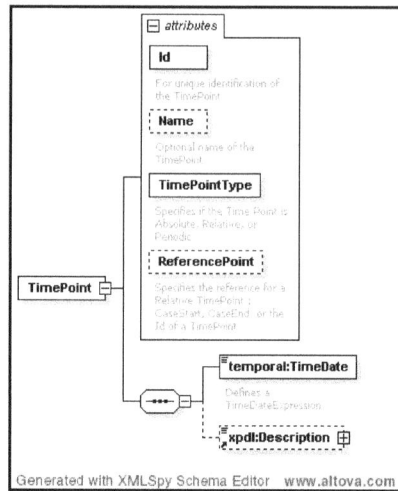

Fig. 1. The TimePoint Element

To specify a time point, we introduce the `TimePoint` element (see figure 1). The attributes are a required `Id`, for unique identification of the time point, an optional `Name`, a required `TimePointType`, and an optional `ReferencePoint`. The `TimePointType` attribute specifies whether the time point is `Absolute`, `Relative`, or `Periodic`. If it is `Relative`, a reference time point needs to be specified in `ReferencePoint`. If it is `Periodic`, a reference time point may be specified. For brevity and clarity, we present elements using a graphical representation rather than a textual schema. The particular graphical representation used is borrowed from XMLSPY [11]. Attributes appear in a large box at the top, followed by the sub-elements. Optional entries are dashed. Solid entries without cardinality must appear exactly once.

The `TimePoint`'s sub-elements are a required `TimeDate` and optional `Description`. Note that the `Description` element is a reference to the XPDL `Description` element.

Again, we do not strongly type our elements in the spirit of the current version of XPDL. For an Absolute time point (i.e., `TimePointType` set to `Absolute`), the `TimeDate` could use the `xsd:dateTime` datatype for time (Gregorian calendar). Its value space is described as a combination of date and time of day in Chapter 5.4 of ISO 8601[10].

Note that we provide the capability to specify an absolute time point, but it does not represent a best practice. It is a best practice in process modeling not to use "concrete values" but rather use abstract concepts when specifying the model. This provides generality to a process definition, so that each instance of the process is bounded within its actual specific runtime context. For example, it is a best practice to identify a role (e.g. a "Professor") as a performer of an activity (e.g. "Correct Homework") rather than a specific individual (e.g. "J.F. Allen"). This allows for the process to be more universal and instantiated multiple times in multiple contexts. The same best practice applies to specifying time points in a process model (e.g. "Next Friday" rather than "Friday February 27th 2009").

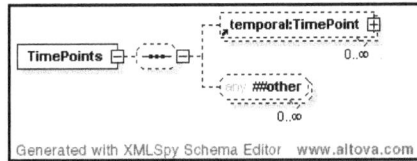

Fig. 2. The TimePoints Element

TimePoint elements are grouped together using a TimePoints element (see Fig. 2). The TimePoints element is added as an any element to the Package element in XPDL. Recall that the "any ##other" element is the generic extension receptacle of various elements in XPDL. It states that elements may come from other namespaces. By placing the various time point definitions at the package level, we provide for simple re-use of these throughout the package.

DURATION

We refer to the time elapsed between the start of an activity and its completion (or end) as the *Duration* of the activity.

The Duration element allows for the specification of an optional Estimated, Minimum and/or Maximum value for the duration of an interval (see figure 3).

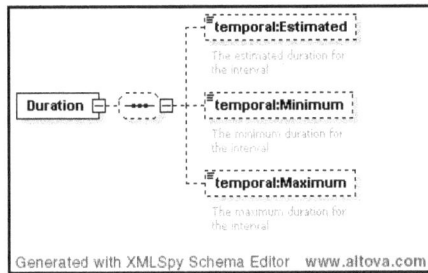

Fig. 3. The Duration Element

Duration could use the xsd:duration datatype. The duration information is added as an any element to the Activity element in XPDL. In this paper, we are only providing for the specification of the duration of the activity. In future work, we will also address the duration of other intervals of interest (e.g. Transfer Time, Queue Time, Wait Time, etc.).

TEMPORAL CONSTRAINTS

Limited capabilities for temporally constraining the start or end of a process or workflow are already provided by XPDL (via BPMN attributes). Note that it is not possible to specify an end point for a process or workflow in XPDL from which one could do backward scheduling (i.e. make sure all activities are scheduled such that the process instance is completed by the specified time point). This extension is beyond the scope of this paper and will be addressed in future work.

Temporal constraints can be specified for activities and sub-processes of a process model or workflow specification. An individual temporal constraint either applies to the start or end of a process or an activity. If it is a start constraint, we use the element StartTemporalConstraint (see Fig. 4). The attributes of a StartTemporalConstraint are a required *Id* for unique identification, an optional *Name*, a required ConstraintDetail which identifies the type of constraint, and a required ReferencePoint. The ConstraintDetail specifies if the constraint is an ASAP (As Soon As Possible), ALAP (As Late As Possible), NET (Not Earlier Than), NLT (Not Later Than), or ON (Must Be On). The constraint is always relative to a time point which is referred to by the attribute `ReferencePoint`. The `ReferencePoint` can either be `CaseStart`, `CaseEnd` or the `id` of a specified `TimePoint`.

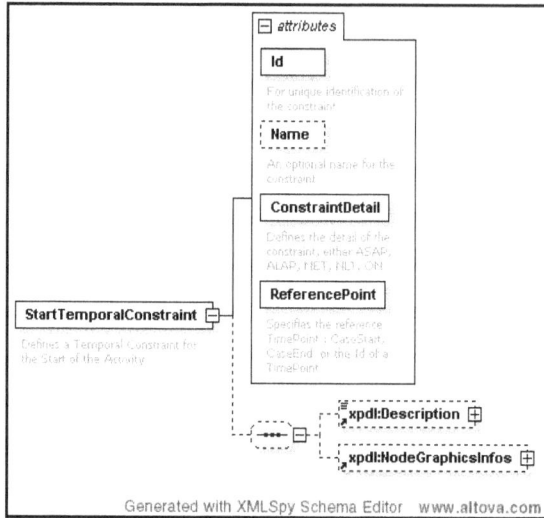

Fig. 4. The StartTemporalConstraint Element

The sub-elements of `StartTemporalConstraint` are optional elements referenced from the XPDL schema. These include a `Description`, and `NodeGraphicsInfos` which can be used to specify how to draw the temporal constraint in the business process diagram.

If the constraint applies to the end of an activity, it is called an `EndTemporalConstraint` and its definition is identical to `StartTemporalConstraint`.

Given that an activity can have more than one temporal constraint (one start and one end), the temporal constraints of an activity are grouped in the `TemporalContraints` element presented in figure5. The `TemporalContraints` element is added to the XPDL `Activity` or `WorkflowProcess` element as an `any` element.

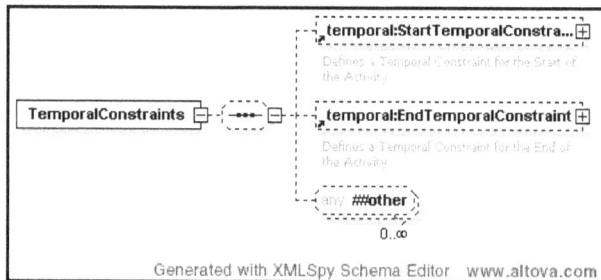

Fig. 5. The TemporalConstraints Element

TEMPORAL DEPENDENCIES

A temporal dependency defines a dependency between two temporal constraints and is specified using a `TemporalDependency` element (see Fig. 6). The attributes of `TemporalDependency` include a required `Id` for unique identification, an optional `Name`, a required `From` and `To` for specifying the source and destination constraints, and an optional `LeadLag`. The `From` and `To` fields identify the two temporal constraints "connected" by the temporal dependency. The optional field

LeadLag specifies a lag when a positive value is provided or a lead when a negative value is provided for the dependency.

The optional sub-elements of TemporalDependency are Description and ConnectorGraphicsInfos. ConnectorGraphicsInfos is used to provide the graphical information related to the depiction of the link that represents the dependency.

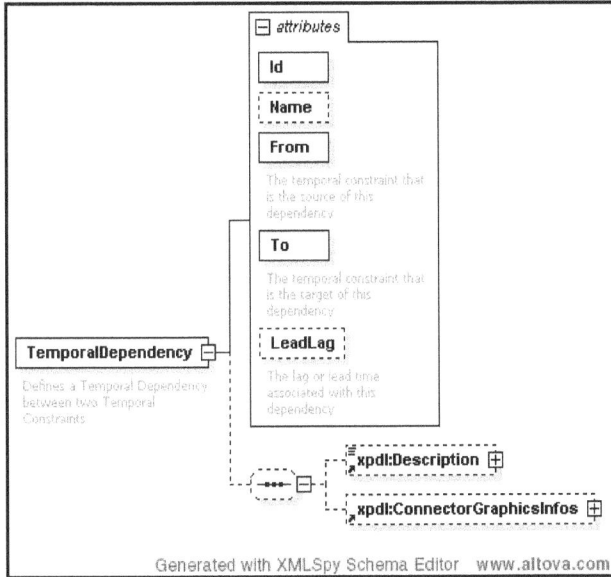

Fig. 6. The TemporalDependency Element

A business process definition may include many temporal dependencies. The individual TemporalDependency elements are thus grouped in a TemporalDependencies element as in figure 7. The TemporalDependencies element is added as an any element in the Package element within XPDL. This allows for the flexible interrelation of temporal constraints from different activities.

Fig. 7. The TemporalDependencies Element

```
<Package ...>
   ...
   <WorkflowProcesses>
      <WorkflowProcess Id="BP27" Name="Final Exam Example">
         ...
         <Activities>
            <Activity Id="A74" Name="Complete Final Exam">
               <Description>The exam is to take place on December
                            1st from 2 to 5 pm</Description>
               ...
               <temporal:TemporalConstraints>
                  <temporal:StartTemporalConstraint Id="STC28"
                          Name="Exam Start" ConstraintDetail="ON"
                          ReferencePoint="TP01">
                     <Description>The exam starts at 2 pm
                     </Description>
                  </temporal:StartTemporalConstraint>
                  <temporal:EndTemporalConstraint Id="ETC48"
                      Name="Exam End" ConstraintDetail="NLT"
                          ReferencePoint="TP44">
                     <Description>The exam ends no later than 5pm
                     </Description>
                  </temporal:EndTemporalConstraint>
               </temporal:TemporalConstraints>
            </Activity>
            <Activity Id="A26" Name="Sign Attendance Sheet">
               ...
               <temporal:TemporalConstraints>
                  <temporal:StartTemporalConstraint Id="STC22"
                      Name="Signing Start" ConstraintDetail="ASAP"
                          ReferencePoint="CaseStart">
                  </temporal: StratTemporalConstraint>
               </temporal:TemporalConstraints>
            </Activity>
         </Activities>
      </WorkflowProcess>
   </WorkflowProcesses>
   ...
   <temporal:TemporalDependencies>
      <temporal:TemporalDependency From="STC28" Id="TD15" LeadLag="1h"
              Name="Tardy Lag" To="STC22">
         <Description>Signing the exam attendance sheet starts 1 hr
                  after the start of the final exam</Description>
      </temporal:TemporalDependency>
   </temporal:TemporalDependencies>
   <temporal:TimePoints>
      <temporal:TimePoint Id="TP01" TimePointType="Relative"
              ReferencePoint="CaseStart">
         <temporal:TimeDate>December 1st at 2pm</temporal:TimeDate>
      </temporal:TimePoint>
      <temporal:TimePoint Id="TP44" TimePointType="Relative"
              ReferencePoint="CaseStart">
         <temporal:TimeDate>December 1st at 5pm</temporal:TimeDate>
      </temporal:TimePoint>
   </temporal:TimePoints>
</Package>
```

Fig. 8. The Final Exam Example

Example

We provide a simple example which uses the temporal perspective extension presented above. The process segment we represent is:

The exam takes place on December 1st from 2 to 5 pm. The exam can finish earlier if all the students complete and leave the exam before 5 pm. The majority of students show up for the exam on time. Tardy students may show up anytime during the first hour of the exam and still be allowed to write the exam. Note that tardy students are not allowed to write beyond 5 pm. University regulations require that each student sign the attendance sheet in case there are tardy students. Signing the exam attendance sheet starts one hour after the start of the exam.

See figure 8 for an excerpt of the extended XPDL file of a potential model of this process segment.

CONCLUSION AND FUTURE WORK

We presented an extension to XPDL that captures the temporal perspective of business processes. This extension deals with the various temporal constraints and dependencies that may occur while characterizing real world business processes. We introduced an XML schema for most of the temporal constructs of the temporal perspective. These individual schemas are integrated into a namespace-qualified extension called "temporal" providing a simple extension to the current XPDL schema. Our proposed extension allows for the specification of the temporal perspective in a fully XPDL compliant fashion. With this extension, XPDL becomes expressive enough to account for a very large set of real world business processes that are time dependent.

The work presented herein represents a first version of the temporal schema. It is part of an on-going project at Trisotech to introduce time as a first class citizen to some of the main Business Process standards. We are currently working at extending the temporal schema to capture all of the temporal constructs that we admittedly left out of this version. We are also working at relaxing the limit of one start and one end temporal constraint per activity. Another avenue of research we are also working on is a BPMN extension to allow the depiction of the temporal constraints and dependencies within a BPMN diagram.

ACKNOWLEDGEMENTS

The contribution of the Trisotech (www.Trisotech.com) Development Team is gratefully acknowledged, Abel Ferreira and Simon Ringuette in particular for the schema. The second author is supported by the Natural Sciences and Engineering Research Council of Canada (NSERC).

REFERENCES

Gagné, D., Trudel, A., "The Temporal Perspective: Expressing Temporal Constraints and Dependencies in Process Models." Fischer, L. (Ed), 2008 BPM and Workflow Handbook, pp. 247-260, Future Strategies Inc., 2008.

Brunt, J., "The Road to XPDL 2.0 Case Study." Fischer, L. (Ed), 2008 BPM and Workflow Handbook, pp. 187-194, Future Strategies Inc., 2008.

Workflow Management Coalition (WfMC): Process Definition Interface – XML Process Definition Language, Document number WfMC-TC-1025, Version 2.1a, 10 October 2008.

Workflow Management Coalition (WfMC): The Workflow Reference Model, Document number WfMC TC-1001, 1995.

Workflow Management Coalition (WfMC): Interface 1 – Process Definition Interchange Process Model, Document number WfMC-TC-1016-P, 1998.

Workflow Management Coalition (WfMC): Current list of XPDL implementations, http://wfmc.org/xpdl-implementations.html

Workflow Management Coalition (WfMC): Workflow Process Definition Interface – XML Process Definition Language, Document number WfMC-TC-1025, Version 1.0, 2002.

Object Management Group (OMG): Business Process Modeling Notation (BPMN) Specification. Version 1.0, OMG report: dtc/06-02-01, OMG, (2006)

Allen, J.F., Maintaining Knowledge about Temporal Intervals. Communications of the ACM 26 (1983) 832-843

International Standard Organization (ISO): Data elements and interchange formats — Information interchange — Representation of dates and times, Reference number: ISO 8601:2004(E), Third edition, 2004-12-01.

Altova XMLSpy XML Editor. Retrieved February 25 2009 from http://www.altova.com/products/xmlspy/xml_editor.html

BPM SAAS as the Foundation of a Cloud-based Post-IT Enterprise

Wolf Rivkin, B-Wave Software LLC, USA

ABSTRACT

In this chapter we are not trying to describe any isolated implementation of BPM but rather making an attempt to find a place and a role for BPM in the whole big orchestra of Enterprise Architecture and Processes (EAP). We believe that only by making this 'orchestra' play in harmony can we help the cause that heavily relies on BPM as well as other 'instrument groups' like SOA and ESB: The Enterprise Architectural and Business Transformation (EATB) from the current ugly Legacy duckling to a gorgeous Elegant swan that can easily reach the Cloud. Despite this rather lyrical tone of the previous sentences, the chapter itself has very precise ontological and methodological considerations and results, which not only lead to definitions of the Desired Post-IT Enterprise State but reveal the decisive role that BPM plays in it.

INTRODUCTION: DESCRIPTION OF THE APPROACH

This article has both a descriptive and a predictive nature. It starts by laying a scientific foundation for the description of the basic properties and behaviors of such a complex system as **IT-Based Enterprise** (ITE), then tries to apply this methodology to the explanation of its past and present, and finally extends to the prediction of its future.

Post-IT Enterprise does not exist yet. We need to show its possibility and necessity, as well as try to describe its features and behaviors, before it comes and catches us, Enterprise analysts, as usual, at unawares. First, here are some absolutely necessary basic definitions:

Ontology (Encarta): '*In Computer and Information Science (IS) is a formal representation of a set of concepts within a domain and the relationships between those concepts*'

Methodology (Encarta): "*The methods or organizing principles underlying a particular art, science, or other area of study*";

Let us note here that ITE is our 'domain' and '*area of study.*'

Architecture (constructional, IT, etc.): The ontological concept of the organization and description of the lower, Design-level Artifacts; more concisely: Architecture is Meta-Design. In its turn, Design is Meta-Development.

Enterprise (ITE): An IT-based company that has reached an Architectural level of operational complexity at which interactions between Design-level artifacts become more important than the Design of each individual artifact.

Enterprise Architecture (EA): A sub-discipline of Information Science (IS) describing scientific approaches to the efficient organization of ITE's Business and IT Design-level artifacts.

Enterprise Processes (EP): An aggregate of all kinds of processes happening inside, outside, and with Enterprise (see elaboration later in this article).

Enterprise Development Methodology (EDM): A Methodology that applies to an ITE's development as a system and as an area of study.

We shall show that Enterprise Architecture and Processes (EAP) constitute the foundation of an exact, scientific EDM. The term 'scientific' is very important here, because we consider EAP to be a scientific sub-discipline of IS, which, in its turn, is considered to be an applied version of its parent theoretical scientific discipline—Cybernetics. We use the word 'scientific' in both senses it is defined by Encarta:

- *relating to, using, or conforming to science or its principles;*
- *proceeding in a systematic and methodical way;*

We understand scientific principles as demanding non-contradictory self-sustained definitions and postulates proven by an experiment or (in our case) practice.

We think that Information Science is the underlying discipline that defines and directs the path of IT as an industry and ITE as its subject. We very much regret that thinking otherwise has brought us to where we, as a community, are right now: to the situation where we can predict what will happen to our Universe billions of years in the future much more accurately than what will happen to our Enterprise one year from now.

Can We Predict the Future of Enterprise?

A Post-IT Enterprise is mostly a matter of the future. An obvious question is: "Can we possibly predict the future of Enterprise and its IT?" Unfortunately, the answer is: "Yes and no":

- Yes, because if we have correct, objective methodology describing ITE we can fully define its features and behaviors, thus explaining its past and present and objectively predicting its future.
- No, because ITE is human-directed, hence not always following the best objective route. It is the same way, for example, in mechanics: we can predict the path of a stone thrown by someone vertically above his own head. However, we cannot guarantee that no one will try to conduct such an exercise, even having been warned of the consequences. The recent history of Enterprise IT is full of examples proving this.

What we can do, though, is show the very existence of the objective path and formulate it in the aforementioned scientific manner, thus, hopefully reducing the number of Enterprise murder- and career suicide- attempts.

EDM's goal is to determine what Enterprise IS and what it DOES. Enterprise Architecture is the answer to the former part, while Enterprise Processes (EP) is the answer to the latter. We can elaborate the notion of EP further by differentiating it into three major categories:

a) External and Internal Enterprise Business Processes (EBP) that constitute the current Enterprise's Business Model (EBM), also called the Mission. These processes provide desired business results to either an external business client, or an internal business unit. This is the area of BPM;

b) The Unified Internal Process of Understanding, Formalizing, Creating, and Executing EBPs. It is the improved version of the former Software Development Life Cycle (SDLC), which is now called Business Process Development Life Cycle (BPDLC), and is described, for example, in [1]. It represents a seamless, well-defined, and detailed

---

[1] W. Rivkin. Closing the Business/IT Gap Once And For All. BPMInstitute.org

cycle of internal Enterprise Activities from the formulation of a business strategy, to its formalization as business processes, to their realization, analysis and optimization, and finally to the provision of an input for the improvement of the strategy.

c) The Process of the Evolution or Transformation of the Enterprise as a whole over time from its current Mission to the desired future EBM, called the Vision. This process defines how EAP must evolve over the Enterprise's lifespan to provide a smooth, predictable, business-safe path from the Mission to the Vision.

The formal representation of EDM as a sum of EA and EP enables the creation of methodologically flawless, practical Enterprise Architectural Transformation Frameworks (EATF), capturing the whole being of an ITE as it functions and evolves over 'business-time.' The postulates and conclusions of this article are very much based on the author's framework called *Enterprise Service Orchestration Framework* (ESOAF) [2]. For a better understanding of these postulates and conclusions, let us briefly consider the Integrated View of ESOAF, shown in Figure 1.

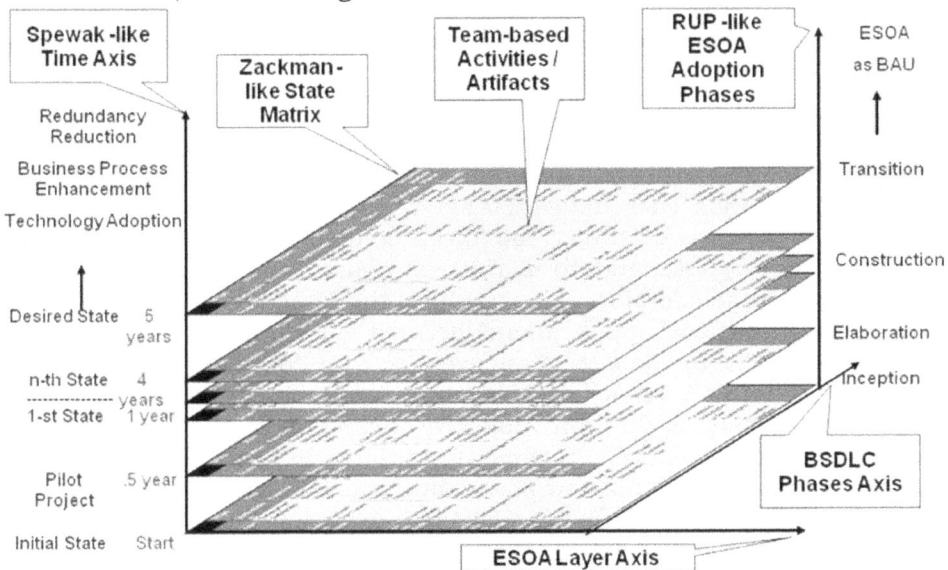

Figure 1. Integrated ESOAF View.

Every two-dimensional matrix layer in Figure 1 represents the Architecture and Processes of types (a) and (b) (BPM and BPDLC, see above) of an Enterprise at some point in its existence. Their entire sequence describes ITE's Transformation (as a process of type (c)) from the Initial, imperfect 'Legacy State' to the desired, 'Elegant' one. Thus, ESOAF puts EA, BPM, BPDLC, and EAT, which together fully describe an Enterprise, into cohesive methodological context.

Now, the scientific approach requires that before predicting the future of our 'domain' we must first check how our methodology explains the known experimental facts (in our case – the history of ITE).

---

[2] http://www.b-wavesoft.com/index_files/esoaf.html

A BRIEF HISTORY OF ENTERPRISE

From an EDM point of view, historically IT has passed through the same three phases of artifact complexity that correspond to today's hierarchy of Enterprise entities (see Table 1):

Phase	Years	Main entities	IS methods	Acceptance
Development	1950s-70s	Code, data, host	Operational systems, programming languages	Good
Design	80s-90s	Meta-code(UML diagrams),meta-data (schemas),meta-host (network)	OOA&D, RDBMS, network protocols	Good
Architecture	2000–present	Business Processes, Services, Data Storages, Internet	EA Frameworks based on BPM/ESB/SOA	Failed

Table 1 Phases of IT development

Every subsequent stage in Table 1 has been caused by Hegelian's dialectical law of 'quantity turning into quality': as the number of primary artifacts in a previous phase rose, it reached the point when their inter-relations became more important than each individual one of them. Then, the meta-artifacts, describing these inter-relations had to be created. They became the main artifacts of a new phase, and, thus, the next phase was initiated.

For example, at the end of the Design phase the inter-relations between lower-level Design artifacts (Applications) became more important than the Design of every individual one, thus the Architectural Phase of IT's development objectively started. A reader of this paper probably understands already what the mentioning of the word 'objective' means: as in the case of the previous two phases, objectively IS came up at the right time with the adequate methods and entities for the new phase, but unlike in those previous phases, the IT community subjectively has failed to implement them.

Subjective, anthropogenic failure to recognize the coming of a new Phase led to the chaotic growth of the infamous 'spaghetti' architectures; this, in turn led to the following main problems of in-house IT, constituting its today's crisis state and pushing Business to outsource it into Cloud:

- High TCO;
- Low agility;
- High exit cost from legacy technologies.
- A Methodological and, hence Informational gap between Business and IT;

Since the first IT crisis in 2000, the in-house Enterprise IT industry has had almost 10 years to resolve these problems. Instead it has let them become graver and graver. So, the Architectural IT Phase has never actually been realized. However, dialectical conflict between the obsolete Design form of the Enterprise and its Architectural contents must somehow be resolved. And it is being resolved right now. Due to the incapacity of in-house IT, it is happening outside of the traditional Enterprise boundaries – in the vendor-supported Cloud. Thus, instead of the Architectural State, the practical IT goes into the Cloud State.

GOING CLOUD

Let us define what Cloud and SAAS mean practically and methodologically:

- **SAAS**: Service Domain (SD) Powerhouses. By SDs we mean the good old CRM, ERP, Billing, ESB, Security, etc.; by their corresponding powerhouses – either existing service providers like Saleforce®.com, or those that are quickly emerging right now like SAP®, Oracle®, IBM®, etc. These computing powerhouses will provide hosted services based on their existing technologies and products such as Netweaver™, Fusion™, and MQ™.
- **Cloud**: Agnostic utility computing companies like Amazon®, Google®, Telemerk®, etc. They are providing, and will continue to provide data storage and dedicated or grid computing infrastructure for your services no matter what their nature and underlying technologies are.

Cloud computing promises to be more efficient because:

- Major vendors are more receptive to the modern IS/EDM approaches and have higher personnel quality, thus they have a better chance to provide Enterprise with the right methodological solutions;
- Every Cloud/SAAS provider can serve several Enterprises, thus offering very attractive prices to each of them.

Both types of companies tend to blend with each other: Cloud companies become certified providers of SAAS vendors' software, while SAAS vendors create their own Cloud computing facilities. So, we shall use the terms Cloud and SAAS interchangeably.

Cloud computing means a possibility for ITE to outsource all or part of its IT operations to external ventures. EDM sees such outsourcing as an Enterprise Cloud-Oriented Transformation (ECOT). From the methodological point of view it may be said that what Enterprises really outsource is their IT Architecture and part of its Processes. Obviously, the outcome of such outsourcing highly depends on the quality of what is being outsourced.

THE IMPORTANCE OF BEING ELEGANT

Every Enterprise naturally creates **Architecture** during its development, whether it cares about it or not. However, if it does not care about it, then ugly, chaotic, and inefficient architectures are naturally created and grow like a jungle or a slum (see, for an example, Figure 2)

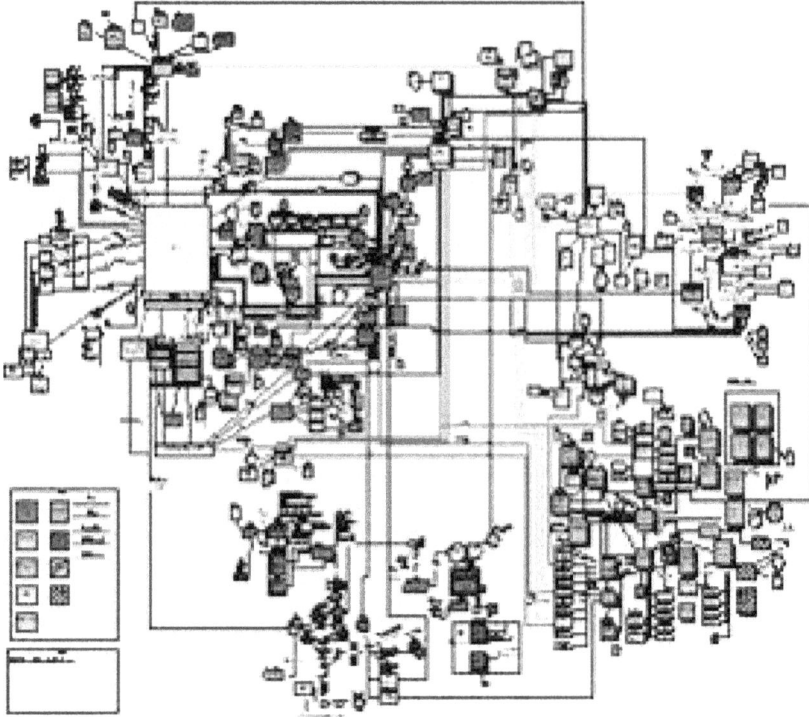

Figure 2. An *example* of typical Legacy Architecture

Such Legacy Business/IT Architectures are composed of a variety of applications chaotically integrated in a point-to-point manner through their APIs. So, there are only two scenarios for direct ECOT of such architecture:

- Outsourcing of non-integrated Applications;
- Outsourcing of the whole structure as-is;

Both scenarios represent methodological dead ends: in both of them Enterprise loses control over non-integrated or poorly-integrated parts of its Architecture and Processes. It is obvious that when immersed into Cloud these parts become inaccessible for future integration. This way Enterprise gains a cost-attractive short-term solution but loses the long-term agility and adaptability of its Architecture. So, we can state that Legacy Architecture is not outsourceable. However, enthusiasts of throwing bricks over their heads are welcome to try.

So, what should Enterprise do to gain all the advantages of ECOT while keeping its architecture agile and adaptive? The answer is simple and evident: first optimize your architecture, make it ready for controlled outsourcing, and only then outsource it. Obviously, this optimized architecture must be SOA-based to facilitate outsourcing its parts as services. Also, it must be BPM-based so that the same can be done with its processes, while regaining control over both domains immersed into the Cloud.

This 'Optimized State' is defined in ESOAF as Elegant Enterprise (EE) (Figure 3).

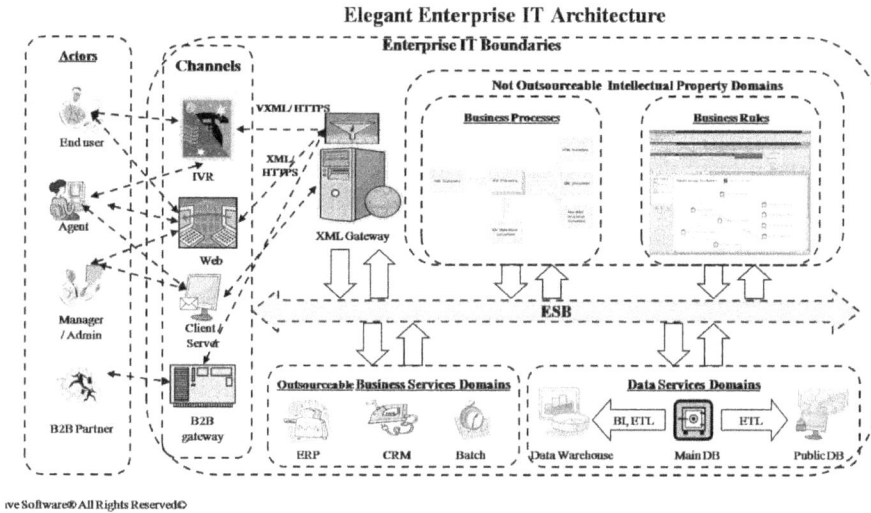

Figure 3. Elegant Enterprise Architecture.

ESOAF sees EE as the Desired State of Pre-Cloud Architecture and, simultaneously, as objectively the best Initial State of Post-IT Architecture. The reason why ESOAF considers this architecture optimal is because it is completely free of the aforementioned disadvantages of Legacy Architecture: it is uncoupled, efficient, and agile. From a methodological perspective it is fully BPM/ESB/SOA based, which is imperative for a proper ECOT.

Here is the operational, dynamic behavior of such an Enterprise, or its common EBP. Let us consider the usual Event-Driven user request scenario:

a) One of the external Actors places a service request through one of the Channels;

b) This request is translated into one of the standard (usually XML-based) formats through XML /Security Gateway and is placed on the ESB as a request message;

c) The corresponding Business Process Flow (BPF) Instance in a BPMS reacts by proceeding through BPF;

d) On the way, it calls, in an uncoupled manner, different services from Business and Data Service Domains, as well as Business Rule Engine (BRE) services.

e) Every service produces some functional activities and reacts with a reply message containing information that eventually reaches the Actor to notify her about the result of her request

This example shows different, seemingly isolated sub-architectural frameworks such as BPM, BRE, ESB, and SOA inter-operating with each other in a cohesive and uncoupled fashion due to their methodologically sound a place and a role. The various service domains of this framework are completely uncoupled, and all architecture is process- and event- driven. Every aforementioned sub-architectural framework is considered to be either a service-requestor or a service-provider domain (or both). EE allows for easy replaceability and reusability of its parts (services, sub-processes, master data signatures, etc.), thus eliminating the infamous 'ripple effect,' reducing the cost of exit from legacy (composite) applications, as well as functional and data redundancy, and projects' time-to market.

So, summarizing the properties of the 'Elegant Enterprise' Architecture we conclude that:

- It is based on a scientific methodology that adequately explains the experimental (in our case historical) facts, parameters, and tendencies in the history of IT;
- It uses only the approaches and methodologies offered by IS and adequate for the current ITE's Architectural phase;
- It addresses all the IT problems mentioned above;

From a scientific point of view it is enough to objectively make this architecture an optimal one.

As was mentioned above, Elegant Enterprise represents the Desired State of In-House Enterprise, allowing for resolving its Architectural problems. However, it has never been implemented as such, and now it is probably too late. By rejecting en masse the approaches and products (like SAP Netweaver or Oracle Fusion), meant for such an architecture, in-house IT made software vendors look for other ways to connect to Business, avoiding the reluctant IT. Thus the Cloud concept was born.

BPM IN THE CLOUD

Elegant Enterprise is not just a catchphrase. It means that every part of the organization works according to the same methodology, meaning common entities, approaches, standards, and rules. It means that Enterprise uses only the methodologically validated types of well defined, organized, and uncoupled artifacts, thus removing barriers to their free and effective flow.

Let us note how uncoupling different domains makes it easy, effective, and efficient to outsource them without disrupting the Business Processes. BPM plays a fundamental role in Elegant Enterprise, but that is nothing compared to the role it is bound to play in its outsourced version

It is clear now how, having this perfect in-house EE Architecture, we can outsource its BSD functionality easily and without a 'ripple effect.' However, the question remains how we are supposed to outsource the WHOLE of IT, without completely cutting it off the Business?

The next paragraph contains references to some concrete products. The author can assure the readers that he is not on salary at the mentioned firms (while sometimes he is sorry about this fact☺). There are many others on the market now like Appian®, Lombardy®, etc. What follows is a real story of discovery, nothing more, nothing less.

Recently, on BPMS Watch, Bruce Silver's blog on business process management, I discovered his notes from Intalio®3 User Conference about the keynote made by Greg Olson, founder of Coghead®," a BPM-in-the-Cloud service that "uses Intalio® as the process engine under the covers."

As Mr. Olson said: "The entire app is Web 2.0, accessible through Google Gadgets or iFrame"(see Figure 4)

---

[3] Intalio® is an Open-Source BPM Engine.

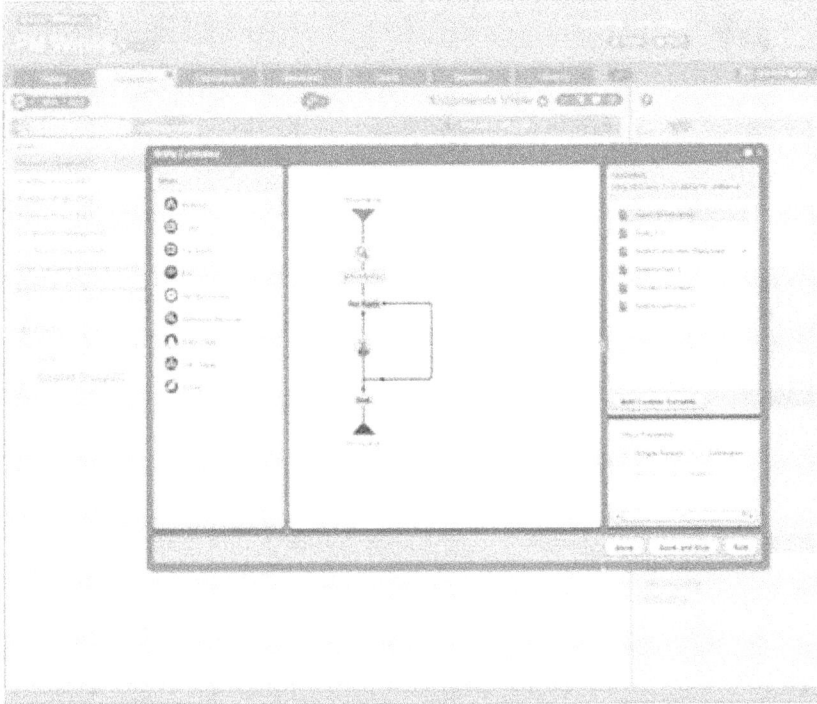

Figure 4. Coghead BP Designer.

As "...all of the data lives in Coghead® ... [it] provides a 'linked application' feature, in which a facade on Coghead communicates with a RESTful API on your app behind the firewall, which ... is based on the Atom Publishing Protocol (APP)."

Voila! That is it! If we change the word 'app' to the more appropriate word 'service,' we have a conceptually complete picture of BPM/ESB/SOA-based Enterprise Architecture and Processes, fully immersed into Cloud, which require only two groups of in-house Enterprise professionals to make the Enterprise-Cloud business structure click:

1. Advanced Business Analysts (BA) who are able to create basic Business Process Flows/Subflows (BPF) and Business Rules, working with Cloud-based tools like Coghead® BPMS and any internal or external Business Rules Engine, connecting them in BPFs through ESB;

2. Cloud company-employed Software Designers, able to make these processes executable and run them through this outsourced BPMS and all SAAS products.

This pattern can easily be achieved right now from the human resources point of view.

My current understanding of the ECOA Desired State (I call it *'Heavenly Enterprise'* because all its operations are in the Clouds ☺) can be represented as in Figure 5

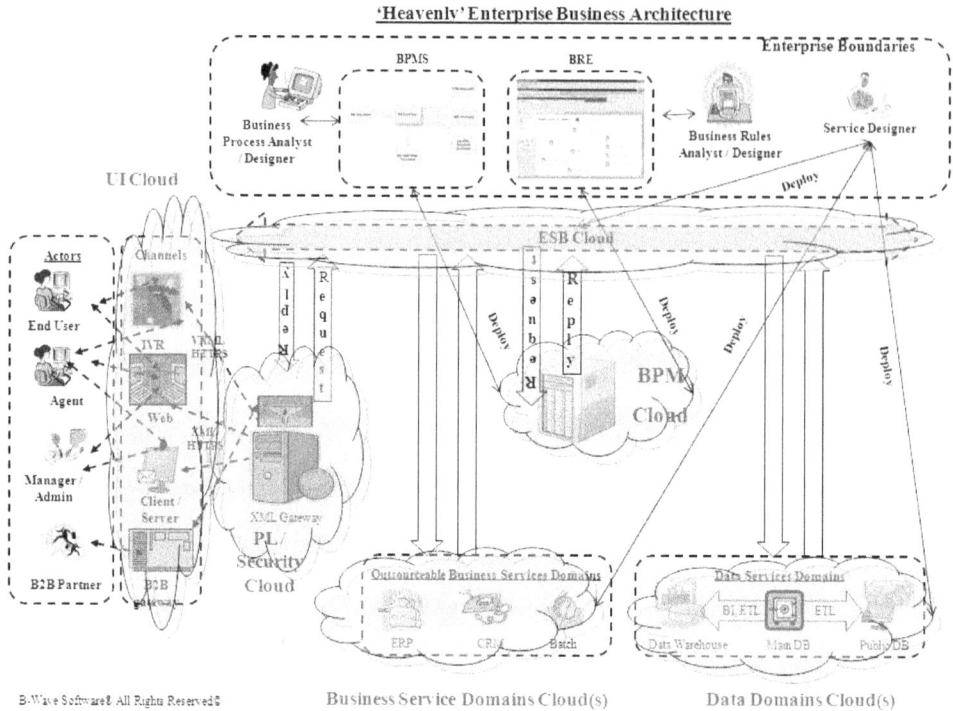

Figure 5 Post-IT Enterprise Architecture.

From the external Actors' perspective this change is absolutely transparent. They see the same User Interface, being absolutely indifferent to the fact that it, like *all* other SDs, is immersed into Cloud. The EBP mentioned above logically stays the same, despite the fact that physically it happens outside the Enterprise's boundaries.

We have introduced here a new entity; **Cloud Service Bus** (CSB). Its purpose is to keep Enterprise and Cloud(s) uncoupled from each other for easy reusability (from the Cloud company's point of view) and replaceability (from that of the Enterprise), which might be especially important during the initial stages of Cloud Transformation, when not all Cloud utilities may prove themselves effective and efficient enough and might need to be replaced swiftly and without fatal trauma for the Enterprise's Business.

It is all fine and dandy, say you, but how do I organize the cooperation of this Enterprise-Cloud symbiosis; how can Enterprise stay on top of what and how Cloud is doing on its behalf? We will get the answer when we compare the BPDLCs for Enterprise with in- and out-of- house IT.

BUSINESS CLOUD MANAGEMENT

Let us show how the two aforementioned groups, responsible for the Enterprise-Cloud artifact/process flow, communicate with each other, by comparing Business Process Development Life Cycles (BPDLC) for the 'Elegant' (Figure 6) and 'Heavenly' (Figure 7) Enterprises.

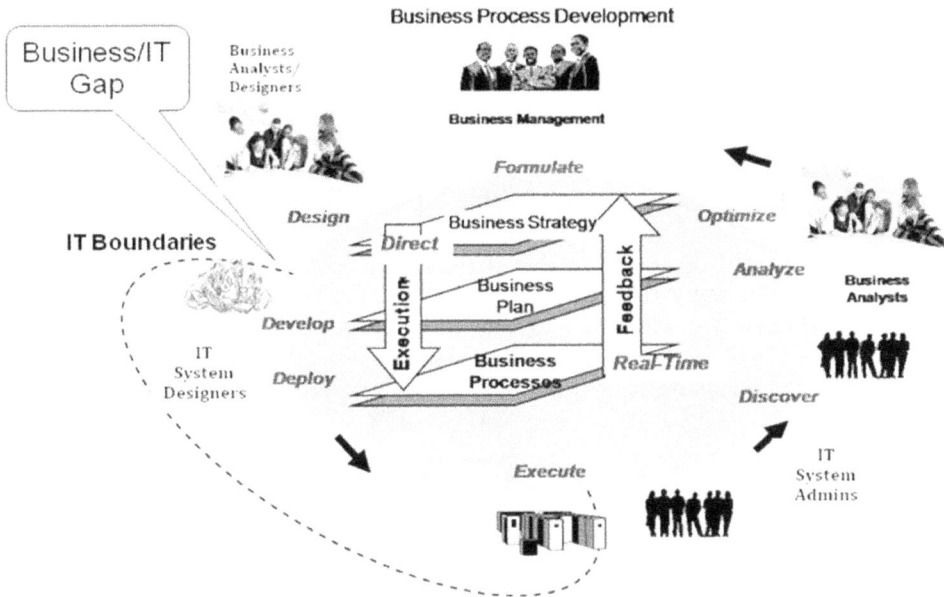

Figure 6. BPDLC for Elegant Enterprise

'EE' BPDLC works by going through the following its phases:

1. **Formulate:** Business Management Team (BMT) formulates an Enterprise's business strategy on the basis of internal BP analysis, market conditions, and other input factors as output textual artifacts.

2. **Design:** Business Analyst/Designer Team (BADT) receives input artifacts from BMT, analyzes them, and creates new or enhances existing BPs in the form of BBPFs by specifying the BP's logic as BPF routes. BBPFs are the BADT's output artifacts; No BPF routes may be changed outside of BADT.

3. **Develop:** IT Systems Designer Team (SDT) receives input artifacts from BADT, analyzes them, and transforms them into Executable BPFs (EBPF), which are analogous to UML's State-Chart Diagrams, by specifying states, transitions, events, message signatures, and all other necessary EBPF features. If they consider changes in the logic, they consult with BADT and let them make the changes then repeat phase (3). After specifying all nested levels of BPFs, SDT creates necessary services supporting the BPFs' execution. EBPFs and services are the BADT's output artifacts.

4. **Deploy:** IT System Admin Team (SADT) in cooperation with SDT creates BPM System (BPMS)/Enterprise Service Bus (ESB) infrastructure and deploys the EBPFs and services into this infrastructure.

5. **Execute:** SADT tests, runs, and maintains the resulting solution.

6. **Discover:** BADT, in cooperation with SADT, specifies points and parameters for running BP analysis, called Business Activity Monitoring (BAM). BAM points enable a feedback data flow that describes the real-time behavior of Enterprise's BPs. This data flow results in output artifacts in the form of reports and diagrams;

7. **Analyze:** BADT uses these artifacts along with Business Intelligence (BI) data analysis to provide BMT with all the information necessary to adjust the company's business strategy.

8. **Optimize:** BADT uses the results of the analysis to create propositions regarding Business Process Optimization within the boundaries of the current strategy as well as providing BMT with all the necessary information to adjust the company's business strategy. Then the BPDLC repeats itself.

A full analysis of the BPDLC can be found in [4]. Just note that its phases form one of the sets of parameters that shape ESOAF 3-D matrices [Figure 1].

As can be seen in Figure 6, steps 3 through 5 are the only ones that happen inside IT. So, the only difference in the BPDLC for 'Heavenly Enterprise' is that these phases are delegated to Cloud (see Figure 7):

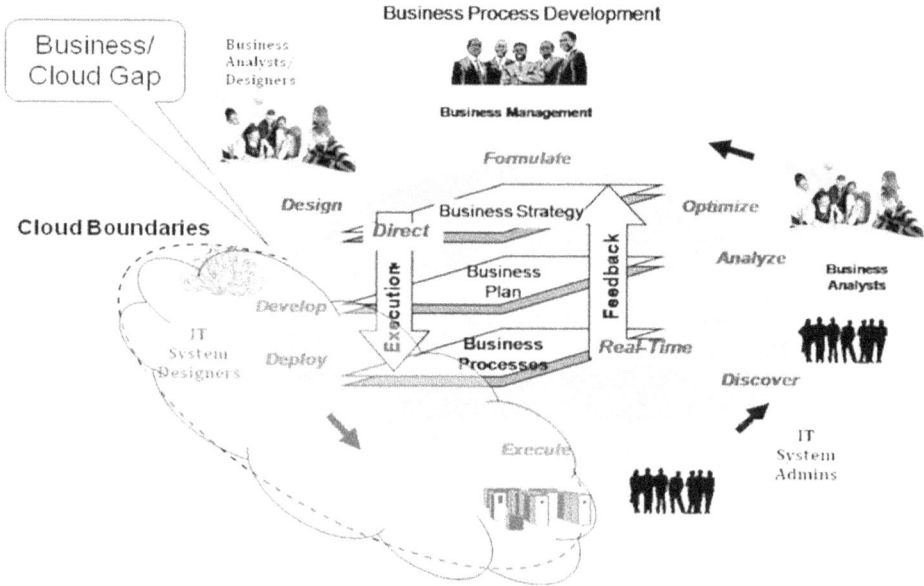

Figure 7. BPDLC for 'Heavenly Enterprise'

There is no difference in the process steps or the teams involved for this scenario. The major difference is that SDT personnel are now SAAS company employees, working as its representatives at the Enterprise, while a SADT team consists of internal SAAS company employees contacting the Enterprise through SDT.

In this scenario, Business Analysts, creating Basic Business Process Flows, become the cornerstone of the whole Enterprise, for it is they who communicate with direct Cloud representatives (SDT) in creating, enhancing, and managing the company's Business Processes and services, thus providing control by the Enterprise over the formalization and improvement of the Enterprise Business Model before and after its execution in the Cloud.

---

4 W. Rivkin 'Closing the Business/IT Gap Once And For All.' BPMI.org http://www.bpminstitute.org/articles/article/article/closing-the-business-it-gap-once-and-for-all.html

Section 4

Appendices

Author Biographies

Our sincere thanks go to the authors who kindly gave their time, effort and expertise into contributing papers that cover methods, concepts, case studies and standards in business process management and workflow. These international industry experts and thought leaders present significant new ideas and concepts to help you plan a successful future for your organization. We also extend our thanks and appreciation to the members of WfMC Review Committee who volunteered many hours of their valuable time in the selection of the final submissions and who helped guide the content of the book.

ROY ALTMAN

roy.altman@peopleservinc.com
President, Peopleserv, Inc., USA
Roy Altman is founder of Peopleserv, Inc (www.PeopleservInc.com), and inventor of its People Relationship Management solution. He has been providing customers with high-value, effective solutions for longer than he cares to mention. He holds an MBA from Pace University in New York, and has taught at Columbia University, and other institutions of higher learning. Altman has published several articles on business automation issues, and is a sought-out speaker for conferences and seminars.

LAURENT BAGNOUD

laurent.bagnoud@hevs.ch
UAS professor Master of Science in Computer Science
Laurent Bagnoud holds a Master of Science in Computer Science from the University of Zurich (2001). He worked as an IT applications instructor for Lloyds TSB Bank in Zurich from 1998 to 1999, and as a business analyst and IT project manager for Swisscom IT Services SA in Berne and in Sierre from 2001 to 2006. He was in co-charge of IT project management methodology in the same company, in particular during the offshoring of the first IT development project to India (October 2004 to August 2006). He has been teaching Business Process Management and Project Management in the degree courses "Business Information Systems" and "Business Administration" of the University of Applied Sciences of Western Switzerland (HES-SO) since September 2006 (www.hes-so.ch). He is also in charge of the CAS "Performance Management" of the HES-SO Masters programme "Quality and Strategy Manager" (www.masterqsm.ch). In his capacity as a UAS professor at the Institute of Business Information Systems of the HES-SO, he carries out applied research projects within the EU research programme (EU-FP). He contributes to technology transfer between academia and the industry by participating in projects supported by the Swiss Confederation's innovation promotion agency (CTI). Laurent Bagnoud is a member of the "administrative processes" team of eCH, which is in charge of standardising the administrative processes of Swiss authorities.

TOM BOBROWSKI

tbobrowski@gmail.com
Principal, Capgemini Financial Services, USA
Tom Bobrowski is a Principal with Capgemini Financial Services. Prior to that he managed a portfolio of clients in Satyam's Global Insurance Practice and has been a major proponent of BPM in Insurance sector. Prior to joining Satyam, Mr. Bobrowski managed property and casualty operations for Rothschild, with a focus on commercial property, casualty, and Directors and Officers liability risks. Mr. Bobrowski was a founding partner in Arc Information Technologies, LLC., a builder of IT platforms for wholesale electricity trading operations.

DR MICHÉLLE BOOYSEN, PH.D, PMP

drmich@petanque-c.com
Managing Director, Pétanque Business Specialists, South Africa
Based in Cape Town, Michélle heads up a team of business professionals who provide services as a Strategy Delivery Office to corporate and medium to small businesses. (www.petanque-c.com and www.tenstepsdo.com).
Trained in economics and the law, Michélle has applied her ability to make difficult or complex matters easier to understand, distilling information into who, what, when and

how. She developed the unique VizPro®/ProcessStep™ process mapping methodology (www.processstep.com) which was launched globally during 2007.

Michélle has a Ph.D in Commerce, is an NQF Assessor and Moderator and a Project Management Professional. In her free time, she enjoys cycling, completing her 4th Argus Cycle Tour in 2008, recently took up surfing and enjoys watching DVDs at home and is a novice painter.

Jorge Cardoso

jorge.cardoso.pt@gmail.com
SAP Research, Germany and University of Coimbra, Portugal

Prof. Dr. Jorge Cardoso joined SAP Research, Germany, in 2007. He previously gave lectures at the University of Madeira (Portugal), the University of Georgia (USA) and at the Instituto Politécnico de Leiria (Portugal). He has worked at the Boeing Company (USA) on enterprise application integration and at CCG, Zentrum für Graphische Datenverarbeitung on Computer Supported Cooperative Work systems. He has published over 90 refereed papers in the areas of workflow management systems, semantic Web, and related fields. He edited several books, and organized several international conferences on Semantics and Information Systems.

Juan Chacón

jchacon@pectra.com
PECTRA Technology, USA

Juan Chacón is PECTRA Technology's Marketing Manager. Graduated from the Universidad Blas Pascal with a degree in Business Administration, he has an MBA from the FUNCER Business School -MBA program designed together with the University of Massachusetts-, among other Strategic Marketing courses he has taken. Among his main objectives are the development and execution of PECTRA Technology's strategic Marketing plan. This is where the campaigns related to demand creation are, client loyalty, and Partner events as well as a media plan to achieve positioning of the brand.

Previously, Juan Chacón worked as the head of Regional Marketing for the company CLARO (Grupo Telmex), and before that at Matriceria Austral and Fiat Argentina.

Michele Chinosi, PhD

michele.chinosi@uninsubria.it
Insubria University, Italy

Dr. Michele Chinosi, PhD has MS in Computer Science from University of Milano in 2004. Currently he is Ph.D. in Computer Science at the Computer Science and Communication Dept. of Insubria University (Varese, Italy). His main research topics are modeling and design methodologies for Business Processes, XML and XML-Schema representation, privacy and security issues in business processes. He was an invited speaker at WfMC Architecture & Process 2008 conference. Now he is contributing to BPMN 2.0 Oracle/SAP/IBM submission proposal.

Linus Chow

linus.chow@bea.com
Co-Chair WfMC Public Sector Chapter
Principal Systems Engineer, BEA Systems, Inc., USA

Linus Chow is the Co-Chair of the WfMC Public Sector Chapter and a Principal Systems Engineer for BEA systems. He has over 15 years of leadership and management experience in information technology internationally with over 8 years in workflow, BPM, and SOA. He has played crucial roles in expanding the growth of BPM and workflow adoption first in the US and then internationally from Australia to Switzerland. Currently, Linus leads the adoption of BPM/SOA solutions for Public Sector customers promoting the WfMC and its standards and best practices. He is a published author and an active speaker on the Best Practices of BPM and SOA frequently engaging with AFCEA, WfMC, BPMI, IQPC, AIIM, Brainstorm, and other industry organizations. A decorated former US Army Officer, Linus has an MBA, a MS in Management Information Systems, and BS in Mathematics.

Martín Dauber Capi

mdauber@integradoc.com
Quality and Process Supervisor, INTEGRADOC, Montevideo – Uruguay.

Martín Dauber is part of INTEGRADOC team (www.integradoc.com), a Business Process Management and Workflow focused company. He has been Quality and Process Responsible of the company for many years, gaining lot of experience in understanding customer processes, specifying requirements and dealing with implementations and expectations. He is an advanced student of Mechanical Engineering in the "Universidad de la República", Uruguay, focusing in the industrial area, complementing business vision with a deep productive processes vision. Having participated in multidisciplinary teams in projects for Telco's, Food Industry and Government between others, he has reached an absolute understanding of BPM risks and strengths when applied to organizations.

TONY DE JESUS

University of Madeira
Tony de Jesus is a senior student majoring in Computer Science at the University of Madeira. During the past five years they were involved in several programming projects. The most relevant one was the development and implementation of a management system for received and sent out "snail" mail inside the University of Madeira.

LAYNA FISCHER

layna@FutStrat.com
Editor and Publisher, Future Strategies Inc.,
As the Official Editor and Publisher to WfMC and Director of the annual Global Awards for Excellence in BPM and Workflow, Layna Fischer works closely with WfMC to promote the mission of the WfMC with respect to industry awareness and educational content. Ms Fischer was also the Executive Director of the Business Process Management Initiative (now merged with OMG) and is on the board of BPM Focus (previously WARIA, Workflow And Reengineering International Association), where she was CEO since 1994.

Future Strategies Inc., (www.futstrat.com) publishers of unique books and papers on business process management and workflow specializes in dissemination of information about BPM and workflow technology, business process redesign and electronic commerce. As such, the company contracts and works closely with individual authors and corporations throughout the USA and the world.

Future Strategies Inc., is the also publisher of the business book series *New Tools for New Times*, as well as the annual *Excellence in Practice* volumes of award-winning case studies and the annual *Workflow Handbook*, published in collaboration with the WfMC. Her experience in the computer industry includes being the president and CEO of a multi-million dollar high-technology export company for seven years, during which time she also founded an offshore franchise distribution company called Computer Direct. Ms. Fischer was also a senior editor of a leading international computer publication for four years and has been involved in international computer journalism and publishing for over 20 years. She was a founding director of the United States Computer Press Association in 1985.

DENIS GAGNÉ

dgagne@trisotech.com
CEO, Trisotech, Canada.
M. Gagné is responsible for the solutions and technology vision at Trisotech. He has led Trisotech through the process of developing unique services and product propositions and provided leadership in plotting out Trisotech's market strategy. M. Gagné's current research interest focus on technological and know-how innovation in the fields of business process management and business transformation.

RICARDO GARCÊS

rgarces@acin.pt
Junior developer, ACIN, Portugal
Ricardo Garcês is currently working in ACIN, a Portuguese software development company. He has majored in Computer Science at the University of Madeira in 2007 and within the scope of his final project, he collaborated in the work "Open Source Workflow Management Systems: A Concise Survey."

During the past seven years he was involved in several programming projects. The most relevant one was the development and implementation of a management system for received and sent out "snail" mail inside the University of Madeira.

HARTMANN GENRICH

hartmann.genrich@gmx.de

Hartmann Genrich worked for Gesellschaft für Mathematik und Datenverarbeitung (GMD), the German National Research Institute for Information Technlogy. He holds a Dr. rer. nat. (PhD) in Mathematics from University of Bonn, and published various papers on the mathematics of Petri Nets. Later he got involved in the modelling, simulation and analysis of workflow systems. He retired from GMD in 2001 and works as a consultant to US-American and German companies.

DANIEL T. HOLT

daniel.holt@afit.edu

Lt Col, USAF, PhD

Air Force Institute of Technology, United States

Lt Col Daniel T. Holt is an active duty Air Force officer who joined the faculty of the Air Force Institute of Technology for the first time in 1999 and currently serves there as Assistant Professor of Management. While on active duty, he has served as an Air Force engineer in Central America, Asia, and the Middle East. Throughout his career, he has developed expertise in change management, corporate entrepreneurship, leadership and executive development, organizational analysis, and human resource management. He holds a Ph.D. in management from the Auburn University. His scholarly work has appeared in such publications as the *Journal of Applied Behavioral Science, Entrepreneurship Theory and Practice, Human Resource Management,* and the *Journal of Leadership and Organization Studies.* In addition, his work has appeared in *Research in Organization Change and Development* (Elsevier, 2007).

STIJN HOPPENBROUWERS

stijnh@cs.ru.nl

Institute of Computing and Information Sciences of Radboud University Nijmegen, Netherlands

Dr. Stijn Hoppenbrouwers is an assistant professor at the Institute of Computing and Information Sciences of Radboud University Nijmegen, the Netherlands. Initially trained as a linguist (Utrecht; Bangor) he obtained his PhD in December 2003 (Nijmegen). He has worked in the field of information systems and enterprise engineering since 1996, both in academia and in industry. He specializes in game-like procedures for collaborative, low-threshold systems modeling, and on the design of software to support such procedures. He teaches various information systems topics, including requirements engineering and an advanced course on BPM and Business Rules.

CHARLES JOESTEN

cjoesten@icorpartners.com

Director, ICOR Partners, LLC, USA.

Charles Joesten is a Director with ICOR Partners and is responsible for delivering strategic consulting services and solutions to Federal Government and Department of Defense (DoD) clients. As a certified Project Management Professional (PMP), Charles leverages industry standards and principles to establish process rigor and workflow efficiency into operational value and improved performance. In his seventeen years of consulting, he has managed numerous projects and complex programs to help guide clients through corporate strategy, enterprise transformation, process improvement, and performance measurement challenges. Charles has built more specific expertise in workflow, document, and records management and provides thought leadership in these disciplines. Some of his key contributions to clients include office automation solutions, integrated performance measurement standards, predictive budgeting models, and workflow and document management system implementations. He has written several white papers and presented at numerous conferences to share and learn in these areas.

Prior to joining ICOR Partners, Charles served in senior management roles with several of the leading management and IT consulting firms. Charles holds a Bachelor of Arts in Economics from Vanderbilt University and a Master of Business Administration in Strategy and Business Process Reengineering from George Mason University.

DR. SETRAG KHOSHAFIAN

setrag@pega.com

VP of BPM Technology, Pegasystems Inc., USA.

Dr. Setrag Khoshafian is Vice President of BPM Technology for Pegasystems Inc. Dr. Khoshafian is a recognized BPM pioneer and thought leader who has done R&D, innovation, and productization in a number of domains including BPMS and DBMS. His expertise spans Business Process Management Suites, Lean Six Sigma, BPM COE/Methodology, BPO, SOA, BI, Analytics, Social Networking, Advanced Databases, and Object Orientation. Dr. Khoshafian is the BPM thought leader at Pega. He is also the program manager for Pega's Government and BPO solutions. Dr. Khoshafian's vision of enterprise software is captured in his recent book *Service Oriented Enterprises*. This vision combines a service-focused way of doing business with the latest BPM technology for a fresh approach in which each party or participant sees itself as a service provider as well as a service consumer integrated through BPM. Dr. Khoshafian holds a PhD in Computer Science from the University of Wisconsin-Madison.

MARIETJIE LANCASTER

marietjie.lancaster@postoffice.co.za
Group Executive: Group Strategy, South African Post Office, South Africa
Marietjie Lancaster is responsible for Group Strategy at the South African Post Office. This includes Post Office subsidiaries Docex, CFG & Postbank. She has more than 15 years experience on senior management level. She completed her MBA in 1999.
Apart from the normal strategic activities, she has also been responsible for a number of major projects within the Post Office during the last few years eg:
- Initiation and implementation of third party payment services (Pay a Bill)
- Introduction of biometrics and smartcard system for pensioners
- Electronic bulk mail lodgement
- Electronic Bill Presentment and Payment
- Electronic airtime at counters
- Postbank Mzansi initiative
- Fully integrated point of sale system
- My SAP ERP 2005 reimplementation across the group

Some of these projects already received more than 20 awards from the industry of which four were International. She strongly believes in teamwork and empowerment of staff through formal and informal training, coaching and mentoring.

VANINA MARCOTE

vmarcote@Pectra.com
Marketing Coordinator, PECTRA Technology, USA
With four-year experience in the IT industry, Vanina is the Marketing Coordinator of PECTRA Technology. Graduated from the Universidad de Buenos Aires with a degree in Social Communication majoring in Marketing and advertising, she has taken several postgraduate courses regarding Marketing and Communication. As a Marketing Coordinator, Vanina is in charge of different tasks in the Latin American region, related to branding, planning and coordination of 360° communication strategies, client satisfaction and loyalty, and sales generation.
Vanina also holds academic experience, working as a researcher at Universidad de Buenos Aires (UBA) and teaching the subject: "Theories and Practices of Communication II" (Communication Science Degree, UBA). She has participated in several Communication Conferences in Argentina and is the author of different articles oriented to ethnic marketing.

DR. ING. JUAN JOSÉ MORENO

jmoreno@integradoc.com
Director. INTEGRADOC.,Montevideo--Uruguay.
Juan J. Moreno is cofounder of INTEGRADOC (www.integradoc.com), a Business Process Management and Workflow focused company, holding the intellectual property of its INTEGRADOC BPM Suite. Having managed dozens of installations in different countries of South America, he has a deep understanding of the benefits organizations may obtain from BPM. He is also professor and researcher at the Engineering and Technologies Faculty of the "Universidad Católica del Uruguay". He holds a PhD in Computer Science, specialized in Software Engineering, from the "Universidad Pontificia de Salamanca", in Spain. He has dozens of technical and arbitrated publications, and has been recognized with the third price of "Innovator of the Year 2003" in his country, Uruguay.

MR. VINAYKUMAR S MUMMIGATTI

vinaymummigatti@gmail.com
Associate Partner, IBM Global Business Services, USA

Mr. Vinaykumar S Mummigatti is an Associate Partner at IBM Global Business Services and responsible for BPM alliances, Delivery and Solutions. Prior to that, he was heading the Consulting and enterprise Solutions business for Financial Services Vertical at Satyam Computers Services. He has more than 16 years experience in IT consulting & delivery management, managing strategic alliances, Marketing, Sales and Operations. A thought leader in BPM space, Vinay has worked with leading clients in developing Technology Strategy and business Solutions involving BPM, ECM, Portals, CRM and Collaboration. Key contributions to BPM practice include BPM methodology, Center of excellence framework, Business case, ROI frameworks and business process templates. He has presented at multiple conferences and authored white papers. He holds a Bachelors degree in Electronics Engineering and MBA in Finance and Marketing.

NATHANIEL PALMER

nathaniel@wfmc.org
President, Transformation+Innovation and
Executive Director, Workflow Management Coalition, USA

Nathaniel Palmer is President of Transformation+Innovation, as well as the Executive Director of the Workflow Management Coalition. Previously he was Director, Business Consulting for Perot Systems Corp, and also spent over a decade with Delphi Group as Vice President and Chief Analyst. He is the author of over 200 research studies and published articles, as well as "The X-Economy" (Texere, 2001). Nathaniel has been featured in numerous media ranging from Fortune to The New York Times. He is on the advisory boards of many relevant industry publications, as well as the Board of Directors of Association of Information Management (AIIM) NE, and was nominated to represent the Governor of Massachusetts on the Commonwealth's IT Advisory Board.

JON PYKE

jpyke@cordys.com
Chief Strategy Officer and Executive Vice President,
Cordys BV, The Netherlands.

Jon is the Chief Strategy Officer and executive Vice President for Cordys BV. Cordys was founded in 2001 and came to market with a completely new genre of BPM technology. Dubbed BPM 2.0 (or total BPM) Cordys has rapidly become a global force in the market and has built an impressive list of blue chip clients around the world in a very short space of time. As an individual, Jon demonstrates an exceptional blend of Business/People Manager; a Technician with a highly developed sense of where technologies fit and how they should be utilized. Jon is a world recognized industry figure; an exceptional public speaker and a seasoned quoted company executive. Prior to joining Cordys, Jon was the CTO and Executive Vice President for Staffware Plc, where he was responsible for product development and overall executive responsibility for product strategy, positioning, public speaking etc. Finally, as a main board director he was heavily involved in PLC board activities including merges and acquisitions, corporate governance, and board director of several subsidiaries. Jon's final piece of work for Staffware was to conceive, design and oversee the development of the IProcess Engine. Staffware was sold to Tibco in 2004.

Jon has over 30 years experience in the field of software development. During his career he has worked for a number of software and hardware companies as well as user organizations. Jon has written and published a number of articles on the subject of Office Automation, BPM and Workflow Technology. More recently Jon has Co-Authored a book covering both technical and business aspects of BPM. The book is published by Cambridge University Press and is called – Mastering you Organization's Processes. Jon cofounded and is the Chair of the Workflow Management Coalition He is an AiiM Laureate for Workflow – and was awarded the Marvin Manheim award for Excellence in workflow in 2003.

LUIS ALFONSO RAMÍREZ VEGA

lramirez@acerti.com.mx
CEO--President, Company Name: Asesoría y Certificación SC (ACERTI), Hidalgo, México

Luis Ramirez is a PECTRA Technology Business Partner, Mexico. He graduated from the Tecnológico de Monterrey (ITESM) with a degree in Systems Engineering; he has an MSc in Technology from the same institution and an MSc in Education from the University of British Columbia, among other Strategic Management courses he has taken.

Among his main objectives is implementation of PECTRA Technology's BPM Solutions. This is where change-management and project management is done in the BPM Industry. Luis Ramirez is a published author in Mexico in subjects such as non linear mathematics, strategic management, team building facilitation and attitude re-engineering.

CLAY RICHARDSON

crichardson@forrester.com
Senior Analyst, Business Process Management,
Forrester Research, USA.

Clay delivers strategic and tactical guidance to Business Process & Applications professionals seeking to automate processes and integrate structured and unstructured information into business processes. Clay specifically helps enterprises establish BPM strategies, governance standards, establish BPM centers of excellence, identify lean and agile methodologies best suited for BPM projects, and identify vendors and technologies that help them optimize mission-critical business processes. Prior to joining Forrester Clay served as BPM practice leader at Project Performance Corporation, a global system integrator based in Washington, D.C., where he launched and managed the company's business process management practice. Prior to that, Clay directed a diverse team of consultants, trainers, and support engineers in delivery and support of BPM solutions, as the director of professional services at HandySoft Global Corporation, a pure-play BPM vendor. Clay is active with several BPM industry associations, including the Workflow Management Coalition, where he served as founder and co-chair of the organization's Public Sector chapter.

WOLF RIVKIN

wrivkin@b-wavesoft.com
B-Wave Software LLC., USA

Wolf Rivkin has a master's degree in applied mathematics and 20+ years of IT experience, including 15 years as a senior level architect and manage with Alltel, IBM, Bellsouth, etc. He is a practitioner, a methodologist and an author, specializing in Enterprise Business Transformation (EBT) Frameworks / Roadmaps as well as the creator of the Enterprise Service Orchestration Architecture Framework (ESOAF). As a Principal/Chief Architect he led EBT efforts for industry leaders in telecomm, financial, media, utilities and hospitality industry verticals. He is the founder and Chief Architect of B-Wave Software LLC, an analytic and consulting firm in the field of EBT. His LinkedIn profile is at: http://www.linkedin.com/in/wolfrivkin

CHRISTINE ROBINSON

Principal consultant
Enterprise Architecture and Emergency Preparedness/Disaster Recovery,
CSC, USA

Christine Robinson, a principal consultant at CSC focusing on Enterprise Architecture and Emergency Preparedness/Business Continuity and Disaster Recovery, is an award-winning senior technology professional whose vision helped inspire Congressional legislation and funding that also became the foundation of some recent government procurements. According to one pre-eminent industry analyst, "this should be a Presidential Order and available to every Federal, state, and local entity." Her diverse Enterprise Architecture background, yet highly specialized Emergency Preparedness/Business Continuity and Disaster Recovery background, enable her to conceptualize at the global and strategic levels down to gathering and assimilating the tiniest details required for both normal and emergency operations.

Before joining CSC, Ms. Robinson held senior technical leadership positions with other notable companies to include SAIC and Verizon. She evaluated the US Treasury's most important IT Contingency Plans and COOPs which helped set the standard for quality for future plans. She led a multitude of first-ever technology initiatives for business and government domestic and international systems. These included designing research networks, new technology deployments from a local to international level, innovative designs for system integrated solutions, and many others.

ROCIO ANGELICA SANCHEZ

rsanchez_a3@hotmail.com
BPM Consultant, Congress of the Republic of Peru

Rocio Angelica Sanchez has twelve years of experience in information technology implementations developing custom software and solutions, including business process management and content management systems, for the implementation of business, quality, and administrative improvements. She is a consultant in the formation of strategic plans, workshop facilitation, indicator management, and long-term consultant participation in studies and projects related to management improvement in the High Direction in diverse organizations in Peru.

ERIC D. SCHABELL

JBoss Solutions Architect Benelux
RedHat
eric@schabell.org

I have been working in software development for over 10 years now, using many languages and in many different industries; from IBM to smaller software companies, from research organizations to the financial industry. I have also continually taught on this subject commercially and at the university level. I enjoy both writing and speaking on these topics as it is of paramount importance to pass on our knowledge to others in the field. The only way to make our industry better is to display the experiences and lessons learned while practicing our craft. I have been active specifically in BPM-related projects for a few years now.

ROBERT SHAPIRO

rshapiro@processanalytica.com

Robert Shapiro is founder and manager of ProcessAnalytica. He is Senior Vice President: Research, for Global 360. He founded Cape Visions which was acquired by Global in 2005. At Cape Visions he directed the development of Analytics and Simulation software used by FileNet/IBM, Fujitsu, PegaSystems and Global 360 Business Process Management products.

Prior to founding Cape Visions, as founder and CEO of Meta Software Corporation, he directed the implementation of a unique suite of graphical modeling and optimization tools for enterprise-wide business process improvement. Products based on these tools are used by Bank America, Wells Fargo, JPMChase and other major banks to optimize their check processing and Lock Box operations.

As a participant in the Workflow Management Coalition and chair of the working groups on conformance and process definition interchange, he plays a critical role in the development of international standards for workflow and business process management.

In 2005 he was awarded the Marvin L. Manheim Award for outstanding contributions in the field of workflow.

KEITH SWENSON

kswenson@wfmc.org
VP of R&D, Fujitsu Computer Systems, USA
Technical Committee Chair, WfMC.

Keith Swenson is Vice President of Research and Development at Fujitsu Computer Systems Corporation for the Interstage family of products. He is known for having been a pioneer in web services, and has helped the development of standards such as WfMC Interface 2, OMG Workflow Interface, SWAP, Wf-XML, AWSP, WSCI, and is currently working on standards such as XPDL and ASAP. He has led efforts to develop software products to support work teams at MS2, Netscape, and Ashton Tate. Mr. Swenson holds both a Master's degree in Computer Science and a Bachelor's degree in Physics from the University of California, San Diego. From 1995 to 1997 he served as Vice Chairman of the ACM Special Interest Group for Group Support Systems (SigGROUP). In 1996, he was elected a Fellow of the Workflow Management Coalition. In 2004 he was awarded the Marvin L. Manheim Award for outstanding contributions in the field of workflow. He is currently the Chairman of the Technical Committee of the Workflow Management Coalition.

PROF. ALBERTO TROMBETTA

Alberto.Trombetta @uninsubria.it

Insubria University, Italy
PhD in Computer Science in 2000 from University of Turin, he is currently Assistant Professor at the Computer Science and Communication Dept. of Insubria University (Varese, Italy). His main research topics are security issues in distributed, data-intensive applications and design methodologies for business processes.

DR. ANDRÉ TRUDEL

Andre.Trudel@acadiau.ca
Professor, Acadia University, Canada.
André's primary research area is Artificial Intelligence, and more specifically temporal knowledge representation and reasoning. Secondary research interests are measuring the exact size of the Web, and building computer interfaces to interact with dogs. This last research project arose from his interest in field-bred English Springer spaniels. He has 12 dogs and competes with them at the highest level in competitions across North America.

CÉDRIC TUMELAIRE

cedric@tumelaire.be
Cédric Tumelaire is prominent in education, of new technologies and is responsible for twin cities of the city of Waterloo (Belgium).
After schools in Wallonia, he pursued advanced studies in industrial engineering and later graduated in computer science. Soon he became very interested in public affairs and as a consequence followed courses in political sciences. Professionally, he started in software analysis and rapidly became consultant for a software company in the banking area. He pursued a number of different missions for the most important clients of the Belgium market. Today he still works as computer science consultant after having been elected as member of the communal council of Waterloo in 1994.

RÉMY TZAUD

remy.tzaud@ti-informatique.com
Xpert.Ivy, Switzerland
Business development manager, software editor of Xpert.Ivy BPM tool, (Switzerland) www.ti-informatique.com and www.xpertline.com

JACOB P. UKELSON D.SC.

jacobu@actionbase.com
ActionBase Inc., USA
Jacob has a proven track record in discovering and developing innovative solutions to real-world customer problems, and then developing them into products. Jacob has fostered innovation in many different environments, including both research and business settings. Jacob is CTO of ActionBase, the leader in Human Process Management Systems, where Jacob oversees ActionBase's innovation, vision and technical strategy.
Previously, Jacob served as CTO of Itemfield until its acquisition by Informatica. Prior to that role, Jacob was CTO and Business Development Executive for IBM's Global Technology Unit. He was also a department general manager at the IBM Thomas J. Watson Research Lab, managing a group of 130 cross-disciplinary researchers. Jacob received his Doctorate of Science in computer science from the Technion University in Israel. Jacob has been published in many technical journals and has spoken at conferences worldwide. In 1997 he received the Alexander C. Williams Ergonomics and Human Factors Award from the Human Factors Society.

PEDRO VALENTE

pvalente@uma.pt
University of Madeira
Pedro Valente joined University of Madeira in May 2001 and worked since then as a project manager, analyst and programmer. He has a post-degree in Informatics Engineering and is currently pursuing his M.Sc on Interactive Information System modeling. He previously worked at Taboada & Barros as a programmer and during 1998 he was a teacher at the Escola Secundária Francisco Franco, Funchal.

CARIEN VENTER

carien.venter@postoffice.co.za
Chief Management Analyst, South African Post Office, South Africa
Carien Venter is a Chief Management Analyst at the South African Post Office.

She has a BSc Hons degree as well as an MBA. Before joining the Post Office Carien worked in the Strategy Department of one of the major South African banks, where amongst other functions she performed the role as Strategy Consultant for the African subsidiaries. She is currently responsible for Management Information, including Research and Benchmarking in the Post Office. She also manages projects, as and when her specific expertise is required.

LUCÍA WAINER ROMANELLI

lwainer@cnd.org.uy

Administration and Operations Manager, National Development Corporation (Corporación Nacional para el Desarrollo, CND), Montevideo, Uruguay.

Lucía Wainer is part of the National Development Corporation (www.cnd.org.uy) leading the administration and operation department. She holds a degree in accountancy from the Economic Sciences Faculty of the "Universidad de la República", in Uruguay. She is actually professor at the Accounting department at the Administration and Economics Faculty of the "Universidad de la República". She has also worked as Auditor for more than 10 years in PricewaterhouseCoopers.

MICHAEL WHITE

michael.white@singularity.co.uk

Head of Marketing, Singularity, United Kingdom

Michael White is head of Marketing at Singularity, a $35m revenue, 240 employee BPM vendor headquartered in Ireland with offices in New York, London, Singapore and Hyderabad India. He recently authored the Singularity technical white paper on the application of BPM to automate Case Management-type process patterns. Prior to joining Singularity in 2004, Michael was Senior Product Manager with Siemens' electronic security group in Dublin, Ireland and Munich, Germany. His other roles have included Senior Business Analyst, Management Consultant and Senior Project Manager. Apart from Singularity and Siemens, Michael has worked with Deloitte Consulting, Misys Corporation, AIB Bank and Elavon. He has managed major public sector and financial services assignments in South America, Africa, the Caribbean and throughout Europe, including the UK, Ireland, Germany, Sweden and Holland.

Michael holds a degree in Computer Science from Trinity College Dublin, a post-graduate diploma in Computing along with a series of other post-graduate qualifications.

AMY WYRON

amy@colosa.com

Marketing Manager, Colosa Inc.

Amy Wyron is a consultant with Colosa Inc., the developer of ProcessMaker Open Source BPM Software. She holds a degree in Public Policy from Duke University, and has provided leadership developing ProcessMaker's marketing strategy and community platforms during its transition to open source. Her current research interests include Business Process Management standards, commercial open source models, and the use of technology initiatives and indicators to achieve optimal process outcomes in public and private organizations.

WfMC Structure and Membership Information

WHAT IS THE WORKFLOW MANAGEMENT COALITION?

The Workflow Management Coalition, founded in August 1993, is a non-profit, international organization of workflow vendors, users, analysts and university/research groups. The Coalition's mission is to promote and develop the use of workflow through the establishment of standards for software terminology, interoperability and connectivity among BPM and workflow products. Comprising more than 250 members worldwide, the Coalition is the primary standards body for this software market.

WORKFLOW STANDARDS FRAMEWORK

The Coalition has developed a framework for the establishment of workflow standards. This framework includes five categories of interoperability and communication standards that will allow multiple workflow products to coexist and interoperate within a user's environment. Technical details are included in the white paper entitled, "The Work of the Coalition," available at www.wfmc.org.

ACHIEVEMENTS

The initial work of the Coalition focused on publishing the Reference Model and Glossary, defining a common architecture and terminology for the industry. A major milestone was achieved with the publication of the first versions of the Workflow API (WAPI) specification, covering the Workflow Client Application Interface, and the Workflow Interoperability specification.

In addition to a series of successful tutorials across the U.S., Asia and Europe, the WfMC spent many hours over 2007 helping to drive awareness, understanding and adoption of XPDL. As a result, it has been cited as the most deployed BPM standard by a number of industry analysts, and continues to receive a growing amount of media attention.

In "Open Formats and Transparency in Business Process Definition" published in the Enterprise Open Source Journal, WfMC Executive Director Nathaniel Palmer discusses the merits of XPDL as means for ensuring process definition transparency and portability. XDPL is being adopted as a requirement for BPM workflow RFPs, with the most recent examples cited as a large federal government project and that of a telecommunications firm.

WORKFLOW MANAGEMENT COALITION STRUCTURE

The Coalition is divided into three major committees, the Technical Committee, the External Relations Committee, and the Steering Committee. Small working groups exist within each committee for the purpose of defining workflow terminology, interoperability and connectivity standards, conformance requirements, and for assisting in the communication of this information to the workflow user community.

The Coalition's major committees meet three times per calendar year for three days at a time, with meetings usually alternating between a North American and a European location. The working group meetings are held during these three days, and as necessary throughout the year.

Coalition membership is open to all interested parties involved in the creation, analysis or deployment of workflow software systems. Membership is governed by a Document of Understanding, which outlines meeting regulations, voting rights etc. Membership material is available at www.wfmc.org.

COALITION WORKING GROUPS

The Coalition has established a number of Working Groups, each working on a particular area of specification. The working groups are loosely structured around the "Workflow Reference Model" which provides the framework for the Coalition's standards program. The Reference Model identifies the common characteristics of workflow systems and defines five discrete functional interfaces through which a workflow management system interacts with its environment—users, computer tools and applications, other software services, etc. Working groups meet individually, and also under the umbrella of the Technical Committee, which is responsible for overall technical direction and co-ordination.

WORKFLOW REFERENCE MODEL DIAGRAM

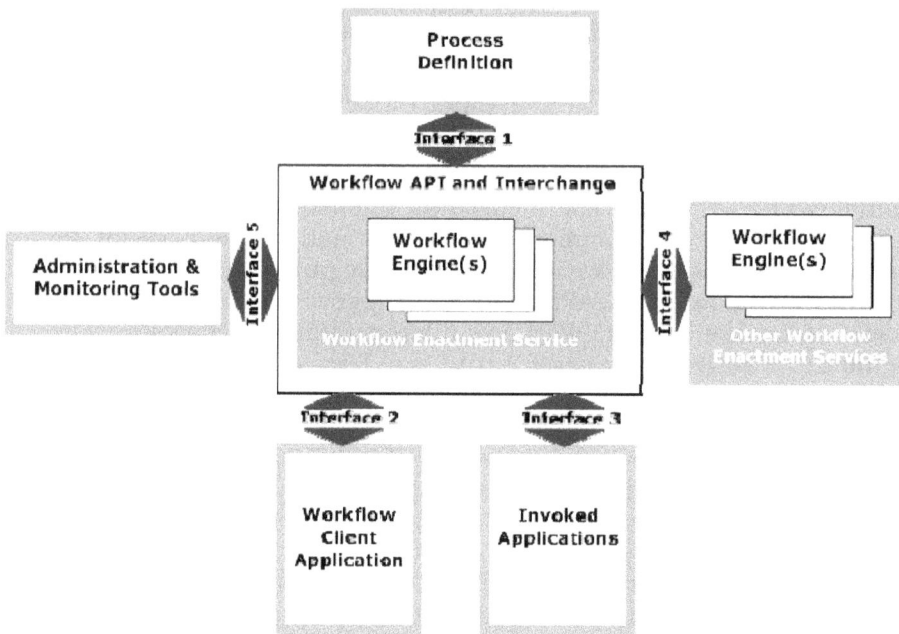

WHY YOU SHOULD JOIN

Being a member of the Workflow Management Coalition gives you the unique opportunity to participate in the creation of standards for the workflow industry as they are developing. Your contributions to our community ensure that progress continues in the adoption of royalty-free workflow and process standards.

MEMBERSHIP CATEGORIES

The Coalition has three major categories of membership per the membership matrix following. **All employees worldwide** are welcome to attend all meetings, and will be permitted access to the *Members Only* area of our web site.

Full Membership is appropriate for Workflow and Business Process Management (BPM) vendors, analysts and consultants. You may include up to three active members from your organization on your application and these may be replaced at any time by notifying us accordingly.

	Full Member	Associate /Academic Member	Individual Member	Fellow (by election only)	Visitor
Annual fee	$3500	$1500	$500	$0	$100 per day
Hold office	Yes	Yes	Yes	Yes	No
Nominate somebody for office	Yes	Yes	No	No	No
Committee membership	Yes	Yes	Yes	Yes	Observer
Voting right on standards	Yes	Yes	Active Participants only	Active Participants only	No
Voting right on WfMC.org business	Yes	Current officers only	Current officers only	Current officers only	No
Company reps in Meetings without visitor fee	4 (transfer-able)	1 (transfer-able)	individual only	individual only	Fee required

FULL MEMBERSHIP

This corporate category offers exclusive visibility in this sector at events and seminars across the world, enhancing your customers' perception of you as an industry authority, on our web site, in the Coalition Handbook and CDROM, by speaking opportunities, access to the Members Only area of our web site, attending the Coalition meetings and most importantly within the workgroups whereby through discussion and personal involvement, using your voting power, you can contribute actively to the development of standards and interfaces.

Full member benefits include:

- Financial incentives: 50 percent discount all "brochure-ware" (such as our annual CDROM Companion to the Workflow Handbook, advertising on our sister-site www.e-workflow.org), $500 credit toward next year's fee for at least 60 percent per year meeting attendance or if you serve as an officer of the WfMC.
- Web Visibility: a paragraph on your company services/products with links to your own company website.
- User RFIs: (Requests for Information) is an exclusive privilege to all full members. We often have queries from user organizations looking for specific workflow solutions. These valuable leads can result in real business benefits for your organization.
- Publicity: full members may choose to have their company logos including collaterals displayed along with WfMC material at conferences / expos we attend. You may also list corporate events and press releases (relating to WfMC issues) on the relevant pages on the website, and have a company entry in the annual Coalition Workflow Handbook
- Speaking Opportunities: We frequently receive calls for speakers at industry events because many of our members are recognized experts in

their fields. These opportunities are forwarded to Full Members for their direct response to the respective conference organizers.

ASSOCIATE AND ACADEMIC MEMBERSHIP

Associate and Academic Membership is appropriate for those (such as IT user organizations) who need to keep abreast of workflow developments, but who are not workflow vendors. It allows voting on decision-making issues, including the publication of standards and interfaces but does not permit anything near the amount of visibility or incentives provided to a Full Member. You may include up to three active members from your organization on your application.

INDIVIDUAL MEMBERSHIP

Individual Membership is appropriate for self-employed persons or small user companies. Employees of workflow vendors, academic institutions or analyst organizations are not typically eligible for this category. Individual membership is held in one person's name only, is not a corporate membership, and is not transferable within the company. If three or more people within a company wish to participate in the WfMC, it would be cost-effective to upgrade to corporate Associate Membership whereby all employees worldwide are granted membership status.

FELLOWS

The WfMC recognizes individuals from within its existing membership who have made sustained and outstanding contributions to WfMC objectives far and above that expected from normal member representation.

VISITORS

We welcome visitors at our meetings; it is an excellent opportunity for you to observe first-hand the process of creating standards and to network with members of the Coalition. Your role will be as an observer only, and you are not eligible for a password, or for special offers available to WfMC members. You must pre-register and prepay your Visitor attendance fee. If you decide to join WfMC within 30 days of the meeting, your membership dues will be credited with your visitor fee.

HOW TO JOIN

Complete the form on the Coalition's website, or contact the Coalition Secretariat, at the address below. All members are required to sign the Coalition's "Document of Understanding" which sets out the contractual rights and obligations between members and the Coalition.

THE SECRETARIAT

Workflow Management Coalition (WfMC)

Nathaniel Palmer, Executive Director,
99 Derby Street, Suite 200
Hingham, MA 02043
+1-781-923-1411 (t), +1-781-735-0491 (f)
wfmc@wfmc.org.

WfMC Membership Directory

ADOBE SYSTEMS INC.
Full Member
345 Park Avenue, San Jose CA 95110, USA
Ashish Agrawal, Senior Product Manager
Tel: [1] 408-536-6262
ashish@adobe.com
Adobe revolutionizes how the world engages with ideas and information. Adobe recently launched LiveCycle Enterprise Suite (ES) is a family of servers and tools for automating external-facing business processes and closing the engagement gap. It enables organizations to automate tasks such as data capture and dissemination, process management, digital rights management, and document generation. It also changes the way organizations think about how they automate the processes that directly or indirectly touch customers, partners, and suppliers. LiveCycle ES drives a new way to develop applications specifically for end users who abandon shopping carts, do not complete forms, or become frustrated with automated ways of interacting with organizations. These engagement applications are enabled through a blend of LiveCycle ES, leveraging Adobe Portable Document Format (PDF) and Flex™ technologies that put a whole new type of interface based on Adobe Flash® on outward-facing applications. LiveCycle ES is the only solution that offers a comprehensive platform for customer engagement, blending industry-leading tools and services with best-in-class partner solutions and enterprise standards to transform business processes that extend to customers, partners, and suppliers.

AIIM INTERNATIONAL
Full Member
1100 Wayne Avenue, Suite 1100, Silver Springs, MD, 20910, USA
Betsy Fanning, Director, Standards & Content Development
Tel: [1] 301-755-2682 / Fax: [1] 301-587-2711
bfanning@aiim.org
AIIM International is the global authority on Enterprise Content Management (ECM). The technologies, tools and methods used to capture, manage, store, preserve and deliver information to support business processes. AIIM promotes the understanding, adoption, and use of ECM technologies through education, networking, marketing, research, standards and advocacy programs.

APPIAN CORPORATION
Full Member
8000 Towers Crescent Drive, 16th Floor, Vienna, VA, 22182, USA
Malcolm Ross, Director of Product Management
Tel: [1] 703-442-1080
malcom.ross@appian.com
Founded in 1999 and headquartered in Vienna, VA, Appian is the first business process management (BPM) company to deliver advanced process, knowledge management, and analytics capabilities in a fully-integrated suite. Designed to extend the value of your existing systems, Appian's process-centric, context-driven solutions align business strategy with execution, and drive quantifiable improvements in business performance. Fortune 500 companies, government agencies, and non-governmental organizations have deployed Appian's award-winning platform–Appian Enterprise–to gain unprecedented visibility and control over their strategic business processes and enable customers to make better-informed decisions about their business.

BIZMANN SYSTEM(S) PTE LTD
Associate Member
73 Science Park Drive, #02-05, CINTECH I, Singapore Science Park I, Singapore 118254
Ken Loke, Director
Tel: [65] 65-62711911
kenloke@bizmann.com

BOC INFORMATION TECHNOLOGIES CONSULTING LTD.

Full Member
80 Haddington Road, Dublin 4, Ireland
www.boc-group.com
Margit Schwab, Managing Director
Tel: [353] 1-6375-240/ Fax: [353] 1- 6375241
Margit.schwab@boc-ie.com
The BOC Group is a software and consulting house specializing in IT-based Management Approaches. From its offices in six different countries and its Headquarters in Vienna, the BOC Group operates on a world-wide basis with Europe as its core market. Anticipating markets needs, the BOC Group offers expertise in Strategy Management by using the Balanced Scorecard concept, product ADOscore®, in Business Process Management based on the Business Process Management System Meta-Modelling concept, ADONIS®, in Supply Chain Management using the SCOR® concept, ADOlog® and in IT Architecture and IT Service Management by using, current concepts like ITIL®, ADOit®. The BOC Group performs projects and offers solutions in the banking, insurance, telecommunication, health care, public administration sectors as well as in the fields of E-Learning and Knowledge Management providing its customers with competence optimizing their processes, identifying their IT potentials, better utilizing their knowledge assets and deployment of their human and IT resources.

CORDYS UK LTD.

Full Member
Abbey House, Wellington Way, Brooklands Business Park • Weybridge, Surrey, KT13 0TT, UK
Jon Pyke, Chief Strategy Officer
Tel: +44 (0)1932 268480 / Fax: +44 (0)1932 268500
jpyke@cordys.com
Cordys provides an industry-leading Business Process Management Suite (BPMS) to Global 2000 companies. Cordys' unique SOA-based solution enables customers to design, execute, monitor and improve business processes more rapidly, with better performance, and with greater adaptability than any other available solution. Companies from major industries worldwide have selected Cordys to support business performance improvement because business executives can continually optimize IT systems in real-time within a code-free environment. Headquartered in the Netherlands, Cordys is a global company with offices throughout the Americas, Europe, China and India.

FLOWRING TECHNOLOGY CO. LTD.

Associate Member
12F, No.120, Sec.2, Gongdao 5th Rd., Hsinchu City, 300 Taiwan
Chi-Tsai Yang, VP and CTO
Tel: [886] 3-5753331 / Fax: [886] 3-5753292
jjyang@flowring.com

FUJITSU SOFTWARE CORPORATION

Full Member
1250 E. Arques Avenue, Sunnyvale, CA 94085, USA
Keith Swenson, Chief Architect
Tel: [1] 408-746-6304 (877) 372-8787) / Fax: [1] 408 746-6344
kswenson@us.fujitsu.com
Ranked as a leader in the Application Infrastructure Software market, the Fujitsu Interstage BPM Suite helps companies build SOA-enabled BPM applications by bringing business and IT professionals together to design, simulate, automate, analyze, and optimize business processes. Fujitsu's Process-Driven Approach to SOA using Interstage Business Process Manager, together with CentraSite, Fujitsu's SOA registry and repository, successfully brings business and IT professionals together. This top-down approach allows for collaboration on translating real business models into optimized, executable business processes while letting an organization reuse their existing Visio process maps, IT infrastructure and other SOA assets to reduce operational costs and maximize business agility and efficiencies. With $43 billion in annual revenues, Fujitsu is the third largest global IT Company. Its Interstage offerings are the enabling technologies of choice for companies building applications that can be shared across the enterprise to lower operating costs, accelerate business processes and react quickly to changing market requirements.

GLOBAL 360, INC

Full Member
2911 Turtle Creek Blvd. Suite 1100 Dallas, TX 75219, USA
Robert M Shapiro, Senior Vice President, Research
Tel: 1-617-823-1055
robert.shapiro@global360.com
Insight 360 is Process Intelligence for BPM, providing bottom-line BPM benefits without the risk and cost of a BI project, and without relying on a competing application infrastructure that attempts to obviate existing investments. While most BPM Suites are not designed to address the management of processes that lie outside of their direct control, Insight 360 is unique because it offers an independent layer that can integrate with BPM Suites and other applications for providing end to end process visibility and alignment. Insight 360 benefits are focused in four distinct areas: Visibility, Alignment, Efficiency, and Agility.

HANDYSOFT GLOBAL CORPORATION

Full Member
1952 Gallows Road, Suite 200, Vienna, VA 22182, USA
H.J. Lee Caffrey, Vice President, Product Management
Tel: [1] 703-442-5690/ Fax: [1] 703-442.5650
hjlee@handysoft.com
HandySoft Global Corporation is leading the way for companies worldwide to develop new strategies for conducting business through the improvement, automation, and optimization of their business processes. As a leading provider of Business Process Management (BPM) software and services, we deliver innovative solutions to both the public and private sectors. Proven to reduce costs while improving quality and productivity, our foundation software platform, BizFlow®, is an award-winning BPM suite of tools used to design, analyze, automate, monitor, and optimize business processes.

IVYTEAM-SORECOGROUP

Associate Member
Alpenstrasse 9, P.O. Box CH-6304, Zug, Switzerland
Tel: [44] 41-417108020
Heinz.lienhard@ivyteam.ch

KOREA INSTITUTE FOR ELECTRONIC COMMERCE (KIEC)

Full Member
Textile Center B/D, 6th Flr, 135-713 Dachi-3Dong Kangnam-gu, Seoul, ROK
Sangwon Lim
Phone: [82] 2-528-5020, Fax: [82] 2-528-5789
swlim@kiec.or.kr
Korea Institute for Electronic Commerce (KIEC) was established under the Korean Government pursuant to the Framework Act on Electronic Transaction legislated in August 1999. The state purpose is to promote Korea's e-Business in line with a rapidly global trend. KIEC has been positioning itself as the hub of Korea's e-Business industry to meet the needs of the times. The institute has created an e-Business-friendly environment nationwide by linking the public and private sectors and facilitating international cooperation.

METASTORM

Full Member
500 East Pratt Street, Suite 1250, Baltimore, MD 21202, USA
Doug Gruber
Tel. [1] 113 871 1300
dgruber@metastorm.com
With a focus on enterprise visibility, optimization, and agility, Metastorm offers market-leading solutions for Enterprise Architecture (EA), Business Process Analysis & Modeling (BPA) and Business Process Management (BPM). As an integrated product portfolio, Metastorm Enterprise™ allows organizations to maximize business results by unifying strategy, analysis and execution. Metastorm is the only solution provider to bring together these critical disciplines on a single software platform to enable an understanding of enterprise architecture and strategy, accurate impact and opportunity assessment, effective process execution, and accelerated value realization for organizations worldwide.

NEC SOFT LTD.

Full Member
1-18-6, Shinkiba, Koto-ku, Tokyo, 136-8608, JAPAN
www.nec.com
Yoshihisa Sadakane, Sales and Marketing Senior Manager
Tel: [81]3-5569-3399 / Fax: [81]3-5569-3286
sadakane@mxw.nes.nec.co.jp
NEC Soft is a subsidiary of NEC Corporation, Japan's leading IT firm. NEC Soft, Ltd. has been providing solutions, mainly System Integration & System Services, Software Development, and Sales of Software Packages & Information Processors, and creating reliable partnerships with our customers for over 30 years since it was established. By offering total, unified services with separate business domains, NEC Soft's Total Services dynamically support the value creation customers seek.

OPENWORK

Full Member
Via Conservatorio 22, Milano, 20122 Italy
Francesco Battista, Marketing Director
Tel: [39] 02-77297558 / Fax: [39] 0805833115
francesco.battista@openworkBPM.com
openwork® is a pure Independent Software Vendor concentrating all efforts exclusively on its openwork Business Process Management suite. openwork features an original methodology that makes use of daily business, non-technical language and approach, introducing high-abstraction tools to map, share and maintain organizations shape and working rules. Those agile tools also allow to reflect organizations evolutions, keeping them always aligned with changing business needs. openwork is then able to act as an interpreter of graphic representation of organizations shape and working rules, enabling paper manual processes to become alive into finalized real-world web applications, integrated with other existing IT systems.

PECTRA TECHNOLOGY, INC.

Full Member
2425 West Loop South, Suite 200, Houston TX 77027, USA
Federico Silva, Marketing Manager
Tel: [1] 713-335-5562 / [54] 351-410-4400, ext 9309
fsilva@pectra.com
PECTRA Technolgy's award-winning Business Process Management system, PECTRA BPM Suite, is a powerful set of tools enabling discovery, design, implementation, maintenance, optimization and analysis of business processes in the organizations. PECTRA BPM Suite automates processes and critical tasks generating optimum levels of operational effectiveness. It fulfills all requirements demanded by today's organization, quickly and efficiently. PECTRA incorporates the follow concepts: BAM, Workflow; EAI, and B2Bim, as well as PECTRA BPM Mobile that allows task execution from any mobile device.

PEGASYSTEMS INC.

Full Member
101 Main Street, Cambridge, MA 02142 United States
Dr. Setrag Khoshafian
Vice President of BPM Technology
Tel: [1] 617-866-6407
Setrag.khoshafian@pega.com
Pegasystems (NASDAQ: PEGA) provides software to drive revenue growth, productivity and agility for the world's most sophisticated organizations. Customers use our award-winning SmartBPM® suite to improve customer service, reach new markets and boost operational effectiveness. Our patented SmartBPM technology makes enterprise applications easy to build and change by directly capturing business objectives and eliminating manual programming. SmartBPM unifies business rules and processes into composite applications that leverage existing systems -- empowering businesspeople and IT staff to Build for Change®, deliver value quickly and outperform their competitors. Pegasystems' suite is complemented by best-practice frameworks designed for leaders in financial services, insurance, healthcare, government, life sciences, communications, manufacturing and other industries. Headquartered in Cambridge, MA, Pegasystems has offices in North America, Europe and Asia.

PERSHING LLC

Associate Member
19 Vreeland Road, Florham Park, NJ 07932, USA
Regina DeGennaro, VP – Process Management Applications
Tel: [1] 973-360-2631
rdegennaro@pershing.com

PROCESSMAKER

Full Member
790 Washington Ave, Suite 210, 11238 Brooklyn, NY USA
Brian Reale
brian@colosa.com

ProcessMaker is an open source business process software tool that allows private and public organizations to automate document intensive, approval-based processes across systems including finance, HR and operations. A web-based application, it allows users across multiple sites to create and share workflows, customize forms, manage processes, and enhance reporting. ProcessMaker includes tools to design forms, create documents, assign roles and users, create routing rules, interconnect with third-party systems including business intelligence (BI), document management (DMS), content management (CMS) and enterprise resource planning (ERP) systems through a service-orientated architecture (SOA), and to map an individual process quickly and easily. It is available free for download at http://sourceforge.net/projects/processmaker/

PROJEKTY BANKOWE POLSOFT

Full Member
Plac Wolnosci 18, Poznan, 61-739 Poland
Boguslaw Rutkowski, Solution Architect
Tel: [48] 61-8599311/ Fax: [48] 61-8516995
boguslaw.rutkowski@pbpolsoft.com.pl

Projekty Bankowe Polsoft Company is part of Sygnity Group, one of the biggest IT services and software vendor for industry and public sectors in Poland. PB Polsoft offers BPB Workflow technology, highly scalable standard-based workflow system with strong EAI capabilities, especially for Web Services, rich process and form (XForms) modeling tools as well as set of components for building workflow client portal applications based on java portlet technology. BPB Workflow was developed in J2EE technology and can be used as both an embedded or a standalone server working in EJB container. It has well defined Java WAPI and Web Services interface and offers web-based administration and modeling tools. The workflow engine is cluster aware and has robust build-in process fail-over and recovery capabilities.

QUALIWARE APS

Full Member
Skovlytoften 9B, P.O. Box 60, DK-2840 Holte, Denmark
Shahid Qader, Sales Manager
+45 4547 0700
sales@qualiware.com

Founded in 1991, QualiWare is a global consulting services and business modeling software provider. Our services and products help our customers succeed with their Quality Management, Business Process Management and Optimization initiatives, Business Excellence programs, Enterprise Architecture initiatives, and/or IT solution development needs, including the QualiWare Lifecycle Manager which supports XPDL 2.1 for process portability. QualiWare is a private company with offices in Denmark, Sweden, Norway, Ukraine and the United States. Our development team is headquartered in Copenhagen, Denmark and Kiev, Ukraine.

SAVVION

Full Member
5104 Old Ironsides Drive, Suite 205, Santa Clara, California 95054, USA
Ajay Khanna, Sr. Director, Product Marketing & Management
Tel: [1] 408-330-3400 / Tel: [1] 408-330-3400
akhanna@savvion.com

Savvion is the leading provider of business process management (BPM) software that improves business performance and reduces costs. Savvion has a proven track record of turning process improvement ideas into real-world solutions quickly, often in as few as 30 days, and delivering a return on investment as high as 300%. More than 300 global business enterprises, public service agencies, and systems integration firms, including 20 of the Fortune 100, use Savvion systems to manage their business. Savvion is recognized by Intelligent Enterprise as one of the most influential companies in information technology today, and is cited as a leader by independent research firms.

TIBCO SOFTWARE, INC.

Full Member
3303 Hillview Avenue, Palo Alto, CA 94304 USA
http://www.tibco.com/software/process_management/default.jsp
Justin Brunt, Sr. Product Manager
Tel: [44] 0-1793-441300 / Fax: [44] 0-1793 441333
jbrunt@tibco.com

TIBCO digitized Wall Street in the '80s with its event-driven "Information Bus" software, which helped make real-time business a strategic differentiator in the '90s. Today, TIBCO's infrastructure software gives customers the ability to constantly innovate by connecting applications and data in a service-oriented architecture, streamlining activities through business process management, and giving people the information and intelligence tools they need to make faster and smarter decisions, what we call The Power of Now®. TIBCO serves more than 3,000 customers around the world with offices in 40 countries and an ecosystem of over 200 partners.

UNIVERSITY OF NEBRASKA

Academic Member
Lincoln, NE 68588
Edwin Mukusha, Administrative Systems Group
Phone: (402) 472-7756
Email: emukusha@nebraska.edu

W4 (WORLD WIDE WEB WORKFLOW)

Full Member
4 rue Emile Baudot, 91873 Palaiseau Cedex, France
www.w4global.com
Philippe Betschart, CTO
Tel: [33] 1-64531760 / Fax: [33] 1-64532898
Philippe.Betschart@w4global.com

W4, one of the leading European software vendors specialized in Business Process Management, supplies more than 270 customers, serving more than 1 million users. For more than 10 years W4 has been widely acclaimed for its expertise in Human Centric BPM. Whatever the particular need, there is a package available allowing customers to take full advantage of W4 technology. W4 BPM Suite is a complete package, from modeling to monitoring, dedicated to the enterprise process automation. This BPM package is managing the automation of complex work processes involving high volumes of users, connections to applications and integration to the IT. Process can be both support (finance, HR, etc) and company-specific (new product launch, modification requests, etc.) W4 BPM Suite provides an easy tool for modeling their processes and generate the presentation layer (application) for both Java and .NET environments. It also offers managers reporting and supervision functionalities.

WORK MANAGEMENT EUROPE

Associate Member
Postbus 168, 3830 AD Leusden, The Netherlands
www.wmeonline.com
Cor H. Visser, Managing Director
Tel: [31] (33) 433 2223 / Fax: [31] (33) 433 2224
cvisser@wmeonline.com

Additional Workflow and BPM Resources

NON-PROFIT ASSOCIATIONS AND RELATED STANDARDS RESEARCH ONLINE

- AIIM (Association for Information and Image Management)
  http://www.aiim.org
- AIS Special Interest Group on Process Automation and Management (SIGPAM)
  http://www.sigpam.org
- BPM and Workflow online news, research, forums
  http://bpm.com
- BPM Research at Stevens Institute of Technology
  http://www.bpm-research.com
- Business Process Management Initiative
  http://www.bpmi.org *see* Object Management Group
- IEEE (Electrical and Electronics Engineers, Inc.)
  http://www.ieee.org
- Institute for Information Management (IIM)
  http://www.iim.org
- ISO (International Organization for Standardization)
  http://www.iso.ch
- Object Management Group
  http://www.omg.org
- Open Document Management Association
  http://nfocentrale.net/dmware
- Organization for the Advancement of Structured Information Standards
  http://www.oasis-open.org
- Society for Human Resource Management
  http://www.shrm.org
- Society for Information Management
  http://www.simnet.org
- Wesley J. Howe School of Technology Management
  http://howe.stevens.edu/research/research-centers/business-process-innovation
- Workflow And Reengineering International Association (WARIA)
  http://www.waria.com
- Workflow Management Coalition (WfMC)
  http://www.wfmc.org
- Workflow Portal
  http://www.e-workflow.org

www.ingramcontent.com/pod-product-compliance
Lightning Source LLC
Chambersburg PA
CBHW080719220326
41520CB00056B/7143